THE GRAND PRIX SABOTEURS

Joe Saward is a Formula 1 journalist. He started his career travelling from race to race in Europe and then joined Autosport magazine in London. He moved through the ranks to become Grand Prix Editor and then created his own agency, establishing the award-winning Business of Motorsport electronic newsletter in 1994 and launching www.grandprix.com – now one of the largest Formula 1 websites - in 2000. The author of several books about motor racing, including the best-selling World Atlas of Motorsport, Saward has lived in France for the last 15 years.

MORIENVAL
PRESS

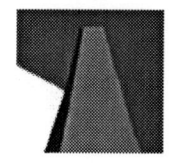

Also by Joe Saward

THE WORLD ATLAS OF MOTOR RACING

BROCK AND MOFFAT ON THE ROAD TO SPA

JAGUAR V12 RACE CARS (with Ian Bamsey)

THE GRAND PRIX SABOTEURS

THE GRAND PRIX DRIVERS WHO BECAME
BRITISH SECRET AGENTS DURING WORLD WAR II

JOE SAWARD

First published in 2006 by Morienval Press

3 5 7 9 8 6 4 2

All rights reserved

Copyright © Joe Saward 2006

The right of Joe Saward to be identified as the author of this work has asserted his right under the Copyright, Designs and Patents Act 1988.

This book is in copyright. Subject to statutory exception and to provisions of relevant collective licensing agreements, no reproduction of any part may take place without the written permission of Morienval Press, 6 Discovery Walk, London E1W 2JG, UK

www.morienval.com

This book is sold subject to the conditions that it shall not, by way of trade or otherwise, be lent, re-sold, hired out, or otherwise circulated without the publisher's prior consent in any form of binding or cover other than that in which it is published and without a similar condition including this condition being imposed on the subsequent purchaser.

ISBN 978-0-9554868-0-7

Typeset in Hoepfler Text

Printed and bound in the United Kingdom by
Lightning Source
6 Precedent Drive, Rooksley,
Milton Keynes, Buckinghamshire
MK13 8PR

FOR MY SON
WILLIAM

IN THE HOPE THAT HIS GENERATION
DOES NOT HAVE TO FIGHT WARS

ACKNOWLEDGMENTS

This book is the work of more than 18 years of research, thought, verification and finding ways to overcome opposition from those who did not want the full story to be told. It became a never-ending labour of love rather than a normal book project and every day, even now it is done, I find myself sub-consciously looking for information. Other writers came along and picked up on elements of the story that I had revealed - but this was never a project that could be done quickly.

There were too many secrets.

Until the summer of 2003 I was piecing together the story but then, after nearly 60 years, the British government decided to release the final secret documents about the SOE. These papers confirmed that my conclusions had been correct and so I would like to thank the government for enabling me to be confident that this really is the true story.

Despite a few who refused to help - and some who hindered progress - there are a long list of people to thank, beginning with Quentin Spurring, the man who first suggested that I should look into the story of "W Williams". He did not know much about the subject, he admitted, but he knew it was something that would interest me. As usual, Q was right.

I would also like to mention Paul Treuthardt, David Tremayne and Brad Spurgeon who not only put up with my constant discussion on the subject but also had the temerity to encourage me to push on. And there was also encouragement, bordering on bullying, from Alan Henry, Maurice Hamilton, Eoin Young, Nigel Roebuck and Richard Williams.

They saw me through the times when I was ready to give up.

The remaining names are in alphabetical order and I apologise to anyone I have missed: the late Michael & Rose Alexander, Squadron Leader the late Vera Atkins, Christopher Balfour, Roger Benoit, Andrew Benson, Matt Bishop, Jeff Bloxham, Anthony Brooks DSO MC, the late Colonel Maurice Buckmaster OBE, the late Robert Burdett MBE MC, the Central Intelligence Agency, Valerie Collins, the late Gervais Cowell, the late Gerard Crombac, John Davenport, Harry Despaigne MC, the De Thieulloy family, Anne Dewe, Mike Doodson, the late René Dreyfus, Martyn Elford, the Foreign and Commonwealth Office, Professor Michael Foot, JMG, Frederic Grover, Serge Guérin, the Guildhall Library, Hammersmith Books, Stéphane Hessel, the late David Hodges, Sir Lewis Hodges, Rachel Hudson, the Imperial War Museum, Denis Johnson, Bruce Jones, Liane Jones, Peter Murray Lee, Dan Knutson, the Mairie de Neuilly Plaisance, the Mairie de Sermaise, Robert Maloubier MC, the Ministry of Defence, William Mearns, Chris Nixon, Jean Overton-Fuller, Heinz Pruller, Sir Brooks Richards, Michael and Jackie Saward, Amy Saward, William Saward, Mark Seaman, Robert Sheppard, the Special Forces Club, Duncan Stuart, Francis Suttill, Swarthmore College, Jessie & Dick Teager, Fay Tresilian, Gill Treuthardt, Jeroen Van der Ploeg, Ernst Vogt, Mick Walsh, Carolyn Way, Major Peter Westrope MBE, Rob Wiedenhoff, Chris Williams, Sir Frank Williams, Chris Willows, the late Derek Wright and Peter Wright.

A word of thanks too to David Wright, Richard Nicholl, Pene Corfield, the late Roger Bullen and Peter Lake who each played an important role along the way.

And, finally, to Cindy Sverrisson, a wise and clever soul who is my constant friend and supporter, who did a great deal to make this happen.

Joe Saward
Paris, December 2006

"To understand the French Resistance you must think of it as an egg-timer which was turned on its head when the Germans invaded France in 1940. In the beginning there was no sand in the bottom section. The first grain of sand was called Charles de Gaulle and gradually others joined him. By the end of the war everyone in France was a member of the Resistance."

A former SOE agent

CHAPTER ONE

Prague, Wednesday, May 27, 1942

If Raymond Chandler had not been living it up in Hollywood at the time, he would have enjoyed meeting SS-Oberscharführer Johannes Klein. Klien would have made a perfect thug in a Chandler novel. In German "klein" means "small" which, assuredly, Johannes Klein was not. He was a huge man, more than six feet tall and broad as an ox. And he looked all the more out of place when his vast frame was squeezed into the driver's seat of a Mercedes-Benz 320 Cabriolet.

There was barely enough room for his pistol.

Klein liked cars and working as the chauffeur for Obergruppenführer Reinhard Heydrich was the perfect job for him. Heydrich was important enough Nazi to have good cars. The 320 had a numberplate that read "SS 4" and back home in the Heydrich's garage was a bigger Mercedes 770 limousine with the numberplate "SS 3". Heydrich, the Reichsprotektor of Bohemia-Moravia, was a man in whom Adolf Hitler had great confidence and great hopes for the future.

The 320 was one of the most attractive cars ever to have come out of the Mercedes-Benz factories in Untertürkheim in Stuttgart. The beautiful two-seater sports car had a long sweeping bonnet and elegant bodywork and that morning, as Klein drove Heydrich to his office in the sinister Hradčany Castle in Prague, everything in Klein's life seemed to be perfect.

Klein had folded back the canvas top of the 320 so that they could enjoy the sunshine. They drove without any bodyguards, convinced that there was no-one in Czechoslovakia brave enough - or, perhaps, mad enough - to attack Heydrich. Everyone knew that retribution for such an attack would be terrible.

Heydrich was an utterly ruthless man and had earned himself the nickname of "The Hangman" during his time in Czechoslovakia.

But now his job was done. The resistance had been beaten. Heydrich wanted only to clear his desk before he flew to Berlin later in the day for a conference with Der Führer. They were going to discuss Heydrich's transfer to Paris.

Klein was enjoying himself while Heydrich was busy finishing off some paperwork. Where Zenklova Street meets the Holesˇovickách Highway, in the east of the city, there is a tight downhill corner, which curls to the right, into an area where the local tram lines meet and passengers switch from one tram to another.

As the Mercedes approached the corner Klein slowed the car. Ahead he saw a man stepping into the roadway, carrying an armful of straw. It seemed a little odd. Klein cursed silently and braked. Heydrich looked up from his paperwork, just in time to see the man throw the straw to one side to reveal a hidden Sten gun.

A British sub machine gun, Heydrich thought.

The gunman, Josef Gabčik, aimed at the Mercedes-Benz and pulled the trigger of the Sten. Nothing happened.

Heydrich was reaching for his pistol as Gabčik scrambled to free the firing mechanism of the temperamental Sten. The Reichsprotektor rose from his seat and took aim at his would-be assassin. As he did so he was aware of swift movement to his right. A second attacker, Jan Kubiš, was running towards the Mercedes-Benz with a hand grenade gripped tightly in his fingers. The Mills bomb was made from cast iron and deeply serrated so that it would break into fragments when it exploded. It had a four second time fuse from the moment Kubiš let go. If the Czech aimed well Heydrich would have only four seconds to live.

In the excitement of the moment Kubiš missed his target. The Mills bomb hit the side of the Mercedes and bounced back on to the road, landing beside the rear wheel of the now-stationary Mercedes. Heydrich turned to fire his pistol at Kubiš, aware that Klein was already climbing out of the door on the other side of the vehicle to chase Gabčik. He had given up with the Sten and had turned and was now running away. Passengers at the tram stop stood opened-mouthed, trying to take in what was happening in front of them.

The hand grenade exploded with a loud bang and a bright flash of light. There was a cloud of smoke but as it cleared it seemed that Heydrich was unharmed. He was standing in the car, shouting instructions at Klein. Then he flung open the door on his side of the car and jumped out, intent on chasing Kubiš, who had turned and was now running for his life. As his feet touched the ground the Reichsprotektor staggered, clutched at his hip and then fell backwards on to the road and lay still as the smoke above him cleared.

For a moment it was quiet. Kubiš had disappeared. Klein had chased Gabčik into a butcher's shop. A woman who had been standing at the tram stop crossed the road to look at the fallen figure in his hated Nazi uniform. As she did so shots were heard from the butcher's shop as Klein and Gabčik exchanged fire.

But then the quiet returned. Klein had been hit twice. He was down on the floor and Gabčik had escaped. No-one wanted to help Heydrich, but they were frightened of what might happen if they did not and so the bystanders waved down a van carrying floor polish and lifted the still-conscious Heydrich into the back. The driver set off to cover the short distance to the Bulovka Hospital.

At the hospital the excitement quickly calmed down. The surgeons went to work to extract a grenade splinter that had pierced Heydrich's diaphragm and broken a rib. Another splinter was lodged close to his spleen. The doctors examined Heydrich and declared that they were not too worried. The Reichsprotektor's injuries were not serious. His life was not in danger.

At Hradčany Castle the Reichsprotektor's staff were alerted but the news they telephoned to Berlin was promising. Heydrich had survived an assassination attempt. They would be launching a manhunt for his attackers. There would be no mercy.

✠

The attack on Heydrich was just one small event in a much bigger conflict. Europe was at war. There was fighting in Russia and in North Africa. The Germans had occupied much of Europe. Britain was under siege. But, come Saturday, all this was forgotten as people everywhere did what they could to amuse themselves. A Saturday night was still a Saturday night and in wartime there is all the more reason to go dancing and have a good time, to forget what is happening.

Over in England, the evening of Saturday May 30 1942 may have seemed like a normal Saturday night and the residents of the besieged island may not have noticed the unusual number of aircraft passing overhead as they went to their beds that night, but the girls in the pubs across the country had known from the early evening that "something big" was going on. There were no bomber pilots to be found.

The only girls who knew the answer to this mystery were in a bunker beneath a grass-covered mound in the gardens of a country estate near High Wycombe in Buckinghamshire. Inside the Royal Air Force's Bomber Command Operations Room the walls were covered with maps of Europe and charts which showed the progress of Operation Millenium. The RAF was launching its biggest ever bombing raid on Germany. More than 1000 bomber aircraft were heading out across the North Sea bound for the ancient city of Cologne. By the morning everyone would know about the Thousand Bomber Raid and within a few days Bomber Command's leader Air Chief Marshal Arthur Harris would become Sir Arthur.

The Thousand Bomber Raid was his idea but he had been forced to fight for it. The bureaucrats in the Air Ministry had opposed the whole concept and had even tried to stop Harris getting his 1000 planes. Despite the opposition he had scraped together 1046 bomber aircraft. But even "Bomber" Harris had not managed to get his hands on the 1047th bomber flying that night.

Heading south across the English Channel towards Occupied France was a lone Handley Page Halifax, flown by 138 Squadron of the Royal Air Force. One Thirty Eight was a special duties unit and the staff at Bomber Command headquarters knew only that the plane was "a special". They did not need to know more. What One Thirty Eight did was "hush-hush".

The man at the controls of the lone Halifax was Pilot Officer Frank Rymills, known to his friends as "Bunny", for reasons that are probably best forgotten. Bunny was only 21 but he seemed a lot older, having been hardened during the 26 bombing raids he had been on to the hot spots of Germany in old Whitleys. They were planes that the aircrew nicknamed "the flying coffins" but Bunny Rymills had lived.

Flying for One Thirty Eight was probably a little less dangerous than being a bomber pilot and Bunny was happy with that. He did not know anything about the men in the back of his plane and he did not want to know. They were "Joes" and, as far as he was concerned, the less he knew the better he felt. If the plane was shot down and he was taken prisoner he would not be able to tell the Germans anything. In this case ignorance really was bliss.

Like many experienced bomber pilots, Rymills felt that life was too short to worry about the petty RAF regulations that existed on the ground. A pilot must always respect the rules of flying, but to enforce a ban on smoking in the planes was, he believed, a little excessive. Bunny liked to smoke and never took off on a mission without at least 50 cigarettes with him in his cockpit. He smoked one every 20 minutes. The nicotine kept him awake and kept him calm.

As the streams of British bombers began to rain destruction on Cologne, Rymills and his crew were searching for their target in the darkness over France. This was to be a "blind" drop with no help from people on the ground and no lights to signal the dropping zone. The navigator had to find four small lakes in a row, to the south of the River Sarthe, near Le Mans. His only navigational aids were his charts and the moonlight, which reflected off any water below. It was not an easy thing to do but that night everything went according to plan. The target was recognized and Rymills flicked on his intercom and informed the crew that it was time for the drop. The radio operator, who also acted as a gunner and as the dispatcher, opened a hatch in the floor of the Halifax. Inside the bomber the noise of the engines suddenly increased.

So did the tension.

The first "Joe" was a fit-looking young man known only as Charles. He was bundled up in parachute gear but was wearing civilian clothes underneath. He sat down by the hole in the floor and carefully dropped his legs down into the 160mph slipstream beneath the plane. He waited for the green light. When Rymills gave the signal, Charles calmly pushed himself forwards and dropped out into the darkness. Hurriedly Sebastien, the second agent, sat down and repeated the manoeuvre. The dispatcher threw a couple of suitcases through the hole after the two men, static lines opening the parachutes attached to them. Rymills was informed that the drop had been completed. The dispatcher hauled in the static lines as Bunny swung the Halifax around and headed for Le Mans. The hatch was left open until they reached the city a few minutes later. The dispatcher had bundles of propaganda leaflets for the population below, to disguise the real purpose of their mission.

As the noise of the Halifax's engines faded away, the two secret agents floated towards the ground. Dropping "blind" was a dangerous business. Without a reception committee there was less chance of being caught in a German trap, but the problem was that if you ran into trouble there was no-one there to help. A few weeks later one of the other Joes landed on the roof of a French police station and was arrested before his feet even touched the ground. One or two others were killed on landing and others suffered serious injuries. There was a very real risk of landing in a pond, getting stuck in a tree or breaking an ankle on uneven ground.

The two men stared into the darkness below them, looking for the first glimpse of the earth. At the same time they had to keep an eye on the other parachutes, so they knew where the suitcases would be landing. Charles, however, had other problems.

"The harness of my parachute sent me askew," he remembered, "but I landed straight and soft not far from a horse."

The startled beast took off, galloping into the darkness. Charles disentangled himself from his parachute and quickly went in search of Sebastien and the suitcases. It took them longer than expected to take care of everything.

"We had landed only a hundred yards from a farm," Charles reported, "so we decided to dispense with the luxury of giving our parachutes a proper burial and left them under fairly deep water in a ditch."

Then they were on their way, fearful that the plane might have attracted a German patrol or that someone might have seen them landing. France was under curfew and to be out on the roads at night was a dangerous game. The German forces of occupation tended to shoot first and ask questions later but the two men knew that in the small hours of the morning most of the Germans would be tucked up in bed. France was a huge country and to have a German garrison capable of checking every district over which a plane had passed was simply not possible, even with half a million German soldiers spread across the country. The good thing was that thanks to Bunny Rymills and his crew the two secret agents knew exactly where they were and were not stumbling around lost, waiting for daybreak to reveal landmarks.

They had landed near a hamlet called Les Quatre Vents. It was the highest point in the area and was dotted with trees and smallholdings. They knew that if they headed south-east along the main road which runs between Sablé-sur-Sarthe and La Flèche they would reach La Flèche before dawn. Before taking-off from England the two men had agreed that they would stick together and walk the eight miles to La Flèche together, then take a bus from there to Le Mans. They walked for two hours, skirting around the village of Crosmières, listening out for the sound of an approaching vehicle or the noise of boots on the road ahead. They heard one German patrol approaching but had time to hide in a field where each had a nip of brandy from a flask they had brought with them. As the sun was rising they arrived in the town. A few early-risers were on their way to church for Sunday morning Mass, but the town was big enough for the two men not to be noticed. The Briefing Officers in London had told them that there would be an early morning bus to take them from La Flèche to Le Mans, but someone in London had made a mistake. On Sundays there was no early bus. The first bus would not leave for Le Mans until midday, and so the two secret agents had to keep out of sight until eventually the bus rumbled into town. They climbed aboard, delighted to finally have the chance to be anonymous. From La Flèche the bus might have run up the RN 23, the main highway from Paris to Nantes, but instead it wound through the side roads, visiting different villages as it worked its way up towards the city of Le Mans.

There were moments when Sebastien thought he remembered places along the route, but the truth was that the roads he knew best were a little further to the east where 12 years earlier he had won the French Grand Prix at the wheel of a factory Bugatti racing car. He found it rather amusing that he was returning to Le Mans as a passenger on a local bus and wondered what the other passengers would make of it all if they knew what he was doing.

He was a former Grand Prix driver who had just been parachuted into France to fight the Germans.

It all seemed rather unlikely.

When the bus pulled up outside the railway station at Le Mans Charles and Sebastien found it was busy with crowds of Parisians, heading back to the capital after a weekend in the country. They had come to escape the claustrophobia of the German occupation - and to buy food. Every Sunday afternoon the trains were jammed with city folk, carrying whatever fresh food they had been able to find out in the country. The trains were not expensive and so they were always crowded and often the passengers would have to stand up all the way to the Gare Montparnasse in Paris. Although the crowd provided them with anonymity, the two agents knew that railway stations were dangerous places because the Germans were always watching closely, knowing that enemy agents needed to move around France. There were security checks to go through. That Sunday afternoon in Le Mans, the German guards did not notice anything strange about the forged identity papers of the two men. The train rattled its way to Paris where, in the early evening, the two men parted with a swift handshake. To a casual observer it was just two friends saying farewell but it was much more significant than that: The French Section of the Special Operations Executive (SOE) was back on active service in Paris.

✠

The SOE had been Prime Minister Winston Churchill's idea. When Britain stood alone, its back to the wall after the defeat of France in June 1940, Churchill had decided that he wanted to hit back at the Germans in any way he could. He had only been Prime Minister for two months and a Nazi invasion of Britain was expected at any moment. He instructed his subordinates that he wanted secret agents to be sent to Europe and set it ablaze with assassinations and bombings. Churchill did not want to fight by the rules.

The Prime Minister had learned the value of guerrilla warfare

40 years earlier while working as a reporter for The Morning Post in the Boer War in South Africa. The Afrikaners had waged a highly effective campaign, ambushing British supply trains and attacking isolated garrisons. The mighty British Army had been incapable of defeating the commandos and Churchill dreamed of creating a similar situation in the German-occupied territories, with secret armies disrupting life and preparing for uprisings that would coincide with the liberation of Europe.

The concept of large scale military action behind enemy lines was still relatively new. Only four years earlier General Emilio Mola Vidal, advancing on Madrid during the Spanish Civil War with four columns of troops, had coined the phrase "the Fifth Column" which, he said, was already inside the city, poised to rise up at the moment his other armies attacked.

The SOE was to be Churchill's Fifth Column.

For Charles and Sebastien, the name SOE meant nothing. They worked for an organization that had no name other than "The Firm". They had been told that they were specially employed by Churchill, but that even he would deny their existence if they were caught. It would be several years after the war before the British Government even acknowledged that people like Charles and Sebastien had ever existed. Even to this day some of the operations mounted by SOE agents remain secret, the files locked away in government vaults, classified in perpetuity. The attack on Obergruppenführer Reinhard Heydrich in Prague was just such an operation. Officially it was an operation mounted by the Czech government-in-exile under Edvard Beneš. But Gabčik and Kubiš, like Charles and Sebastien, had been trained in secret SOE sabotage schools in Britain. They had been delivered to Czechoslovakia in a British plane. They were using British weapons.

Assassination was a weapon that helped to foster the spirit of resistance, or at least that is what the SOE instructors argued in the Special Training Schools in England. The need to build up resistance was particularly important in France where there was almost no desire to fight the Germans. The French had lost one and a half million men in World War I. In every town and village across the nation there are war memorials to the dead and so many names on each one that it seems impossible that so many men could have gone from such small communities. In some areas the war so devastated the population that there was no-one left to work the land.

After the rapid defeat of France in the spring of 1940 the French did not want to fight. That summer SOE analysts in London estimated that only one Frenchman in 100 would be willing to play an active role in a resistance movement against the Germans. It was more than a year before there was any overt action. The first attack came in August 1941 when a communist resistance fighter called Pierre Georges - later known as "Colonel Fabien" - walked up to a German naval officer at the Barbès Métro Station in the north of Paris and shot him. The German response was vicious: Honoré d'Estienne d'Orves, Maurice Barlier and Yan Doornik, three intelligence officers of Général de Gaulle's Deuxième Bureau, who had been captured earlier that year while trying to set up a spy network in France, were executed at the Mont-Valérien fortress in Suresnes. The communists responded by killing six more German officers in the weeks that followed and towards the end of the month the French Prime Minister Pierre Laval was shot and injured during a military parade at Versailles. Whenever there were reprisals French anger increased, and so did the number of recruits for the resistance movements. The first suggestion of a national resistance movement can be traced to the outcry that followed the execution of 48 hostages after the assassination of German Lt-Col Karl Holz in a bomb attack in Nantes in October 1941.

The SOE argued that assassination would deprive the enemy of important officers and force the Germans to replace the dead with other talented men. It also meant that top-level German officers had to be guarded day and night, which meant that thousands of German soldiers were taken away from front line duty in Russia and in North Africa.

Churchill's idea of a Fifth Column in Europe was not an easy one to turn into a reality. In the early months of its existence the SOE's biggest problem was recruitment: one cannot advertise for an organization that does not exist. Candidates had to be found by word of mouth or through social connections. Later a system of questionnaires was introduced which revealed which servicemen and women spoke the various different languages needed.

The other major problem was that from the very beginning Britain's professional intelligence community was opposed to the idea of the SOE. It was no different to the reaction one would get if one invited the Stratford-Upon-Avon Amateur Dramatic Society to take the stage at the Royal Shakespeare Company. The professional spies believed that the job ought to be done by them. Claude Dansey, the deputy head of the Secret Intelligence Service, took to referring to the SOE as "the Stately 'Omes of England" because it requisitioned so many country houses to use as its Secret Training Schools.

Dansey was a powerful man but he could not argue with the Prime Minister. The SIS had no control over SOE budgets. The secret army was part of Ministry of Economic Warfare although officially it was a division of the War Office, known as Military Operations 1 (Special Projects). On the brass plaque outside the door of SOE headquarters in Baker Street in London, the name of the organization was the "Inter Services Research Bureau". This was so that no-one would think it odd when they saw visitors in different uniforms of the different services coming and going. Inside the building the SOE was divided into different country sections. The French Section came under the command of a rather gawky-looking 31-year-old Eton-educated officer by the name of Maurice Buckmaster. He had been a reporter and then a merchant banker before he found his niche with the Ford Motor Company. After a period in the chairman's office at Ford of Great Britain he had been posted to Bordeaux to run Ford's assembly plant there during the period when Ford France joined forces with the Mathis company to establish a manufacturing company called Matford.

When the war came Buckmaster joined the British Army and was appointed an intelligence officer with the 50th Division, part of the British Expeditionary Force in France in 1940. He escaped to Britain after the German invasion of France and in March 1941 was put in charge of the Belgian Section of the SOE. Two months later he was transferred to head the French department, known as F Section.

Buckmaster's appointment marked a new beginning for F Section, which in its early days had been split by internal politics and had achieved almost nothing. When Buckmaster took over he had a staff of only eight. The organization had sent only a couple of agents into France, the first of which was a 30-year-old radio operator called Georges Bégué, who had parachuted into France in May 1941. A few days later he was followed to France by F Section's first network organizer, Pierre de Vomécourt, who was to be the driving force behind Autogiro, the first French Section sabotage network. Charles had been sent to France to work for Autogiro.

What no-one in England knew in May 1942 was that de Vomécourt's network had been penetrated by German counter-intelligence. Charles would discover the bad news only when he arrived in Normandy. He was soon on the run, with the German security police on his tail.

Sebastien was more fortunate. His orders were to avoid all contact with Autogiro and to build up an entirely new network in and around Paris. This organization was to be code named Chestnut.

That Sunday evening, as Sebastien made his way through the streets of Paris, his thoughts were not on the task ahead but rather that he would be soon be seeing his wife Yvonne again. They had been apart since he had left France with the remnants of the British Expeditionary Force after the German invasion two years earlier. She had continued to live in their pre-war home on the rue Weber, just around the corner from the Porte Maillot, in the 16ème arrondissement. She had no idea that he would be returning to France. There had been no way that Sebastien could have warned her.

He found it rather strange that Paris under German occupation seemed much more relaxed than it had done in the years leading up to the war. He realized as he walked that it was because the streets were almost empty. In peacetime there had always been automobiles, trucks and buses but by the spring of 1942 the great boulevards designed by Baron Georges-Eugène Haussmann were dominated by the bicycle. The war had brought austerity. Fuel was needed for the military and only a few privileged civilians had access to gasoline. There were German military trucks and staff cars. There were some buses, some fitted with curious-looking gas bubbles on the roof. From time to time horse drawn carts passed by and there were occasional velo-taxis, old taxis that had been cut in half and the rear end attached to a bicycle.

Sebastien knew that whatever pleasure was gained from living in a quieter city was offset by the heavy-handed nature of the German occupation. The French were not allowed to forget their defeat in 1940. No French flags flew over the city. On every public building was the sinister red and black swastika banner of the Nazis. Every day at midday a German marching band paraded down the Champs-Élysées and at every major intersection the French sign posting had become cluttered with small wooden signs in German, indicating to the occupation forces where they needed to go. All the best hotels in Paris had been taken over by the Germans and many of these establishments now housed departments of the military bureaucracy. Security was tight. There were numerous wooden barricades on the pavements at which German military policemen checked the papers of each passer-by.

"Paris was far and away the most dangerous place in which to work," Maurice Buckmaster wrote years later. "It was swarming with Germans and security police of every description."

Sebastien walked quickly down the rue Weber, aware that he might be recognized by someone in his old neighbourhood. When he reached the house he rang the doorbell and heard the sound of his beloved Aberdeen terriers. He had missed the dogs as well. Yvonne - known to Sebastien as Didi - opened the door and stared at him in amazement, putting together in her mind what his presence in Paris must mean. Then she threw her arms around him. Worried that they would be seen, he closed the door behind them and took her downstairs to the little bar in the basement where they seemed to spend most of their time. They had always rented out the apartment on the top floor, preferring to live downstairs. Didi explained that the apartment had been requisitioned and that a German officer was now living there with his French mistress. In hushed tones, Sebastien told Didi that he had been sent to France by Winston Churchill to work as a secret agent.

That evening he told her the rest of his story and explained that the following day he would begin a new life in Paris as Charles Lelong, an engineer who had to travel around France. This would be enough to explain his absences. He would find himself an apartment and then Didi would be able to visit him. No-one would think it strange that the shy engineer had found himself a lady friend.

The following morning Sebastien left the rue Weber and walked quickly down the rue Pergolèse to the Avenue Foch. As he crossed the great tree-lined avenue he glanced down towards the elegant mansions set back from the road on the northern side of the street. Numbers 82, 84 and 86 were buildings which he hoped he would never visit, the headquarters of the Nazi Party's security police force, the Sicherheitsdienst (SD).

✠

The SD had been created in 1931 when Heinrich Himmler, the man in charge of the Schutzstaffel (SS), Adolf Hitler's bodyguard, decided that the elite paramilitary division of the Nazi party needed a counter-intelligence service. He picked a 27-year-old SS officer called Reinhard Heydrich to take charge. Heydrich was so effective in this role that by September 1939 he had taken control of all Nazi Germany's security services and had become head of an organization known as the Reichssicherheitshauptamt (RHSA). The SD were the men Sebastien had come to Paris to defeat and, if necessary, to kill. Their job was to stop him.

As Sebastien set off to start his career as a saboteur, Heydrich lay in the University Hospital in Prague. The doctors who had performed the operation on the Reichsprotektor were mystified that the patient had developed a high fever. Himmler sent his personal physician SS-Brigadeführer Prof Dr Karl Gebhardt to Prague, accompanied by two other eminent physicians: Dr Ludwig Stumpfegger and Professor Ferdinand Sauerbruch. The doctors had never seen anything like it before and did not know how to treat the condition. The situation did not improve. An infection spread slowly through Heydrich's body. His face became paralysed and the muscles in his arms, legs and respiratory system all weakened. Soon he had lapsed into a coma.

On June 3 Heydrich rallied briefly, regained consciousness and spoke to his pregnant wife Lina, but then he fell back into the coma again and died just before dawn the following day. The post-mortem revealed that he had died from "septicaemia caused by bacteria and possibly by poisons carried into the vital organs by the bomb splinters".

Heydrich's death remained a mystery for more than 30 years until Alvin Pappenheimer, a highly-respected professor of biology at Harvard University, revealed that a British colleague called Paul Fildes had once bragged to him that the death of Heydrich had been "the first notch on my pistol".

Fildes, who died in 1971, had been the head of the Medical Research Council's bacterial chemistry department at London's Middlesex Hospital before the war but was soon appointed the director of biology at the British Chemical and Biological Warfare research centre at Porton Down. It was there that a botulism toxin called BTX was developed. It is probable that Jan Kubiš's grenade contained clostridium botulinum spores which germinated in one of Heydrich's wounds. There are, however, no official details of Porton Down's involvement.

Nazi Germany was shocked by the assassination. On June 7 the Reichsprotektor's coffin was transported by train from Prague to Berlin where Heydrich lay in state in the Mosaic Hall of the new Reich Chancellery. There was a state funeral at which both Hitler and Himmler made stirring speeches and, to the strains of the Funeral March from Ludwig van Beethoven's "Eroica" symphony, the coffin was carried from the hall by Heydrich's SS colleagues. It was placed on a gun carriage, pulled by six black horses, which took Heydrich to his final resting place in the Invalidenfriedhof cemetery.

The day after the funeral the SS descended on the village of Lidice, outside Prague: 173 men were shot. The women and children were taken away to concentration camps. The village was burned to the ground and the remaining buildings were blown up and bulldozed.

Nothing was left. The message was clear.

The assassins survived only another week. The Germans had offered a huge reward for information leading to the arrest of the men involved in the attack and on June 18, their hiding place was discovered to be in the crypt of the Church of Sts Cyril and Methodius in Prague's Resslova Street. For six hours, seven men held off Nazi troops who tried to gain entry to the church. In the end the

Germans pumped water into the crypt in an attempt to flush out the assassins. Those left alive turned their guns on themselves rather than face capture by the Nazis.

SOE agents knew the dangers involved and they accepted them, just as the racing drivers accept that there is always a chance that things will go wrong and they will be killed.

Sebastien understood the rules of the game.

He had been a good racing driver, perhaps even a great one. He had won more Grand Prix victories than any Englishman before him but because he lived in France and insisted on racing with the pseudonym "W Williams" he received almost no recognition at home in England.

At the start of his career he had adopted the name because he did not want his mother to know that he was risking his life in motorcycle races and when he switched to car racing it was useful to keep the same name because there were some who had heard of the bike racer "Williams". Later, when success brought him fame, secrecy became a habit and he liked to cultivate an air of mystery.

"Some said he was a wealthy sportsman because he drove a magnificent town car - an Hispano Suiza," remembered René Dreyfus, one of his rivals. "Others thought that he was one of the livery men who operated from the Place de l'Opéra in Paris and hired out his car and his services as a chauffeur to wealthy clients. No-one knew for sure. What we did know was that he was a charming, but very reserved, gentleman. A lovely man."

The instructors at the secret SOE schools in Britain did not agree with Dreyfus's generous assessment.

They thought that Willy Grover was a killer.

CHAPTER TWO

Until the Metropolitan Railway Company built a branch line to Chesham in 1889, it was a small country town. It was only 30 miles to the north west of London but in a world without cars 30 miles was a very long way. Chesham, hidden away in the wooded valley of the River Chess, a tributary of the River Thames, was off the beaten track and had a strong tradition of non-conformism. In the churchyard stands a monument to Thomas Harding, a non-conformist who was burned at the stake in the town in 1532.

The Chess Valley is flat and rather marshy, but it provided a place to grow cress and reeds. The sides of the valley offered a little more potential as they were covered with groves of beech trees. The timber from these was used to produce wooden items, including brushes, shovels, yokes and spoons. Chesham produced all of these and wooden shoes as well, for the people of London. For themselves there was beer, which was brewed with the waters of the Chess.

In the 1580s the name Grover first started to appear in the local records, the name being applied to the people who lived in the beech groves on the slopes of the valley. As Chesham developed so the Grover name spread along the valley and, as the years flowed quietly by, the name spread over the hill to Amersham and then along the valley of the River Misbourne to Great Missenden, and Chalfont St Giles.

By the 1880s Grover smallholdings dotted the entire region.

Unlike sleepy Chesham, the Misbourne valley was on a major road from London to Birmingham and when the stagecoaches began to link the big towns of England, the coaching inns of Great Missenden found that they needed a constant supply of horses and it was on one of the horse farms in the area in the 1880s that a young man called Frederick Grover learned how to breed horses. Within a few years he had moved south and established a small stud farm near the town of Taplow, on the River Thames.

Taplow is not a big place but the area is famed for its horses, if only because the parish of Taplow contains several magnificent country estates, the most notable being Cliveden, once the home of Hugh Lupus Grosvenor, the Duke of Westminster, the richest man in England. Although he enjoyed a long career in parliament, the Duke was most famous for his racehorses: Bend Or won the Derby in 1880, ridden by the famous jockey Fred Archer, and six years later Archer rode another Westminster horse, Ormonde, to victory in the Two Thousand Guineas, the Derby and the St Leger. Ormonde is remembered as the greatest racehorse of the nineteenth century.

The main Westminster stud was at the family's Eaton estate in Cheshire, one hundred and fifty miles to the north-west of Taplow but from 1870 onwards the Duke ran a 250-acre stud on the Cliveden estate. There was a constant stream of important visitors and large house parties every year during Royal Ascot. Often the Duke did business with foreign visitors and made handsome profits from his horses. In 1884, for example, he sold a stallion called Doncaster to the Hungarian government for the sum of £5,000 (around £335,000 at modern prices). Frederick Grover must have mixed with people at the Cliveden stud and this probably explains how it was that the humble horse-breeder in Taplow became close friends with the Imperial Russian government's military attaché in London, Prince Ivan Yurievich Trubetskoy.

The Trubetskoys had been one of the most influential families in Russia for several centuries and, before being posted to the London embassy, the Prince had served as a colonel in the Imperial Guard in St Petersburg. Once in London he found a quieter life. In that era a diplomat had plenty of time to indulge his hobbies and Trubetskoy was fascinated by the possibility that he might be able to breed the perfect horse. He believed this would be a cross between the British Anglo-Arab and the Don horses from Russia, which had been bred for centuries by the Cossacks. The Anglo-Arab, a cross between an English thoroughbred and an Arabian mare, was famed for its stamina and speed but tended to be highly-strung. The Don horses were renowned for their toughness and ability to cope with different climates. As their experiments went on Grover and Trubetskoy became close and the horse-breeder was soon invited to the Prince's vast estates near Kiev to continue the work. Frederick even learned to speak Russian and in 1895 was a guest at the coronation of Tsar Nicholas II. The arrival of the new Tsar was to have a dramatic effect on Grover's life because he decided that Trubetskoy should move to the Russian Embassy in Paris and appointed him the Russian military attaché to France.

The Prince, keen to continue his experiments, convinced Grover to follow him across the English Channel and not long afterwards Frederick Grover settled in Montrouge, a small country town close to Paris, which, within a few years, would be swallowed up the expanding city. Frederick met and soon married a French girl called Hermance Dagan and in 1897 they became the parents of a daughter whom they named Elizabeth, although from an early age she was always known as Lizzie.

When Lizzie was six Hermance gave birth to a second child, a son born on January 16, 1903. Frederick registered the birth at the town hall in Montrouge, choosing the names William Charles Frederick although the new youngster was always known as Willy.

Frederick and Trubetskoy continued their horse breeding experiments in Paris but each summer Grover left his family and went to Kiev in Russia. Hermance took the children south to the Dagan family home, a vineyard at Grands Fonds, near Agen in the southwest of France. Willy loved his days in Agen, even if his was a rather solitary childhood. Lizzie was too old to join his games and Willy was 10 before another sister Alice was born and 17 when a brother called Frederic (without a k) joined the family.

Although he was a loner, Willy had inherited his father's easy charm. In his childhood he was an outsider. He had been born in France but never felt like a Frenchman. He was an Englishman but he never lived in England. His brother and sisters belonged to different generations. As an outsider, he liked to keep a low profile. Later when people discovered what he had done in his life he became the centre of attention but it was not a role that came easily to him. He was different and his attitude to life was unlike many others. To him, nothing was impossible.

When Willy was 11 France was plunged into war with Germany and, alarmed by the German invasion of France, the Grover family despatched Willy to England, to stay with relatives in Hertfordshire. He was there long enough to become a member of the local Boy Scout troop. After the German invasion had been checked at the Battle of the Marne, and the war had bogged down in the trenches of the Western Front, Willy returned to France. It was not long afterwards that Trubetskoy died and, without his patron, there was little reason for Grover and the family to stay in Paris. Many of the Russian émigrés that Frederick knew had moved to Monte Carlo during the war and he decided to move the family there. The tiny principality had been famous for 50 years for its spectacular casino and its luxury hotels. The rich and famous of Europe gathered there to pass the winter in the sub-tropical climate beneath the great corniche.

Lizzie was 19 years of age when the family arrived in Monte Carlo and she soon met a dashing Englishman called Richard Whitworth. Before the war Whitworth, who came from a famous engineering family, had been an engineer with Sir Henry Royce's luxury automobile company. Royce kept a design office next to his Villa Mimosa at Le Canadel, along the coast towards Toulon, and often sent his engineers out to test his vehicles on the roads of France. Whitworth had even taken part in one of the early long distance automobile races between Paris and Moscow.

Willy was fascinated with the automobiles he saw in the Principality and his sister's boyfriend quickly became his hero, particularly after he taught Willy how to drive a Rolls Royce. The ability to drive was still a rare talent at the time and as manpower was short because of the war Willy soon discovered that he could earn good money working as a chauffeur for some of Whitworth's clients. He was required to pass a driving test under the watchful eye of a local Monaco official but he manoeuvred the automobile with sufficient skill to be granted a licence immediately.

When the war ended the Grover family returned to Paris and moved into a new apartment in the Rue de la Pompe, in the 16ème arrondissement. Willy was sent to school just down the road at the Lycée Janson de Sailly. This was a famous Parisian school but the military-style education and discipline left little room for imagination and the 15-year-old Willy Grover was not a good pupil. He was becoming more and more interested in mechanics. Initially he was fascinated by photography but then he acquired a motorcycle, one of the thousands left behind in France when the US Army went home in 1919. Manufactured by the Indian Motorcycle Company of Springfield, Massachusetts, the motorcycle became Willy Grover's pride and joy. He loved nothing better than to strip down his Indian and rebuild it, time and time again. His brother Frederic, although only a toddler, remembered Willy working on the motorcycle in the early 1920s.

"The parts would be everywhere," he recalled, "but somehow Willy would manage to put it all together again. He was a very good mechanic."

Willy was something of a disappointment to his parents. They might have had dreams of a proper profession but Willy had no time for school. He wanted to be a chauffeur. Paris was full of potential customers, thanks to the many hundreds of delegates at the international conferences, which dragged on into the summer of 1920. The city was also attracting the idle rich, people who had lived through the war and now wanted just to have fun. Paris cared little for the strict moral codes adopted elsewhere, like Prohibition in America, and thousands of wild and interesting characters flocked to the city in the early 1920s. It was a hotbed of art, literature, fashion and sex.

Willy's connections with Rolls Royce resulted in a job to drive for the famous Irish portrait painter Sir William Orpen, who, before the war, had made a fortune painting portraits of London's high society. During the war Orpen had worked as a war artist for the British Government and then, having been knighted in 1918, he became the official artist of the Paris Peace Conference. Orpen was rich and famous and he wanted the world to know it. He bought himself a Rolls Royce and hired the 16-year-old Willy Grover to drive it. Willy was happy to wear the smart brown uniform, complete with peaked cap, which Orpen organized for him.

The artist kept a suite of rooms at the Hotel Majestic, painted in a studio at the Hotel Astoria, on the Avenue de Champs-Élysées, and kept a mistress in a house which he owned on the Rue Weber, near the Porte Maillot. Sir William's mistress was a very striking young woman.

"She was tall and pale with blue eyes and blonde hair," remembered Simona Packenham, one of the British visitors of the era. "She was very beautiful and a woman of quite exceptional charm and sweetness."

Her name was Yvonne Aupicq and she had met Orpen when she was working as a nurse in Paris in 1917. She was 21. He was 39. He had a wife and daughter living in England but this did not seem to matter to either of them. Orpen was fascinated and asked Yvonne to model for his paintings. One of the first was called "The Rape" which, Orpen said, was based on the experiences of his model in Lille when the Germans invaded at the start of the war. The girl was beautiful and haunted and she appeared again in "The Refugee" and "The Spy" although in the post-war era, Orpen's "Disappointing Letter" and "Early Morning" featured a much warmer and happier Yvonne.

The relationship between the artist and his model was to last for 12 years and in that time the couple mixed with many of the famous names in Paris, notably the author James Joyce. The writer and the artist were close in age and were both Dublin men. Later Samuel Beckett, another Dublin writer, arrived. His aunt had been taught to paint by Orpen at the Dublin Metropolitan School of Art.

From the United States came many youngsters. Sylvia Beach established her famous Shakespeare and Company bookshop and young American writers, including Ezra Pound, Ernest Hemingway, F Scott Fitzgerald and many more who failed, established their own expatriate society. Gertrude Stein, who had been in Paris since 1903, looked upon the newcomers as "The Lost Generation". Willy Grover knew many of them and spent much time in Hemingway's favourite bar, the Trou dans le Mur - The Hole in the Wall - just opposite the Café de la Paix at 23 Boulevard des Capucines. This was an English bar where the English chauffeurs whiled away their time, waiting for rich clients in the Place de l'Opéra and where, so they say, the croque monsieur had been invented in 1910.

Driving the Rolls Royce in his strange uniform, Willy Grover became a well known figure in Parisian society as he ferried Orpen and his mistress around Paris and, at weekends, took them to the fashionable seaside resort of Dieppe, where they played golf at Pourville. When Orpen returned to Ireland Willy looked after the Rolls Royce but was free to work for other clients. His aim in life in those years was to raise enough money to buy his own automobile. He lived at home with his parents and saved every penny he could. Orpen's absences also meant that Willy could indulge his love of speed, which had developed after he bought the Indian motorcycle. In the early 1920s he began competing in motorcycle races, although he never told his family and chose to race under the pseudonym "W Williams".

Willy's brother Frederic remembers rumours about a race at Pau one summer when they were all down in the south-west, but none in the family knew for sure if it had been Willy.

"I have never figured out where this flirting with death came from," recalled Frederic many years later. "I suppose that was what it took to be a racing car driver in the 1920s."

✠

Willy's dream was to race cars and he took a step closer to fulfilling that ambition in the autumn of 1924 when he scraped together enough money to buy a second hand Hispano Suiza H6 automobile. This was the most expensive car in Europe at the time. It had been first unveiled at the Paris Salon in 1919 and featured a 6.5-litre straight six engine, incorporating many of the lessons that designer Marc Birkigt had learned while developing aero-engines during World War I. It was a big car but was nonetheless sufficiently powerful to be raced, as drinks heir André Dubonnet proved in 1921 by winning a sports car race at Boulogne at the wheel of his H6. The new car was a huge financial gamble for Willy Grover but it attracted more clients than the old Rolls Royce and also meant that Willy could go racing.

In January 1925 Willy Grover entered the Hispano-Suiza in the Monte Carlo Rally and was one of the 32 finishers in the gruelling event. After he reached Monaco he spent several weeks working as a chauffeur on the Riviera and, when "The Season" was coming to a close, he took part in a number of local hillclimb events. The man to beat that year was a rising star with the Delage team called Robert Benoist and Willy had no chance against the nimble little Delage. Benoist won at La Turbie, Mi-Corniche, Mont Agel, Esterel and Le Camp. Willy went back to Paris to prepare for the summer visitors and to dream of racing a car like the Delage.

It was perhaps inevitable that Orpen's chauffeur and mistress should become friends. They lived in the same neighbourhood and although the shy Willy was overawed by the confident and beautiful Yvonne, he gradually overcame his natural reticence and their friendship grew. He gave her the nickname "Didi" and when Orpen was not in Paris they spent a great deal of time together.

"They were very good dancers and they won all kinds of prizes for dancing at the big hotels," remembered Willy's brother Frederic. "Willy was also very gifted at sports and played a lot of tennis and golf. Yvonne always said he could have been a golf champion."

Inspired yet frustrated by his efforts on the hill climbs of the Riviera in 1925, Willy set his heart on acquiring a racing machine which he could use to beat Benoist and the other heroes of the day. He wanted a Bugatti Type 35 and was convinced that if he acquired such a car he would be able to use it to make a name for himself in the sport and by doing so secure a salaried drive with one of the factory racing teams and so pay for the purchase. He had all the confidence of youth but a 22-year-old without a family fortune could barely dream of buying a Bugatti. And yet he did. To Willy nothing was ever impossible. How he did it we will probably never know. Ettore Bugatti was a man who appreciated racers and perhaps allowed himself to be talked into giving Grover a deal on an old car. Perhaps Yvonne had some money saved. Whatever the details, Willy took the risk and acquired a 35B in the autumn of 1925 and began driving the car in hill climb events all over France. Many of these events were won by Bugatti 35Bs, but none was won by the mysterious "W Williams". It was not until January 1926 that Willy made his breakthrough with victory in the Hispano-Suiza on the Mont des Mules hillclimb, an event that always followed the end of the Monte Carlo Rally.

Two months later Willy entered the Bugatti in the Grand Prix de Provence at Miramas.

The Miramas speedway sits at the edge of the vast flood plain of the River Rhône. Near at hand is the French Air Force base at Istres, opened in 1917 as a flying school. It was the existence of the aerodrome that helped former racer Paul Bablot to convince the local authorities that the noise of an autodrome would not be a problem for the local residents. Having raced in the Indianapolis 500 in 1919 with the Ballot team, Bablot was convinced that France needed a speedway like Indianapolis and began raising money to build one as soon as had returned home. It took several years to raise the cash for such ambitious project but in 1924 Bablot's dream became a reality. The Grand Prix de Provence of 1926 was the first major event at Miramas and although the entry was rather disappointing there were still 29 cars for the five heats; one for each of the different classes. The smallest class was for 1100cc-engined cars but as only one was present there was no need to hold the race; in the 1500cc class there were only three cars and one broke down.

"W Williams" appeared in Heat 3, the class for 2000cc cars. There were four cars but the quality was exceptional. Two were driven by men who would go on to much greater things: Marcel Lehoux from Algeria and the local hero Louis Chiron, from Monte Carlo. The other driver was a privateer called François Eysserman. Willy completed the 10 laps but was more than a minute and a half behind Lehoux at the finish. He had a lot to learn.

The fourth heat featured the Sunbeam Talbot Darracq (STD) team which was expected to win the race with its potent Talbot 70s. The team had new Sunbeams under development but for the Miramas race STD's star driver Major Henry Segrave and his team mates Edmond Bourlier and Jules Moriceau were still using the older cars. They finished 1-2-3 in the heat, well ahead of the next runner. The lap times had been fairly close in the heats and although everyone expected the STD team to win without too much trouble they hoped that the 50-lap race was going to be a good battle. At the start the newcomer "W Williams" surprised everyone by taking the lead, chased by Chiron. What was even more surprising was that the mysterious Williams stayed in the lead until eventually he had to stop for new tyres. This dropped him behind the Talbots but he chased and caught Bourlier and was closing on Segrave, a big star at the time, when he had to stop again for more tyres. Segrave was safe but Willy rejoined in second place and stayed there all the way to the finish.

As soon as the race was over Louis Coatalen, the renowned competition manager of Sunbeam Talbot Darracq, slipped away from his team and went in search of "W Williams". Coatalen was so impressed, in fact, that he offered Willy a factory drive for the 1927 season.

Willy's crazy plan had worked.

After a few days of complete euphoria Willy Grover became frustrated. He did not want to wait a year to go racing. He went back to work in Paris and did more hillclimb events but he could not afford to race with the big stars. After a few weeks he approached Ettore Bugatti and talked him into letting him take one of the factory Type 35s which had been raced in the Targa Florio. He enlisted Yvonne to help him out and in July the pair drove down to the Basque city of San Sebastian for the Spanish GP. The big event was the Grand Prix of Europe that was run on the first weekend for a handful of new Grand Prix cars. The Spanish GP, a week later, was open to a variety of different machines although Willy knew that there was little chance of success, because he was up against the factory teams from both Delage and Bugatti. STD had turned up to give the new Sunbeam Grand Prix car a run and Willy was keen to see how well the car he would be driving in 1927 would do. The race was disrupted by rain and although Willy ran as high as fourth he dropped back with mechanical trouble and finished 10 laps behind.

Despite the poor result, these were nonetheless exciting times for Willy and Yvonne, who were swept along in "The Roaring Twenties".

"On the road back to Paris they were constantly frustrated by all the barriers at the railway crossings," remembered Willy's brother Frederic. "My brother used to shout out "Duck!" to Yvonne and they would go straight through them without stopping."

The autumn and winter seemed to Willy to drag on forever but finally spring came and Willy began to prepare for life as an STD driver. The team was not ready for the Grand Prix de l'Ouverture, the first big race of the year at Montlhéry in March, and Willy went back to Ettore Bugatti and begged Le Patron for a car. There were none available. STD went to the Grand Prix de Provence two weeks later with the old Talbots and Willy finished right behind Moriceau in his heat. On race day the weather was so bad that the team withdrew from the main event.

It was not until the first week of July that Willy was finally in a position to go racing again. On the day before the Grand Prix de l'ACF at Montlhéry, the race organizers decided to put on a Formula Libre event to entertain the crowds and convinced some of the teams to run cars. STD agreed to field Willy and the veteran Louis Wagner in Sunbeams and ran an old Talbot for Alberto Divo. Willy took the lead and was ahead for two laps before he retired with a gearbox failure. As he was climbing out of his car the wealthy aristocrat Gerard de Courcelles suffered a steering failure on his Guyot Special out at the back of the circuit and went off at high speed and hit a tree. "Couc" died on his way to the hospital. The crash cast a dark shadow over the meeting but the main event went ahead as planned on the Sunday. Practice had shown that the new Delage 15-S-B was an extraordinary piece of machinery. In fact Ettore Bugatti was so worried by what he saw that he decided to avoid the humiliation and withdrew his three factory cars from the event. This meant that the field consisted of the three Talbots, driven by Divo, Willy and Louis Wagner up against the three Delages of Benoist, Bourlier and André Morel. The only other car was a slow Halford, driven by England's George Eyston.

At the start six cars got away cleanly but Wagner was left sitting on the grid trying to start his Talbot. First he tried to crank the handle but then opened up the bonnet to try to find the problem. Finally he concluded that brute force was the only way and the car was push-started by a gang of frenzied STD mechanics. As Wagner disappeared from the stadium area, the race leaders reappeared on the other side of the oval with Divo ahead as they went up on the high banking. Benoist was next and then Willy. For three laps the order remained the same but then Benoist grabbed the lead and Willy followed him through, pushing Divo back into third position.

For the next five laps Willy pushed Benoist as hard as he knew how but the more experienced Delage star responded with a new lap record on each lap. If Willy had any illusions of beating France's hero, they would soon evaporate. On the 10th lap the Talbot began to misfire and Willy began to fall back. In the end he came into the pits and handed the car over to the reserve driver Moriceau. They would end up back in fourth place, behind the three Delages. Coatalen was, nonetheless, impressed by what he had seen and so too was Benoist. The mysterious newcomer was good.

But if he had any fears about "W Williams" becoming a threat to his success, they were short-lived. A few days after the race at Montlhéry Coatalen reluctantly announced that STD was suspending its racing activities because the company was in big financial trouble. Willy was released from his contract. It was a huge blow to the young man but Willy immediately began to badger Ettore Bugatti, hoping for a chance to drive with Le Patron's factory team. It was a long summer but Willy never gave up and eventually Bugatti relented and offered Willy the job of being the team's reserve driver at the RAC Grand Prix in England in October.

The vast banked Brooklands speedway near Weybridge was the home of British motor racing and the world's first permanent motor racing facility. All the other great speedways that followed Brooklands had been inspired by the Surrey track.

Despite his European background, Willy was very British at heart and it was a proud moment for him as the cars lined up for the start of his "home" Grand Prix. British racing at the time was not as advanced as in Europe and there were few drivers of international note and, once Sunbeam was gone, no serious British teams. Segrave had retired from racing not long after setting a new Land Speed Record of 203.7mph on Daytona Beach in Florida but his rival Malcolm Campbell was racing a private Bugatti. George Eyston was there too in his private Bugatti. There were two British-built Thomas Specials, which had been completed that year despite the death earlier in the year of John Parry-Thomas while attempting a Land Speed Record. The cars were driven by William "Bummer" Scott and Harold Purdy but neither was competitive. The weather was awful although a huge crowd turned up at Brooklands to see whether Benoist could complete the task of winning every major Grand Prix race in the same season.

The Delages were, of course, dominant after an initial attack from Bugatti's Emilio Materassi and it was left to Sunbeam refugee Alberto Divo to lead most of the event. Benoist was never far behind him and took the lead with around 20 laps to go. Willy watched the race hoping to get a chance to drive but the factory Bugatti drivers Materassi, Louis Chiron and Count Caberto Conelli seemed not to need his help. But then, at half distance, Conelli ran out of fuel just before his pit stop and was faced with the job of pushing the Bugatti more than a mile back to the pits. The Italian aristocrat completed the task but he was so tired from the exertion that he was unable to drive any more. Bugatti turned to Willy. There was no hope of a good finishing position by then but he was ordered to bring the car home. The mysterious "W Williams" finished 20 laps behind Benoist.

The 1927 international racing season was over. The 1.5-litre formula had been a failure and the manufacturers were leaving the sport. The international automobile federation had become so concerned about the state of affairs that it took the controversial decision to announce a new Grand Prix formula for 1928. In the long term this would be a success but the immediate result was a disaster, as the last of the big manufacturers withdrew, leaving all the top drivers out of work. The drivers who could not afford to buy their own cars were left with little choice: even the great Benoist found himself unemployed and had to accept a job running a garage in Paris.

Willy refused to give up and once again Ettore Bugatti was the man under siege and, if only to buy himself a little respite, Le Patron loaned Willy a four-seater Bugatti Type 43 with which to compete on the Monte Carlo Rally at the start of 1928.

Willy took Didi and some friends with him down to the Riviera and he then turned his attentions on Ernest Friderich, Bugatti's agent in Nice. Within a few days Willy was sent up to the Bugatti factory at Molsheim to collect a new Bugatti 35C for Friderich. In the weeks that followed Willy raced this new car in all the usual events at the end of "The Season" on the Riviera, doing valuable promotional work for Friderich's agency. A deal was struck over prize money and Willy ended up owning the car.

In April he finished runner-up to Louis Chiron in the Grand Prix d'Antibes, a new event on a road course called the Circuit de la Garoupe. A few days later he won the hill climb of the 17 Tournants, in the valley of the Chevreuse, near Paris and not long after that added another victory at the Vernon hillclimb, up near Rouen.

That year the Automobile Club de France ran its Grand Prix

on the Comminges circuit, near St Gaudens, in the shadow of the Pyrénées. Worried that there would not be enough Grand Prix cars, the ACF decided to run the event for sports cars and so Willy fitted his Grand Prix Bugatti with a windscreen, mudguards and headlights. On July 1 he drove the car to his first major victory in Europe. It might have been a bad year for the French GP but victory in the event was the best result a driver could hope for in his career. Willy had ceased to be a promising young driver – he had arrived.

Racing success was very good for sales and, keen to gain from the reflected glory of success, Ettore Bugatti agreed to supply Willy with factory racing cars for the rest of the season. Three weeks later Willy went to San Sebastian and took on eight other Bugattis, including a factory car which Ettore Bugatti had made available to Robert Benoist. But there was no chance for the new team mates to renew their rivalry as Willy's car caught fire early in the race and Benoist finished second to his team-mate Louis Chiron.

At the start of September the Bugatti team headed to Monza to take part in the Grand Prix of Europe. Willy led the first four laps of the race, ahead of Tazio Nuvolari, Baconin Borzacchini and Emilio Materassi but then his engine failed and he was forced to watch the rest of the race from the garages. On the 17th lap he watched as Materassi's Talbot tried to pass Ernesto Maserati and Giulio Foresti on the main straight. The Talbot went out of control and cart wheeled off the track and across the ditch which separated the crowd from the track. Materassi was thrown from the car and the wreck bounced through a spectator area before coming to rest back in the ditch beside the circuit. Materassi was dead, but so too were 27 others, in what was the worst accident motor racing had ever seen. It was a shocking and bitter end to the season and a reminder of the dangers of motor racing.

Willy went back to Paris for the winter. The winner of the Grand Prix de l'ACF did not work as a chauffeur and Willy found new employment with Bugatti, teaching the company's customers how to drive the powerful cars without hurting themselves.

"Willy was a glorified salesman," remembered Frederic Grover, "but many of the people who bought those expensive cars could not drive them at speed and had to be shown how to do it."

That winter Didi announced to Orpen that their relationship was over. She was not happy. He had been under pressure from a never-ending stream of clients and had developed a serious problem with alcohol. He still had his wife in England and there was talk of another mistress. Yvonne wanted more than the artist could offer.

At 32 she wanted to lead a more respectable life. Perhaps by then her relationship with Willy had gone beyond friendship. He was no longer the boy in the brown uniform and peaked cap. He had become a very successful motor racing driver.

Sir William was generous to his former mistress. He gave her the house in the rue Weber and the old Rolls Royce and he wished her well. Three years later Orpen died from cirrhosis of the liver at the age of only 52.

✠

Willy Grover did not waste any time in asking Didi if she would be his wife. She was only too happy to accept and the couple began planning for a wedding in the autumn of 1929, after the racing season was finished. That season Ettore Bugatti was the only French manufacturer left in Grand Prix racing - and he was having financial difficulties. Alfa Romeo and Maserati both had very competitive machinery so winning was not easy and in order to justify the racing programme Bugatti needed to sell more cars. Bugatti concluded that the only way to make things work would be to reduce his factory's involvement in Grand Prix racing and thus generate more sales by giving his customers a better chance of success. That was tough on professional racing drivers but a necessary evil for the company. If Willy Grover wanted to win races, he would have to buy a car.

That was bad news and meant that at the start of the 1929 season Willy was not on the Riviera for the annual early season events because he did not have the money to buy a car. It was not until April that he managed to do a deal with Le Patron. The car was an old one that Louis Chiron and Robert Benoist has raced in 1928 but it was better than nothing. In order to make the point that this was not a factory car Willy agreed that he would paint the car British

Racing Green and then he and his crew – which consisted of Didi and Bugatti mechanic Ernest Zirn – set off for Monaco to take part in an interesting new event on the streets of the city. They arrived so late that they completely missed all of the practice but as Willy knew all the right people in the Principality, he was able to get permission to do a few laps of the track very early on the morning of the race.

There were 15 cars present, most of them privately-owned Bugattis, although there were four old Alfa Romeo P2s, a couple of Maseratis and even an old Delage. The most intriguing entry, however, was a supposedly-private 7.1-litre Mercedes SSK for Germany's rising star Rudi Caracciola.

The grid positions were drawn in a lottery and Willy found himself in the middle of the second row behind Marcel Lehoux, Christian Dauvergne and Philippe Étancelin, all in Bugattis. Alongside him was Baron Philippe de Rothschild, the famous French playboy who was racing under the pseudonym "Philippe", and on the inside was a little known Italian called Guglielmo Sandri, in a Maserati. Caracciola was on the back row of the grid.

Willy was confident that he had a good chance of victory.

There was a big crowd for the new event and much excitement as the cars lined up on the grid. When the flag dropped Willy burst through between the men on the front row and was second before they reached the corner by the church of Ste Devote and turned uphill towards the Hotel de Paris and the famous Casino. Lehoux was ahead but there was nothing he could do to keep Willy behind him and by the end of the lap "W Williams" was leading the race.

Lehoux crashed on the second lap which left the Maserati of Diego de Sterlich in second place until Caracciola overtook the Italian car on the fifth lap. From then on it was a straight fight between Willy and the German. The gap remained at around four seconds until lap 30 when Caracciola closed in and got alongside Willy in the tunnel. He took an inside line for the chicane on the waterfront and took the lead. Willy fought back and regained the lead on lap 35 but then he decided that he was going to slow down. Watching the Mercedes-Benz he had realized that the big car was going to use a lot of fuel and would therefore spend more time in the pits. If he could save his fuel and waste less time in the pits he would gain a big advantage. He backed off and let the German car get away. Willy went into the pits on lap 49 and was quickly back on the race track. Caracciola came in two laps later but refuelling the car took him a full four minutes and so by the time he was back in the race he was fourth behind Georges Bouriano and "Philippe". It took him eight laps to catch and pass de Rothchild but he was too far behind to catch either Willy or Bouriano. It was a great victory and gave "W Williams" a new status both with the French public and within the racing fraternity. He had won a spectacular triumph of brains over brawn.

Willy was a star.

His next major appearance would not be until the Grand Prix de l'ACF at the end of June. By then Ettore Bugatti had decided that he would once again enter a factory team and had three cars for Willy, Divo and Conelli. Grover did not disappoint Le Patron, going from the last row of the grid to second place during the first lap of the Le Mans circuit and then taking the lead after a spirited battle with veteran André Boillot. Willy won the race by 40 seconds. It had been another magnificent result for Willy and for Automobiles Bugatti. Demand for the Bugatti 35B was soaring and a few days later Willy took the opportunity to sell the Monaco-winning car to Ernest Friderich, who made a quick profit by turning around and selling the car to a wealthy Swiss playboy.

As he stood in front of the mayor of the 16ème arrondissement in Paris that autumn Willy Grover was the picture of success. His bride was a stunning beauty. He was a famous sportsman and was on his way to becoming a wealthy man. He had made it to the top of the sport without a rich family and despite a shortage of paid drives. The Lycée Janson de Sailly had had many famous pupils and Willy, the boy who wanted to be a chauffeur, had become one of them.

✠

The Roaring Twenties came to a dramatic end in October 1929 when the stock market on Wall Street crashed. The confidence which had been building around the world since the end of World War I suddenly vanished. The Great Depression began. The effects would soon be felt across Europe. But for Willy and Didi these were happy times. They went looking for a place to live near the fashionable Atlantic resort of La Baule, in southern Brittany, and found Le Ramby, a large manor house in the country that looked out across a valley but was hidden from the road by a small wood, through which a driveway curved behind a pair of manorial gates. The house boasted a private chapel and close by, hidden from the main house by trees, was a cottage and outbuildings that they decided would be turned into kennels.

Their plan was to breed Aberdeen terriers.

"There was a farm attached to the property," remembered Willy's niece Jessie, "and there were woods where my uncle went shooting. He was a very good shot."

The chauffeur had become a country gentleman and, for the first time, the couple began to use the name "Grover-Williams". They kept the house in the rue Weber for when they were in Paris and added to their income by renting out another apartment that Didi owned in the nearby rue Berlioz.

In the racing world William Grover-Williams remained "W Williams" and for the 1930 season, he was signed by Ettore Bugatti. He raced at Monaco and ran second to Chiron before retiring with mechanical problems. A month later he competed in the Targa Florio road race in the mountains of Sicily.

But then three weeks later at the Tre Fontane circuit near Rome Willy had a big accident and was injured. It would be five months before he was able to return to action and there were many in the racing world who believed that after the crash in Rome, Willy was never the same driver he had been beforehand. It was as if he had realized the dangers and was holding back, aware that he had other things in life which were as important as racing.

Such changes in attitude are common in racing and sometimes a little caution creates a more complete driver. The wildness of youth may have gone but knowing when to push and when to hold back can also bring great rewards. When Willy returned to action in the autumn of 1930 at Pau, it seemed as though nothing had changed. He charged through the field to run second, despite having started at the back of the grid. But then mechanical trouble stopped his progress. Ettore Bugatti, ever the businessman, provided Willy with fewer racing opportunities after that and Willy had to use all his skills as a deal maker to secure drives. In 1931 he landed a seat with the Bugatti sports car team by getting hold of a supply of Dunlop tyres to replace the Michelins that been blamed for causing a major accident during the Le Mans 24 Hours. One spectator had been killed, and Bugatti driver Maurice Rost so badly injured that he never raced again.

Driving with Count Conelli, Willy won the 10-hour Belgian GP at Spa-Francorchamps and ended the year taking part in a local event on the sands of La Baule. The race was run along the five-mile curved beach in front of the casino and Willy led from start to finish in his Bugatti Type 35. He would win the race again in 1932 and 1933. For both seasons he remained a member of the Bugatti factory Grand Prix team, alongside his old rival Benoist, the Italian Achille Varzi and rising star René Dreyfus. Willy had no desire to race cars other than Bugattis and told his brother Frederic that he felt much safer driving for Le Patron.

At the end of the 1933 season Willy announced that he was retiring from the sport. He was 30 years old and he wanted a quieter life. He had seen a lot of fellow racers killed and wanted to enjoy his new found wealth. The Grover-Williamses sold Le Ramby to a hairdresser who had won France's first national lottery and, with the money from the sale, Willy and Didi bought a villa in Beaulieu-sur-Mer, in a bay just along the Côte d'Azur from Monte Carlo.

Beaulieu enjoys one of the mildest climates in France yet retains an old world charm which has been lost by many of the other towns on the Riviera. In the 1860s, when the first road and railway link was built along the coastline, the small fishing village began to grow and quickly became a playground for English and Russian royalty in the winter months. There was land available to build elegant residences and villas and by the 1890s Beaulieu was playing host to the rich and famous from across the world. The visitors included the Prince of Wales, British Prime Minister the Marquis of Salisbury, the writer Count Leo Tolstoy, the engineer Gustave Eiffel and the owner of the New York Herald James Gordon Bennett.

Beaulieu became known as "the jewel of the Riviera".

The Grover-Williamses named their new home the Villa Ramby and from then on they split their time between Paris and the

Riviera, wintering in the south and often renting out the villa in the summer months. When they were in the south, they mixed with the rich and famous on the Riviera, appearing with the very latest Bugatti models, and they charmed the wealthy on behalf of Ernest Friderich, Bugatti's agent in Nice. They were very well connected.

"It was a nice villa," remembered Frederic Grover. "They used to rent it to the family of the Prince of Monaco. He had a sister and she lived there sometimes with some kind of gigolo."

Willy's niece Jessie Teager remembered other advantages of Willy's fame.

"They would sometimes go driving in Monaco in two cars," she said. "Willy would be in the first and Yvonne in the second. She would be stopped for speeding and would say: "What about him? Why don't you stop him?" And the police would reply: "He is Williams, we don't stop Williams". They used to jump all the red lights. Yvonne used to say: "Don't bother with them!" but in the end they took away her licence and we had to drive her around when she came to Paris."

When they were in Paris Willy continued to work from time to time as a glorified salesman for Le Patron at the Avenue Montaigne. It impressed the clients no end to be able to meet a big racing star and "W Williams" had certainly become that.

CHAPTER THREE

The Avenue Montaigne is the home of Parisian chic and it has been since 1911 when the Hotel Plaza Athenée first opened for business. It rapidly became known as one of the best hotels in the world. The following year dressmaker Madeleine Vionnet opened her first boutique just up the road from the Plaza and revolutionized fashion by designing glamorous gowns that fitted the bodies of her clients rather than squeezing them into dresses as had previously been the style.

At the same time the Théâtre des Champs-Élysées opened with Serge Diaghilev's production of Igor Stravinsky's Rite of Spring, choreographed by Vaslav Nijinsky. This so shocked the audience that fights broke out in the auditorium.

The Avenue Montaigne was exciting, new, elegant and glamorous. In the years that followed all the great fashion houses opened stores on the same street and so when Ettore Bugatti decided that he needed a showroom in Paris in order to sell his beautiful cars to the rich, the Avenue Montaigne was the obvious location.

Bugatti's creations were beautiful works of art and wildly expensive. Customers were rare and Bugatti liked to make sure that they felt special when they visited his firm and so he staffed the showroom with Grand Prix drivers. Willy was one of the big names, but the biggest star was Robert Benoist.

Willy and Robert had been fierce competitors in the 1920s and then, for a while, had been team mates at Bugatti. By the time Benoist was appointed the manager of the Bugatti showroom in Paris, in the middle of 1932, they had become friends.

They had much in common: both came from modest backgrounds although close association with wealthy and extraordinary people had given them the desire to succeed; Willy's father had been friends with a Russian prince; Robert's had been the gamekeeper of the Rothschild family, at a property in the valley of the Chevreuse, to the south of Paris.

Robert's grandfather came from the small town of Lurcy-Lévis where, in the early 1800s, André de Sinéty had built an impressive estate. When Baroness Charlotte de Rothschild, the widow of Baron Nathaniel, decided to transform an old Cistercian abbey into the grandest estate in the region, she hired Benoist to be her steward. The baroness was one of the richest women in the world and no expense was spared on the Abbaye des Vaux de Cernay. It had vast imposing gateways, sweeping driveways through the woods and even a vast man-made lake. Robert's father Gaston (who was always known as Georges) followed his father into service and lived in one of the hunting lodges on the estate.

The old baroness lived until 1899 and then the estate passed to her grandson Baron Henri de Rothschild. He was not a banker like most of his relatives but had studied medicine and he was an important patron of the work carried out by Marie and Pierre Curie. He had established two hospitals, built a soap factory, and even experimented with the canning of different foods, in an effort to improve the diet of the French nation. Educated in the finest schools, Baron Henri was also passionate about the theatre and was a moderately-successful playwright under the pseudonym of André Pascal.

He and Georges Benoist were the same age. They married at the same time and had identical young families each boasting two sons and a daughter. Robert Benoist and Baron Henri's son James shared the same birthday, although they were born a year apart. Robert and his older brother Maurice and the two Rothschild boys James and Philippe may have played together during the summers of their childhood, unaffected by social convention. If not, they certainly grew up in parallel. Robert knew every inch of the woods around the Abbaye and by the age of six was already a remarkable hunter.

One evening, when his parents were entertaining, he gave everyone a shock when he shot a hare that was lurking just outside the dining room window.

By the time Robert was in his teens, Georges Benoist had decided that it was time to leave the employ of the Rothschilds and established kennels for hunting dogs outside the village of Auffargis, a few miles further down the Chevreuse Valley from the Abbaye, close to the town of Rambouillet.

The Rothschild boys and their wealthy friends from Paris were often in the valley with their latest playthings and the Benoist boys were able to see their first automobiles. Robert may have dreamed of owning such magnificent machines but he and Maurice had to make do with the more affordable bicycle. Robert cycled to school in Rambouillet and later undertook the longer journey to the Lycée in Versailles. In time he became a member of the Versailles Cycling Club and was very successful in local bicycle races. At 18 he left school and went to work in a garage in Versailles.

It was 1913 and automobiles were new and exciting.

That summer Robert and some of his friends from the cycling club decided to travel to Amiens to watch the Grand Prix de l'Automobile Club de France on the Circuit de Picardie. Before the event two drivers had been killed in testing accidents, emphasizing the dangers of the era. A huge crowd gathered for the eight-hour spectacle and Robert and his friends camped out overnight at the corner in the town of Moreuil, so that they would be there when the race began early in the morning.

Benoist and his pals were thrilled as Jules Goux took the lead in his Peugeot but then Albert Guyot moved ahead in a Delage and seemed to be on his way to an emphatic victory when he suffered a tyre failure. As the car slowed down Guyot's riding mechanic misjudged the speed they were travelling and jumped out too early. He fell under the wheels of the car and Guyot had to fit a new wheel and then drive his injured colleague back to the pits. The delay meant that the race was won by Georges Boillot in a Peugeot. For Benoist's little group of fans, however, the hero of the day was Guyot.

Robert went home telling his pals that one day he would race in Grands Prix for Automobiles Delage. It was not just a teenage boast. Benoist had convinced himself that he could become a Grand Prix driver. He knew that self-belief was not enough and that, without money, he would have to work his way up through the automobile world. But he was determined, and decided that the first step on the ladder to success would be to get a job with Delage. After a few months gaining experience in the garage at Versailles, he found work with Jean-Albert Grégoire's automobile company in Poissy. He stayed only a few months before moving on to Unic in Puteaux. It was closer to the Delage workshops in Courbevoie and Robert began visiting the Delage factory on a regular basis, asking about a job.

In August 1914 Robert's dreams had to be put on hold when France went to war with Germany. Benoist was called up in December and should have joined the 131ème Régiment Infanterie. But because he was working at Unic, which was building much-needed trucks for the military, Robert did not join the army until August 1915 when he was sent off to the St Avold airfield, near Bourges, to become a pilot in the new Armée de l'Air. The idea of flying around the sky in one of the dangerous new flying machines, made from wood and canvas, was not very appealing to many recruits but for Benoist it was an adventure. Robert wanted to become a fighter pilot.

He qualified as a pilot in November 1915 and soon afterwards was promoted to the rank of corporal. It was not until April 1916 that he finally joined the 50ème Escadrille at the Vaubecourt aerodrome to the south of Verdun. Known at the time as MF50, as it was using Maurice Farman aeroplanes, the squadron flew reconnaissance missions over the German lines, pinpointing targets for the French artillery. A month after joining the squadron Benoist was promoted to the rank of flight sergeant.

From time to time Benoist and his observer Lt Georges Domino took hand-held bombs with them on their trips, but they generally flew with nothing but revolvers as weapons. In November that year Robert received a commendation when he went to the assistance of a colleague who had been attacked by enemy planes and by doing so frightened the German planes away.

Then in May 1917 Benoist and Domino were given a brand new Morane-Parasol monoplane with which to experiment. It was light and fast but, most importantly, it carried a Lewis machine-gun that Domino could fire at the Germans. It was not long before the two adventurers found themselves in aerial combat with a German fighter over Montfaucon d'Argonne. The enemy plane was shot down and the two young heroes celebrated their first victory.

Two days later, while machine-gunning the German lines in

the middle of the Verdun battle zone, their plane was hit by ground fire and Robert was forced to crash land between the two front lines near the Fort de Souville. The pair crawled through the mud of No Mans Land to the relative safety of the French trenches.

Robert had been inspired by his first dogfight and was delighted to be promoted to the rank of Adjutant at the end of June. But he was bored with flying reconnaissance missions. He wanted to be in combat and began badgering his commanding officer to transfer him to a fighter pilot training school. Eventually the besieged officer gave up and Robert was posted to the Le Plessis-Belleville aerodrome near Senlis where he learned to fly fighter aircraft. In November 1917 he was assigned to the 463ème Escadrille, but his dreams of battling German aces in the skies did not become a reality. The squadron spent its time patrolling the airspace over Paris.

And then, in March 1918, Robert was posted to the famous aerobatic school at Pont Long, near Pau in the shadow of the Pyrénées where he found himself training young pilots. One of them was Marcel Doret, who became a close friend and in the 1920s and 1930s was to become France's foremost test pilot with the Dewoitine company. Benoist stayed in the Armée de l'Air until September 1919. He had become an impressive and confident individual. He had a huge number of flying hours to his name and left the air force looking for a job that would give him the same thrill as aviation.

The idea of being a mechanic was simply not appealing.

Robert wanted to race.

For 18 months he failed to find a job. He wrote to all the major automobile companies in France, offering his services as a test and racing driver and explaining about his experience as a mechanic and his wartime adventures. It was not until early 1921 that he received a reply from the little-known De Marçay automotive company in the Avenue de Suffren in Paris. The aircraft firm had built an 1100cc cycle car and wanted someone to test it. Benoist agreed immediately and was soon doing his test runs on the streets in the École Militaire district. De Marçay had found a cheap daredevil to help it promote its products in racing.

Robert made his competition debut that summer in the Paris-Nice trial, an endurance test for both man and machine. He finished eighth but the performance was enough to attract the attention of the Société des Moteurs Salmson, an aero-engine company which had grown dramatically during the war and wanted to continue to expand by diversifying into new businesses. The company founder Émile Salmson was dead but a salesman called André Lombard convinced Georges Salmson, one of Émile's sons, that the automobile business was a good idea. The man running the firm was Jean Heinrich and Lombard and Salmson convinced him to buy a license to produce British GN cyclecars for the French market. The first GN-Salmson had been unveiled at the Paris Salon in 1919 and by 1921 Salmson had built more than 350 vehicles. To show off the cars Lombard himself took part in racing events. He also laid the foundations for the future by hiring an engineer called Émile Petit to establish a competition department. Petit designed an 1100cc air-cooled engine and GN-Salmson quickly became successful with its works driver Joseph "Pepino" Honel. As sales increased, Heinrich was convinced that it was time for Salmson to build its own cars and end the relationship with GN. Petit was ordered to design two completely new models: a cycle car and a slightly bigger voiturette.

Rather than paying a lot of money to hire well known racing drivers, the company decided to look for cheap new stars and, with a background in aviation, the Salmson management concluded that former pilots were the right kind of people for racing. Benoist found that he was one of three former Armée de l'Air pilots chosen to partner Honel although fighter aces Lionel de Marmier and Albert Perrot quickly faded from the scene, de Marmier returning to aviation to become a famous test pilot between the wars.

With a Salmson contract Robert Benoist had become a professional racing driver and, with sufficient financial security, was finally in a position to think about settling down and starting a family. He was 27 years old and was ready to marry his girlfriend Paule Ajustron, who came from Toulouse. The couple lived briefly in the village of St Léger-en-Yvelines, a few miles from Auffargis, but then moved on to a rented apartment in the rue Ordener in the 18ème arrondissement of Paris. Paule was soon pregnant but the child, a son, died at birth. Later she would give birth to a daughter called Jacqueline.

Early in 1922 Honel was killed and so Robert became the lead driver and in August travelled to the famous Brooklands circuit in England to make his international debut. He was not overawed at all and won the Junior Car Club Cyclecar 200 with apparent ease. A month later he won again at Le Mans and finished off his first racing season with a third victory at Tarragona in Spain.

The victories established Robert as a promising young racer, but he knew that 1923 would have to be better if he wanted to move up from the lightweight cyclecars to race in Grands Prix. He was confident he could do it and as the year progressed he became a consistent winner and the star of the Salmson team. His biggest victory was in the Bol d'Or race in St Germain-en-Laye, but the win brought an element of farce. During the race he was sliding around so much in his seat that he wore out the seat of his trousers. At the end of the race the French Minister of Sport Henry Paté was waiting to present Benoist with the trophy and did not understand why the driver seemed unwilling to climb out of the car. Fortunately Robert Letorey, the director of the Montlhéry circuit, saved the day by putting a mackintosh around Robert's shoulders to spare his blushes.

But while things were going well for Benoist, behind the scenes Salmson was having difficulties. Lombard and Petit were unable to work together and in the end it was decided that the engineer was more valuable than the man who had come up with the idea of going racing. Dropping Lombard, the wily salesman, meant that Salmson sales began to fall and the reason for the company's involvement in the sport disappeared. If winning races was not enough to increase sales, there was little point in spending the money to compete. There were cheaper ways to advertise the company products.

✠

That summer Louis Delage unveiled his new Grand Prix challenger. After the war France's previous domination of racing had been challenged. In 1921 the Grand Prix de l'ACF had been won by the American Duesenberg company with driver Jimmy Murphy. The following year Felice Nazzaro had won the event in an Italian-built

Fiat. France needed to re-establish its dominance. That year the Grand Prix de l'ACF took place at Tours and 38-year-old veteran René Thomas appeared at the wheel of the new Delage.

The new 2LCV was the work of Charles Planchon, an engineer who had joined Delage after learning his trade with Peugeot, Charron, Gnome & Rhône and Panhard. It was a good-looking car with an impressive V12 engine, but it had a string of teething problems at Tours that left Louis Delage so angry that he fired Planchon and promoted Albert Lory to head the competition department. The British firm Sunbeam won the Grand Prix de l'ACF with Major Henry Segrave driving.

Delage demanded a better car for 1924 from his engineers and Lory decided to refine Planchon's design. Lory was another man who had cut his teeth with Panhard but had moved to Salmson during the war to work on the development of aero-engines. He was briefly involved with the Salmson racing programme before becoming Planchon's assistant.

As Lory worked to refine the 2LCV, Louis Delage went out looking for a new star to race alongside the ageing Thomas. Delage approached Benoist and Robert, unable to believe that his dream was about to come true, agreed a deal almost immediately.

Benoist and René Thomas were soon firm friends. This was no surprise as the pair were made for one another. Thomas had been a pioneer of aviation with the Wright Brothers. Later he joined the Antoinette company and survived an accident in Milan in 1910 when his flying machine suffered a structural failure and plummeted 600ft to the ground. He was seriously injured and could fly no longer and so he returned to motor racing, driving a Schneider automobile in the 1913 French GP at Amiens, where Benoist and his friends had gone as spectators. The following year Thomas was taken to the United States by Delage and won the Indianapolis 500, the biggest event on the US calendar.

Coached by Thomas in the spring of 1924, Benoist quickly began to break hillclimb records all over France, winning at Mont Agel, Argenteuil, Le Camp, Bourges, Limonest and Montaigu. By the beginning of August the Delage team was ready for the Grand Prix de l'ACF on the Lyons circuit, where 10 years earlier Georges Boillot had fought his famous battle for Peugeot against five Mercedes. The 14.38 mile circuit on public highways was a shorter version of the original track but ran from Givors along the valley of the River Gier before climbing up the hillside to the undulating plateau that led the racers back to the famous descent at Les Sept Chemins.

There was an impressive entry of 22 cars including a team of Sunbeams, which had been designed by former Fiat man Vincent Bertarione. Fiat had its supercharged 805s from the previous year but the rising power in Italian motor sport was Alfa Romeo, which had employed another former Fiat man, Vittorio Jano, to design a car called the P2. The P2s were driven in practice by Antonio Ascari, Giuseppe Campari, Louis Wagner and Enzo Ferrari, although the future Formula 1 mogul mysteriously withdrew before the race. Delage had three cars for Benoist, Thomas and Alberto Divo while the Rolland-Pilain team, which had appeared in 1922 and 1923, had been taken over by engine designer Dr Schmid and was racing under the Schmid banner. Giulio Foresti crashed his car heavily in practice leaving only Jules Goux to race for Schmid.

The most exciting entry was a new Bugatti called the Type 35. Bugatti hated supercharging and so the cars were not powerful enough to compete but there was little doubt that the beautiful Type 35 was going to be an important car.

The four-day Grand Prix de l'ACF meeting was a jamboree with races for motorcycles, sidecars and even bicycles. And emotions were running high. The Sunbeam team, which had won the GP de l'ACF the previous year, got into trouble with the local authorities for traffic infringements which the drivers swore had been invented by the French police. Segrave, Dario Resta and Kenelm Lee Guinness responded by revving their engines loudly when the band played La Marseillaise in the lead-up to the race.

Segrave was keen to repeat his success of the previous year and took off into the lead, chased by Ascari, Guinness, Campari and Pietro Bordino in his Fiat. The Delages were next but in the early stages Bordino took command of the race, passing Campari and Guinness and catching Ascari. The two Italians battled for several laps and then Bordino went ahead and by the end of the third lap he had taken the lead from Segrave. After 10 laps of the track the Fiat then began to fade as Bordino's brakes gave out and so Ascari took the lead and held on until the mid-race refuelling stops began. In the closing stages Ascari was caught and overtaken by Campari.

The Delages were reliable but not quick enough although Divo and Benoist were both still running and finished second and third after Ascari lost time pitting for water.

It was a promising start for Robert's Grand Prix career.

In the weeks that followed he added more hillclimb wins at Laffrey, near Grenoble and at Saint Alban les Eaux, near Roanne. Then at the end of September the team went to Spain for the San Sebastian Grand Prix where despite torrential rain Robert led a Grand Prix for the first time. After five laps he crashed but escaped unharmed. Not long afterwards Guinness slid wide in the village of Aldeamuro, hit a wall and rolled his Sunbeam. His riding mechanic Thomas Barrett was thrown from the car and fell into a railway cutting. He was killed instantly. Guinness suffered serious head injuries. Segrave stopped to help his team mate but medical attention was at hand and so he rejoined the race and went on to win after six hours of racing. Guinness never raced again.

Robert went home to Paris knowing that he had what it took to beat the very best and was enormously frustrated when Louis Delage informed him that the team was not going to compete in the Italian Grand Prix in October.

Robert was hungrier than ever as he waited that winter. In the spring he kicked off the season with a string of victories in hillclimb events on the Riviera and got ready to contest the new World Championship, which had been devised by the AIACR, the international automobile federation. This began at the Belgian Grand Prix but neither Bugatti nor Sunbeam sent a works team to Spa and so the entry was down to just seven cars and was a straight fight between the Alfa Romeos of Ascari, Campari and new recruit Gastone Brilli-Peri and the four Delage drivers Benoist, Alberto Divo, Thomas and Paul Torchy. Robert was out early with a broken fuel tank and the same problem hit the other Delages and in the end there were only two Alfa Romeos left to score an unchallenged 1-2. It had been a humiliating event for Delage and there was little hope of a much better result at the Grand Prix de l'ACF at Montlhéry.

This time there were teams from Alfa Romeo, Delage, Sunbeam and Bugatti.

Sunbeam was still suffering from the loss of both Guinness and Dario Resta, the latter having been killed in a testing crash at Brooklands not long after Guinness's crash in Spain. Bugatti was still persisting without supercharged engines and the cars were just not fast enough.

The crowd was small, numbering only around 30,000 people, a tiny number compared to the huge crowds that there had been at Lyons the previous summer. Ascari took off into the lead, being chased by Segrave's Sunbeam and Divo's Delage but it was not long before the Delage driver was in the pits for a change of plugs. Campari had moved up to second place and although the Alfa Romeos then both lost ground with pit stops they were still ahead at one quarter distance.

Rain began to spit and then Ascari failed to appear. Word began to filter back that the Alfa Romeo star had been caught out by the tricky conditions and had gone off in the high-speed left-hander on the way back to the oval. The front wheel of the Alfa had snagged a wooden fence beside the circuit, put there to keep the spectators off the race track, and the car had flipped. Ascari had been thrown out as the P2 tore down 100m of the fencing and was then crushed when the cart-wheeling machine landed on him. He was carried from the scene gravely injured and died on his way to hospital.

When word of his death arrived back at Montlhéry Alfa Romeo gave up. Campari drove to the garages, climbed from his car and walked away. Brilli-Peri was called in. The Alfa Romeo team packed away its equipment. The disaster left Delage unchallenged and Benoist's car, which had been taken over by Divo, came home five minutes ahead of its sister car after nine hours of racing. The crowd was happy to celebrate the victory of a French driver in a French car for the first time since Georges Boillot had triumphed at Amiens in 1913. Robert received the trophy and the winner's bouquet from the French President Gaston Doumergue, but then, as a tribute to Ascari, he drove to the scene of the accident and left the flowers there.

The death of Ascari was a terrible blow to Italian racing but the team regrouped and picked a new man to join the team: Tazio Nuvolari was a little man with a big reputation in motorcycle racing and he was the star of the practice days at the Italian Grand Prix. He then crashed violently, overturned his car, but escaped with only cracked ribs. Delage had not bothered to attend and so the only challenge to Alfa Romeo domination came from the US car company Duesenberg, which had won at Indianapolis and wanted to take on Alfa Romeo for the World Championship. The Alfas were quicker and it was left to Brilli-Peri to win his greatest victory.

The World Championship was secured for Alfa Romeo and almost immediately the company announced that it was withdrawing from the sport. Delage was left on its own. The Delage team took four cars down to Spain for the Gran Premio de San Sebastian and ran Benoist, Divo, Thomas and Torchy but the opposition was not competitive. Bugatti had a four-car factory team but the Type 35s were still not powerful enough and so the only real challenge came from Count Guilio Masetti in a privately-entered Sunbeam. Divo, Benoist and Thomas were soon out ahead but Torchy was stuck behind Masetti until the fifth lap when he tried a risky overtaking manoeuvre. The car went off and hit a tree. Torchy was taken to hospital but the team kept running with Divo and Benoist fighting for victory until Robert's car broke down. Then news came from the hospital: Torchy was dead, another victim of a lethal season of Grand Prix racing.

The international automobile federation had decided on a new Grand Prix formula for 1926 and had come up with rules for 1.5-litre supercharged engines. Delage planned the 15S8 but it was not ready at the start of the year and so Robert raced the 1925 cars on the hillclimbs at the start of the season. At Mont Agel he produced a sensational result when he spun at the final corner and, rather than wasting time turning the car, selected reverse and crossed the line backwards, still being quick enough to beat the hill record.

While waiting for the new Grand Prix cars Delage took old ones down to Sicily for the Targa Florio. For the second time in just a few months Benoist lost a team-mate when new recruit Masetti went off the road and was killed when his car overturned. In later years such a death toll would have scared drivers into demanding change but in the 1920s it was simply accepted as part of the game. There was never a shortage of drivers wanting to race. The problem was that there was not enough money to go around.

The Grand Prix de l'ACF at Miramas in 1926 marked a low point in Grand Prix racing: only three cars turned up and all were from Bugatti, which was taking advantage of the situation to turn the event into a publicity stunt. Only Jules Goux finished.

In July the Delage team was finally ready and made its first appearance with the new 15S8 at San Sebastian. The team had been completely restructured since 1925 with Divo going back to join Sunbeam Talbot Darracq leaving Robert as the undisputed Delage team leader. For San Sebastian his team mates were Edmond Bourlier and André Morel while opposition came from Bugatti with Goux, Meo Costantini and Ferdinando Minoia.

Benoist soon rid himself of the Bugattis and was hoping to shrug off the frustrations of the year with a proper Grand Prix victory. He knew that the French win in 1925 had been lucky and wanted more. But even as his thoughts were turning to the possibility of victory, Robert began to get hotter and hotter. The metal of the cockpit was heating up to such an extent that he burned himself when he touched the sides. He could live with the burns but the heat also started to sap his energy. His feet were burnt and he soon found that he was having a problem concentrating. He knew that he had to stop and when he climbed from the car he had to steady himself on the pit wall. It did not help. He fainted. Morel and Bourlier had had similar problems and Louis Delage was running out of drivers. He was forced to ask visiting drivers Louis Wagner and Robert Sénéchal if they would take over. The Bugattis went ahead and although Robert did later go out again and set a new lap record, it was a bad defeat for Delage. The car had a problem: the exhaust pipes were running too close to the cockpit. It was a design problem and there was nothing that could be done.

The problem returned a week later when the team raced again in the Spanish GP at San Sebastian. Bugatti won again. The Delage team was faced with a terrible decision. The problem was such that it could not be fixed before the end of the year. The team could withdraw or try to fight through, knowing that success was unlikely, even if the cars were faster than the opposition. In August the team went to Brooklands for the inaugural RAC English Grand Prix and faced serious opposition from Sunbeam Talbot Darracq, which had three new straight-eight Talbots for Segrave, Divo and Jules Moriceau. The Delage team featured Robert, Wagner and Sénéchal and after an early burst of speed from the Talbots, Benoist moved up and was right on Segrave's tail when the British driver headed for the pits. Benoist stayed in the lead until his stop and was surprised to find himself still ahead when he rejoined. After 15 more laps, however, he found himself being bombarded by red hot flakes of metal which were breaking off the exhaust pipe. Robert refused to be beaten and drove on until it became impossible to go on.

It was the same story all over again. The drivers came in from time to time to bathe their burning feet in cool water but even that proved not to be enough and in the end Louis Delage had to ask André Dubonnet to help out. He was dressed in a lounge suit rather than racing overalls but gamely took up the challenge. Wagner struggled through to win the race while Robert had to settle for third.

It was not enough. Louis Delage was fed up and decided not to send his cars to the Gran Premio d'Italia at Monza in September. But that winter asked his engineers to come up with a solution to the problem. They turned the 15S8 engine through 180-degrees, moving the exhaust pipes away from the driver. The redesigned 15S8 was an extraordinary Grand Prix car.

The long-suffering Benoist had Bourlier and Morel as team mates once again in 1927 and it was Bourlier who was given the chance to show the racing world the speed of the new car. He won the Mi-Corniche, Moyenne Corniche and La Turbie hillclimb races. In March Benoist led the way for the Formula Libre Grand Prix de l'Ouverture at Montlhéry, and lapped the entire field three times in just 30 laps. There was no overheating.

The World Championship kicked off that year at Indianapolis but Delage did not enter a team for the American classic and so the team was not seen in action again until the Grand Prix de l'ACF at Montlhéry at the start of July. The Delages were so fast that after practice Ettore Bugatti withdrew his cars from the race to avoid embarrassment. The crowds at Montlhéry did not take kindly to the news but hoped that Delage and Talbot would somehow manage to put on a decent show. The STD team was running Divo, Wagner and a new signing called "W Williams". Robert knew Divo and Wagner well but the new man was intriguing. He had seen him on a few hillclimbs and he knew that "W Williams" was quick and he wanted to race him.

At the start of the race the old devil Divo led the way but Robert stayed with him while "W Williams" was right behind him. When Benoist overtook Divo and went into the lead "W Williams" followed him, overtaking Divo and starting to put pressure on Benoist. Robert was impressed but he was not about to be intimidated by a novice. He began to set new lap records. "W Williams" stayed with him. For nearly an hour the two men jousted and then Robert saw the Talbot begin to fall away with a mechanical problem. Benoist went on to lead a dominant Delage 1-2-3. It was a big victory and for a few days Robert did not have time to think about "W Williams". But then came the unexpected news that STD had run into financial trouble and was stopping its racing programme immediately.

Robert would not have to worry about "W Williams" again but the news came as a serious blow. Some drivers might have rejoiced at the demise of Talbot but Robert wanted to race the best. Without Talbot, the Delage achievement would be undermined even if Bugatti still had good cars. The situation was highlighted when the Grand Prix teams gathered at the end of the month in San Sebastian. Robert found himself in a fairly comfortable position, leading until the mid-race pit when Bugatti's Emilio Materassi found his way into the lead. For seven laps Robert battled with the Italian. It was a spectacular fight, one of the best that Grand Prix racing had ever seen, and then Materassi spun and threw up a huge cloud of dust. Unable to see anything at all Robert also went off the road and spun to a halt. As the dust began to settle both men were scrambling to get their cars going again. And then something extraordinary occurred: Materassi set off in one direction and Benoist set off in the other!

Fortunately Robert realized his mistake before he encountered any cars coming the opposite direction and spun the car around and chased after Materassi once again. Despite the mishap Benoist was able to win again.

At the start of September the Delage team travelled south to Italy, to take part in the European Grand Prix at Monza. There were only six cars present for the event and it was raining heavily but Benoist won again, lapping the famous Milan circuit at over 90mph. Robert was delighted but even at his moment of triumph he was frustrated. He knew that the opposition was weak. That day at Monza, the organizers ran a second race for Italian machinery under the Gran Premio di Milano banner. This was a showdown between the Alfa Romeo and Fiat factory teams. The old Alfa Romeo P2 was still a very potent piece of machinery but it met its match with the new Fiat Tipo 806, which had been designed for the 1.5-litre World Championship but had never been raced. After a series of heats the final was a showdown in pouring rain between Count Aymo Maggi in a Bugatti, Giuseppe Campari in an Alfa Romeo and Pietro Bordino in the new Fiat. Bordino produced a brilliant display and drove to victory at an average speed of 96.5mph. It was hard to compare conditions but clearly the Fiats would have been strong challengers.

After the race Fiat announced that it was withdrawing from Grand Prix racing once and for all, claiming that the 1.5-litre formula was too expensive and had no relevance to the company's road-going products. All Robert could do was to go on winning and at the end of the month the Delage team set off for England where the RAC English Grand Prix was to be held at Brooklands on October 2.

Motor racing had really taken off in Britain and the entry for the race was much better than the previous year with Bugatti appearing with a factory team for Louis Chiron, Materassi and Conelli and private cars for Malcolm Campbell, George Eyston and Prince Ghica. Benoist spotted "W Williams" as the Bugatti reserve driver. Delage had also made some changes with Divo being taken on after the demise of STD as team mate to Robert and Bourlier.

The weather was terrible with high winds and drizzling rain. Materassi was his usual fiery self and took off into the lead but Divo soon came out of the spray and went into the lead and before long the Delages were soon running 1-2-3. Robert was happy to sit in third place. The Bugattis were scrapping amongst themselves but could not keep up and as the track dried so the Delages pulled further and further ahead. It was a massacre. The Bugatti teams kept the crowd amused with George Eyston handing over his car to Le Mans winner Sammy Davis while Conelli ran out of fuel, some say deliberately, and pushed the Bugatti back to the pits. He was so tired that he handed the car over to "W Williams".

Eventually Robert moved into the lead and the three Delages thundered on to a dominant win and to victory in the World Championship. There was no Drivers' Championship but this did not stop the French press dubbing Robert "The World Champion".

In December 1927 he was appointed a Chevalier of the Légion d'honneur, the French equivalent of a knighthood.

It was the first time that a racing car champion had received such recognition from the French government.

Not bad for a gamekeeper's son.

CHAPTER FOUR

Robert Benoist's moment of glory was but fleeting. The accountants at Automobiles Delage reached the conclusion that, despite all the success on the racing circuits, the firm could not afford the luxury of a competition department and Louis Delage was forced to accept that if he wanted his company to survive he had to stop racing. There could be no compromise. The international automobile federation had decided that the 1.5-litre Grand Prix formula was never going to work but by changing the rules for 1928 gave everyone the excuse to withdraw and not build new cars.

The 1928 season would be run with only Bugatti offering a serious challenger. Rather than produce a string of victories, Le Patron realized that he would make more money if he did not run a strong factory team against his own customers. For the small group of professional racing drivers this decision was a disaster. There were no jobs left, even for the "World Champion". Benoist did not have the kind of money that he needed to run his own team and he could not find a drive. His only option was to wait and hope that a new opportunity would come along. Robert was a big name and there was no shortage of promotional work to be done but there was no permanent position on offer until he was asked if he would like to become the Sales Manager at the Garage Banville in Paris's 17ème arrondissement. It was a good job. The Banville was the height of style and modernity and the ultimate in chic at a time when fashion was becoming more and more important.

The Garage Banville had been idea of a group of rich young men who were members of an unofficial dining club which met at the Pharamon restaurant in Les Halles on Friday nights in the years leading up to World War I. Louis Risacher, Christian Dauvergne, Georges Virolle and Gaston Sigrand had all been at school together at the Lycée Michelet in Vanves and all shared a passion for the automobile and for aviation. When the war came they went their separate ways. Risacher and Dauvergne joined the Armée de l'Air and by the end of the war Risacher had become a member of Georges Guynemer's Escadrille des Cigognes and a fighter ace.

They all survived the war and entered the optimistic world of the Twenties convinced that after the war to end all wars the world would be a better place. It was a golden age for new ideas and new architecture. It was in this exciting and creative era that Risacher and his friends came up with the radical idea of building a garage in which the wealthy could store their exquisite luxury cars which, at the same time, would double up as a sports and social club.

Sigrand, the heir to a department store fortune, established a corporation in March 1925 to fund the construction of the Garage Banville. The others became shareholders and once the idea was off the ground new partners were attracted, including Louis Courbaize, a businessman who saw the commercial potential of the idea and wanted to use the garage to sell cars. He was the French importer for the Italian firm Itala. As Sigrand had to run his own family's company he soon stood down and Henri Terrisse became the director. Land was acquired at the corner of the rue Pierre Demours and the rue de Courcelles and work began on what they wanted to be a palace for the automobile.

The Banville project reflected all of their interests. On the ground floor was a spacious exhibition hall and showroom, where the latest luxury cars were to be sold. Downstairs was a service department where the luxury cars were lovingly repaired. There were an additional six floors, linked by a curling ramp, wide enough for two cars, with a 10% incline between each floor. The clients of the Banville Corporation rented cages in which they locked their beloved new automobiles. There was room for 600 cars. But what made the Banville extraordinary was that up on the sixth floor there were facilities for golfers (a pitch-and-put area, complete with a bunker and a driving range). There were three indoor tennis courts, plenty of space for table tennis, a gymnasium and a restaurant. There had been plans for a swimming pool but these were abandoned because of the cost. When the construction was nearing completion Terrisse hired a young man who would run the garage for him: Gaëtan Baille was only 28 but he understood exactly what kind of clients were needed. He loved the association with the likes of Risacher and Dauvergne and believed that for the French the fighter pilots of World War I were the modern equivalents of medieval knights in shining armour. He felt that the garage would greatly benefit from an association with them and their friends. It was not long before Baille was drawn into Dauvergne's circle of friends, which included Robert Benoist.

Baille was keen for the Banville to make a big impression when it opened and asked Dauvergne and Benoist to organise an extraordinary promotional event: a hillclimb competition *inside* the garage, using the sweeping ramps from the ground to the roof. A section of the course even ran across the roof, the drivers' only protection from the six-storey drop being a pile of sandbags on which spectators sat to watch the action. The course was 600 metres in length and 15 cars were entered, all of them sporting models. Some were driven by the big names of the day, but we will never know who won the Banville hillclimb because it was decided that, on the grounds of safety, it would be unwise to record times lest the competitive urges of those involved got the better of them. The Banville hillclimb remains one of the strangest motor racing competitions ever held - but it was a huge success.

When Benoist found himself looking for work at the end of that year Baille suggested that he would be the perfect man to become the sales manager of the Banville. His very presence would sell cars. Robert reluctantly agreed and moved his family from the rue Ordener to a new apartment block in the rue Dardanelles, a street which had just been laid out on land beside the old fortifications of Paris, at the Porte de Ternes.

The Garage Banville quickly became a magnet for Paris's racing community and provided Robert with occasional chances to race. In June 1928 he and Dauvergne represented Itala in the Le Mans 24 Hours. They were up against the big English Bentleys and a selection of competitive American cars from Stutz and Chrysler. the Itala was not in the running for overall honours but managed to win its class and finish eighth overall. It kept Robert's name in the limelight. The other thing it did was to remind Benoist how much he loved the sport and how much he missed racing. He soon began to pester Ettore Bugatti to let him race a factory Bugatti Type 35.

Bugatti understood racing drivers. He had competed himself when he was a designer with the Stucchi & Prinetti motorized tricycle company in Milan, and had long been a believer in employing racing drivers in his company. Racers were extraordinary people and much more ambitious than the average person. Bugatti's first employee had been Ernest Friderich, the man who won the first important race victory for Bugatti in Brescia in 1921. He would end up as Bugatti's sales representative on the French Riviera, a major market for a luxury car company.

The Bugatti Competition department was run by Italian Meo Costantini, who had been a successful member of La Squadriglia degli Assi (The Squadron of Aces) during World War I. Piloting Spads alongside Francesco Baracca (from whom Enzo Ferrari acquired his prancing horse logo), Costantini ended the war as an ace with the rank of captain and two of Italy's top decorations. He then went racing and enjoyed considerable success, including scoring victories on the Targa Florio, the Coppa Florio and in the Spanish GP.

Costantini joined the Bugatti management at the end of 1926 and came up with the plan to build up the customer car business by not running a factory-entered team in 1927. This was so successful that Bugatti was soon able to organize his own "Bugatti Grand Prix" at Le Mans for his customers. With money pouring in, Le Patron decided in the summer of 1928 that he could again afford occasional factory cars and entered one for Robert at San Sebastian, which was being run as a sports car event that year. After a stirring battle with Louis Chiron, Robert was beaten. He was out of practice.

That race would be Robert's last Grand Prix for five years. He settled down to promote the Garage Banville and raced only on occasion in the years that followed. In 1929 the Banville company became a Chrysler distributor and so Robert teamed up with Henri Stoffel and raced a Chrysler in the Le Mans 24 Hours. Once again the Bentleys dominated, finishing 1-2-3-4. Benoist and Stoffel finished sixth ahead of a second car entered for Cyril de Vere and Marcel Mongin. That summer Enzo Ferrari asked him to drive for the Alfa Romeo factory team for the Spa 24 Hours, sharing one of Vittorio

Jano's new Alfa Romeo 6C 1750s with Attilio Marinoni.

The pair led home an Alfa Romeo 1-2-3.

On September 3, 1929, the New York Stock Exchange suffered a sharp drop in prices. The market recovered within a matter of days but there were still signs of trouble. In the course of October confidence ebbed away and then panic set in. On October 24 the Exchange was overwhelmed by the number of transactions as investors sold their shares. Within a few days $30 billion dollars was wiped off the value of the US economy. The ripples spread and gradually the world economy slipped into what would become known as the Great Depression.

People stopped spending money and selling luxury cars became a very difficult business. Money to go motor racing dried up. It would be two years before Robert received a telephone call from Meo Costantini asking him if he would be interested in doing some development work for Bugatti. Costantini proposed that Robert do tests and a few French national events but it was not long before Guy Bouriat, the manager of the Bugatti showroom in Paris, decided that he did not have the time to race Grand Prix cars and announced that he would only race in France. Ettore Bugatti offered Robert a Grand Prix drive for 1933.

That year the Bugatti works team featured Benoist, Achille Varzi, René Dreyfus and Willy Williams. It was a brilliant line-up. Varzi was one of Italy's biggest stars who had moved to Bugatti in order to be the clear number one driver in a team. He wanted only to beat his bitter rival Tazio Nuvolari. Dreyfus had joined the team after two poor years with Maserati, hoping to revive his career.

"Benoist was the oldest member of the team," remembered Dreyfus. "All of 38. I thought that was old at the time! He was the team's foundation. Its solid rock. He was still a good driver if not as quick as he used to be. He had the most striking face, the profile of an eagle, with sharp features, piercing eyes. Through his face you could see something beautiful, his honesty, his nobility, his class. He was a true chevalier.

"I liked him a lot."

Robert continued working at the Garage Banville in the early part of the year but in May 1933 Bouriat was killed in a high-speed accident during the Grand Prix of Picardie at the Péronne circuit. Ettore Bugatti and his son Jean, who was beginning to play a more important role in the company, needed a replacement and concluded that Benoist was the obvious candidate. He was racing well and he had experience of running a showroom at the Garage Banville.

The Banville did not have a racing programme and Baille was forced to accept that it was impossible to keep Benoist. Robert served out his notice period and in January 1934 he became a full time employee of Automobiles Bugatti.

The 1933 driving team had already broken up: Varzi had gone back to Alfa Romeo, following a fall-out between Tazio Nuvolari and Enzo Ferrari which resulted in Nuvolari going to Maserati. Willy Williams had decided to retire and moved away to La Baule, although Benoist did manage to convince him to become a part-time Bugatti salesman. Bugatti was again scaling back its Grand Prix programme but the team still needed a new driver to race alongside Dreyfus.

Benoist advised Costantini that he should look at a youngster called Jean-Pierre Wimille.

✠

A fan of Benoist during the Delage days, Wimille had first made his name in voiturette racing in 1930, his progress drawing him to the attention of Ernest Friderich, Bugatti's man in Nice. Wimille was wild but he was fast. He calmed down and after a solid year in 1933 he looked like a man who was ready for major success.

The problem was that the world of Grand Prix racing was changing fast and the 1934 season would be a tough one for Automobiles Bugatti. The domination that the French had enjoyed in the 1920s had already been challenged by the Italians and in 1934 the big German teams arrived, supported by Germany's new Chancellor, Adolf Hitler. Within days of taking power Hitler had announced plans to build a network of fast highways that would criss-cross the country: to build a car for the people (a project which would ultimately result in the birth of the Volkswagen company); and to encourage motor racing activities by providing funding for the Mercedes-Benz and

AutoUnion Grand Prix teams. This allowed the engineers to explore and develop new technologies and the arrival of the new cars had an immediate impact at the Internationales Avus-Rennen event in Berlin in the spring of 1934.

Seeing the writing on the wall Meo Costantini resigned at the end of the year and went back to Italy. Ettore Bugatti asked Benoist if he would like to run the competition department as well as the Bugatti showroom. From then on Robert would race only occasionally.

Bugatti was facing a difficult future in racing and that would inevitably affect the company's sales of production cars. The French government would not help and in the end Benoist and Jean Bugatti concluded that the company had to find a way to sidestep the German challenge in Grand Prix racing and yet keep Bugatti in the spotlight, without huge investment being necessary. Their decision was to withdraw from Grand Prix racing and concentrate Bugatti's efforts on winning the Le Mans 24 Hours. The new car was to be based on the chassis of the Bugatti Type 57 but this was fitted with a dramatic streamlined body. The cars were designated 57G and while the engineers assembled them, Benoist went out to hire the best team of drivers he could find. When the first 57Gs appeared at Montlhéry in the spring of 1936 Robert shared one car with his childhood friend Philippe de Rothschild, a quick driver who had stopped racing because of pressure from his family. Willy Williams came out of retirement to share a second car with voiturette racing star Pierre Veyron while a third car was driven by rising stars Wimille and Raymond Sommer.

The distinctive blue cars quickly gained the nickname "Tanks" but the French public loved them. They were winners and with France split by social and political unrest, they gave the nation something to be proud of. The plan to win Le Mans in 1936 went awry when the race was cancelled because of the industrial action which paralysed the whole of France that summer.

The strikers went so far as to blockade Ettore Bugatti's famous factory at Molsheim and even refused entrance to Le Patron himself. Ettore was outraged and announced that he was leaving Molsheim and would never return. He moved his offices to Paris and left his son Jean in charge of the factory in Alsace.

Benoist was not a man to allow his plans to be ruined by the strikers and, despite the blockades, he produced a team of Tanks for a series of long-distance record attempts that autumn at Montlhéry. Then his attention turned to the 1937 Le Mans programme for which Bugatti entered two Tanks: the first to be shared by Benoist and Wimille, the second for Robert's old friend Roger Labric and Veyron.

Saturday, June 19, 1937 was a stormy day but that did not deter around 150,000 fanatical Frenchmen from turning up at Le Mans. They had come to see a blue car win. Although the Bugattis went off into the lead, the early part of the race was dominated by a terrible accident at Maison Blanche where, in the course of the ninth lap, Rene Kippeurt lost control of his old Bugatti and rolled, throwing Kippeurt out on to the road. A group of six other cars arrived on the scene at speed: Pat Fairfield in his Frazer-Nash BMW328 hit Kippeurt's wreck head-on. The impact tore the Bugatti in half. Fritz Roth swerved his BMW to avoid hitting anything and went off into a field. He was thrown out of the car. The remains of Fairfield's car were hit by a Delahaye, driven by Jean Tremoulet, sending it end over end into a field. At the same time Tremoulet's car was hit by the Talbot driven by "Raph" and his car was hit by a Riley driven by Raoul Forestier.

Kippeurt had been killed instantly in the impact and Fairfield was barely alive. He was rushed to hospital with internal injuries and for two days the doctors fought unsuccessfully to keep him alive. "Raph" was badly injured and his legs remained paralyzed for six months. Roth suffered concussion and a serious facial injuries.

Despite the sombre news the race continued and in the cool of the evening Benoist lapped the track in a record 96.42mph, a speed which left the opposition astonished. Half an hour later rain began to fall and by nightfall half of the 60-car field was gone. The Wimille-Benoist car continued to lap at around 90mph. There was a scare during the night when Wimille came into the pits with a damaged wing but it was quickly repaired and he was soon on his way again. In the early morning the team suffered a setback when the Labric-Veyron car retired but throughout Sunday morning Benoist and Wimille thundered on as excitement grew in expectation of the first

French win at Le Mans in 11 years.

At four in the afternoon the Tank crossed the finishing line, amid scenes of much celebration. Benoist and Wimille had covered 2043 miles, ninety miles more than the previous record. Bugatti was back in the limelight again after years of German domination of the sport. Benoist was a national hero again.

But at 42, he recognised that it was time to announce his retirement. There was much to be done in Paris and with Grand Prix racing dominated by the Germans, it was a good moment to stop. He continued to run both the competition department and the Bugatti showroom in the Avenue Montaigne while Ettore Bugatti set up an experimental department in the old Zenith Carburetor works at 15 rue du Débarcadère, not far from the Porte Maillot, where his engineers were researching aero-engines and drawing up plans for a motor torpedo boat. The feeling was that war was coming and Bugatti began discussions to move the factory from Molsheim - close to the German border - to Belgium.

In September 1938 the Munich Crisis caused the French government to call up its reserve officers. Robert Benoist was ordered to report to Toulon where he learned about the latest German warplanes. He wanted to fly again but at 44 the Armée de l'Air decided that he would be better off "flying" a desk.

☩

When the international tension eased, Robert was demobilized and returned to Bugatti, which was by then beginning preparation for the 1939 Le Mans 24 Hours. The programme was to be a huge success with Wimille and Veyron winning the race, but almost immediately afterwards Robert was back in uniform with orders to attend an officer training course at the École de Perfectionnement des Officiers de Reserve de l'Air in the rue St Didier in Paris. After that he was posted south to the Istres air force base, not far from the old Miramas race track. He was not happy. He wanted to be back to Paris, to be nearer the action.

By August he had used his network of old friends to get himself transferred to the Le Bourget aerodrome to the north of Paris where he began working for his old World War I observer Georges Domino, now a colonel in the munitions service of the 5ième escadre.

The Bugatti racing programme went on without him. In the middle of the summer holidays Wimille was scheduled to race on the sands at La Baule. There were delays at Molsheim and the Tank that he was to race was not finished until 10pm on the night of Friday, August 11. It needed to be shaken down before being sent to La Baule for the weekend and so Jean Bugatti took it out for a run on a stretch of public highway near the Bugatti factory.

Jean had been forbidden to race by his father and had competed only in the hillclimb at Shelsley Walsh in England but he had done many similar tests in the past. There were only two junctions that needed to be watched and Jean stationed mechanic Robert Aumaître at one and asked his 16-year-old brother Roland to oversee the other. People who arrived were happy to wait, keen to see a racing Bugatti being tested.

Joseph Metz, a radio operator from the nearby Entzheim Airfield, was in a hurry. He had had a little to drink and wanted to go home. He told Roland Bugatti that he would keep to the grass verge, out of the way, but for some reason he was cycling in the middle of the road when Jean Bugatti arrived behind him at 125mph. Jean swerved at the last minute, missed Metz by a fraction, but the Tank veered at unabated speed into a large plane tree. The car was torn apart by the impact, the engine was ripped off and catapulted into a field and Jean's body was thrown 60 feet from the wreck. Metz, shocked by the arrival of the racing car, had fallen off his bicycle and broken his wrist.

Nothing could be done for Jean Bugatti. A couple of years later, unable to live with what he had done, Metz committed suicide.

Ettore Bugatti, who was away in Belgium visiting King Leopold to discuss moving the company's production facilities to Belgium, was dealt a terrible blow. He had lost not only his beloved son but also the man who was going to take over Automobiles Bugatti when Ettore decided it was time to retire.

Within a few days of Jean's death, Europe went to war again when German armies marched into Poland. The British and the

French declared war on the Nazis.

At the Paris Peace Conference in 1919 France's Marshal Ferdinand Foch was so appalled by the terms of the peace treaty imposed on the defeated Germans that he warned the other delegates that the Treaty of Versailles was so punitive that it would inevitably lead to another war.

"This is not peace," declared the old tiger. "This is a truce for 20 years."

Foch's prediction was correct to within two months.

In Paris the outbreak of war was greeted with something close to panic. For three consecutive nights there were air raid warnings but when the Luftwaffe failed to appear life in the French capital returned gradually to normal.

Bugatti busied himself with his work, organising the transfer of his factory from Molsheim to Bordeaux. This was done at night - to avoid German bombing raids - using special trains provided for him by the Air Ministry. The move was completed by February 1940 and Bugatti put the factory to work, producing crankshafts for Hispano Suiza aero-engines.

That autumn a few British troops arrived in France as an Expeditionary Force. It may have helped French morale but everyone knew what was coming. The French did not want to fight. The slaughter of the Great War was too recent a memory and when the chief of the French defence staff General Maurice-Gustave Gamelin suggested attacking Germany while its troops were busy in Poland he was overruled. The French army, he was told, was a defensive army.

France would rely on the Maginot Line, a system of fortresses that ran down France's eastern border from the Belgian frontier to Switzerland. Autumn gave way to a bitterly cold winter - the coldest for 50 years. The invasion of France, which Hitler had planned for the start of November, was delayed because of snow and freezing fog. Each new deadline for the attack came and went.

As a frustrated Benoist pushed papers around his desk at Le Bourget, his friend and sometime Bugatti colleague Willy Grover-Williams was also finding it hard to deal with bureaucracy. He wanted to enlist in the British Army and presented himself at the British Embassy in Paris only to be told by the military attaché that volunteers were not being accepted, unless they wished to travel to England at their own expense.

In the middle of January 1940 the weather began to improve. A German attack was scheduled for January 17 but a plane carrying plans of the invasion crashed in Belgium and Hitler hesitated. The bad weather returned.

On February 28 Willy went to the British Embassy in Paris again. The rules had been changed and this time he was allowed to enlist and he became a member of the Royal Army Service Corps, being posted to the Central Purchasing Board as a driver. It was not the most glamorous work that the British Army had to offer, but Willy was happy to do it.

After a couple of months in Paris he was posted north to work as a driver with Major General Roger Evans's 1st Armoured Division, which was part of the British Expeditionary Force. Willy was based at Doullens, his job being to drive staff officers to meetings.

He had been in Doullens for only a couple of days when the Nazi invasion began. The Germans ignored the French fortresses on the eastern frontier and attacked through Holland and Belgium. The local defence crumbled in the face of the Blitzkrieg. Within days General Heinz Guderian's Panzers had smashed through the French defences at Sedan and, turning west, raced towards the Channel Ports, cutting behind the bulk of the British forces. The Allies were disorganised. There were rifts between French and British commanders and matters were not helped when General Gaston Billotte, the man in charge of the French First Army Group, was killed when the staff car in which he was travelling collided with a truck. The roads were highly dangerous.

Within days Guderian's tanks had reached the sea and the 1st Armoured Division had been badly mauled while attempting to break through the German lines at Abbeville. Around Calais, Boulogne and Dunkirk 400,000 Allied troops were trapped with their back to the sea. In the south the Allies tried to organise a counter-attack but there was chaos. Willy drove to Paris, delivering staff officers to meetings there. It gave him a chance to see his family.

"He came to have lunch," remembered his niece Jessie Teager. "He told us that we were losing the war and that the Germans were coming. Luckily my father (Richard Wright Whitworth) had already gone to England."

Willy's brother Frederic also remembered that visit.

"He came at the end of May and told the family not to stay, saying it was finished and it would be better for them to go to the south."

While Willy was in Paris the Allied forces trapped on the Channel coast began evacuating from the beaches of Dunkirk. Ships of every kind came across from England to save the army. By the time the evacuation was over nearly 340,000 soldiers had got out of the Dunkirk pocket. Seventy thousand had been killed, captured or were missing.

At lunchtime on June 3, as the last battles were being fought at Dunkirk, the Luftwaffe bombers turned on Paris. At Le Bourget large numbers of French warplanes were destroyed on the ground. The Air Ministry on the Boulevard Victor received several direct hits and the railway junctions at Versailles and St Cyr were seriously damaged. German armour began moving south towards Paris. By the weekend of June 8/9, German guns could be heard from Paris as the invaders broke through the French lines in a vicious battle on the River Aisne.

The French authorities parked vehicles across the great Parisian boulevards to stop gliders landing and an unprecedented exodus of people began, as the population headed out of the city across the Pont de Sèvres and down the RN10 to Versailles and on to Chartres. They used whatever means of transport was available and the road quickly became clogged with cars, trucks, limousines, taxis, hearses, tractors and even hand carts. The traffic moved at barely walking pace and along the road all shops were stripped of provisions. Petrol was almost impossible to find.

On the Monday morning the French Government pulled out of Paris. Benoist received orders to leave Le Bourget and report to an air base near Blois. He was given permission to make the journey in his supercharged Bugatti 57 Atalante, one of the most dramatic sports cars that Bugatti had ever built. The traffic jams meant that Benoist made slow progress although he took the opportunity to stop briefly to see his parents at Auffargis, the house being just a short distance from the highway.

On Friday June 14 the Germans took control of Paris and the following evening, meeting in the Hotel Splendide in Bordeaux, the French cabinet voted 14 to 9 in favour of asking the Germans for peace. Prime Minister Paul Reynaud resigned and 84-year-old Maréchal Henri Philippe Pétain became the new head of state.

The German advance continued and as the armies advanced towards Blois, Robert received further orders to report to an air base near Tarbes, in the shadow of the Pyrénées. The refugee convoys were slower than ever, the roads blocked and the verges strewn with abandoned vehicles. Pétain went on the radio telling the French that it was time to stop the fighting.

For the British units that had been left behind in northern France, the only escape route was to head to the west to the Atlantic coast ports of Cherbourg, Saint Malo, Brest and Saint Nazaire, 400 miles from Dunkirk. Ships were sent to rescue them. Willy Grover ended up in Cherbourg and escaped on June 17. Under heavy attack from German bomber aircraft, Willy's vessel slipped away in the night and he arrived at Falmouth the following day.

✠

In France Robert tried to stay ahead of the German advance but his progress to Tours and Chatellerault was slow. On the night of the 18th, broadcasting from London, Général Charles de Gaulle, France's under-secretary of state for defence, appealed to Frenchmen and women to continue the fight. Not many heard him. At Saumur the 2000 officers and pupils of the famous Cadre Noir Cavalry School held up the German advance for three days in desperate actions to defend the bridges along a 30-mile stretch of the Loire river.

Robert was nearly at Poitiers before a German convoy, its sirens blaring as it tried to get through the refugees, finally caught up with him. The Germans paid little attention to most of the refugees but the unusual Bugatti sports car, being driven by an officer in the Armée de l'Air attracted their attention. Benoist was pulled over and ordered to join the German convoy. That evening they stopped in a field beside the main road. A stream of admiring German soldiers came to look at the Bugatti and that night Robert slept in the car.

He was woken at dawn and given some fuel for the day ahead. Soon the convoy was moving again, heading on towards Angoulême but progress was slow and Robert began to consider his alternatives. He had no desire to remain a prisoner and wanted to try to make an escape before his fuel supply ran low. As the convoy slowed down for yet another obstruction, Robert spotted a small lane off to the side of the main road. Without a second thought he floored the throttle launching the powerful Bugatti across the road and into the country lane. The move was so swift that it took the Germans completely by surprise. Worried that the Germans might try to send a plane to look for him, Robert drove very quickly, aiming for the country estate of one of his friends, where he knew he would be able to hide the car in a barn. After that, like most of the French nation, he waited to find out what the Germans were going to do next.

The French government was collapsing and on June 22 France's General Charles Huntziger signed an armistice at Rethondes, near Compiègne. The armistice came into effect just after midnight on June 25. The French army was disbanded and French citizens were instructed not to fight the Germans. Benoist was free to go home to Paris.

Under the terms of the surrender France was divided into two zones: the Occupied area which came under German control and the Unoccupied area which was to be administered by a government led by Pétain. This was to be based in Vichy and it quickly adopted right wing policies, believing that France's defeat had been caused by weakness created by the socialism in the 1930s. Pétain may have believed that he was independent and preparing France for its revenge on the Germans but rapidly that veneer was stripped away and the Vichy government became increasingly pro-Nazi.

Robert returned to Paris and went back to work at Bugatti in the Avenue Montaigne. To help fill the time he also started running a haulage company in Bois-Colombes.

Morale in France was low, particularly among the generations who had fought in World War I. Defeatism had taken over. The fighting had been intense and the French had fought fiercely. It is often forgotten that in the six weeks after the invasion began 130,000 Frenchmen died fighting - twice as many casualties as the Americans suffered in the battle for Normandy four years later.

Some of the younger generations wanted to resist the Germans but there was little that they could do against such a mighty occupation force. With France subdued, the Germans turned their attention to the invasion of Britain.

The British were weak and as the High Command frantically tried to re-organise the Home Forces, Willy Grover-Williams was posted to Royal Tunbridge Wells in Kent, where the remains of Britain's armoured forces were in the process of being re-equipped with new tanks.

That summer in the skies above Kent the Royal Air Force fighter squadrons clashed with the Luftwaffe in what became known as the Battle of Britain. The losses on both sides were heavy but the German decision to switch from attacking the RAF fighter stations and bomb the city of London gave Fighter Command the chance to recover and the Spitfire and Hurricanes wrought havoc with the German bombers.

Willy continued his work as a driver, spending his free time reading up on tank warfare, a subject which had fascinated him since the campaign in France. His letters home to the family in France were depressing. His brother Frederic, who had left Paris and was working as forester in the Vichy Zone, remembered Willy's mood.

"He was very bored," he recalled. "He wanted to get back to France to see Yvonne. He told me that one day a General who he was driving about was holding some big tank manoeuvres. I believe that even Winston Churchill was there. At one point the General gave an order and Willy realised that it had been misunderstood and that the troops were not doing what the General had ordered. He hesitated for a while and then finally took his courage in both hands and said: 'Sir, you said something and they are doing something different'. He was right and his intervention avoided a major mistake."

Willy later told his brother that on the way back from the manoeuvres the General asked how Willy knew so much about tactics. They began talking and the General asked if there was anything he could do for Willy in order to say thank you. Willy told him that he wanted to go back to France and fight behind enemy lines.

If he had hoped to be whisked back across the Channel within weeks Willy was to be disappointed. Nothing happened. Many of the tank regiments were sent off to Egypt and went into action in the Western Desert but Willy stayed in England. The Home Forces were re-equipped and training continued and then, In July 1941, Willy was posted to a remote Royal Army Service Corps unit in Kinross in Scotland.

✠

Back in France the country was firmly under German control. Ettore Bugatti found himself in a very difficult and unpleasant situation. He was an Italian and with Italy allied to Germany he was under pressure to turn over his factory to help the German war effort.

If he did not comply he knew that the factory would be confiscated from him and used by the Germans. Faced with this threat Bugatti came up with an unusual solution and offered to sell his works to the Germans for half of what it was actually worth. That way he did not incur their wrath but at the same time left the way open to argue after the war that he had not dealt willingly with the Occupation forces.

Bugatti needed the money. In November 1940 the RAF had bombed the factory in Bordeaux which left the business with no income. Ettore moved some of his design staff into one of two apartments he owned in a building on the Avenue Hoche, not far from the Arc de Triomphe in Paris. He lived in one and worked in the other. The designs were turned into prototypes at the experimental department in the Rue du Débarcadère. The Germans visited the offices once to see if Bugatti had anything of any value under development but then he was left alone.

His plan was to design and build small and cheap cars for after the war, when there would be little money around. He set to work designing two very small engines: the 370cc Type 68 and the 1500cc Type 73. With the money he received from the Germans Bugatti purchased the Corre factory in Courbevoie, which had previously produced cars under the La Licorne name, and he began to manufacture small vans. There was very little demand as fuel was almost impossible to find but it provided some income.

Robert Benoist was often a visitor at the design office in the Avenue Hoche and at the rue du Débarcadère. He did not have much to do at the Avenue Montaigne. He looked after the personnel side of the business and, when it was necessary, travelled across France when Bugatti customers needed their cars repaired or serviced.

He was frustrated. He hated the German occupation but there was no resistance movement for him to join.

Up in Scotland, Willy Grover-Williams was also frustrated. He wanted to see Yvonne and was bored of sitting around doing nothing, but that was all about to change.

In the autumn of 1941 Willy received a letter from the Ministry of Works, requesting that he present himself for an interview at the requisitioned Hotel Victoria on Northumberland Avenue in London. Willy had no idea what it was about but set off to London in the hope that it was something interesting.

CHAPTER FIVE

Frederick Gordon was an ambitious man. In the 1880s he built the largest hotel chain in the world, several of them on a new street called Northumberland Avenue, which cut through from Trafalgar Square to the Embankment on land that had previously been the private estate of the Duke of Northumberland. This was within easy walking distance of the Charing Cross railway station and Gordon believed that this would keep the hotels filled with travellers, arriving in London from the south and from Europe.

In order to get a monopoly in Northumberland Avenue he acquired the Hotel Victoria from the Northumberland Avenue Hotel Company in 1893. This was the second largest hotel in London and boasted 500 rooms. It was a great success and Gordon became very wealthy.

During World War I the hotels were requisitioned by the government in order to house the extra departments needed and in 1940 the same thing happened again. The Hotel Victoria was taken over by the War Office.

Willy Grover presented himself at the reception desk on arrival from Scotland and was directed to a room at the back of the building, overlooking the courtyard which lay between the old hotel and the rear of Scotland Yard, London's famed police headquarters. He was invited into the room by a Major.

He used a false name but Willy would later discover that his real name was Lewis Gielgud. Before the war he had been a poet and then a senior official in the International Red Cross in Geneva. He came from a talented family. His brother Val had been head of

William Grover was a man of much mystery. His father was English and his mother French. He grew up in France. When he started racing motorbikes he used the name "W Williams" so that his family would not know the risks he was taking. In World War II William Grover-Williams, as he had by then become, joined the British Army. In 1942 he was parachuted into France to work as a secret agent for the Special Operations Executive in Paris.

Dressed as a French cavalryman, Willy poses for a photo in his childhood. Later, fascinated by machinery, he bought an ex-US Army Indian motorbike (top right) and began racing. At the same time he worked as a chauffeur and saved enough to buy an Hispano-Suiza, with which he started competing on the Monte Carlo Rally in 1925 (below right).

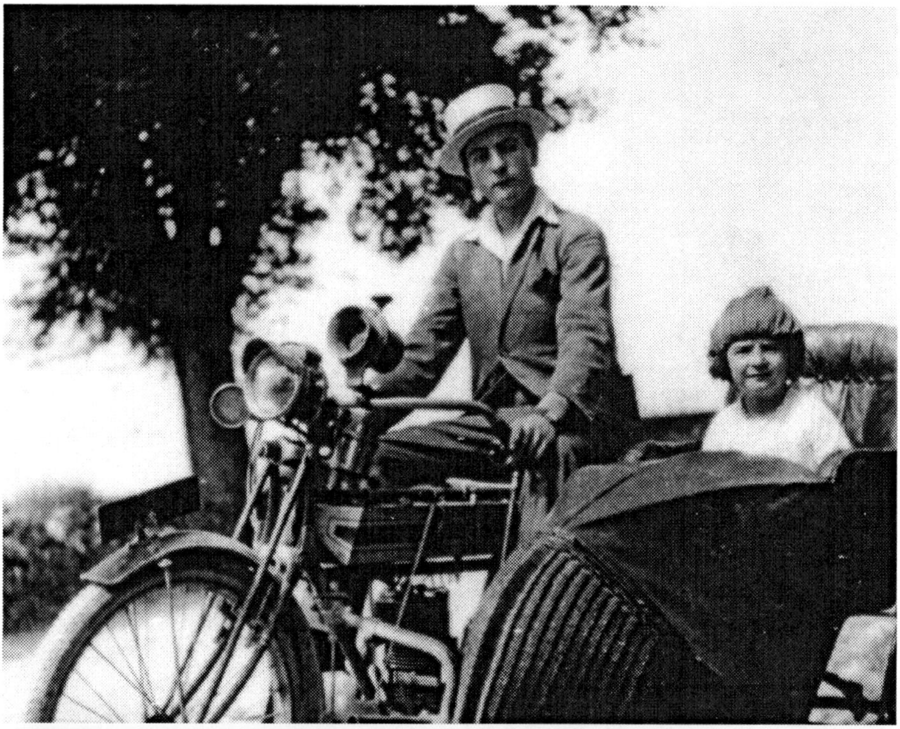

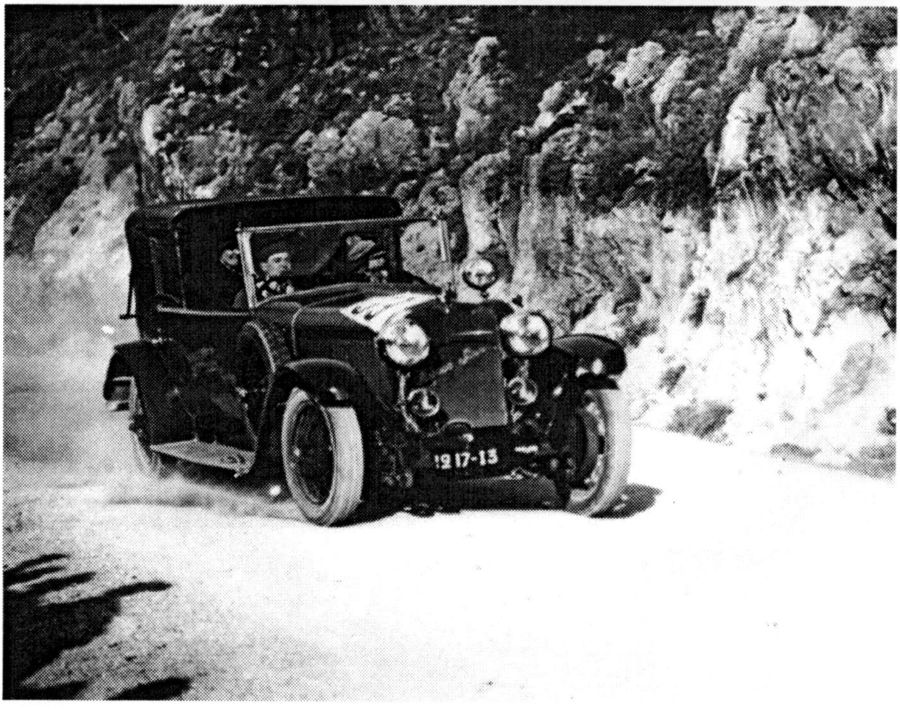

84- The Grand Prix Saboteurs

The beautiful Yvonne Aupicq (left) was a nurse during World War I, but when she met the Irish war artist Sir William Orpen she became his model - and his mistress. Being painted as a nun (above left) was a private joke between them. Yvonne lived in a house on the rue Weber in Paris (above right) and spent much time with Orpen's chauffeur Willy Grover. In 1926 Grover became a Grand Prix driver (below). Yvonne and Willy married in 1929.

St Gaudens 1928: Willy Grover takes the chequered flag to win the first of two French Grand Prix victories. Grand Prix racing was troubled that year with only a few cars racing, so the Automobile Club de France held the race for sports cars. The top drivers all raced Grand Prix Bugattis, but these were fitted with mudguards and headlights!

production at the BBC and his younger brother John was a well known actor. Gielgud offered Willy a cigarette and started asking mundane questions. Willy replied, wondering what the interview was all about. The room, he noted, was barely furnished at all, featuring a trestle table, which had been covered by a grey blanket, two chairs and a single filing cabinet. It was not a real office at all.

Gielgud continued to ask him innocent questions: Where did he come from? Which languages did he speak? How well did he know France? Finally Gielgud came to the point. Would Willy be interested in helping the Allied cause rather than just being a chauffeur? He explained that Willy's flawless French was a very useful talent and Willy replied that he was very keen to help. Gielgud mentioned that it might be rather dangerous work but Willy laughed. He was not worried about danger. Gielgud then explained, in a conspiratorial manner, that what he was about to say was top secret information and must not be repeated to anyone. Every effort was being made to tie down German soldiers in France and disrupt the German war effort, he said. There might be a job for Willy working behind enemy lines, organizing sabotage.

The risks, he added, would be enormous. Willy replied that he was used to a more exciting life than the one he had in Scotland and said that he would be delighted to go back to Paris. It was not for Gielgud to make the decision and he explained to Willy that he ought to take a few days to think about it and proposed another interview a week later. He would organise things with Willy's commanding officer. In fact this was a ruse. The time was used by the Security Service (MI5) to investigate Willy Grover and discover if there was anything in the government files to suggest that he might be a threat to national security. The search produced nothing and after a second interview Gielgud gave Willy an address in Portman Square and told him to be there a few days later.

Orchard Court was a fashionable apartment building on Portman Square. With the bombing of London, most of the wealthy residents had departed to homes in the country and the building was all but empty. The War Office had requisitioned some of the apartments and employed the uniformed porters. Willy followed the instructions he had been given by Gielgud and took the elevator to the third floor. He rang the bell of apartment number six and a slightly balding middle-aged man opened the door. Willy was ushered into a room that had just a desk and two chairs.

The organisation, he noted, did not have much in the way of furniture. After several hours of interviews with various members of the organisation he was finally informed that he was going to be sent away for training. His name, they said, was no longer Willy Grover. He would be known in future as Vladimir Gatacre. Even more extraordinary was a promotion that instantly turned a Private soldier into a Second Lieutenant. He then had to learn his cover story and was fitted for a new uniform before being shown into another room where he found a group of 10 other men.

They were then introduced to an RAF officer who swept into the room and began speaking in French. He was Flight Lieutenant André Simon, who said that he would be acting as their conducting officer in the weeks ahead. They were going to a house in the country for a training course. Simon gave them instructions to meet him, but not to acknowledge him, at Waterloo Station.

Travelling around Britain in wartime was not easy. The authorities had removed all the signposts in case there was an invasion. Inside every railway carriage was a poster, instructing passengers to keep one another informed of where they were. At each station the railway staff would walk up and down the platforms, shouting the name of the town. When he heard shouts of "Guildford" Willy climbed out of the train and made his way to the forecourt where he found Simon standing beside an army truck. The candidates climbed aboard the truck and then the canvas back was tied down tightly and the vehicle set off into the descending darkness. It was about an hour before the journey ended, although the trip could have been made in

15 minutes if the truck driver had not been ordered to drive around aimlessly so that no-one in the back had any idea where they were when they arrived.

The destination was Wanborough Manor, a large vine-covered country house, hidden away on the north side of the Hog's Back, a narrow ridge of chalk hills at the western end of the North Downs. It was located in a restricted zone in which the public was not allowed.

This was the SOE's Special Training School Number 5.

It was dark when the passengers were finally released from the back of the truck to be greeted at the door of the manor by Major Roger de Wesselow, a former Coldstream Guards officer. The sleeping arrangements were organised alphabetically and Grover-Williams (now known as Vladimir Gatacre) found himself sharing a room with a man called Raymond Hamilton. Willy would never know it but his new room mate was a former timber trader called Richard Heslop. He had served in the Military Police during the fall of France and had then been sent to Africa where he was serving when he was selected for an officer training course, where his talents were spotted and referred to SOE.

Wanborough Manor turned out to be a surprisingly civilized place. That evening over drinks and dinner the trainee secret agents got to know one another's cover stories. They all knew that what they were being told was not true but they were amused nonetheless. They were told that they should always speak in French and very quickly it emerged that some of the group were never going to be able to survive in France.

Early the next morning they discovered that the fine food, hot water and soft beds were the good part of the training. The bad part were physical exercises early every morning, which ranged from cross-country runs and assault courses to self-defence techniques. This would be followed by breakfast and then they would move on to map-reading work in the woods along the Hog's Back. They were also trained to use grenades and explosives and even did a small amount of target shooting in a couple of old chalk quarries hidden away at the back of the Wanborough estate. Later in the day there were lectures in sabotage techniques and in Morse Code. No contact was allowed with the outside world. Letters were censored and the trainees were not allowed to use the telephone.

Everything was done under the watchful eyes of André Simon and Roger de Wesselow. As the course progressed they learned that Simon was well-versed in underground activities: he had not only worked underground in France, but had also been arrested and had escaped from the Vichy police. What was not revealed until years later was that Simon's mission had been to rescue former French Prime Minister Édouard Daladier, who had been placed under arrest by Pétain in 1940.

During their time at Wanborough, a ritual developed among the trainee agents of listening to the BBC radio news each evening at nine o'clock. It was through this that they learned of the assassination of German officers in Nantes on October 20 and the executions of 50 hostages, mostly Communists, which followed in Nantes and Châteaubriant. The killings disgusted not only France but also the Americans and a few days later the US State Department issued a bulletin condemning the Germans.

"The practice of executing scores of innocent hostages in reprisal for isolated attacks on Germans in countries temporarily under the Nazi heel revolts a world already inured to suffering and brutality," it said. "These are the acts of desperate men who know in their hearts that they cannot win. Frightfulness can never bring peace to Europe. It only sows the seeds of hatred, which will one day bring fearful retribution."

The executions shocked the trainees at Wanborough and made them realize that when Gielgud had spoken of the dangers of the job, he had been serious.

Willy and Raymond found themselves drawn to two other trainees - Ely and Roland - and the four men formed their own little team. Ely Mountford was about the same age as Willy and had a slight American accent. His real name was Ernest Wilkinson and he had been born to British parents in Missouri. In the 1930s he had settled in France and married a Frenchwoman. When war broke out he had joined the Royal Air Force and had fled France when the German invasion came. To avoid being interned by the Germans, his wife had gone through the motions of divorcing him and was by then running a boarding house in the town of Angers, on the Loire.

Roland was a fun-loving and lively 19-year-old. His real name was Robert Sheppard and after the German invasion of France in 1940 he had crossed into Spain where the Spaniards had interned him for a while before he was allowed to travel to Gibraltar. When he arrived there he enlisted in the British Army and had spent nearly a year on The Rock before filling in a questionnaire asking for foreign language speakers. Not long afterwards he received a letter from the War Office, inviting him to an interview in London.

"I don't really remember the others on the course at all," said Sheppard. "What I remember about Vladimir is that right from the beginning we got along very well together. He was a good chap. I was a young man and for me Vladimir was already quite old. He was very sophisticated and had the air of a Parisian. We were all very security-minded. I had no idea that his name was Grover-Williams and he didn't know my name. But we were the group that liked to have a beer in the bar in the evenings."

Even then they knew that they had to keep under control because André Simon was always keeping an eye on them.

"We knew we were being trained for secret action but we were not given any details," remembered Sheppard. "We were told that we would learn the rest at the right time. Wanborough was the preparatory training so that we knew everything you ought to know when you are in the army."

Willy's training reports reveal that he worked hard and was very keen to do well. He was described as "an efficient soldier who liked discipline and who was fond of planning things and seeing that the plan was carried out meticulously". His wireless training was handicapped by a "great dislike of Morse Code and a lack of confidence in learning it". As Christmas approached the course at Wanborough came to an end. The trainees were put back into the army truck and driven back to Guildford. When they reached London they were sent on leave. While they had some rest, the instructors decided which candidates should go on to the next stage of training. Only five of the 11 were picked: the Wanborough "Gang of Four" and a Frenchman who was known only as Guy.

Willy spent Christmas in London and reported to Orchard Court early in the New Year. He met Simon and the four survivors of the Wanborough course and they immediately set off for Euston Station from where the London Midland and Scottish Railway took them north on what seemed to be an interminable journey. The train was full of people but the trainees had two compartments to themselves and after a day of travel the train finally rattled into Glasgow. After an hour's wait the express headed off again, through the suburbs of the city, alongside the River Clyde to Dumbarton and then, as night fell, it turned north beside Loch Long. At the top end of the Loch the railway cut through the hills to Loch Lomond and then disappeared into the Grampian mountains to emerge in the town of Fort William, in the shadow of Ben Nevis. They changed trains and this time set off for the coastal town of Arisaig.

This was spectacular countryside, some of the wildest in Britain, and was where Bonnie Prince Charlie hid out while escaping from the English after his defeat at the Battle of Culloden Moor in 1746. For five months the Young Pretender had remained at liberty, assisted by local supporters, as the English Red Coats searched for him.

It was late at night by the time they arrived in Arisaig and found another army truck waiting for them. The Arisaig Peninsular, to the north of the town, was another restricted zone, closed off to the general public. The truck took them down the winding coastal road, through rough rocky country, broken up by small ravines, until it pulled up outside a small house, close to the road but screened from it by a grove of trees. This was Garramor, the French Section's commando training school, part of Special Training School No 25.

Garramor was to be their home for the next six weeks. Conditions were much less comfortable than they had been at Wanborough Manor, with agents sleeping five or six to a room and the only heating coming from log fires. But when the weather cleared there were spectacular views across the water to the towering mountains of Skye. The trainee agents worked night and day and the exercises were much more physical than they had been at Wanborough. They learned how to climb cliffs and to move quietly across country without being spotted. They were taught how to drive trains, how to shoot off locks and given a very thorough training in the use of explosives.

"It was a very interesting and sporting type of training," remembered Sheppard. "We were up at dawn training in the snow. It was the same sort of thing as at Wanborough but on a much larger scale."

The trainees were usually worn out after a day of training but they found some time and energy to play practical jokes on the commandant of Garramor, Major Millar.

"We put a very small piece of gelignite on the bottom of a toilet seat," remembered Sheppard, "and when the Major went to the toilet we triggered it!"

The Major was not happy.

"He had a few words about that," remembered Sheppard.

When they were not blowing up their instructors, the trainee agents were kept busy blasting holes in old railway locomotives. All day long there were muffled explosions up and down the Arisaig Peninsular as groups of saboteurs from different nations practised their dangerous new skills.

Part of the training involved a small arms training centre

which had been established in a farm called Camusdarach.

"They had all kinds of mechanical devices which made targets jump out at you all over the place," recalled Sheppard. "You would enter with a Sten gun. You did this in the daylight, at night, even in smoke. It taught you all the different moves when you were firing and was part of the psychological hardening process."

On Sundays they were allowed to relax.

While they were there news came through that the Japanese had attacked the US naval base at Pearl Harbour. No-one had ever heard of it before then and they had to fetch maps to find out what happened. They knew that after that America was in the war. Towards the end of the course the agents were sent on cross-country missions with instructions to avoid their instructors and blow up a number of designated targets. During one of these exercises Heslop had a heavy fall and broke a bone in his leg. He disappeared from the course. At the end of the Arisaig course there was a 36-hour exercise during which each agent in turn took charge of a different operation. Willy's training reports emphasized his loathing for signals work but noted that he was very keen on demolition. The conclusion was that he was "a very good all-round man" and "the star turn of this party". His fitness was a little suspect but the report concluded that he had "lots of guts". There were conflicting assessments from different instructors about his leadership ability, but all agreed he was "a tough resourceful individual who would probably work best on his own".

The four survivors headed south, with railway warrants that took them to Warrington in Lancashire. Outside the railway station there was another army truck, which took them east towards Altrincham. After a few miles it turned off the main road and arrived at the gates of Dunham Massey Hall, the SOE's parachute training school. The old manor house was surrounded by its own walled deer park in which the trainee agents were able to go about their business without the world outside knowing anything at all. Inside the hall some of the larger rooms had been converted into gymnasiums and a curious collection of parachute training apparatus had been installed. This included a terrifying trapeze device, which would catapult the trainees across the room. It was designed to teach them how to fall without injuring themselves, but it caused many injuries.

There were several groups of SOE trainees at Dunham Massey Hall at any one time but the different groups were never encouraged to mix. The courses lasted only a week and when Willy's group was there the weather was bad, with snow on the ground. After a couple of days working on the evil trapeze the trainee agents were taken out into the grounds of the house and taught how to jump from moving trucks. They then tried jumping from a parachute tower and once that had been completed it was time to move on to actual parachute jumps. These were carried out at the nearby Ringway aerodrome. In peacetime Ringway was Manchester's civil airport but from June 1940 it had been the home of the British Parachute Training School. The shock of the German invasion of Holland and Belgium had alerted the British to the fact that they needed parachute troops and it was at Ringway that the legend of the Parachute Regiment began. These were the elite soldiers of the British Army and to win the coveted parachute wings and a red beret was something that many dreamed of doing. In its first fortnight of operation at Ringway an RASC driver became the Parachute Training School's first victim when his chute failed to open properly in what is known in parachuting circles as "a Roman candle". Even 18 months later parachuting was still new and dangerous and there was some trepidation among the SOE trainees. The instructors did not help. They were men who were used to taking risks and enjoyed a certain black humour when asked by the pupils if the parachutes had ever failed to open. They replied that no-one had ever come back to complain.

On the first day at Ringway the trainees were taken up in a Wellington bomber and flown around the airfield. Some of them had never flown before. The next day they made their first jumps. There were no worries about having to open the parachutes themselves.

They had static lines. The drama of the whipping slipstream and the deafening noise inside the plane left them all in a state of high excitement as the jump approached. And then they were outside drifting towards the ground and, for the first time, able to enjoy the flying sensation which is so addictive for parachuting fanatics.

"That evening we had a dinner party in the village of Ringway to celebrate," remembered Sheppard. "We went with André Simon and we all felt really good."

The days that followed were rather more difficult as the trainee agents had to do a series of jumps from low-level barrage balloons.

"It was absolutely mad," recalled Sheppard. "There were four of you in this basket, one in each corner and a sergeant in the middle. You went up and up, sitting on a plywood platform and hanging on to your corner because it was bumping around and you were worried that you might fall through the hole in the floor. Then the balloon stopped and the sergeant said: "Now, gentlemen, whenever you want". There was absolute silence. You just had to suicide yourself. You could hear everything when you were doing it: the crack of the static line, the parachute whooshing open. You got the impression it was never going to open up in time but then you would hear the instructors on the ground yelling at you to keep you legs together before you hit the ground."

Willy suffered a typical parachute injury, banging his nose with his knees during one of the landings. He later told his brother Frederic that low-level parachuting was not much fun. In total there would be seven jumps for each trainee during the course, including one in which the jumper had a kit bag strapped to his or her leg and another - the most terrifying of all - a low level jump at night although sometimes there was not time for that and so the trainee agents were given darkened motorcycle goggles and jumped in the daylight!

Once that was done they were qualified parachutists. There were two days to go before Christmas when they learned that they were going back to London and would get 14 days of leave. There was little time for celebration and soon they were back in the army truck on the way back to Warrington.

The four would lose Guy the Frenchman at this point. He had done well in all the radio courses and they later heard that he had been sent off to the advanced signals training course at Special Training School 53 in Aylesbury. The others never did discover his identity and all that Sheppard and his friends remember is that they heard that he had had an accident when he parachuted into France. In all probability he was an agent called Orabona who was dropped into France to work for Général de Gaulle's RF (République Francaise) section in July 1942. His parachute failed to open and he was killed, although after the war his SOE file was destroyed so no trace remains.

When they reached London's Euston Station, Grover-Williams, Sheppard and Wilkinson went their separate ways.

"The security was very good," remembered Sheppard. "I had no idea where Vladimir was staying. We said goodbye at the station and we did not meet up again until we went back to Orchard Court."

✠

It was in this period that Willy met up with his sister Lizzie and her family in London. They had escaped from Paris and, with the help of the American Embassy in Marseilles, had been put in contact with one of the escape lines into Spain. Once in England they had settled in an apartment near Grosvenor Square. Willy's niece Jessie Teager remembered Willy's visit.

"He came in civilian clothes," she recalled, "he had dark glasses on and a moustache to try to disguise himself but I immediately said: 'Hello Willy'."

Jessie was working with a Free Dutch newspaper based in Mayfair and one day while looking out of the window she saw her uncle walk by. She mentioned it to him later and he asked: "Was I in uniform? You can always talk to me when I am in uniform."

Jessie remembered being aware of what Willy was doing.

"He told me that I was not supposed to tell anyone or I could end up being interned," she recalled. "He would come to visit us very late at night but he never stayed with us. We never knew where he was staying."

After the short leave Willy, Sheppard and Wilkinson met up again at Orchard Court and discovered that Heslop - their old friend Raymond Hamilton who had broken his leg in Scotland - had managed to catch up with them, despite having been out of action for a month. Heslop had missed the parachute training because the doctors had decided that his leg would not stand up to a rough landing and so if he was going to go to France in the future, he would be going in by boat or by aircraft rather than by parachute.

The cheerful foursome and the ever-present André Simon departed from Orchard Court once again, bound for Waterloo Station and from there they took a train to Southampton. They transferred to a smaller train that steamed through the New Forest to the station at Brockenhurst. Outside was a half-tracked vehicle. They climbed aboard and the half-track took off into the New Forest, another restricted area.

"I was sitting next to the driver," remembered Sheppard, "and he was going like mad. Vladimir was next to me and I said in French: "My God, he is driving like hell, this chap". It struck me that Vladimir had a little smile. He looked at the driver and he said: 'No, it's all right. He knows what he is doing'."

Sheppard still had no idea that the man next to him had won Grands Prix in the 1920s and 1930s.

Their destination on this occasion was Beaulieu Abbey, the home of the Montagu Family, which had been taken over by the SOE and turned into Special Training School 31 - the saboteur's finishing school. The Montagu estates had been requisitioned early in the war and to begin with the SOE used only four or five of the houses. As the organisation grew, more and more houses were requisitioned until there were around 20 being used for trainee secret agents. Each SOE Section had its own house and every attempt was made to make sure that there was no contact between the different groups. This was not as difficult as it may sound because the Beaulieu estates include large areas of deserted heath land. The four trainees stayed in a house called Vineyards and once again Willy roomed with Heslop; Wilkinson with Sheppard.

"Vladimir was always cheerful," Heslop remembered. "He was very philosophical but he was impatient to rejoin his wife in Paris."

They knew that the weeding-out process at Wanborough Manor and Arisaig was now over. They were all going to go to France and it was just a matter of working out which job they would do best when they got there. The plum job for an SOE agent was that of "network organiser", but there was also a demand for assistant organisers, couriers and radio operators.

The course at Beaulieu was designed to ensure that a secret agent knew as much as possible about daily life in Occupied Europe. There were endless courses about the structure of the German army, about the SS and the agents had to learn all the various divisional badges and uniforms. There were lessons on aeroplane identification. All information they could gather would help the overall war effort. They learned about the French police forces and other officialdom and about the necessary local regulations and community information. They were taught the art of clandestine propaganda and given guidance on who would be the right kind of people to recruit and how to approach the problem in a world where everyone was afraid to show their true colours for fear of being betrayed.

The instructors at Beaulieu were an extraordinary group of talented individuals, including experts with the most unusual skills. The man who taught the secret agents about the German uniforms was fashion designer Hardy Amies; there was also the journalist Paul Dehn, who would later become the award-winning script writer of films such as Goldfinger, The Spy Who Came In From The Cold and Murder on the Orient Express. There were professional policemen who taught them the tricks of the trade and even members of the criminal community who had been let out of prison to help the war effort by imparting their knowledge on breaking and entering and cracking safes. The SOE agents were taught all manner of dangerous skills.

The French house was under the command of Captain Nobby Clark, who specialised in field crafts. He taught the agents how to live off the land and how to poach game if they ran short of food when on the run. He had been the gamekeeper on the Royal estates at Sandringham. They say that a poacher-turned-gamekeeper is a dangerous man, but the reverse is just as effective. Their education in demolition techniques continued with classes in how to manufacture their own home made explosives if their supplies from Britain ran out and they were also taught how to deal with the huge metal containers which were dropped by parachute. Another important lesson was how to shake off pursuers if they found themselves being followed. The SOE had learned that often the Germans did not arrest agents immediately after identifying them, in the hope that they would lead the security forces to others in the network. The trainees were thus taught how to spot if they were being followed and how to get away from a tail without attracting attention. When the lessons were over they were taken to the nearby town of Bournemouth where the ideas were put into practice. Department stores, which had doors on several sides, were particularly useful.

Towards the end of the course there was a four-day exercise over a weekend during which the agents were sent off from Beaulieu and told that they had to break into a restricted area and bring back as much secret material as they could find. During the exercise they had to be at a specific rendezvous and make contact with someone they did not know. They were given the name and address of someone with whom they had to discreetly discuss the possibility of anti-British resistance. To aid them they were given false identity papers, £10 in cash and a railway warrant. They were told to come up with their own cover stories. They were also given an envelope, which they were instructed to give to the police if they were arrested. This explained that they were in training to be secret agents and gave the police an address to contact to verify the story.

Usually the SOE instructors gave details of the agents to the police forces to see if the trainees could stay ahead of the law. That helped everyone stay alert.

"I cheated terribly," remembered Sheppard. "The police were going around checking all the hotels but I was never caught because I went to stay with my aunt."

Such resourcefulness was exactly what the SOE wanted to see from its secret agents. If they had an advantage to be exploited they should use it. Willy certainly did. He decided on his secret mission that he would travel to Derby, the site of a Rolls Royce factory, which was producing aero-engines for Spitfires and the Lancaster bombers of the Royal Air Force, and that by using his brother-in-law's name and other connections he would try to get into the factory and see what he could steal. When he got there he discovered that he knew the director of the plant from the old days in Paris and so he was able to steal some Rolls Royce documents and returned to Beaulieu, avoiding all the traps which had been set. It was an excellent performance. After another short leave it was back at Beaulieu again for another course. This was designed to help the secret agents to immerse themselves in their cover stories and how to behave if they were arrested. This included simulated interrogation sessions at strange hours of the night, with instructors dressed as Germans, trying to catch out the trainees.

"To be quite frank we couldn't take this very seriously," remembered Sheppard, who was much more interested in the exercises in which the students had to break into other Beaulieu houses at night and steal things without being caught.

Willy Grover-Williams and his three friends graduated from Beaulieu at the end of March 1942. In the final report from his instructors he was described as having been "surprisingly fit and agile. Very good at close combat. Knows field craft, but inclined not to bother, and good at weapons". He had been chosen to be an F Section organizer. He would have his own network and was commissioned as a Second Lieutenant on the Army's General List.

Willy Grover was ready to go back to France.

CHAPTER SIX

Maurice Buckmaster had one recurring problem during his period as the man in charge of the SOE's French Section: how could he deliver his agents to France? There was no way of sneaking across the borders by land: Nazi Germany occupied virtually all of Continental Europe with only Spain and Switzerland remaining at liberty. The Spanish government under General Francisco Franco was sympathetic to Adolf Hitler, although it carefully avoided any active involvement in the war. This meant that the British could not mount operations from Spanish soil and even escapers crossing the Pyrénées between France and Spain ran the risk of being arrested and incarcerated in the infamous prison at Miranda de Ebro. The Swiss remained completely neutral and so cross-border operations into France or Germany were simply not possible.

Initially the British tried to land agents by boat on the heavily-defended and rocky north coast of France but it soon became obvious that these operations were extremely hazardous. The Germans had built The Atlantic Wall, a series of fortifications designed to prevent any landings and the beaches were under constant surveillance. There were obstacles and minefields. Where the coast was rocky the British faced the age-old danger that smugglers had struggled with for centuries. Navigating in dangerous waters during the night would inevitably result in the loss of valuable agents who has spent months in training.

In the end the British came up with the idea of flying agents aboard civilian airliners to Gibraltar where the Royal Navy had a small fleet of vessels which ran clandestine operations in the Mediterranean.

These included the trawler called Tarana which would leave port in Royal Navy colours and be repainted during the first night at sea and have the profile of its funnels changed. It thus became a local fishing boat, sailing under a neutral flag. The Tarana worked in conjunction with a number of Polish-run feluccas, small fishing vessels which had been acquired locally, to land agents on the beaches of southern France. This was a lengthy process but the security was much better as the Germans were not expecting visitors from the south and at that time the coastline was not as tightly guarded as the north. From the south of France the secret agents could travel north and sneak across the Demarcation Line between Vichy France and the Occupied Zone. There were dangers but it was still seen as being safer than landing in Brittany or on the coastline of Normandy.

As the war went on the conclusion was reached that the only really effective way to get secret agents in and out of France was by plane, either being dropped by parachute or landing them by small aircraft in remote areas. As early as September 1940 the Air Ministry had established a secret unit for clandestine work. It was known as 419 Flight and it undertook its first operation in October 1940. This was not a success. The engine got lost on the return trip from France and eventually crash-landed in Scotland. Four One Nine Flight was later renamed 1419 Flight and was stationed at various different aerodromes before settling in Newmarket in August 1941. After that it was renamed again, becoming known as 138 Squadron.

By that time there were an increasing number of highly-trained and experienced pilots who had served their time on bombers and survived a series of raids. The Royal Air Force had a policy of moving pilots on after they had completed a tour of duty on bombers. The risks were too great and the RAF wanted to keep morale high, particularly when the casualty rates went up as bombing raids went deeper and deeper into the German heart lands. As the number of pilots increased so did the potential for clandestine operations and in February 1942 the RAF established a second Special Duties Squadron, known as 161. The two secret units soon became known as The Moon Squadrons because they could only operate when the moon provided them with sufficient light to navigate.

Taking secret agents to France involved a lot of risk for all concerned. Dropping agents by parachute was easier than landing a plane, but it created the risk that a highly-trained agent might be hurt or even killed. If there was a reception committee on the ground there was less danger of an accident but more chance of a trap.

Flying small planes in and out required people on the ground to act as guides. The little planes, notably the Westland Lysander, were slow and could easily be hit by anti-aircraft fire or shot down by German night fighters. Landings in France were not easy and several pilots and secret agents were killed when Moon Squadron planes crashed while touching down in difficult conditions. Ground fog was often a problem although, as the war went on, it was unsuitable ground which proved to be the biggest danger for the Moon Squadron pilots. Aircraft would flip over when they landed or would become stuck in the mud on a landing field. Several had to be destroyed on the ground and the crews had to try to get back to Britain by way of the escape lines which were set up to help Allied airmen get away.

All of these factors meant that often there were long delays in delivering secret agents because conditions had to be right. At the same time, the highly-trained and very valuable agents wanted to get into action immediately rather than sit around in England, mulling over what they were about to do and the risks they were about to expose themselves to. To make sure agents did not get bored the SOE introduced a number of additional training courses and exercises to pass the time. Willy and his friend Wilkinson, who had also been chosen to be a network organiser, were sent to Secret Training School 17, situated on a country estate just outside the county town of Hertford. Brickendon Bury was hidden away in its own wooded parkland and served as the SOE's school of assassination and explosives techniques. At Brickendon Bury, the SOE network organisers were taught the philosophy of assassination and how it should be used only to foster the spirit of resistance. Too many killings would lead to excessive German retribution and the resistance would be blamed. It would mean fewer long-term recruits. Occasional assassinations were sufficient to keep the Germans worried.

The philosophy was similar to that taught on the industrial demolition course held at Brickendon Bury by George Rheam, formerly of the Central Electricity Board. He argued that while large bombs made a lot of noise and attracted attention, they often caused little serious real damage and factories could be put back into operation very quickly. Rheam's theory was that the saboteurs should be taught to identify vital parts of important machines, which would be difficult or impossible to replace. These could be stolen or destroyed either by hand or, if necessary, using a very small explosive charge. Entire production lines could be stopped if one small component could not be replaced. Rheam believed that if the saboteurs followed his strategy they would more easily be able to smuggle explosive devices into important factories and, perhaps more importantly, it would be much more difficult to pin down what had happened. If a part went missing, any retribution was more likely be seen as being a bad thing, which would help to foster the spirit of resistance.

Rheam also argued that attacks on railway lines did not need to involve blasting away the railway tracks and derailing trains because the same effect could be achieved by damaging rolling stock and sabotaging signalling systems. One of the SOE's most effective weapons was a specially-formulated "abrasive grease" which was used on locomotives. This grease rapidly wore out machinery parts and caused the locomotives to grind to a halt. It left no trace as to who had carried out the sabotage as the Germans could not pin down who had applied the special grease. Guarding every single railway marshalling yard tied up more soldiers.

The industrial demolition course lasted for three weeks and after that Willy and Wilkinson returned to London to await the start of their missions.

Willy's brother Frederic recalled a strange story his brother told him later when they were together in Paris but it is impossible to determine whether or not there is any truth it. Frederic said that Willy was sent to France on a raid to kidnap German officers and bring them back to Britain so that the Allies could get information about the French coastal defences, presumably in preparation for a future invasion.

"He told me that he had something like 40 men for the operation," Frederic said. "There was an isolated house on top of a cliff. There was a young Scotsman who was only about 18. My brother wanted to leave him with the boats but he wanted to go on the mission and my brother was weak enough to allow him to come. They went and everything went as planned. They arrested two German officers and were on their way back to the boats when they met a patrol. They dropped quietly to the ground to let the Germans pass but the Scottish boy couldn't stand the pressure and broke. He was killed and the others had to shoot their way back to the boats."

According to Jessie Teager, who later heard the same story, they managed to get one of the German officers back to Britain. The British authorities say that no such missions took place and argue that Willy may have been talking about an exercise and that his story was misunderstood. It is however hard to imagine that the raid described in such detail was a figment of Willy's imagination or a misinterpretation by members of his family. There is no denying that cross-Channel raids were going on at the time. As early as July 1941 commandos from an SOE unit based in Dorset crossed the English Channel and landed near Cap Gris Nez. The operation scouted the coast but failed to find a single German. A month later other raids took place at Merlimont and Onival and during the second a German officer was taken back to Britain. The commandos soon became known as The Maid Honour Force, named after the trawler they used for the raids. This took part in a number of raids early in 1942, mainly to the coast of Brittany. In February of that year Lord Louis Mountbatten, the chief of combined operations, took control of the Maid Honour Force and turned it into the Small Scale Raiding Force, which he described as an "amphibious sabotage force" of 50 men, which was directly under his command.

That same month members of the newly-formed 1st Parachute Brigade parachuted into a remote area of the French coast and attacked a German radar station at Bruneval which had been identified as having the latest German "Würzburg " radar system. Components were seized and an operator was taken prisoner and the paratroopers then escaped in landing craft beneath the cliffs. The German equipment was examined and it was discovered that the device would only work within a narrow frequency range and could be jammed with the use of aluminium strips known as chaff. This was used with great effect in 1943 and it saved many lives as it rendered the German air defences completely blind and allowed bombers to come and go without being tracked. The value of commando raids was proven and at the end of March 1942 there was a major commando operation on the docks at St Nazaire in southern Brittany, to block the port and stop the Germans using the vast Normandy Dock to refit the Tirpitz, its latest new battleship. The close proximity of civilian population made the Royal Air Force reluctant to bomb the dock and so it was decided to send in a force of Commandos to destroy the docks gates by ramming them with an old destroyer and then blowing up the ship. There were heavy casualties but the raid was a success and an important boost for British morale.

There is no record of a commando raid that fits the description given to Frederic Grover and Jessie Teager, but the nearest seems to have been in April 1942 when No 4 Commando under Major The Lord Lovat landed around 50 men on the beaches closed to the village of Hardelot, near Boulogne. Their aim was to capture prisoners and to inflict as much damage as possible on the German defences. The only injury was a soldier who was shot in the leg after failing to identify himself. The mystery remains unsolved but it is worth noting that the cross-Channel raiding activities were to have an important effect on the future of the SOE as a raid in October 1942 on the Channel Island of Sark resulted in several Germans being killed, two of them apparently shot when their hands were tied. This led to Adolf Hitler's infamous Kommandobefehl order later that month in which he declared that since Germany's enemies were using "methods which are outside the Geneva Convention" in the future anyone caught while involved in sabotage activity was "to be slaughtered to the last man".

If Willy did go on a raid to France, Bob Sheppard was not included. He had gone back to Scotland after Beaulieu but was back in London in May, waiting for his mission to begin. With the training complete the agents sat around in London, waiting for a call from Orchard Court. They were at liberty to do as they pleased.

"We really had nothing to do," remembered Sheppard. "All our missions were in hand, except for the final details which we got only on the day. We were on stand-by. One day I saw Vladimir at Orchard Court and we decided to have lunch together the following day at the Café Royal. We knew from the Moon that we would probably both be going to France within 48 hours."

✠

The two men met at the Café Royal at the bottom of Regent Street. Established by Frenchman Daniel Thevenon in 1885, the restaurant was reputed to have the best food and wine in London and while it was an extravagant thing to do, both men felt it was perfect in the circumstances. They took lunch in the mezzanine restaurant and while they could not discuss their missions, nor talk of their past lives, they were like schoolboys who have lived through the worst boarding school together, their friendship had been forged during the training.

"We really were like school friends," said Sheppard. "We had had a very good time in training. It was during that lunch that Vladimir suddenly said: 'We never know what is going to happen, but we must meet after the war is over'. He asked me if I knew the Bugatti showroom in Paris, on the Avenue Montaigne. I said I did. He said: 'Just opposite there is a bar where I used to go. At the first occasion you are in Paris after the liberation, leave a message at the bar. We will meet there and have a drink'."

The two agents finished lunch, shook hands, wished each other well and went their separate ways.

"I didn't find out until after the war was over that he had been a famous racing driver," remembered Sheppard.

The following day Willy was called to Orchard Court for his final briefing before being sent to France. There was a lot more activity than there had been in the apartment the previous autumn and this meant that the F Section Briefing Officer and a departing agent were often forced to use the black-tiled bathroom to go over details of the mission ahead. One perched on the bidet, the other on the edge of the bathtub. The lavatory seat served them as a map table. When the briefing was over Willy was informed that if caught by the Germans he was on his own. The British government would deny his existence. He was offered a cyanide pill in case he felt at some point that death was the best option available to him. Usually Buckmaster appeared at the end of the briefing. He liked to make a point of presenting each departing agent with a small gift. It was not an affectionate gesture but a practical gift, usually a gold cigarette case, cuff links or a pen. If an agent was on the run in France Buckmaster's gift could be sold or bartered to help them escape.

Soon it was time to depart. Willy was introduced to a young man who used the code name Charles. Together they got into a staff car which left London, heading north. On the journey they had time to talk, but there was nothing for them to talk about. Charles looked a lot more like a secret agent than did Willy Grover-Williams.

His real name was Christopher Burney and although only 25 he had already seen action as a subaltern with 12 Commando at Narvik in Norway in 1940. Burney was rather surprised to be in the company of a man who looked like a bank manager and he later wrote that he felt that Willy "seemed rather suspicious but, when you looked a little closer, you could see that there was something very respectable about him".

The journey took this unlikely pair north through the drab and bomb-damaged suburbs of London and out into the countryside of Hertfordshire on the Great North Road. The journey was only 50 miles but it took a couple of hours before the driver finally turned off the main road and drove through country lanes until they arrived at the gates of a country estate. Inside the wooded park at the top of a hill was Hazells Hall, the last stop for SOE agents on their way to Europe.

Hazells Hall had been the home of the Pym Family and had been requisitioned in 1940 when the Air Ministry decided to build an airfield on secluded marsh land nearby. The aerodrome was disguised from the air and no-one outside the base knew that it was any different to any of the other bases that sprung up in the area. The road to the airfield was closed to the public and although there was occasional discussion in The Anchor and the Wheatsheaf public house in Tempsford village the secret remained safe. Planes came and went at strange hours but no-one knew anything about the passengers.

Hazells Hall served as the quarters for the senior officers from the aerodrome as well as for the passing SOE agents. It was lavishly decorated and in the tense hours before a mission began the agents were afforded every luxury available. Chefs were on stand-by 24 hours a day and the bar was well-stocked. Girls from the First Aid Nursing Yeomanry kept the atmosphere cheerful.

The departure of the agents was then entirely dependent on the weather. Grover-Williams and Burney dined that evening with some of the pilots. There was much talk of "a flap" that was going on that night in Bomber Command and they hoped that whatever was happening in the skies of Europe would deflect attention from their plane.

After dinner Willy and Charles were driven through the darkness to a barn on the Old Gibraltar Farm, which was away from the other buildings of the air station. This was the newly-established preparation centre for agents being despatched to France. Tempsford had been the home of 138 Special Duty Squadron for only two months and it was only six weeks since the squadron had received its specially-modified Handley Page Halifaxes.

For the next three hours the two secret agents underwent a series of checks as SOE officers ensured that they carried nothing incriminating, nor anything that would be out of place in France. Their clothing was searched for ticket stubs, English matchboxes and clothing labels. Their French identity cards and papers were closely examined and they were constantly questioned in French. When the inspectors were satisfied, the agents squeezed themselves into the special flying suits, which could be worn over normal clothes, and then made their way out into the darkness where Bunny Rymills and his crew were waiting to take them to France.

Rymills taxied quickly away into the darkness.

✠

Twenty-four hours later Willy looked back and remembered the darkened faces of Tempsford as being only a distant memory. He was back in Paris with Yvonne and nothing else much mattered.

His new life began that Monday morning when he slipped quietly out of the house on the rue Weber and went in search of a place to live. The French Section in London had given him plenty of money with which to operate and he quickly found and rented a suitable apartment in the rue Vineuse, a street that led from the

Place du Trocadéro down towards the Passy Métro station. It was close enough to home to be convenient but far enough away to be anonymous. He explained to the concierge that he was an engineer and that he travelled a great deal and thus began his new life as Charles Lelong. For the first few days, he settled in and began to create the right impression. He left for work in the mornings and returned every evening. Yvonne visited him.

Soon he was accustomed to life under the German Occupation. His orders were not to do too much in a hurry. The French Section chiefs in London had planned that Willy's network would be a "sleeper" organization and would aim to still be there ready to disrupt German troop movements and communications when the Allied forces began the liberation of Occupied Europe. The Allies may not have known when that would be, but they wanted a sabotage group to be ready. Other groups could do immediate damage to the German war machine. Willy had been told that once he had recruited and trained groups for his specific targets, he could allow the Chestnut network to engage in as much quiet disruption as possible in and around Paris, so long as there was no trace of what they were doing.

The Sicherheitsdienst and the Abwehr, the German military intelligence, had already proved to be a dangerous opponent and played a clever game with resistance networks. The intelligence officers followed up every lead they were given which hinted at resistance work but they almost never made arrests, allowing the networks to continue their activities under surveillance. This led to additional members of the group being identified and to the Germans being able to build up an in-depth knowledge of the networks. This meant that those arrested were often stunned by how much the Germans knew and that always made them more willing to talk, which in turn led to more information. It also resulted in many resistance people being convinced that there had been traitors in the networks. Even if some of those in a network did escape arrest, there was always uncertainty and fear about those who remained at liberty.

Anyone organising a secret sabotage network is faced with the problem that as the group grows it becomes more exposed. Each new recruit increases the risk. Each might be a collaborator, might simply talk too much; or might brag to their friends about clandestine activities. To protect themselves from this, the SOE network organisers had been taught to create numerous "sub-networks" and try to ensure that there was no contact between each different cell.

Each sub-network had a leader and only he or she would know the network organiser. The rest of the cell would report only to the cell leader. To prevent organizers and sub-network leaders from being caught together they often used couriers to pass messages between them or established "letter boxes" where written instructions could be deposited for later collection. The essential element in the construction of a solid sabotage network was to make the right choice of cell leaders. The fewer people who were involved at the centre, the stronger an organisation could be.

Willy's aim was to have links with only a handful of his helpers, leaving his assistants on the ground to recruit and train groups of saboteurs. Once these cells were ready to go into action, they would go to ground and wait. He would then set up new cells to do immediate sabotage work. For a sabotage cell to be effective it needs to be supplied with arms and explosives. These would have obvious uses later on, but they were also of huge psychological value because they proved to the rank and file of the organization that the unknown people at the centre of the network were serious about what they were doing. The French Resistance had been built on talk but there had been very little action. A supply of guns or explosives from England gave an organiser instant credibility.

In order to obtain the weapons he needed, Willy needed a supply route and so his first task was to recruit a team to deal with parachute receptions. This group would be notified of parachute drops and would provide the necessary signals for the Royal Air Force planes. The group would then collect the arms and transport them to hiding places. Establishing a reception team was, therefore, a priority, but in order for such a network to be used properly once they were trained, Willy needed to have radio contact with London. The Briefing Officer in London had told him that F Section would send him a radio operator as soon as one became available. He had also been told that he would be getting a fully trained assistant to help him in his work. The intention was clearly for Willy to build a big network.

✠

In the early part of the war resistance had seemed hopeless to the French population. It was better to stay quiet, look after one's family and not get involved. For the average Frenchman it was difficult to accept that the collapse in 1940 had been quite so quick and defeat so comprehensive. There was a feeling that France had been let down by the British. The Germans were quick to exploit the fact that in July 1940, soon after the British fled France in disarray, the Royal Navy attacked and destroyed most of the French fleet at the Mers-el-Kebir naval base in Algeria. It had been a necessary step to prevent the French ships from falling into German hands but there had been many French casualties and there remained bad feeling about what the British had done.

At the same time, the average Frenchman was no fool. The forces of occupation were not popular. The people did not trust the German-controlled media and, as the war progressed, more and more of the French population began to listen to the nightly BBC French Service broadcasts from London. These were considered to be the most reliable source of news. But while they listened with interest as the war developed, most Frenchmen were preoccupied with making life as comfortable as possible for themselves and their families rather going to war themselves. Everyone, be they French or German, was dealing on the black market. The rations dictated by the authorities never lasted for an entire month and the shop windows in Paris were depressingly devoid of goods. There were always queues for food and every so often there would be food riots when supply was exceeded by demand. Coffee was so scarce that everyone now drank a bitter substance made from acorns. One could get used to drinking it, but real coffee was a treat. Tobacco was also scarce and many Parisians fell into the habit of collecting up the cigarette butts in order to save every precious ounce of tobacco. Looking for something to help brighten up this depressing lifestyle, the French turned to horse racing, which enjoyed a boom with tens of thousands of Parisians regularly flocking to the racecourses at Longchamps and Auteuil to forget their predicament and have a little fun. It was a lot easier than trying to take on the Germans.

The execution of hostages in the winter of 1941 had stirred up some resentment but not as much as one might imagine. Often the hostages were Communist activists and they had done so much to disrupt France in the years before the war and were so closely connected with Soviet Russia that there was a widespread distrust of their motives. Other hostages were black market dealers, who had been caught breaking the midnight-to-six curfew. Everyone relied on the black market but there was not much sympathy for those who got caught. They were making fortunes from the sale of rare commodities.

Willy quickly learned about Paris life with help from Didi. He made sure that she was seen at the rue Vineuse by the concierge and so became a part of Charles Lelong's life. To her friends nothing seemed to be out of the ordinary and in the rue Vineuse it was perfectly natural that the busy engineer should have a lady friend. These were good times for Willy but at the time he felt increasing frustration as he waited for London to send him an assistant organiser and a radio operator. Willy had been through all his old pre-war Parisian friends and analysed whether he felt they might be interested in working for the British, whether they could be trusted and whether they were suited to clandestine work.

His first choice was Albert Fremont, a garage owner whom Willy had known since the early 1930s. He was certain that Fremont would agree to work with him and would be a good man to lead a cell. But Willy still had to be careful. There was always the possibility that Fremont might refuse the offer and if that were to happen he did not want Fremont to know where he was living. The SOE training schools had taught him that it was best to hold all his recruitment meetings on neutral ground, in neighbourhoods that he rarely frequented. The best method was to telephone a potential recruit and arrange to meet in a café. Alternatively, an agent could also manufacture a "chance" encounter on a street and retire with his potential recruit to a café to have a little chat. Willy decided that to make contact with Fremont, he would simply call in at Fremont's garage and ask him if he would be interested in working for the British.

Fremont agreed immediately and very quickly the two men began to consider who would be other potential recruits. The first name they discussed was that of Robert Benoist.

CHAPTER SEVEN

Albert Fremont and Robert Benoist had been in the Armée de l'Air together during World War I and the two men had a great deal in common. Fremont was sure that Robert would be a willing recruit but Willy, who had been taught to be very cautious, even with his friends, wanted to be certain that there was no danger before revealing his presence to Benoist. He asked Fremont to make an initial vague approach to Robert to find out what he thought about working for the British, without mentioning that Willy was back in Paris. They need not have worried. Robert was delighted to be asked, and explained to Fremont that he was already in contact with a resistance group known as Action Vengeance, although he told Albert that the group could do nothing because it had no weapons.

Action Vengeance had begun life in January 1941 as an escape line, under the guidance of Dr Nicolas Vic-Dupont. All the leading people in the organisation were doctors but Vic-Dupont made contact with a group of officers who were working in the Intelligence Service of the Armée de l'Air de Vichy, notably Colonel Georges Ronin and Captain Robert Masson and together they were working with the Red Cross to get prisoners out of France - and to gather information that might be useful for the Allied cause.

Benoist was useful to Action Vengeance because his work with Automobiles Bugatti allowed him considerable freedom to travel where he pleased. Ettore Bugatti had no desire to help the Germans and turned a blind eye to Robert's clandestine activities and arranged for Benoist to have whatever documentation he needed to visit restricted areas and to be out at night during the curfew. If the Germans checked on Benoist's activities, Bugatti would confirm that Robert was indeed his service manager and had to travel around France to see Bugatti customers, to test their cars and ensure that they were working properly. The problem was that Robert was not content just collecting information. He wanted to fight.

On hearing Fremont's report of the meeting, Grover agreed that Robert would be a first-class recruit for the Chestnut network and so a few days later, Albert telephoned Benoist at the Bugatti showroom and arranged to meet him in a café a few blocks away. Willy accompanied Fremont and explained quietly to Robert that he was in France as "an agent of Winston Churchill" and was planning to build up a secret network that would eventually take the fight to the Germans. Robert could hardly contain his enthusiasm for the idea. He wanted to get into action as soon as possible.

Within a few days of the meeting Willy was contacted by the man who was to be his assistant network organiser: Richard Heslop, his old room mate from Wanborough and Beaulieu. Being unable to parachute because of his leg injury while training in Scotland, Heslop had been forced to fly to Gibraltar and was then a passenger on one of the feluccas that landed him on a beach near Antibes. It had taken Heslop a couple of weeks to get from the Côte d'Azur to Paris, including crossing the Demarcation Line. He had rented an apartment in Paris and was living under the name of Rene Garrat. Willy was delighted to have another friend in Paris to help him, but discussions between the two men soon highlighted the fact that there was not going to be much that they could do until a radio operator arrived. They could build up a network to receive parachute drops but if nothing then happened the team would soon lose heart. The resistance movement had the reputation of talking a lot, but doing very little, and Willy wanted to taken seriously.

As there was no sign of a radio operator Willy decided that the best course of action was to try and make contact with London via the emergency contact he had been given by F Section before he left for France. The problem was that the contact was in the city of Lyon, on the other side of the Demarcation Line. Crossing the line was not easy. There were designated crossing points between the two zones but these were heavily guarded and without the right documentation it was impossible to bluff one's way through. The alternative was to cross the line illegally, but this was highly dangerous as the police in the Vichy Zone were as ruthless as the Germans.

Grover family members remember hearing tales of a trip to Lyon on Willy's behalf by Yvonne to meet the mysterious "Marie Monin" who Willy had been told could be contacted by leaving a message in one of the cafés in the city. There are no details of this visit but, according to SOE chief Major-General Colin Gubbins, in a recommendation for a medal made after the war, Willy himself went to Lyon that summer and had a narrow escape while crossing the Demarcation Line, being stopped and searched but getting through "by the exercise of great coolness and self-control."

There are no details of the meeting but Willy was no doubt surprised when he met Monin as she was a most unlikely secret agent – and not French at all.

Her real name was Virginia Hall and she was an American. Originally from Baltimore, Hall was in her mid-thirties, was living under her own name (except when meeting SOE agents) and was tall with flaming red hair and walked with a very conspicuous limp because of a wooden leg. Educated at both Radcliffe and Barnard Colleges, Hall had emigrated to Europe in the 1930s to study in Vienna and later in Paris before returning to the US to study French and economics at George Washington University.

Hoping for a career in the Foreign Service, she had then begun to work as a clerk at the American Embassy in Warsaw, Poland but, while on a holiday in Turkey, she had lost the lower part of her left leg in a hunting accident and after that discovered that the Foreign Service had lost interest in her. She was turned down for a diplomatic career and so moved to Paris and began working as a journalist.

When the war broke out she escaped to London and it was there in January 1941 that she met Nick Bodington, the pre-war Paris correspondent of the Reuters news service, who had worked for the Secret Intelligence Service. He was by then involved with the French Section of the SOE and thought Hall would make a good agent. Americans were still considered to be neutrals so she had free access to move around France. It was arranged that Hall would work as the Vichy France correspondent of the New York Post newspaper and, in order to avoid suspicion, she travelled to Lyon via Portugal and Spain. She arrived in the city in August 1941 and, as a result of her journalism, had immediate and valuable access to many of the top names in Marshal Pétain's government. Unlike most SOE agents, who strove to go unnoticed, Hall used her high profile as a disguise. It was inconceivable that such an obvious figure would be engaged in clandestine work, yet for 18 months she was the pivotal figure in the history of F Section and proved to be enormously capable in that role. The only problem she had was that as her reputation spread she had to cope with more and more British agents who had run into trouble. Eventually the Germans concluded that she had to be working for the British but they could do nothing about her because they did not control the Vichy Zone.

When Willy got through to Lyon he was delighted to discover that, by a happy coincidence, Virginia Hall had a radio transmitter available and even had a stray operator looking for something to do. London was contacted and it was agreed that the logical thing to do was to hand the two over to Chestnut. The only problem was how to get the radio and the operator across the Demarcation Line and up to Paris. Willy was introduced to Marcel Clech, the radio operator who before the war had been a taxi driver in Brittany. He had been involved in resistance work from very soon after the invasion of France and had been sent to Britain for training. He returned by submarine and had landed in Provence at around the same time as Willy parachuted into France, his orders being to join the Autogiro network. Three days after his arrival Autogiro collapsed, a fact that Clech discovered only by chance when he stopped off to visit Hall in Lyon. They had sent a message to London asking for instructions and were told that Clech should stay in Lyon and help Hall run her operations until an alternative assignment could be organized.

Willy had turned up at exactly the right moment.

Encouraged by the news, he returned to Paris, expecting Clech to follow within a few days but, shortly after his departure, things changed when another SOE wireless operator arrived in Lyon and contacted Hall. The new man was called Denis Rake and he worked under the code name of Dieudonné. He was a very colourful character who, before the war, had been an actor and nightclub performer. Fluent in French, he had spent the first part of the war working as a radio operator on a minesweeper before being singled out for his language skills and sent off to Wanborough Manor for evaluation.

The SOE was in for a rude shock.

"Our escorting officer's report was that Rake was hopeless," Buckmaster wrote after the war. But that did not stop the commander of F Section deciding that Rake should continue his training, despite the reservations of other senior officers. At the time radio operators were desperately needed and, despite the opposition, Buckmaster had a hunch that Rake would develop into a good secret agent. It was a dangerous leap of faith.

Rake completed his training and was delivered by felucca to a beach near Antibes in the middle of May 1942, before Willy had been parachuted into France. His orders were to wait in the south until a new network had been established in the Vichy Zone. He would then receive orders from London. Lake was met by members of an F Section network known as Urchin, which was operating in Provence. He had nothing to do and soon started sending messages for Urchin. Unfortunately the Vichy police were quickly on his tail and, after a series of adventures, he was forced to head north, leaving his radio set hidden in Cannes. He made contact with Virginia Hall in the hope that she could find a way to get him out of France. Hall put him to work alongside Clech, the two men sharing a single transmitter.

Within a few days, Rake's talent for getting into trouble led to his arrest and he was forced to bribe a Vichy policeman to allow him to escape. When he told Hall about this close call she demanded that he leave Lyon immediately. It was suggested that it might be a good idea for him to go to Paris in place of Clech and the switch was approved by London. Rake was ordered to go ahead and cross the Demarcation Line while plans were laid for his transmitter to follow by way of "a French Countess".

There is little doubt that this was Countess Anne-Marie de Bernard, who operated from the Château de Nanteuil, a large country house to the south-east of Blois. She was a Frenchwoman who had married a young Englishman called William Gaynor-Beard in 1921. They had moved to Nanteuil where they established a school, helping to educate young English students in the language and culture of France. Gaynor-Beard had died and Anne-Marie had married Count Pierre de Bernard de la Fosse, a Frenchman who had been a pilot during World War I. After the German invasion they decided to stay in France as both were French, even though Anne-Marie's children and some of the staff were English.

The household soon became involved in helping stray English soldiers and later airmen to escape from France, assisting them in crossing the nearby Demarcation Line into the Vichy Zone. These activities grew into more overt resistance work and it was not long before the Countess was drawn into the activities of the Monkeypuzzle network, which was being formed in and around Tours. This was not a very successful SOE network because of internal disputes between the organizer Raymond Flower (Gaspard) and the head of its parachute reception team Pierre Culioli.

Rake's ability to get into trouble led to another disaster when he tried to cross the Demarcation Line near Montceau-les-Mines in early July. He was arrested and told the Germans that he had been trying to get into the Vichy Zone, rather than vice versa. By doing this he hoped that he would be taken into the Occupied Zone. The plan went awry when he made up an address where he said he had been staying. The ever-efficient Germans checked the details and found that he was not known there. He was photographed and fingerprinted and was sent to the SD headquarters in Dijon.

In his biography after the war Rake claimed that he was badly beaten up by the Germans before being rescued by the local resistance, which arranged for him to be smuggled out of the prison in a swill bin. However in his official report to F Section he said that he had bribed a guard on his way to Dijon and had been allowed to get away. Whatever the case, Rake went straight to Paris with the aim of contacting the Chestnut network. In his book Rake claimed that the contact was made at the Bar de la Faubourg St Honoré where he met Heslop, but once again this is at odds with the records which show that the first contact was made via Ernest Wilkinson.

Wilkinson - who as Ely Mountford had been trained with Grover and Heslop - had been parachuted into the Limousin region just a few days after Willy. He had travelled immediately to Angers, where his wife was living under the assumed name of Keller. He settled down with her and, using the code name of Alexandre, began setting up a resistance network in the region. Wilkinson was very keen to get into action but suffered the same problem as Willy because London had been unable to get him a radio operator. Wilkinson felt even more under pressure because a number of his early recruits had begun to question whether he really had links with London and so he decided that he would go to Paris and make contact with the only emergency contact he had in the organization – Willy Grover.

Rake's arrival in Paris without a radio transmitter came as a huge disappointment for all concerned and the story of his arrest at Montceau-les-Mines made the group very wary of the nightclub performer. To make matters worse, Wilkinson discovered that Rake was a homosexual and had started a relationship with a German officer called Max Halder on his very first night in Paris, even before he had made contact with Chestnut.

Wilkinson was so keen to establish communications with London that he decided to stick with Rake until they found a transmitter, regardless of the risks involved. Willy was less willing to take a risk but despite his concerns he arranged for an approach to be made to the Countess Anne-Marie de Bernard in Blois, to determine whether she had received the transmitter. This contact was not successful and Willy decided that further attempts to follow up on the plan described by Rake were too risky.

It was at this point that Christopher Burney, the young commando officer known as Charles, who had travelled with Willy to France, turned up in Paris needing help. The trip to Normandy had been a complete disaster. The Autogiro network, for which he was supposed to be working, had collapsed before he arrived in Caen and he had had a series of close calls in the city as he tried to make contact with Autogiro survivors. The Germans had a description of him and he decided that the only sensible course of action was to get out of Normandy and seek shelter in Paris, where Willy was his emergency contact. Willy and Burney agreed that there was no point in trying to revive the Normandy network and that it would be best if Burney went to Lyon and made contact with "Marie Monin" to get new identity papers. Willy suggested that he try to get hold of a radio transmitter and could then return to Paris to work with Chestnut and supply Rake with the radio set he needed.

The Germans must have concluded that the agent they were chasing in Normandy had gone to ground in Paris because on the very day that Burney was due to depart for Lyon he was arrested at his lodgings and taken to the Gestapo headquarters in the Rue de Saussaies. That afternoon, as Burney sat in a cell, waiting for his interrogation, Willy sat in a café half a mile away, waiting for a final meeting with Burney before his departure. When Burney failed to appear Willy knew that the plan was ruined.

Fate then intervened again, as Rake reported that he had been tailed by Germans after passing through one of the street checkpoints in Paris. When he had been arrested crossing the Demarcation Line, Rake had destroyed his false identity papers and when he arrived in Paris he had found a forger to make him new ones. These were not high quality and Rake concluded that this is what made the Germans suspicious. He used the techniques he had been taught during his SOE training to shake off the tail but Willy was worried that the Germans now had Rake's new name and so ordered the accident-prone actor to leave Paris immediately and try to return to Lyon, concluding that Chestnut would be better off without Rake. Wilkinson did not agree and wanted Rake to stay and so Willy agreed to hand him over to Wilkinson's network in Angers.

The decision was a difficult one because it meant that despite all the efforts made Chestnut was still without a radio transmitter. Willy had no faith in Rake and decided that the best course of action was to send Heslop to visit Virginia Hall in Lyon, to see if he could convince her to go back to the original plan and send Clech to Paris. By this point Chestnut had found a safe way to get across the Demarcation Line, using the Paris-Toulouse trains, which ran out of the Gare d'Austerlitz. These were unusual in that they were electrified and it was discovered that inside the engine compartment of each locomotive there was sufficient room to hide several men. The agents would simply go to the marshalling yards at Juvisy, in the south of Paris, where they would be shut inside the locomotives. The trains then went into Paris, loaded up with passengers and headed south to Orleans and Vierzon. They crossed the Demarcation Line at Chery-Lury, where the trains were searched but the Germans never checked the locomotives. At the end of the journey in Limoges passengers switched to conventional steam trains to continue on to Toulouse and the electric locomotives were sent to the local marshalling yards where the agents were released from their hiding place and could then make their way to Lyon by train, via Clermont-Ferrand.

It was decided that Heslop, Rake and Wilkinson would travel together and the trip went without a hitch but, once again, Fate was to play a part. Shortly before the three men arrived in Lyon, Virginia Hall was inundated by a wave of SOE agents on the run from the Vichy authorities. Most of the group had been arrested in October 1941 when the French authorities located an SOE safe house in the south. They had been held in a prison camp at Mauzac in the Dordogne, but had managed to convince the guards there that if the Germans took over the Vichy Zone the agents would be executed and the guards would be held responsible. They had been allowed to escape and had used the only contact they had: "Marie Monin" in Lyon.

One of the Mauzac escapers was Georges Bégué, the SOE's first radio operator in France, and when he arrived in Lyon he explained to Virginia Hall that he knew of a radio transmitter hidden near Châteauroux. Hall immediately despatched Clech to collect it, with orders from London being to then settle down in the area and make contact with the Monkeypuzzle network. This meant that when Rake, Wilkinson and Heslop arrived in Lyon a few days later Hall had neither a radio transmitter nor an operator for Chestnut.

There was, however, some good news. Hall told Heslop that she was due to travel to Cannes a couple of days later to meet Buckmaster's deputy Nicholas Bodington, who was in the Vichy Zone to ascertain F Section's situation on the ground. Bodington gave her a radio transmitter for Rake to use and sent orders for Heslop to return to Paris. Bodington said that Chestnut would get a radio as soon as it was possible. Wilkinson and Rake were ordered to Angers.

As they all needed to get across the Demarcation Line, the three men decided to travel together once again and take the same electric train that they used on the outward journey. Before they could cross the line they were forced to wait in Limoges because of the Fête de l'Assomption national holiday on August 15. That day Rake's poor quality identity papers, which Hall had not had time to replace, led to his arrest by the Vichy police. A hotel bill found in one of his pockets led the police to Wilkinson and Heslop and although they all claimed not to know one another, a sharp-eyed Vichy policeman noticed that the bank notes in their pockets bore serial numbers in sequence.

When an agent was arrested in France in 1942 there was no word of it in any newspaper. They simply disappeared and no-one knew what had happened. There was no way of finding out. Often it was weeks after the arrests before any word was received, usually through other prisoners who had seen the missing agents in detention. All that the surviving agents knew up to that point was that if a colleague disappeared, all links must immediately be cut. If there were documents or transmitters that could be saved this was done as quickly as possible, but that was a dangerous game because one never knew whether the Germans would have got to the equipment first.

While Heslop was away in Lyon, Willy, Fremont and Benoist concentrated their efforts on using the long summer days to find good sites for parachute drops in the area around the Benoist family properties outside Auffargis, and to gather whatever information they could find about what was going on in and around Paris. In August Benoist travelled to Dieppe, using a special Bugatti pass – to try to gather information about what had happened when British and Canadian commandos raided the town.

As the days went by it became increasingly clear that something had gone wrong with Heslop. Having lost his assistant Willy decided that there had been too many close calls and that his best course of action was to wait for London to deliver a radio transmitter and an operator. Chestnut would take no further risks which might compromise the long-term success of the mission. The network had at least managed to establish a route by which messages could be sent back to London, via the Perrier company, which was owned by the Harmsworth Family. The system was slow but it enabled there to be some form of contact between Chestnut and F Section in London.

Willy's biggest challenge from that point on was not trying to find a radio transmitter but rather to restrain Benoist's desire to expand the network as quickly as possible. Robert was a man in a hurry and although Willy tried to convince him to be more cautious, Robert wanted to go to war with the Germans as quickly as he could and began recruiting amongst his friends and workmates.

His first recruit was 45-year-old Thérèse Lethias, a childhood friend who had grown up in Auffargis. Her family had made a great deal of money in publishing at the turn of the century and she had become a very wealthy woman. She had married Ernest Lethias and had left Auffargis to move to the enormous 2,220-acre Ferme de la Haute Borne, near the village of Mery sur Oise, in the country to the north of Paris. The farm produced vegetables for Paris and employed 500 workers. Sadly, Thérèse's husband had died in December 1940 and so she was living on the farm with her parents.

Robert approached her asking for money to help Chestnut fund operations and Lethias agreed immediately. She also offered to supply work permits and housing as the farm had workers of many different nationalities and would provide a perfect hiding place for a radio operator. Willy was delighted with Lethias but when Benoist suggested Jean-Pierre Wimille, he refused point blank.

"Willy had no confidence in Wimille and expressly opposed this," remembered Madame Fremont.

The rejection of Wimille did not stop Benoist. He was finding it more and more difficult to hide his resistance activities from those around him and concluded that the best thing to do was to take them into his confidence and recruit them to help. The first two recruits were Stella Tayssedre, his secretary at the Bugatti showroom, and Marcel L'Antoine, his chauffeur. Robert was no longer living with his wife Paule but instead was sharing an apartment with his brother Maurice, on the Boulevard Berthier, near the Porte de Champerret. According to Robert's son-in-law André Garnier, Robert had asked his wife Paule for a divorce but only because he was worried that she and his daughter Jacqueline - Garnier's wife - might be implicated if he was arrested. Paule was still living in the family apartment on the

Boulevard Gouvion St Cyr.

Robert felt Maurice could be trusted completely and did not even consult Willy before telling his brother about his secret work for the British. Maurice Benoist was five years older than his illustrious brother although when Robert was growing up, Maurice had been the hero. In 1910, when Robert was 15, Maurice went to the town hall in Versailles and volunteered for three years service in the elite Chasseurs d'Afriques cavalry regiment. The unit was in action in Morocco at the time, defending French interests in the region, and Maurice was a dashing cavalryman, until he was shot in the knee in the summer of 1912. He came home with a Médaille de Maroc and a permanent limp. As a reservist he was called up again in August 1914 and went back the Chasseurs before being transferred in October 1915 to the 1st Aviation Group at Dijon. Unfortunately his knee injury meant that he was unfit for active service and in 1916 it was recommended that he be given an honourable discharge. This was a blow for Maurice, particularly as Robert's career as a flyer was much more successful. In the 1920s, as Robert became a racing star, Maurice tried his hand at the wheel of an EHP cycle car. Later he would race a variety of other small cars and would compete at Le Mans, but his success was nothing in comparison to his younger brother.

In the late 1920s his marriage failed and he went to work in the French colonies where he married a younger woman - Suzanne Auvety. She was not well-liked by the family and that created friction but his business ventures abroad were very successful and when he returned to France in the late 1930s he began investing in a variety of automotive-related businesses, notably funding the design of a five-cylinder star-shaped engine that was the brainchild of Émile Petit, who had worked so successfully with Robert at Salmson. That project was not a success. And that was the story of his life.

"The problem," said a family member years later, "was that Maurice was not Robert."

Maurice was successful in other ways. He was an active

member of the Touring Club de France and as a result had access to many influential people. He liked to entertain and was an amusing and charming man.

✠

To begin with there was little for Robert's new recruits to do. Action Vengeance had no weapons and Chestnut could not operate effectively without a radio operator, but as they waited for something to happen the shape of the war was changing.

In North Africa Erwin Rommel's Afrika Korps had tried to break through British lines and attack Egypt and the Suez Canal, but at the start of July 1942 his attack was checked by the British Eighth Army under General Claude Auchinleck. A series of smaller battles in the month that followed achieved nothing and the two armies were left, facing one another in the desert.

In the Pacific, the Japanese Navy had taken heavy losses in June at the Battle of Midway and the US commanders were beginning to prepare for a Marine assault on the island of Guadalcanal. It was scheduled to begin in August.

In Russia the German summer offensive (Operation Blue) took the German armies to the banks of the River Don. Hitler was pushing his armies on towards Stalingrad, wanting to seize the city in order to cut off the links between Moscow and the oilfields in the Caucasus and to conquer the city bearing the name of the Russian dictator. The panzers met little opposition as the Russians retreated in front of them. But in the middle of July the Russian resistance became fiercer with a series of bloody battles as the Germans tried to advance from the Don. For a while the advance was halted but then the Sixth Army began once again to move on towards Stalingrad. The battle for the city, the turning point on the Eastern Front, would begin in August.

The tide was beginning to turn.

CHAPTER EIGHT

William J Vanderkloot was a civilian, but perhaps a better description was that he was a soldier of fortune. The 26-year-old American was being paid $1000 a month, an enormous amount of money at the time, for doing a dangerous job for Britain's Royal Air Force.

He had joined the RAF's Ferry Command in January 1941 in Montreal, Canada, with a contract to fly a converted B-24 Liberator, code named Commando, wherever it needed to go.

The reason the job was dangerous was sitting in the co-pilot's seat that night in August 1942 as Commando flew across southern Russia. Winston Churchill liked to fly up front with the pilot and saying no to the British Prime Minister was not something that Vanderkloot was planning to do.

They had flown from England to Gibraltar and from there to Cairo. In Egypt Churchill had removed Auchinleck as the head of the Eighth Army and appointed Lieutenant-General William "Strafer" Gott in his place. Twenty-four hours later Gott was on his way to Cairo when the plane in which he was travelling was ambushed by German fighters and shot down. The General survived the landing but was killed by the German pilots who machine-gunned the crash site, as he tried to pull others from the wreckage And so Churchill turned the Eighth Army over to Lieutenant-General Bernard Montgomery.

From Cairo Churchill and Vanderkloot flew on to Teheran and from there, accompanied by US President Franklin D Roosevelt's representative, Averill Harriman, they were flying to Moscow to meet Soviet Premier Joseph Stalin. They were not looking forward to the meeting because they knew that they had to tell Stalin that Britain and the United States were not in a position to open a Second Front in Europe and ease the pressure on the beleaguered Russians, who had been taking the brunt of the German military might for more than a year.

The deafening noise inside the converted bomber on the flight up to Moscow was such that Churchill and Harriman could only communicate by writing pencilled notes to one another. Stalin, as expected, was not happy when he heard the news and launched into a verbal assault on the British for having failed to take on the Germans. Churchill exploded with rage and a torrent of words burst forth that completely overwhelmed the interpreter. Stalin did not understand all the words but he recognized Churchill's fighting spirit and was impressed. When Churchill calmed down he explained to Stalin that the Allies did not have the manpower to go ahead with an attack in the west of Europe, but he agreed to do everything he could to help the Russians.

When he returned to London, via Teheran and Africa, Churchill started to look for ways in which he could escalate attacks on German targets in Occupied Europe. His aim was to tie down as many German units as possible. The result was that Churchill asked the SOE to intensify its action in France. After studying the situation, the F Section staff in London concluded that it must accelerate its plans for a second sabotage network in Paris. The new organization would go into action as soon as possible rather than wait for D-Day.

Chestnut network would remain in place but the new network, which would be called Physician, would be given the priority.

Willy Grover would simply have to wait.

The new network has passed into history as Prosper, the code name used by its organiser Francis Suttill, a 32-year-old Englishman who fitted the moment perfectly. He was brave, ambitious, quick-witted and charming. Like Willy, his father had been British and his mother French. He had been an outstanding pupil at the SOE training schools but, most importantly as far as F Section was concerned, his enthusiasm for the job was infectious.

"Prosper was magnificent," remembered Henri Déricourt, himself an important figure in the short and unhappy history of the Prosper network. "He was strong, young, courageous and decisive, a kind of Ivanhoe; but he should have been a cavalry officer, not a spy. He was not sufficiently trained in these things."

But F Section was dazzled and in the months that followed F Section gave everything to Prosper as it tried to please Churchill, as he tried to please Stalin.

The first Prosper agent had been delivered to the south of France by boat on July 30, 1942, just two months after Willy Grover arrived. Yvonne Rudellat was the first woman SOE agent to be sent to France. She was French by birth, and at 45 was considered to be too old to parachute. Her orders were to work for the troubled Monkeypuzzle network until Prosper was ready to employ her in Paris.

Working under the name of Jacqueline Gautier, she quickly became a key member of Pierre Culioli's parachute reception group, known as the Réseau Adolphe. This group received parachute drops in the Sologne region, south of the Loire, and because Monkeypuzzle had none of the communication problems which plagued Chestnut, it was well-supplied and able to carry out sabotage work.

The decision to accelerate the Prosper network meant that at the end of September the Réseau Adolphe laid on a parachute reception for a second Prosper agent, a 22-year-old French girl named Andrée Borrel. She was as fervent and as talented as Suttill and went immediately to Paris to begin to recruit people from the contacts she had been given in London. One of the first meetings she had was with Madeleine and Germaine Tambour, two sisters who had been members of the Autogiro network. A few days later Borrel returned to the Sologne to join a Réseau Adolphe reception for Suttill and his deputy Jean Amps, who parachuted together.

With Suttill as the priority, F Section in London wasted little time in sending him a radio operator. Just a month after Francis Suttill's arrival, Gilbert Norman (code named Archambaud) was dropped to another Réseau Adolphe reception. Prosper was in business and soon weapons and explosives were being parachuted to the new network. Suttill and Borrel were constantly on the move, making contact with a wide variety of different resistance groups in and around Paris. Suttill used the name François Desprée and the cover story that he was a travelling salesman of agricultural products. The brave and resourceful Borrel went with him, posing as his sister, a nurse called Denise Urbain.

"Everyone who has come into contact with her in her work agrees that she is the best of us all," Suttill once told Madeleine Tambour.

Suttill was heavily reliant on Borrell because it soon emerged that he spoke French with such a strong English accent that the best he could do was to pass himself off as a Belgian. To avoid problems Borrel did the talking whenever possible. Their aim was to quickly build a secret army and they did not care if the fighters in the different groups had different backgrounds and contradictory political beliefs. Suttill has often been criticized for having spread his net too wide and for not having sufficient security in his network, but that is hardly fair. Suttill understood very well the need to keep his different sub-networks isolated from one another and, while some of his subordinates can be accused of security lapses, there is no doubt that only he and Borrel really knew all the different people involved with Prosper. To this day Suttill's connections with the powerful Communist resistance around Paris remain a mystery. All that is really known is that large quantities of British arms and explosives found their way into the hands of the Communists.

For Chestnut these were frustrating times. Little progress was made. Willy and Robert continued their recruitment of men who would be willing to work with the resistance when the invasion came but while they were able to give some basic instruction as to the use of various weapons, but they had no weapons to give to the recruits.

They did, however, succeed in setting up a small sabotage network inside the Citroën factory. All the French automobile manufacturers were, to a lesser or greater extent, forced to work for the Germans and this was to cause much trouble after the war. Citroën has always played down its activities, citing the fact that German air raids in June 1940 stopped production in Paris. The reality, however, is that the company built around 37,000 cars and trucks under German control, including military trucks and half-tracks. What was important was that sabotage efforts dropped that production from nearly 14,000 vehicles in 1941 to 9,320 in 1942 and just 4,500 in 1943.

Much of this can be credited to Citroën design engineer Jean Aron, who had made his name transforming the designs of Italian sculptor Flaminio Bertoni into the Citroën Traction Avant. Aron was recruited to the British networks in 1941 by Pierre de Vomécourt, the leader of the Autogiro network. He worked under the code name of Joseph and survived the collapse of Autogiro and thus was able to begin working with Willy Grover soon after Chestnut began operating. In the autumn of 1942, however, Aron was arrested in Lyon, although Willy was able to keep up contact with other members of the group and teach them how to disrupt production by damaging or removing important pieces of machinery, as he had been taught at the SOE explosives school at Brickendon Bury.

Benoist and Fremont continued to scout out parachute landing sites and to wait for a radio operator but London continued to favour Prosper, a fact that was underlined when a second radio operator was parachuted to Suttill's network just a month after Gilbert Norman arrived. Jack Agazarian (code named Marcel) immediately went to work alongside Norman. It had by that point become clear that Suttill's deputy Jean Amps was not suited to running clandestine operations.

F Section tried hard to recruit the best people, Buckmaster

and his team in London did not always get it right. In the spring of 1942, for example, an agent called Nigel Low was parachuted into France, carrying a large sum of money which he was supposed to use to build up a sabotage network. Low disappeared without trace but it was not until after the war that the F Section investigation team discovered that the Germans knew nothing of any such agent. Finally it emerged that in pre-war days Low had been a confidence trickster and had simply gone through the SOE training and being parachuted into France in order to get his hands on a large sum of money.

No trace of Nigel Low was ever found.

Other F Section agents were lonely or scared and sought out company to help them overcome their weaknesses. There were often love affairs between male agents and their female couriers and even the very best agents made serious mistakes. One important SOE man in Paris was seen one evening walking down the Champs-Élysées, with a girl on each arm, singing Rule Britannia.

Suttill was more serious in his work and one evening, while demonstrating how to use Sten guns to new recruits, in a back room at the famous Hot Club in Montmartre, he met a poet called Armel Guerne and decided that Guerne would be the right man to be his assistant. Through Guerne, Suttill came into contact with a whole range of new people including the sculptor Octave Simon who would quickly become the leader of the Satirist network, an offshoot of Prosper. He also met the distinguished biologist Professor Alfred Balachowsky.

Born in Russia, Balachowsky became a naturalised Frenchman in 1932 and worked at the École Nationale d'Agriculture at Grignon, near Versailles where, assisted by the principal Professor Maurice Vanderwynckt, he set up another Prosper sub-network. The school quickly became Suttill's country headquarters.

F Section at this point decided that it would be a good idea to send over a senior officer to get an overview of how things were developing across the north of France and to report back how things were going and what was needed.

The man chosen for the job was France Antelme, although he is best remembered by his code name Antoine. He was parachuted to France in mid-November 1942. Antelme was from a well known family in the British colony of Mauritius, in the Indian Ocean. The family was in the sugar trade, but France busied himself in the manufacture of ice cream on the nearby island of Madagascar. This was French and when war broke out the authorities supported the Vichy government and so the SOE began to look for people to disrupt life on the island and recruited Antelme. Then in May 1942 the British liberated the island and so Antelme was sent to Britain to see if his talents could be used in the European theatre. He ended up with F Section and was very highly regarded at the SOE training schools, being described by one instructor as "one of the best types I have met".

Maurice Buckmaster had enormous faith in him and decided that his job would be to make contact with different networks in an effort to bring them all under the control of Suttill. Antelme was very effective, quickly establishing a string of new reception committees and recruiting several important new agents for F Section. In addition he made contact with a variety of non-Gaullist resistance movements and with the banking and business communities. Antelme's connections and courage undoubtedly helped Suttill to quickly build up Physician but at the same time the rate of growth created new problems.

Contacts between different resistance groups went against everything the network organisers had been taught at the SOE training schools but because of the lack of radios, links developed between the SOE networks in Paris and these became so complicated that sometimes even the organizers themselves did not know that they were using the same people. Whatever the details, a connection was made during this period between Chestnut and Agazarian. This almost certainly came about after Antelme met with Willy Grover and realised that Chestnut could do nothing until it had a radio. Although it was a highly-dangerous link, Antelme believed that it was the best course of action in the circumstances as it gave Chestnut the chance to start operating as it should have been months earlier.

But already the clouds were gathering around Prosper and in the summer of 1943 hundreds of resistance workers would be arrested when the network imploded. Even today the collapse of the Prosper network remains a subject of much bitterness. In order to understand what happened one must look at the bigger picture. The process which led to the collapse of Prosper began at the end of October 1942 when Montgomery broke the Afrika Korps at the Second Battle of El Alamein and advanced along the north coast of Africa, pushing the Germans backwards towards Tripoli. On November 8 the Americans launched Operation Torch, landing troops in Morocco and Algeria, countries which were in the hands of the Vichy government.

Initially the Vichy French fought the Americans but then French commander Admiral Jean-François Darlan agreed to an armistice. The effect of this was that the Germans realized that the Allies could now use North Africa as a base for an attack on France's Mediterranean coastline so Hitler ordered his troops in France to invade the Vichy zone. By mid-November 1942 France's partition was over and the Germans were in full control of the country.

The effect of this was that thousands of people who had been separated from their families and friends for over two years rushed to visit one another as Christmas approached. Reunification should have been good news for the secret armies because there was no longer the need to make the risky journeys across the Demarcation Line but there were a number of important side-effects which would be disastrous for Prosper and F Section.

One of the early travellers from Marseilles to Paris was André Marsac, a member of a secret network called Carte. This was not originally a British organization but had been adopted by F Section. As he travelled north Marsac carried with him a complete list of the 200 members of Carte, with all their addresses and their descriptions. The information was not even in code. On the long train journey Marsac fell asleep and while he slept a German agent stole the briefcase Marsac had with him. It was delivered to German military intelligence in Paris. The list included the names of the Tambour sisters, Borrel's first contact when she arrived in Paris. From that moment on Suttill and the Prosper network were doomed. The Germans decided not to move immediately but instead were content to watch and learn about the British network.

The invasion of the Vichy Zone had one other important side-effect for the F Section networks because Virginia Hall, F Section's agony aunt in Lyon, had to make a quick getaway from France. Thanks to her connections within the Vichy government she found out about the invasion immediately it began and was able to escape before the Germans could arrest her. This remarkable woman used her experiences with the SOE in France to get a job with Bill Donovan's Office of Strategic Services and, in the spring of 1944, returned to Occupied France to run an OSS sabotage network in and around the town of Nevers. In 1945 she became the only female civilian in World War II to be awarded the US Distinguished Service Cross, the country's highest military award after the Medal of Honor. After the war she went on to become one of the first female officers of the new Central Intelligence Agency.

Hall was fortunate to get away. When the Germans swept into the Vichy Zone they were able to arrest an important member of the Soviet spying network, which was known as the Red Orchestra. The Nazis had been tracking down the organisation for most of the war. The arrest of the agent Victor Sukulov (who was also known as Anatoli Gurewitsch and by the code name Kent) on November 12 signalled the beginning of the end for the Red Orchestra. There were further arrests in the days that followed and eventually at the end of the month German security police caught Leopold Trepper, the head of the Red Orchestra. The remaining members of the organization were either arrested or went to ground. This meant that the Germans in Paris no longer had to worry about the Soviet underground movement and could concentrate fully on breaking down the British networks, which they knew were operating in the region.

For Willy Grover the invasion of the Vichy Zone meant more visitors. The Vichy authorities had released Heslop, Wilkinson and Rake from prison in Lyon, not wanting to be held responsible for what might happen to the British secret agents if they fell into German hands, and, having little time to do anything other than run, Heslop and Wilkinson headed for the hills in the centre of France, ending up in the town of Le Puy en Velay. They had refused to travel with Rake, whom they blamed for their arrest the previous August and whom they considered to be dangerous. Rake decided that he must get out of France and teamed up with two British soldiers who had been prisoners since the fall of France and the three men headed for the Spanish border.

Once Wilkinson and Heslop had found somewhere safe to hide in Le Puy en Velay, Wilkinson decided that he wanted to go back to Angers to make sure all was well with his wife. He set off to Paris, planning to make contract with Willy Grover and get instructions as to what he should do. Messages were exchanged with London and Wilkinson was ordered to go back to Angers and continue the work to build up the Privet circuit in Angers as had been intended before his arrest. Heslop was to join him there. Wilkinson sent word to Le Puy en Velay and in March 1943 Heslop joined Wilkinson in Angers.

Frederic Grover - who still believed that his brother was away in England - was another man to make the journey north, sent from Agen by the Grover family to visit Yvonne at the rue Weber to make sure that she was all right.

"We had a little conversation," he remembered. "I suppose she wanted to make sure that I was not a collaborator or something like that and then she said: 'You know your brother is in Paris' and then Willy came into the room. He had a moustache and I thought he had aged a lot in a rather short time."

They had dinner together and then, before the curfew

began, the two brothers set off to walk back through the 16eme arrondissement to the apartment on the rue Vineuse. That night Willy told his brother all about his adventures in England and explained about the problems he had had with the radios and told Frederic how difficult it was to recruit people to his network. He even showed Frederic some microfilm that had arrived for him from England. During the night the two of them decoded the messages. Although happy to see his brother, Frederic was alarmed at what Willy was doing but as his brother would not listen to his arguments there was little he could do. After a couple of days Frederic returned to the south, knowing that Willy was happy to be with Yvonne. He could only hope that the Germans would not catch up with them.

With a link to Agazarian, Willy was finally able to organise Chestnut's first arms drops. This was a small operation and involved only Willy, Robert Benoist and Fremont. The landing site chosen was in the middle of the forest of Rambouillet, not far from Auffargis. The dropping zone was chosen because it could be spotted from the air at the end of a series of three ponds. Although most reception committees operated without vehicles, Robert's access to various permits and vehicles that allowed Chestnut to used a small Citroën van. Benoist was fortunate that, in addition to his Bugatti work, he owned a small transport company, headquartered in the suburb of Bois Colombes, which had several trucks which were constantly on the move. These wood-burning devices were frequently seen in Auffargis where Robert owned a dozen hectares of woodland, which provided fuel for the business.

There was a network of forest roads and Robert was certain that it would be safe to transport the arms away from the dropping zone to the Benoist property in Auffargis. An old well on the estate belonging to Robert's parents had been prepared as an arms dump. It was 30 ft deep and covered by large flagstones, which were then covered with earth and leaves. That evening they listened to the BBC French Service news, waiting to hear the personal messages broadcast each evening after the news to resistance fighters all over France. These were meaningless phrases that were only significant to the individual groups which were listening for a particular message. If the correct message was broadcast the group would go into action. Willy, Benoist and Fremont waited until nine fifteen when the BBC broadcast a second set of messages to confirm that the drop was going ahead as planned and then they departed for the dropping zone and waited in the quiet woods, hoping that the plane would be able to find them. The arms drops were usually made at around one o'clock in the morning and as the deadline approached three men split up and formed a large triangle in the clearing they had chosen. Each man had a torch: two white, one red. The red light would be upwind and if the plane dropped its containers as it passed over the red light the containers would then drift down within the triangle. But with the plane travelling at 130mph a delay of a second could result in the parachutes being off target.

Willy had been taught in England that the most important thing for those on the ground was to count the number of parachutes that opened so that they knew how many containers had to be found. Leaving extra ones lying around the woods was asking for trouble because if that happened the drop zone could not be used again. The plane arrived on time that first night and the three men switched on their lights. The pilot swung around, checked the position and flew back across the dropping zone at around 500ft. There were four parachutes. As the plane disappeared into the night, Willy, Benoist and Fremont rushed to find the containers. On that occasion all went well. None of the parachutes came down in the trees and Willy quickly showed his colleagues how to open the six feet long containers. Inside were three cylindrical canisters, each of which could be carried to the Citroën truck. This should have been easy but the wire handles on the canisters cut into their hands. Once the containers had been emptied it was necessary to get rid of them. The parachutes were packed inside and the containers were buried. On later operations the three men concluded that it was more efficient to weigh the containers down with rocks and dump them into the nearby lakes. In the spring of 1943 a fisherman in one of the reservoirs to the west of Auffargis hooked a container and rumours went around that parachutes had also been found but the Germans were never able to find the culprits.

Once the dropping zone had been cleared the heavily-laden Citroën van set off along the forest roads. They had to be careful that the van did not become bogged down in the mud but the main danger came when they had to cross the RN10 and the main railway line. They stopped to check for German guards before they crossed and then went quickly to the Benoist estate in the woods at Auffargis. They had time to go through the canisters, admiring the Sten guns and pistols. There were Mills bombs and Gammon grenades in addition to plastic explosive, detonators and incendiary devices. There were medical supplies and armbands to be used by resistance fighters when their uprisings began and in the spare corners of the canisters were a few luxury items sent over to help build up morale among the resistance men: cigarettes, chocolate and tinned fruit, all useful rewards for the underground army.

Antelme's influence in London and his enthusiasm to build up Chestnut proved to be very helpful and soon after the first arms drop - eight and a half months after Willy Grover's arrival in France - F Section finally sent Chestnut its own radio operator. Roland Dowlen (code named Achille) was delivered to France in a Westland Lysander in the early hours of the morning on Thursday, March 18, 1943. Two Lysanders came and went, depositing four new SOE agents and whisking away Antelme and three others. It was the first operation to be run by F Section's newly-appointed Air Movements Officer, Henri Déricourt (code named Gilbert). In the months that followed Déricourt would become one of the most controversial figures of the war. He would end up in front of a French military tribunal in 1948, facing charges of having worked for the Germans.

Much has been written of Déricourt's allegiances and treacheries and controversy still surrounds him: some claim that he was a German agent, betraying British networks in France; others say he was a Secret Intelligence Service agent under orders from London to damage the rival SOE; his defenders accept that he was working with the Germans but argue that this was necessary and that most of the time he misled them by promising to reveal details of the Allied invasion of Europe, in exchange for free passage for SOE agents.

It is unlikely that anyone will ever know the truth but Henri Déricourt seems to have been trying to serve two masters: it cannot be doubted that he did a remarkable job for F Section in the course of the next few months, organising a total of 17 clandestine operations, involving 21 aircraft. In his care 43 British agents were delivered to France and 67 were sent back to England. Late in 1943 he was recommended for a Distinguished Service Order, the first member of F Section to be nominated for such an award. The citation highlighted his "great ability and complete disregard of danger" and his need to work with "many very dangerous acquaintances".

At the same time, there is no doubt that Déricourt did give the Germans access to some of the F Section mail which was being sent to and from France and there is little doubt that he was directly implicated in the arrest of at least three F Section agents.

When he was parachuted to France at the end of January 1943 Déricourt was 33 years old. His orders were to establish a network called Farrier, which would do nothing except organize the passengers and landing fields for the increasing number of secret flights between France and England. He settled into an apartment in the rue Pergolèse - just around the corner from Yvonne Grover's house on the rue Weber - and immediately began to build his network. One of his first recruits was a former lover called Julienne Aisner. Another was Rémy Clément (code name Marc), a car fanatic who in the late 1920s had built his own automobiles under the Clément-Rochelle name, at a small factory in Clamart. The cars, which were powered by Ruby engines, were not bad but his timing was wrong and after the 1929 economic crisis the company survived for only a few months. Clément went on to become an Air France pilot. Déricourt and Clément instantly hit it off with Robert Benoist.

Later, when it was suggested that Déricourt was a traitor, Benoist was outraged and refused to believe it was possible but although there is no evidence that Chestnut suffered from any treachery on the part of Déricourt, there is little doubt that he diverted papers, bound for London, to German counter-intelligence officers at the Avenue Foch. At least two Chestnut documents did fall into German hands: a report on the damage caused by an Allied bombing raid of the Paris suburbs of Boulogne and Courbevoie and a German pass which had belonged to Maurice Benoist.

Yet none of the Chestnut operations were compromised by Déricourt and the presence of Dowlen was not known to the Germans, despite the fact that he and Déricourt travelled to Paris together after that first operation, although the two men pretended not to know one another.

When they reached Paris Dowlen went off to make contact with Chestnut and was quickly put into action. A transmitter was installed at Fremont's house in Le Vésinet, although this was later sent down to Auffargis. Before long Dowlen moved to a house which was owned by Thérèse Lethias in the hamlet of Vaux, close to her farm. It was arranged that he would always be late paying his rent so that Thérèse could pretend that she did not wish to tackle him alone and could take either Willy or Robert Benoist with her when she visited her tenant. A transmitter was installed at Vaux and it was agreed that if Dowlen was arrested he would say that he knew Benoist and that they had been introduced by a Monsieur Qualliot, a man Benoist had known in the Air Force who had died a few months previously.

Dowlen had impressed the SOE instructors during his training, although they reported that he tended to stay aloof from the other trainees on his course. This, they concluded, was because of shyness.

"He is thoughtful, observant and vigilant," said one report. "His character and morale are satisfactory. He is reliable in all ways, although has the tendency to sacrifice speed for accuracy and is very slow in taking decisions. He is very security-minded. He takes his work very seriously, is deft and a complete master of every situation in which he finds himself."

Dowlen had a very international background. Born in Sicily, the son of an American mother and an Italian father, he was adopted by an Englishman at the age of five and grew up in Britain. In 1923 he started working at the Royal Bank of Canada in Paris and stayed there until 1933 when he moved to London to take up a new appointment with the bank. He became a naturalised British citizen in 1936 and enlisted in the Royal Army Service Corps in September 1941.

He was 35 and spoke fluent French with only a hint of an accent and, like Willy Grover, he did not look like a secret agent, needing spectacles because of his poor eyesight. He settled into the villa in Vaux and carefully hid his radio set in a corner of the kitchen.

The SOE wireless operators used a short-wave Morse Code transceiver. It weighed 30lbs and could be fitted into a normal-looking suitcase but the signal was weak and needed 70ft of aerial. The sets also needed delicate crystals that could be easily broken.

Dowlen organised a number of escape routes from the villa and even trimmed the hedges in the garden in such a way that they would grow thickly and form what amounted to a small maze, which he thought would be useful to aid his escape. The garden gate was always locked but he hid a key nearby in case he needed it in a hurry and he cultivated the habit of swimming in the River Oise, telling Willy and Robert that it might one day prove to be useful if he needed to get away in a hurry.

A month after he arrived - on April 17 - Dowlen sent his first message to London and from then on he was on the air a great deal, sending 39 messages in just three months, working not only for Chestnut but also for Wilkinson's Privet network in Angers.

CHAPTER NINE

In 1841 the French Government voted to build a vast system of fortifications around the city of Paris. Inside these solid ramparts, they built a military road but 20 years later, when tensions had eased, this was widened and turned into the Boulevards des Maréchaux, each section named after one of Napoleon's marshals. In time this became Paris's first ring road. Where the boulevard passes the Hippodrome d'Auteuil in the west of the city, it is known as the Boulevard Suchet, in honour of Maréchal Louis-Gabriel Suchet, a great military strategist who made his name during Napoleon's campaigns in Spain.

At number 64 Boulevard Suchet there was a large building which the Germans requisitioned and transformed into the headquarters of the Peilfunkdienst, the German army's wireless direction-finding service. This facility was a sophisticated radio-listening centre, designed to monitor all illegal radio traffic in the Paris area. It was in operation around the clock, scanning the air waves, trying to pick up all illegal radio transmissions. If a secret radio operator stayed on the air for long enough the Germans at the Boulevard Suchet were able to alert a second listening station in northern France and the two stations could then take bearings. In theory the bearings met on the site of the secret transmitter. In reality it was rather more complicated than that because at the time radio direction-finding was still a very imprecise art. Although the location of a transmitter could be narrowed down to a search area of only a few hundred square metres, the Germans had no idea where to look if that location was in a densely-populated city, with many apartments in different buildings. They could flood the area with troops but there was no guarantee that they would find anything and the presence of troops would normally cause any transmissions to close down. Once the signal was lost there was little they could do. The Germans did use radio direction-finding vans and hand-held equipment to narrow down the search area further but this usually meant that the radio transmitter had to be operating on several occasions from the same location and British agents were trained to avoid doing that whenever possible. This was never very practical. The better-established SOE radio operators had lookouts, keeping an eye on the neighbourhood and the Germans found that when radio direction-finding vans arrived in an area, the signals would disappear. If the Germans were not spotted they could locate the exact house from which messages were being transmitted, but even then they needed to be careful. Bursting in on an operator was an option but the British agents kept a revolver by their side when transmitting because they knew that if they were caught in the act there would be no doubt about what they were doing and they preferred to try to shoot their way out of trouble. A gun fight would give them time to destroy their codes so that the Germans could not use their transmitters to send fake messages back to Britain.

The existence of the direction-finding services meant that the F Section radio operators were always under pressure. The more time an operator spent working a transmitter, the more likely it was that he or she would be caught. In March and April 1943 the German operators recorded a five-fold increase in the number of illegal radio transmissions in Paris. One of those responsible for the new activity was Chestnut's new radio operator Roland Dowlen. He was busy organizing more arms drops for the network. The first had been hard work for three men and Robert Benoist suggested that they should take his brother Maurice along with them for the second drop.

That took place in April 1943 and, in the months that followed, the group received a further four arms drops, one of which consisted of an extraordinary 17 containers. Robert later reported that this had been far too much for four men to handle. They had done it nonetheless, working through the night to get everything hidden away.

After the first three receptions the old well at Auffargis was full of weapons – there were an amazing 51 canisters - and Benoist had to find a new place to hide his arms. Fortunately, at the start of the war, he had been building a stable block which had been left unfinished when the Germans ordered his builders to work on other projects. This meant that working alone Robert was able to build a false wall in the unfinished stables behind which there was plenty of space for more weapons. Eventually this would conceal a further 47 canisters. For one of the arms drops Maurice recruited a Parisian neighbour called Georges Laurent, who had been a friend for 20 years. Laurent was a director of the Pathephone gramophone company, headquartered at the Boulevard des Italiens in Paris. He was not by nature an adventurer and did not really want to be involved in resistance activity, but he had been unable to find a way to say no to Maurice. He did not help them out again.

With a radio operator and arms arriving from England the Chestnut network could begin to broaden its horizons, although it remained small and secure.

"Grover-Williams built up a successful circuit," SOE chief General Colin Gubbins noted after the war. "He formed a number of sabotage cells and reception committees for parachute operations of which he received a large number. He established a particularly effective sabotage group in the Citroën factory in Paris, where successful sabotage was carried out, which could not be traced to the group."

The Prosper network in comparison was growing at an alarming rate and in April 1943 the Abwehr, German military intelligence service, decided to do some damage and arrested the Tambour sisters. There was talk of treachery but the truth was that the names of the sisters had appeared on the list of Carte agents lost by André Marsac the previous autumn and it was this that was the reason for their arrests. Suttill was particularly distressed at the arrests and determined to find a way to save the two women. His first move was to try bribery, organizing for a Swiss businessman called Jean Worms to deliver a million francs (around £70,000 at today's values) to the Germans in exchange for the captives. The Abwehr found this amusing and took the money, only to deliver two rather mature Paris prostitutes into the safekeeping of Worms. Then they asked for more money.

Perhaps Suttill should have left the sisters to their fate but he refused to give up, unwisely believing that the Germans were still willing to do a deal. The second time he tried to buy the release of the sisters the Germans asked for a rendezvous with both Suttill and his radio operator Gilbert Norman. Incredibly, Suttill agreed, despite the fact that there was a danger that the Germans would double-cross them and arrest the pair. Instead the Abwehr decided to play games with the British agents, like a cat playing with a captured mouse.

Suttill and Norman waited in a café. A car drew up and a German inside photographed the pair before they realized what was happening and fled. In such a situation the two men should perhaps have been withdrawn to Britain for their own safety but that did not happen, although in the middle of May Suttill did fly back to London for consultations with F Section chiefs. When he returned to France he seemed convinced that an Allied landing in France would be coming later that summer. His orders from England were to push ahead and have his units ready to go into action when the landings began.

There are many in France who believe that Prosper was deliberately misled by the British, who had decided after the incident with the Tambour sisters that the Prosper network was doomed and should therefore be sacrificed in an attempt to convince the Germans that the invasion of Europe would come in the summer of 1943. If that ruse was successful the Germans would have to keep more troops in France for the whole of the summer rather than sending them to help on the Eastern Front. Suttill was even rumoured to have met Prime Minister Winston Churchill who, it is claimed, had calculated that a defeat in the East would be more damaging than the loss of a few agents in France.

"Our story was a terrible one," concluded one Prosper sub-agent Jacques Bureau. "The network was used for deception."

Suttill must have believed that the invasion would come that summer because returning to France was tantamount to suicide. Some say that Suttill returned only because he was unwilling to desert the people in his networks and perhaps there is something to this argument, but the concept that he willingly accepted arrest and probably death in order to mislead the Germans is difficult to believe. What is much more likely is that he went back to Paris, believing that the network still had a fighting chance in the months before the landings. When he got back to France the first thing he did was to alter all the security arrangements of the network. His most important move was to order Jack Agazarian back to England with immediate effect. The radio operator had transmitted messages for no fewer than 24 different F Section agents and he knew far too much. London wanted him out of reach of the Germans.

While Suttill was in London, Willy Grover had other problems to deal with. In Angers the Germans were on the trail of Wilkinson, asking questions about him at the boarding house run by his ex-wife Mme Keller. Wilkinson decided that he should move to Nantes and planned to establish a new network in that city. He made the decision to leave Heslop in charge of the activities in Angers but that arrangement did not last very long. Within a matter of days Heslop had been arrested by the Germans and was being questioned. He stuck doggedly to his cover story and the Germans were taken in. Heslop was released and was brave enough to organize another arms drop a few days later. The equipment delivered included two transmitters intended for Chestnut in Paris. The plan was to make Dowlen less dependent on the single transmitter he was using in Mery sur Oise.

Heslop cycled home from the parachute drop with the two radio sets strapped to the back of his bicycle but German security measures in Angers had become such that he had been forced to move out of the city and had settled in the small village of Marcé, just off the main road from Angers to La Flèche. From there he sent a messenger to Paris, informing Willy that the radio sets had arrived.

On Saturday June 5 Willy and Robert drove from Paris in a Bugatti to a rendezvous with Heslop at Marcé. They fitted the two radios into a hidden compartment in the car and informed Heslop that they had received orders to take him back to Paris as well to meet with France Antelme (Antoine). Heslop climbed aboard and was surprised by how quickly they got back to Paris. He thought that the car did not look particularly fast and did not realize that his two drivers were both Grand Prix winners. They were stopped once by police on the way back to Paris but bluffed their way through the blockade and arrived at Albert Fremont's house in Le Vésinet, a chic suburb in the west of the city, with plenty of time to enable them to be back in the centre of Paris before the midnight curfew. Heslop stayed with Fremont and the following day travelled into the city to meet Antelme at Yvonne's house on the rue Weber. Antelme listened to Heslop's story and concluded that it was too dangerous to allow him stay in Angers.

Heslop refused to return to England until he had been back to Angers to tell his network what was happening and so it was agreed that he would be contacted as soon as a flight to London could be organized. Antelme took the opportunity to ask Heslop if he knew of a French police inspector by the name of Imar, explaining that the latter had contacted Wilkinson asking for a meeting. Heslop knew the name and warned Antelme that when he, Wilkinson and Rake had been in jail in Limoges, Imar had been paid 25,000 Francs (£2,800 at today's prices) to organize an escape. The money had been paid but they had remained in prison. Heslop asked Antelme to ensure that Wilkinson did not go to a meeting with Imar. That evening

Antelme met Wilkinson and tried to convince him not to meet the police inspector. Wilkinson refused to listen, saying that he would take the necessary precautions. The following day Antelme watched Wilkinson enter the café where the rendezvous was due to take place. The agent did not re-emerge. They later discovered that he had sent his ex-wife ahead of him to act as a scout. When he entered the café she signalled that there were no signs of a trap. Imar and another man arrived and after a long conversation Wilkinson and the pair got up and went to the cloakroom. As he passed his ex-wife Wilkinson gave her a signal indicating that all was well.

She never saw him again.

He was taken out of a back door of the café and driven to 84 Avenue Foch where captured F Section agents were interrogated.

✠

Originally, when the house had been a private residence, the fifth floor had been reserved for the domestic staff but in the summer of 1943 these had been converted into cells for the prisoners. A slightly larger room became a waiting area for prisoners and another was the office of Ernst Vogt, the interpreter for Obersturmbannführer Josef Kieffer, the head of the SD in France.

Kieffer was a counter-espionage expert who before the war had run the SD office in Karlsruhe in Germany before being posted to Austria and then to Paris. He lived in an apartment on the fourth floor. Kieffer and his team of interrogators were intelligence officers and were not usually involved in the arrest of secret agents nor in any heavy-handed treatment that they received. There were others in the buildings to do their dirty work for them. Wilkinson was treated roughly but, according to Buckmaster, was "the toughest of the tough" and gave nothing away. His arrest sent agents scurrying for safety, notably Antelme who wisely got out of Paris as fast as possible. Grover stayed, trusting that his old friend would say nothing, knowing that

Wilkinson had given nothing away during his first term in prison.

A few days after Wilkinson's arrest, Benoist accidentally came into contact with another resistance network in the south-eastern suburbs of Paris. The meeting came about thanks to an old friend called Charles Escoffier, a garage owner in Paris who had known Robert since his days at the Garage Banville. Escoffier invited him to a party in Servon, a small town near Brie-Comte-Robert, to the south of Paris. The two were accompanied by Maurice Benoist. During a conversation at the home of rose-grower Henri Guérin they discovered that Guérin's son Pierre was actively involved with a local resistance network called the Réseau Cohors Asturies, which had been founded by Suzanne Tony-Robert, the owner of the Château de Forcilles, in the autumn of 1941. This numbered around 50 people and enjoyed strong links with the local police and the gendarmerie. One of its members was Police Commissioner Raymond Morel. The network gathered information about the activities at the German airfields at Melun-Villaroche and Coulommiers-Voisin and had found a way to intercept messages from the German U-Boat headquarters in the Boulevard Suchet in Paris. The man responsible for this was Fernard Cauvin, who worked with Radio France at Villecresne. The quality of his information so impressed the British that he received a special BBC message thanking him and asking him to keep up the good work. The group also organized parachute drops in the grounds of the Château de Forcilles and the nearby Château de Lésigny. Robert departed that afternoon wondering whether the Servon network might be integrated into Chestnut's field of operations.

Robert's enthusiasm for the task was undimmed, but Willy Grover was beginning to worry about Dowlen. A few days after Wilkinson was arrested, Frederic Grover returned to Paris and lunched with Willy at the little restaurant on the corner of the rue Weber and the rue Pergolèse. Willy explained that he was seriously worried about the radio operator, whom he felt was lonely. Although he did not name him, he said that Dowlen had had a very hard time adjusting to life in France and that one evening had got drunk and started talking.

Frederic Grover was worried.

"I told Willy that he should go back to England," he remembered. "He said that perhaps he should but added that the landing was coming soon. He was convinced that the Allies would land in the summer of 1943 and he said that this was when his real work in France would begin."

During the period while Francis Suttill was away in London the Prosper network had gone on running much as before, with Norman, Borrel and Agazarian in the habit of regularly eating together and routinely playing cards at an apartment in the Square Clignancourt. Their schedules were so well known to their friends that when two German intelligence officers using the identities of captured SOE agents Arnaud and Anton tried to infiltrate the Prosper network they stumbled right into the centre of the organisation completely by accident. Acting on a tip-off they had gone to a café called Chez Tutulle on the rue Troyon, near the Arc de Triomphe, and had asked to speak to Gilbert – which was Henri Déricourt's code name. The barman mistook the request as an attempt to contact Gilbert Norman and told the two Germans that at that time of day Gilbert would be playing poker at the apartment in the Square Clignancourt. The Abwehr agents had been directed to Gilbert Norman rather than to Déricourt. When the Germans arrived at the Square Clignancourt they found not only Norman but also Borrel, Agazarian and his wife Francine (Marguerite) and another member of the group.

The Abwehr did not want to make immediate arrests and arranged for the Prosper agents to be put under surveillance, hoping that they would reveal more of the network. It was a clever move and was put into effect with such skill that the only hint of danger came when Borrel heard that a couple of Frenchmen had been asking questions about her in a bar in the rue des Petits Écuries, beneath the apartment in which she was living. When Prosper returned from

London, he immediately moved to change the security arrangements in his network. He insisted that Agazarian and his wife leave for London and a Lysander pick-up was organised for June 16.

That operation brought more SOE agents to France, including a radio operator called Noor Inayat Khan (Madeleine). She travelled to Paris with Déricourt's assistant Rémy Clément and that evening arrived on the doorstep of a flat belonging to Émile-Henri Garry (Cinema) in the rue Erlanger in the Auteuil district. Garry had been brought into contact with the Prosper network by Antelme, who had been staying at Garry's apartment after the arrest of Wilkinson convinced him to leave Yvonne Grover-Williams's house in the rue Weber. On the night that Noor Khan arrived, Antelme was out of Paris, organizing a major arms drop in the Le Mans area. A few days later he led a successful attack on the locomotive turntables in the marshalling yards at Le Mans. But when the raid was over he hurried back to Paris to keep his appointment with Heslop to tell him the bad news about Wilkinson. At that meeting Antelme warned Heslop that the Germans were on the verge of a big round-up of British secret agents in Paris and told him to keep a very low profile. Heslop went back to the Fremont's house in Le Vésinet and waited. He would be there for eight days.

That same week there arrived from England two new agents with orders to join Suttill's organisation. Captain John McAlister (Valentin) and Captain Frank Pickersgill (Bertrand) were both Canadians who had both won high praise at the F Section training schools. Their arrival by parachute to a Réseau Adolphe reception at Châtillon-sur-Cher was problematic with both men having to be rescued from the trees. They were then hidden in a small village in the Sologne and spent the weekend of June 19/20 with Yvonne Rudellat and Pierre Culioli at a remote cottage. Early in the morning on Monday June 21 the four set off in an old Citroën van, heading for the railway station at Beaugency. When they reached the outskirts of Dhuizon, they encountered a German road block. A few nights previously some hand grenades in one of the containers being dropped in the area had exploded on impact, forcing the reception committee to disperse immediately, leaving behind the evidence of a parachute drop. The Germans had set up a road block and earlier that morning had arrested members of one of the local parachute reception teams with a van loaded full of weapons.

McAlister and Pickersgill were immediately arrested but Culioli and Rudellat decided to make a run for it and raced away in the Citroën van, being pursued by the Germans. They ran into another German checkpoint six miles down the road and were both shot and wounded. Before news of this disaster reached Paris, Suttill discovered that Noor Inayat Khan, who was operating under the cover name of Jeanne-Marie Régnier, had been sent to France with a contact address which he had personally reported as being dangerous when he was in London four months earlier. He had even confirmed that the address was no longer valid when he had been in London a few days earlier. Suttill, suffering perhaps from a little paranoia, concluded that F Section was trying to destroy Prosper and on the Saturday travelled to his country headquarters in Grignon and sent a fiery message to London, announcing that he was cancelling all his regular contact points and changing all his passwords.

When he returned to Paris on the Sunday, travelling with Madame Balachowsky, he told her that he suspected treachery in London and that he had returned to France only to protect the French people in his networks. Their conversation ended on the steps of the Gare Montparnasse and Suttill disappeared to his rooms in the rue Hautefeuille, just off the Boulevard St Germain on the Left Bank. He packed up his belongings and moved to the Hotel Magrazan, in the rue Magrazan, close to the Porte St Denis. There were still meetings that he had to attend and the following morning he was at the Gare d'Austerlitz to introduce Heslop and an RAF escaper called Philip Taylor to Henri Déricourt and his assistant Rémy Clément. He went on to meet Gilbert Norman and Andrée Borrel. There is little doubt that at the second meeting he was observed by German intelligence agents, who had been shadowing Norman and Borrell since the affair in the Square Clignancourt. Suttill was followed back to his new lodgings. He had been there for less than 24 hours and already the Germans knew where to find him.

Once again they decided not to act, hoping that if left at liberty a little longer Suttill would lead them to others in his networks. The Germans did not have unlimited manpower and once they had discovered Suttill's hideout they did not follow him when he left Paris on the Tuesday.

For several days he had been worried about the two missing Canadians and having heard rumours that Rudellat and Culioli had been arrested, was trying to find out what had happened to Pickersgill and McAlister. Their first contact with the network should have been with Captain George Darling, one of Suttill's sub-agents in Gisors. Darling, who had been left behind by the British Expeditionary Force in 1940 and had worked for escape lines until becoming a member of the Prosper network, lived at a house in Triechâteau, owned by Madame Renee Guépin. Suttill visited them and discovered that Darling had heard nothing. The worried Prosper chief spent the Tuesday night at Mme Guépin's house, departing for Paris at seven o'clock the following morning.

Madame Guépin remembered his departure.

"He looked grey and strained," she said. "He seemed to have a presentiment that this was the end for having said goodbye he came back twice to say goodbye again."

What Francis Suttill did not know as his train rattled into Paris that Wednesday morning was that during the night the Germans had swooped on the Prosper network: Gilbert Norman and Andrée Borrel had been caught red-handed, decoding messages from London. At the Avenue Foch, Borrel proved to be a fierce prisoner, treating her captors with a fearless contempt and refusing to say anything. The Germans were impressed by her bravery and realised that it was pointless to try to extract information by brutal means. They simply locked her up and left her. Instead they concentrated on Norman.

Suttill's train took him into the Gare du Nord from where he set off on foot to the Hotel Magrazan and there walked straight into a German trap. SD officers had been waiting all night for him to return. Suttill was taken to the Avenue Foch where a team of interrogators led by Kieffer was ready for him. They knew exactly who he was. After the war there were suggestions that Suttill had been betrayed by one of his own team because only a handful of people knew that he had changed his address but it is much more likely that he had been followed to the hotel the previous Monday after his meeting with Norman and Borrell at the Gare d'Austerlitz.

There are many myths about the treatment of captured secret agents at the hands of the SD in France. Some were tortured and even killed. Klaus Barbie and his thugs in Lyon did Germany more harm than good when they beat Jean Moulin to death. If Moulin had talked the process of uniting the French Resistance would have been irreparably damaged but he died with his secrets. The Germans knew that all British agents were under instructions not to give anything away for their first 48 hours of their time in captivity. This was a realistic tactic designed to give other agents time to escape or to destroy any incriminating evidence, while giving the prisoners the knowledge that they could start giving away small details if the treatment became too rough. The drawback was that after the Germans discovered about the 48 hour limit, they tended to push hard for information as quickly as possible. Suttill's first interrogation continued without a break for 64 hours. He was allowed no rest, no food and no water.

The psychological battle that goes on between interrogators and their victims is a fascinating one and the SD men had honed their skills to a fine art. There were "hard" interrogators and "soft" reassuring men. They alternated. There was always the threat of torture but often this was left unstated by the Germans. The initial shock of arrest, followed by a civilised welcome, would often have the desired effect on captured agents, acting as a form of release from the pressures of a secret life. The aim of the "soft" men was to plant seeds of doubt so that a sense of hopelessness would quickly grow in the mind of the prisoners and convince them that it did not matter whether they talked or not. The Germans tried to give the impression that they knew everything there was to know about the British networks. It was a very successful ploy and many prisoners were convinced that London had sold them out and that their friends were really their enemies. Suttill was shown documents that had come from within the Prosper network - probably from Déricourt - and the Germans described everything they knew about the organization in London, most of which had been picked up from earlier interrogations. But it had no effect.

As the hours ticked by it became clear that Suttill was not going to talk. Fear is often a more persuasive weapon than violence and so it was arranged that Suttill would be led down one of the corridors and "accidentally" bump into someone who had been seriously beaten. The gentle interrogation stopped and the treatment became more violent. One of Suttill's arms was broken. And then the "soft" men returned and tried to convince the battered prisoner that it was pointless undergoing the pain when everyone else was talking; that there was nothing to be gained from heroism. Gilbert Norman proved to be a rather easier prisoner. He said very little for the first 48 hours and then he began to talk.

"Norman did not have the integrity of Suttill," Kieffer told SOE officer Vera Atkins after the war. "He made a very full statement."

Suttill however refused to give anything away and it was not until the small hours of Saturday morning that Suttill, unable to function coherently by that point, was finally thrown into a cell and allowed to rest. A few hours later the interrogations began again.

On the Monday, Kieffer showed him copies of his letters and reports to London and a complete list of the personal messages sent to him since the start of the year. It is said that Suttill became ever more convinced that there must be a German spy in London who had sold out his network and that Kieffer - under instruction from Berlin - offered Suttill a deal: if he agreed to reveal the names of the people in his networks and the location of his transmitters and arms dumps, the Germans promised that members of the Prosper network would be treated as prisoners of war and not as spies.

Suttill is thought to have discussed the pact with Norman but no-one knows exactly what happened at that point. Some say that a letter arrived from Berlin bearing the signature of Reichsführer Heinrich Himmler, the head of the SS, and that the two men made the disastrous decision to trust the Germans. Others say that Suttill would never have done such a thing and that Norman must have gone ahead without him.

Whatever the case, a round-up began almost immediately: At Triechâteau Josef Placke and Karl Holdorf - disguised as the missing Canadians Pickersgill and McAlister - made contact with George Darling, requesting that arms be handed over to them. They showed Darling a letter they said was written by Suttill and so he took them to an arms dump in one of the local woods. After the truck was loaded he attempted to leave on his motorcycle but was ordered to stop by the Germans. He realized that he had fallen into a trap, and made a dash for freedom. He was gunned down and killed. In the days that followed the Germans arrested hundreds of people associated with the Prosper networks. As disaster followed disaster, the surviving agents went to ground.

Because the only connection between Prosper and Chestnut had been Jack Agazarian, Willy's team remained at large but many of the Prosper network were arrested. One of the few who escaped was the young radio operator Noor Inayat Khan who had been in Paris for only a week. She was unknown to the Germans and as unlikely a secret agent as one could possibly imagine, although she remains to this day one of the most famous and most decorated of all the F Section personnel.

The 29-year-old Indian princess was the daughter of a Sufi Muslim missionary who had married an American woman. There was certainly adventurous blood in Noor's family as she was descended from the Muslim adventurer Hyder Ali Khan, who in 1762 had declared himself sultan of the Hindu state of Mysore and had set about extending his territories eastward, across the Indian sub-continent to the Bay of Bengal and the city of Madras. This put him into conflict with the East India Company, which represented British interests in India. The result was the four Mysore Wars, which stretched over the next 35 years. After Hyder Ali Khan died in 1782, his son Tippu, who was nicknamed "The Tiger of Mysore", continued the campaigns until British-led troops stormed his capital at Seringapatam in May 1799 and killed him.

In contrast to some of his forebears, Noor's father was a man of peace and his travels to spread the word about Islam took him and his wife to Russia. It was there in 1914 that Noor Khan was born. Soon afterwards the family left turbulent Moscow behind and moved to London, where they stayed throughout World War I. Two sons and another daughter were born during those years and when the war ended and Europe began to recover the family moved to France, settling in 1920 in the Paris suburb of Suresnes, in a house donated to the family by one of Noor's father's followers. For the next seven years the family lived happily in Paris but in 1927, during a trip to India, Noor's father died suddenly. Her mother was grief-stricken and it was left to Noor - the eldest child - to run the family. In the years that followed Noor became increasingly westernised. She went to school in Saint Cloud where one of her schoolmates was Gilbert Norman - and then went on to the École Normale de Musique, close to the Place Malesherbes. After that she read child psychology at the Sorbonne and upon graduation began to write children's stories for newspapers and radio stations.

When the German invasion came in 1940, the family left Paris for England, three of the children having British citizenship. They were fortunate to find space on a boat from Bordeaux to Falmouth. In England Noor worked as a nurse before enlisting in the Women's Auxiliary Air Force in November 1940. She was trained as a radio operator and in June 1941 was posted to RAF Abingdon. At the end of that year she applied for a commission and, during the selection process, her name was passed on to the SOE and so in the autumn of 1942 she received a letter requesting her to attend an interview at the War Office. During her SOE training not all her instructors agreed that she would be a good secret agent. One of them insisted that she was not up to the job. He was overruled because radio operators were needed so desperately. Chestnut was not the only circuit which did not have "a pianist". The instructor - Colonel Frank Spooner - was so incensed at being overruled that he appealed over Buckmaster's head to SOE staff officer Robin Brook. Spooner's comments about Noor were rejected for a second time and she was despatched to Paris where she made contact with Émile-Henri Garry, who explained that he worked with Prosper and was in charge of a sabotage network in the Sarthe department, around Le Mans. He travelled between Paris and Le Mans, using the cover story that he was an engineer but he lived under his own name, sharing the apartment in Paris with his sister Renée.

The following day Garry handed Noor over to her old school friend Gilbert Norman and the two travelled to Prosper's country headquarters at the École Nationale d'Agriculture at Grignon. He showed her a greenhouse from which he regularly transmitted and, using Norman's radio, she sent her first message back to London, confirming her safe arrival. It was while she was at Grignon that she made her first fundamental mistake, leaving her codes unattended in a briefcase. Later she shocked Madame Balachowsky by handing over documents in the street and on another occasion she left her code books lying out on a table. This lack of a sense of security was combined with a certain rashness which led her to regularly visit her old neighbourhood in Suresnes and to an extraordinary situation

Above: The grid forms up for the very first Grand Prix of Monaco in 1929, with Willy Grover in the middle of the second row in Bugatti number 12. During the race he would battle with the celebrated German ace Rudi Caracciola in his huge white Mercedes, which started at the back of the grid. Below: Willy, seen here at the Tabac Corner, won a brilliant strategic victory in his Bugatti and after the race (right) his satisfaction was evident. The victory established him as one of the top racers of the era.

When Willy became successful he gave up his work as a chauffeur. He and Yvonne settled in La Baule in Brittany. They adopted the name "Grover-Williams" and Yvonne indulged her passion for breeding terriers (right). Willy was the local hero at the Grand Prix of La Baule (above), a beach race that he won three times. The couple also enjoyed golf and often played at Pourville, near Dieppe, a chic place to go for weekends when they were in Paris.

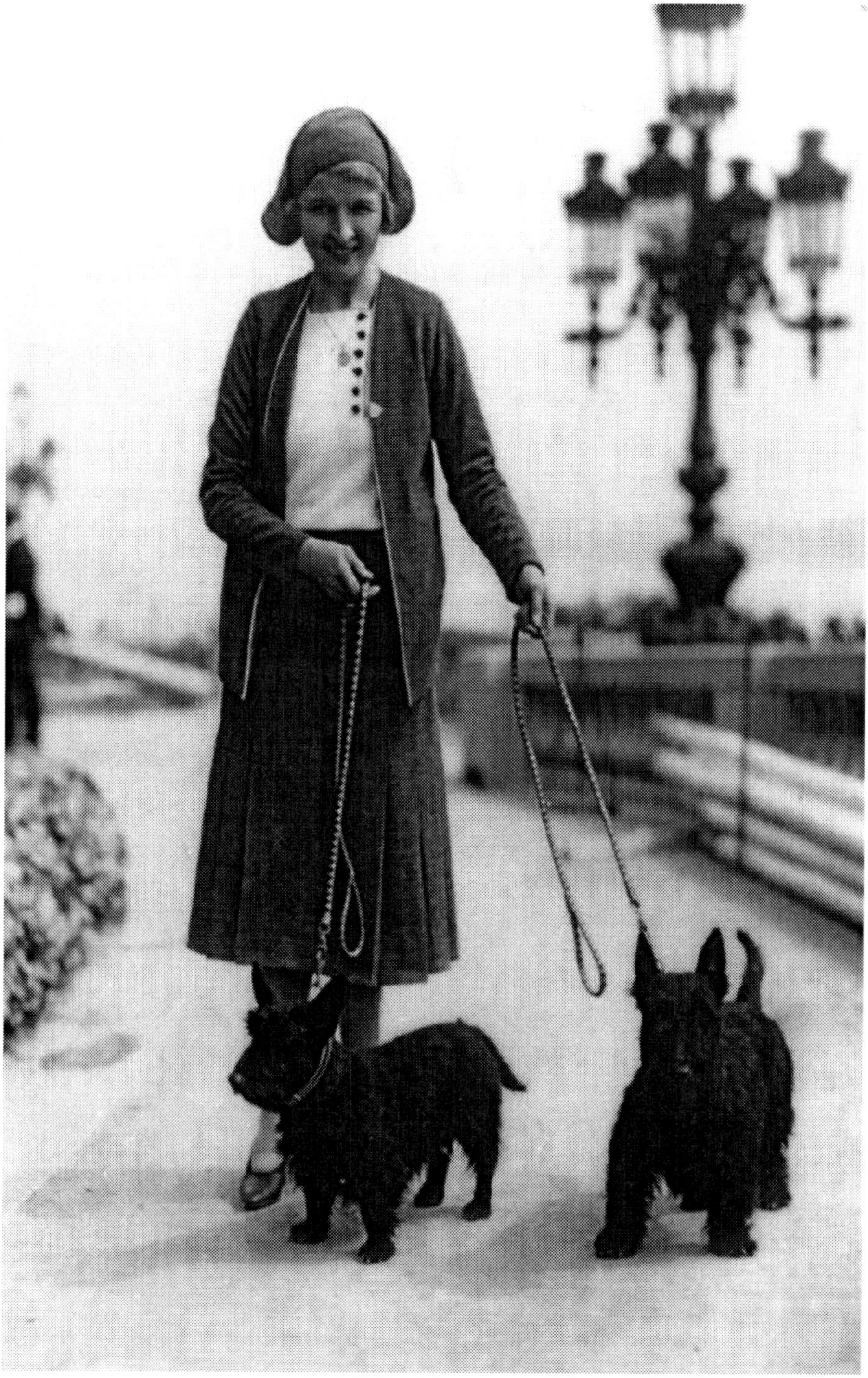

Above: Le Manoir Ramby was not far from the town of Herbignac, near La Baule. It featured its own private chapel and outbuildings which were turned into kennels. The Grover-Williamses added a bar in the basement. Opposite: The distinctive features of Robert Benoist, France's top driver of the 1920s and winner of the 1937 Le Mans 24 Hours.

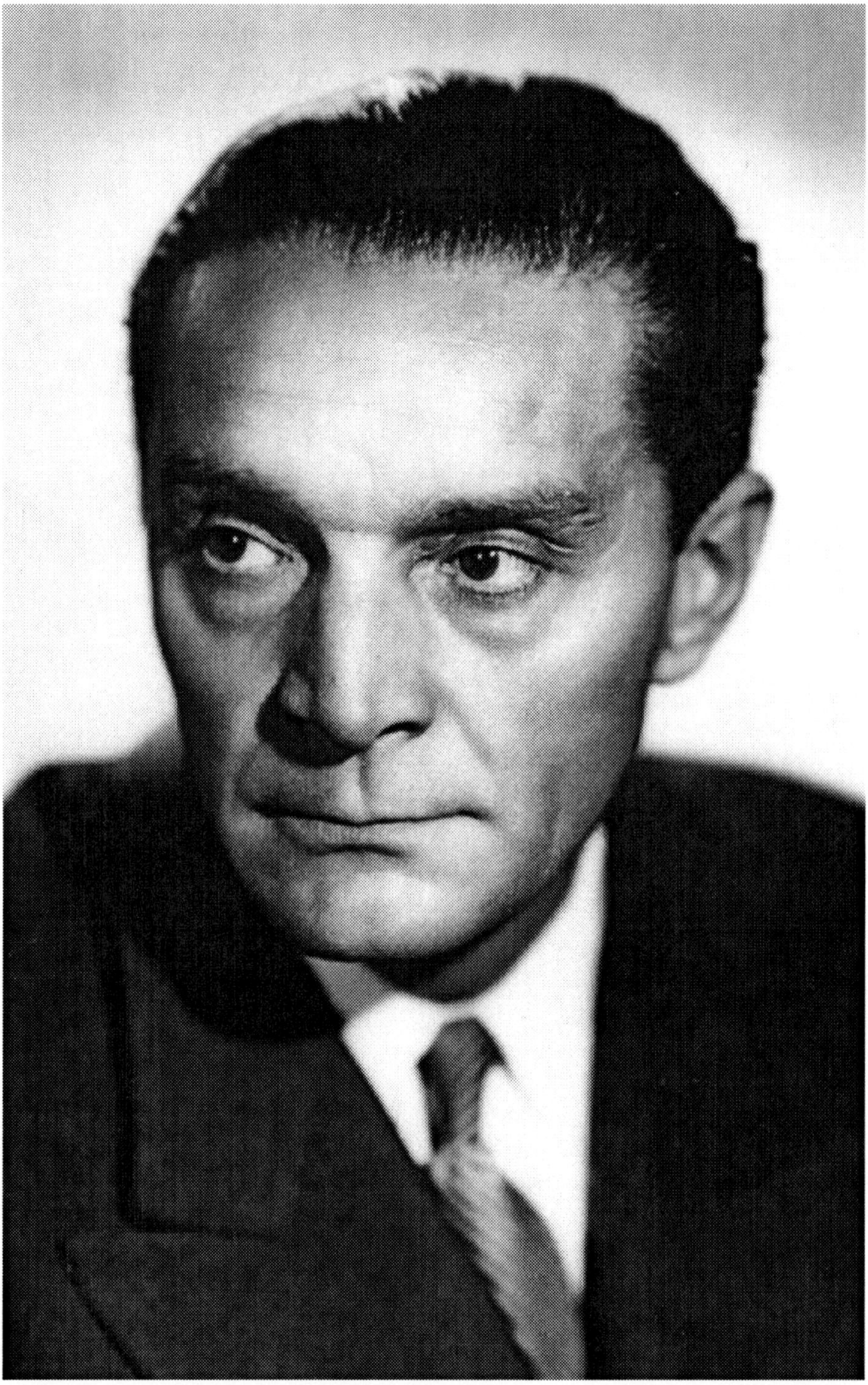

Robert Benoist was a pilot during World War I, initially flying the ungainly Maurice Farman MF.11, a reconnaissance and light bomber aircraft (above). He later moved on to fighters and ended the war as a flying instructor. Benoist then turned his attention to racing and in 1927 became the dominant force in Grand Prix racing with the potent Delage (right). That year he helped to organise one of the strangest races ever - up the ramps of the Banville garage in Paris. The racers ended up on the roof of the garage, six floors above the streets of Paris (opposite page). In 1928 Benoist became the sales manager of the Banville and remained there until 1934 when Ettore Bugatti offered him a job. He became the head of the competition department and in 1937 led the celebrated team to victory in the Le Mans 24 Hours, running the team and sharing one of the Bugatti "Tanks" with rising star Jean-Pierre Wimille (below). The two men would go on to work together during World War II.

The Grand Prix Saboteurs · 171

Maurice Buckmaster *Nicholas Bodington* *Virginia Hall (Marie Monin)*

Andrée Borrell (Denise) *William Grover (Sebastien)* *Francis Suttill (Prosper)*

Noor Inayat Khan (Madeleine) *Henri Déricourt (Gilbert)* *Roland Dowlen (Achille)* when she was putting up a radio aerial outside the building in which she was staying and was surprised by a German officer. Noor was brave and cool under pressure and convinced the German to help her with her task, saying that she could not get her wireless to work properly. Noor's most disastrous error would not be discovered until after her arrest that autumn. Rather than destroying all evidence of her messages to London she had recorded them all in code and en clair in an exercise book. Why she did this has never been explained, although it may have been that she misunderstood the meaning of her orders which said that she must be careful with "the filing" of her messages. This was intended to mean the sending of messages - the journalistic sense of the word "filing" - but she seems to have understood it to mean storing - the secretarial sense of the word. Whatever the details, when Noor was finally arrested the Germans acquired a full set of codes and her radio transmitter and were able to continue using her radio transmitter to confuse London. They did this with great success. Several British agents were parachuted to German receptions as a result of what has become known as "The Radio Game".

In the early days of her mission, Noor stayed with the Vanderwynckt family at Grignon, and during that first weekend met other members of the networks. On the Monday night her radio transmitters were parachuted to a reception a few miles north of Grignon and were delivered to her at the agricultural college. When the Prosper arrests began, at the end of her first week in France, Professor Balachowsky immediately instructed Noor to leave Grignon and not return. Garry put her in touch with Germaine Aigrain, the manager of the Toile d'Avion clothing store on the Champs-Élysées, who agreed to let her stay in an apartment in the Place Malesherbes. Garry was due to be married that week and, despite the disasters going on in Paris, he went ahead with the ceremony. Antelme, who was to have been a witness, was unwell and unable to attend but Noor Khan was at the wedding. The following day SD agents visited Garry's apartment in Auteuil, asking for Monsieur Rattier - Antelme's cover name. Fortunately both Garry and Antelme were out at the time and the concierge was able to intercept Garry before he returned home. He, in turn, was able to stop Antelme from walking into a trap. Garry and his new wife took off to their headquarters in Le Mans while Antelme moved into Germaine Aigrain's apartment in the Place Malesherbes with Noor Khan. The day after the raid in the rue Erlanger, the Germans descended on the École Nationale d'Agriculture at Grignon, arresting Professor Vanderwynckt and his helpers. Although she had been warned to stay away from the school by Professor Balachowsky, Noor visited the school that day and apparently had to shoot her way out of an ambush. The incident was mentioned in the citation for her Croix de Guerre that was published in 1946.

Noor fled to Paris and hid out with Antelme in the apartment on the Place Malesherbes. She made cautious visits to some of her pre-war Parisian friends and broadcast from their houses. One of her few remaining contacts in the networks was Robert Gieules who drove her to different locations in the suburbs so she could transmit to London in relative safety.

Her messages told London of the disasters that had occurred in Paris.

CHAPTER TEN

When Willy Grover heard that France Antelme and the new radio girl Noor Inayat Khan were in trouble, he knew that he needed to do something to help. Antelme was a senior British officer and knew too much about a large number of different SOE networks. He needed protection. Willy rang Maurice Benoist and asked him to call at the apartment in the Place Malesherbes and take the two people he found there back to his own apartment on the Boulevard Berthier. By doing this, Willy concluded, there would be no link between Antelme and Noor and the collapsing Prosper networks. No-one involved in Prosper would know where to find them.

That evening Willy and Yvonne joined Antelme and Noor, Robert, Maurice and Suzy for dinner at Maurice's apartment. Robert immediately offered the fugitives another hiding place: an apartment down in the École Militaire district on the other side of the Seine. This was outside the area in which Antelme and Noor had been operating and was located on a quiet street called the Rue Chevert, which ran between the École Militaire and the Hotel des Invalides. This apartment was actually owned by Robert's mistress Huguette Stocker, who lived most of the time in another house in Saint Nazaire in Brittany. Antelme and Noor moved there for a few days and then joined Robert, Willy, Yvonne, Maurice and Suzy for a weekend house party at Robert's property near Auffargis. The Benoist property was so secluded that no-one would stumble across the fugitives. While they were out in the country Noor was able to transmit and receive messages and was given instructions from London that Antelme must get out of France as quickly as possible to avoid capture. The loss of

Prosper had been a disastrous blow and F Section did not want other networks to be compromised.

Robert made contact with Henri Déricourt, seeking a date to get Antelme out of France, but the Air Movements Officer said that the earliest that an operation could take place would be on the night of Saturday July 17 when he would organize a Lysander operation. For two weeks Antelme would have to lie low. It was decided that Antelme and Noor should remain in the country for a few days and then the same group would reconvene at Auffargis for the traditional Bastille Day holidays. That year July 14 fell on a Wednesday and many Frenchmen and women decided to take extra time off work and extend their break to six days. This meant that between July 13 and July 19 there were a lot of people out in the countryside and the visitors did not stand out. During this period Antelme was shown the preparations made by Chestnut for its arms drops. He saw the arms caches on the Benoist Family estates and when he got back to London reported to the SOE debriefing officers that the Chestnut network was a good circuit, which had about 30 men involved and had already made all the necessary preparations for its D-Day targets. Antelme added that Willy Grover was a cautious man and would be unlikely to get into trouble.

Antelme's stay in Auffargis continued beyond the planned departure date because Déricourt failed to make the rendezvous on July 17 and so the Lysander operation was moved back to Monday July 19. That morning Robert and Willy accompanied Antelme and Noor back to Paris and they went their separate ways: Antelme taking a train to Tours and Noor heading off to meet Robert Gieules, who had found her a new apartment from which to operate in Neuilly-sur-Seine. This was in one of the big apartment blocks that lined the northern side of the Boulevard Richard Wallace, overlooking the Bois de Boulogne. The building housed many Germans, but Noor was soon transmitting messages, doing whatever work London asked her to do. Even with Antelme safely back in England, the F Section chiefs in London did not know which of its agents were at liberty and which had been arrested. Several of those who had been reported to be in custody were still sending radio messages - the Germans were operating the captured radio transmitters - and London felt that it was essential for someone who knew the people involved to go to Paris to discover the extent of the Prosper disaster. The problem was that F Section needed someone who knew everyone and there were only a handful of people with that knowledge. One was Buckmaster's deputy Nick Bodington, the former Reuter news agency man; another was Jack Agazarian, who had been withdrawn from France because he knew too many people. Agazarian's knowledge, once a danger, was suddenly of huge value and London decided that he and Bodington should go back to Paris together. It was a desperate move and the risks were enormous but as the Germans were not looking for either man, it was concluded that if they were careful, they would able to gather the necessary information and get out before the Germans realized they had been there. The biggest danger was that Bodington knew all the F Section networks in France and, if captured, might be forced to reveal everything.

Maurice Buckmaster faced a tough decision but concluded that it was a risk that had to be taken. The two men landed in a Déricourt-organized operation at Angers on the night of July 22. Déricourt did everything in his power to protect the pair from the Germans, but within a matter of days the SD had heard that Buckmaster's deputy was in Paris and began strenuous efforts to find him. Bodington, a professional spy, recognised the danger he was in and was extremely cautious. F Section's primary objective was to discover whether Gilbert Norman, Prosper's radio operator, was at liberty and whether the messages being sent to London were coming from him or from the Germans. London sent a message asking Norman for a rendezvous address. The Germans responded with the details of an apartment belonging to Mme Ferdi Filipowski in the rue de Rome, not far from the Gare St Lazare. The details of the meeting were forwarded to Bodington and Agazarian. The Germans at this point did not appear to realise that Agazarian was back in Paris and thought that the rendezvous would get them only Bodington. They were happy to give away the information that Norman's radio was under their control if they had Buckmaster's number two.

One question that has never been properly answered is why Bodington did not go to the rendezvous in the rue de Rome. Instead he sent Agazarian into the trap. The radio operator was arrested immediately and the Germans quickly recognized that the prisoner was of great value and wasted no time in trying to get the courageous radio operator to reveal the names of the different network chiefs for whom he had transmitted. Agazarian refused to say anything despite being given a terrible working-over at the Avenue Foch. He never broke and later was deported to Germany where he was hanged with 12 other F Sections agents on March 29, 1945.

In later years evidence emerged that Bodington perhaps knew in advance that the rendezvous was a trap because Henri Déricourt had confessed to him as soon as he arrived in Paris that he was in contact with the Germans and was playing a double game. This put Bodington in a difficult situation because a rendezvous had been arranged and if someone did not appear at the apartment in the rue de Rome, the Germans would arrest Déricourt, and thus deprive F Section not only of the man who ran its transport operations in France but also enabled the SOE to plant misleading information in the German camp. Déricourt had told General Karl Boemelberg, the head of the Gestapo in France that he would give the Germans the date of the Allied invasion in exchange for them steering clear of his activities. The sacrifice of Agazarian was a cynical move but one which Bodington seems to have deemed necessary. As time went on this decision was used to create fanciful theories about Prosper having been deliberately betrayed by MI6 and that the Paris networks were sold down the river by London in order to convince the Germans that the Allied invasion was coming in the autumn of 1943.

The arrest of Agazarian left Bodington without a radio operator but the ever-resourceful Déricourt put him in touch with Noor Inayat Khan, who soon began sending messages to London on his behalf. Back in London, Buckmaster was worried that Noor was in great danger and should be recalled to London but the Indian princess insisted on staying in Paris. As a result she was drawn into work not only with Bodington, but also with Général de Gaulle's RF Section and, as more and more of the SOE radio operators were arrested, she became increasingly important to the British. They knew that Noor was a source that could be trusted at a time when other SOE transmitters were uncertain.

One of the radios sending messages to London at that point was the transmitter that had gone to France with Pickersgill and McAlister. London did not know that they had been captured and as a result sent word to Noor Khan to make contact with the two men at the Café Colisée, just off the Champs-Élysées. There, without realising it, she met SD officers Josef Placke and Karl Holdorf - who were posing as Pickersgill and McAlister, as they had done when they tricked George Darling. Noor accepted them at face value and later introduced them to a number of her contacts, notably Robert Gieules. Later he was arrested as a result of the meeting.

With Noor having been identified by the Germans, the Chestnut network was directly in the firing line. Noor remained in regular contact with Willy and Yvonne but as long as the Indian Princess remained at liberty, and not under surveillance, Chestnut was safe. The best way for the operators to avoid capture was to broadcast as little as possible, but the collapse of Prosper and its sub-networks meant that the surviving members of the organization needed to contact London to inform them of the arrests and seek instructions as to what to do. Faced with this problem the SOE operators made their messages as short as possible and changed their frequencies and locations as often as they could. If an operator transmitted at the same time from the same place for more than a couple of days, no matter what frequency was being used, the chances were that the Germans would get a good fix on the location of the wireless set. The better-organized operators had more than one transmitter and moved from one machine to the other, always changing the times of the transmissions, but this had its own risks as each new radio post meant another apartment to be rented and a greater chance that someone would stumble upon something incriminating. Even if they could not always catch the British operators, the Germans learned how to distinguish between the different operators by the way in which they used the Morse Code key of their transmitters. This meant that whenever a new operator went on the air the Germans knew about it immediately, even if they could not break the codes. The British agents used the "one-time pad" system of encryption; each operator using a pad of paper (or a piece of silk) in which every sheet was printed with a different grid of letters. The only copy of the grid was on an identical pad in London. This meant that every message was coded differently and after use the grids were thrown away. For the Germans to be able to use the radio after the arrest of an operator, they had to get their hands on the one-time pad before it was destroyed. If they were successful, a German operator would feed London false information about what was happening in France.

The acknowledged expert of "playing back" captured transmitters was a German translator and interrogator called Dr Joseph Goetz, who had begun sending false messages during the final days of the Red Orchestra. He was not always successful in convincing the British that a transmitter was being operated by an F Section agent, but by the time France was liberated Goetz had successfully used 15 different British transmitters. The British had a number of security checks that were supposed to be included in every message to prevent this from happening but the security was often lax because the radio operators were under pressure to send messages quickly. When Goetz began working Gilbert Norman's transmitter, for example, he received a reminder from London that he had forgotten his security check and that he should be more careful in the future.

Noor Khan stayed free by being constantly on the move, rushing from one location to another as she tried to keep up with her timetable of transmissions. Often she carried a radio set with her. Gieules was very helpful in this respect, driving her to different locations, but at other times she cycled from one site to another. Transmitting from the countryside around Paris was often a good idea because, although there were fewer houses in which to hide, the operators were able to move on before any German patrols arrived.

✠

Chestnut's radio operator Roland Dowlen obviously felt less threatened than Noor. He had been in Paris for several months when the Prosper arrests began and had sent a lot of messages using two different transmitters: one at the villa he rented from Thérèse Lethias in Mery sur Oise and another at a safe house in Paris. At the end of July, however, the Peilfunkdienst picked up some of his transmissions from Mery sur Oise and, using the bearings from two radio-detection units in France, narrowed the search area to the Lethias farm.

On July 29, Lethias spotted two men she did not recognize hanging around near Dowlen's villa in Vaux. She was deeply suspicious and immediately sent word to Dowlen, who was in Paris, that he should be aware that the villa was under surveillance. Dowlen was either too relaxed or under too much pressure to change his habits and two days later - on the morning of Saturday July 31 - he transmitted from Mery sur Oise as usual. As he was working at the wireless transmitter, four cars full of Germans drove up to the villa and around 15 SD men burst into the house. No-one is quite sure what happened after that but some of the labourers on Madame Lethias's farm reported that they had heard shots being fired. There were conflicting reports as to whether or not Dowlen had been captured. Some of the farm workers were convinced that he had shot his way out of the ambush but others reported seeing him being led away by the Germans. No-one was certain what had happened. The only known fact was that Dowlen had disappeared and was either on the run or in German custody. His transmitter at Mery sur Oise was out of action. Knowing that Robert Benoist usually visited Dowlen on Saturday afternoons to discuss messages which needed to be transmitted to London, Lethias sent her father to Paris to warn Robert not to visit that day.

Back in Paris Yvonne Grover-Williams went for lunch that day at Chez Tutulle on the rue Troyon, a restaurant that Willy sometimes used as a place to leave messages. Yvonne was surprised to bump into Noor Khan, who told her that she had a couple of messages which were intended for Dowlen. Then Robert and Maurice Benoist appeared and so Noor gave the messages to Robert.

It was only later in the afternoon that Robert learned about the German raid on Dowlen's villa and he went immediately to Thérèse's farm in Mery-sur-Oise, arriving there in the late afternoon. While Robert and Thérèse tried to piece together what had happened, Dowlen was on the fifth floor at 84 Avenue Foch, being interrogated by the Germans. As usual the SD concentrated on getting as much information as possible in the first 48 hours after the arrest.

That evening Yvonne Grover-Williams caught the train to Le Perray en Yvelines. She was met at the station by Willy, who had ridden there on Robert's motorcycle. They set off for Auffargis and on the way were overtaken by a car with Robert and Thérèse inside. They pulled over and were told the news about Dowlen. That night the Grover-Williamses spent the night in Robert's house in Auffargis with Suzy Benoist. Sunday was quiet and towards the evening Yvonne went back to Paris where she met Maurice and told him about what had happened to Dowlen. She then hurried on to dine with Noor Inayat Khan and warn her about what was happening. The two women agreed to meet again the following day.

Despite the doubts he had expressed to his brother Frederic, Willy Grover was convinced that the Germans would not make any connection between Dowlen and the other members of Chestnut. He stayed where he was at Robert's country house in the woods and on the night of Dowlen's arrest told Maurice's wife Suzy that there was no reason to be alarmed because Dowlen would not give anything away. His arrest would not be a disaster.

At seven o'clock in the morning on Monday August 2 the Germans raided Maurice Benoist's apartment in the Boulevard Berthier and took him away to the Avenue Foch. The investigator Ernst Vogt asked Maurice where his brother Robert could be found. Maurice later claimed that the Germans had a map on which were clearly marked all of the Benoist Family estates in Auffargis. Maurice's testimony suggested that the Germans had a good understanding of Chestnut and its operations, but other evidence does not back this up. If that had been the case the Germans would have planned a more successful raid than the one that occurred two hours later at Auffargis.

Maurice later tried to create the impression that it was Dowlen who had given away the gang's hiding place. The radio operator held out to German pressure throughout the weekend despite the fact that during the interrogations Chestnut's operator would have been introduced to the captured Gilbert Norman, with whom he had been trained in England. Although some protest his innocence, there were many witnesses after the war who reported that during this period Norman seemed to be working with the Germans. Marcel Gouju, a member of the network from Evreux, reported that: "I do not think I have known a more painful moment in my life than when Gilbert Norman came towards me and said with the most beautiful poise: 'You can tell them everything. They are stronger than we are'."

For the morale of a captured agent such behaviour would have been crushing. Even so Dowlen was not a willing helper. The Germans had his transmitter and his codes and wanted him to transmit to London but he refused to do so and it was left to Goetz to transmit six messages in the course of the next two months without the help of Dowlen.

When he was not being questioned at the Avenue Foch Dowlen was kept in the makeshift SD prison at 3bis Place des États-Unis, just off the Avenue Iéna. The cells in the Avenue Foch were much in demand and the Germans did not want newly-captured resistance agents to communicate with the outside world - which was possible from inside the main prison at Fresnes – and so they had converted a large house into a prison, in order to keep prisoners in "cold storage". Despite this Dowlen was still able to tell a fellow prisoner, Marcel Rousset, that he had been arrested by the German radio direction-finding service.

✠

At about nine thirty on the Monday morning a convoy of German vehicles arrived at Robert Benoist's house near Auffargis. There were 15 German police officers in plain clothes. The Germans were under the command of Karl Langer, a caricature of an SS officer, who strutted around in a shiny black mackintosh, barking orders. They immediately arrested Willy Grover. Langer did not believe in subtle methods and, as his men searched the house, he ordered a Spaniard called "Monsieur Jean" to soften up the prisoner. It was not unusual for the SD to use foreigners to do their dirty work against the SOE and there are records of many such renegades from a variety of different countries, including Algerians, Russians and even, later in the war, an English traitor called Harold Cole.

Willy gave nothing away and Langer took most of the party to the nearby Benoist family home where they found Robert's parents, his wife Paule, Maurice's wife Suzy and her maid Chiquita Vilain. Also present were Paule Benoist's brother André Ajustron, his wife Marie and their two children Paulette and Robert, who had been living there since the autumn of 1941. Langer questioned Paule and Marie first but they did not appear to know anything about the resistance work.

Langer then ordered "Monsieur Jean" to attack Georges and Jeanne Benoist, demanding to know where the arms dumps were located.

While this was happening, Maurice arrived at Auffargis, accompanied by Vogt and a Frenchman called Peters, who was working for the SD. Peters was a very dangerous man. His real name was Pierre Cartaud and he knew all about the British-backed resistance movements in France for the simple reason that he had been part of one of the networks until his arrest in May 1942. Prior to that, using the code name Capri, he had worked as a courier in one of Colonel Rémy's intelligence networks in Bordeaux, supplying information to the British about German naval movements. After his arrest he agreed to work for the Germans and the information he supplied led to the arrest of hundreds of people in Rémy's networks. After that there was no going back. Peters threw himself wholeheartedly into the job of catching British secret agents. After a year in their service, the Germans trusted him completely and he even began to use the name Von Kapri.

After the war Maurice admitted to Allied investigators that he had been at Auffargis with the Germans on the morning of the raid, He said that his parents were interrogated for eight hours before his father revealed where the arms were hidden. Georges Benoist was involved to some extent in the activities of Action Vengeance, and appears in the records of the network having been given the code name "Pape", but it is not certain that he knew where the SOE weapons were hidden. Robert told F Section debriefing officers in London that he thought his father had probably guessed there were arms dumps, having been very curious about what Robert was doing when he was examining the disused well at Auffargis.

In a second post-war interrogation Maurice contradicted himself, saying that the Germans took him to Robert's house, which was the next house along the wooded valley and, after arresting everyone there, showed him the arms hidden in the stable block.

Suzy Benoist's maid Chiquita Vilain later told Robert that

she had seen a very dishevelled-looking Dowlen in one of the cars. Robert noted that Chiquita's description of Dowlen was perfect, except that she made no mention of the spectacles Dowlen always wore and concluded that these had probably been broken during his arrest or perhaps in the course of his interrogation over the weekend. In later reports Dowlen was not mentioned by anyone involved and Robert later admitted to SOE officers in London that he thought it strange that the maid should have recognised the radio operator when she had never met him. Robert reported that she had also used the name Achille – which was the correct code name but was never used by members of the Chestnut group.

What Robert did not consider was that Chiquita may not have been telling the truth and was acting under instructions from her employers and that it had been Maurice, rather than Dowlen, who had revealed that the leader of Chestnut was at Auffargis. Later in the war, accusations flew between those involved. Maurice was accused of having worked for the Germans from early in the war, when a former business partner Achille Boitel tricked him into a meeting with Boemelburg. Boitel was later murdered by Resistance fighters. His dealings included working with Walter Hofer and Bruno Lohse, the men responsible for putting together Hermann Goering's stolen art collection.

Boemelburg had wanted to know about Maurice's dealings with members of the Vichy Government, whom he knew from the Touring Club de France. After the war Maurice explained to Allied investigators that he was worried he would be arrested and so told Boemelburg all about his connections with Vichy Interior Minister Marcel Peyrouton and the chief of the Vichy police force René Bousquet. Maurice said that after the meeting he was always careful what he said and did because he believed the Germans were keeping an eye on him.

Maurice nonetheless tried to use his connection to Boemelburg to win his release, writing to the Gestapo chief a week after his arrest, asking to be freed.

It is not clear how the Germans at Auffargis discovered the arms dumps but it seems that searches revealed three revolvers hidden in flower pots on the property. After that they found 51 canisters full of weapons in the old well and a further 47 behind a false wall in the stable block. They also found a dozen parachutes.

By the time these were discovered Maurice and Willy Grover had been driven back to Paris by Vogt and Peters. The two prisoners were put into the cells on the fifth floor at the Avenue Foch to await questioning.

Down at Auffargis there was further questioning for those arrested. Marie Ajustron told Langer that the stable building was always locked and that Robert Benoist must have built the false wall himself. It was established that two months prior to the raid bales of hay had been piled up in front of the false wall, replacing a pile of wood. The Germans concluded from this that the arms had probably been there for only three months. The captured weapons and supplies were then loaded into trucks and taken away and the Germans departed at six in the evening.

Robert had spent the previous night out of Paris and in the morning rang Maurice's apartment and found himself speaking to a man with a German accent who told him that Maurice was out but would be back later. Robert immediately recognised the danger and began telephoning around to try to find out what was happening. Yvonne Grover-Williams also telephoned Maurice's apartment that morning and she too realised that Maurice must have been arrested. She tried to contact Auffargis, but the telephone lines were busy. Yvonne knew that at lunchtime Maurice was due to be at the Brasserie aux Coupoles at the Porte de Champerret to take a call from Auffargis and so she went there to see if the call came through. Yvonne expected that the call would come from either Suzy or Willy and was surprised when Robert came on the phone. He said that he was worried and they agreed to meet in the Métro station at Étoile to talk. The conversation offered little hope for either. Robert promised to send Fremont to Auffargis to discover what was happening and advised Yvonne to get out of Paris and go to ground. That afternoon, after sending a frantic message to Frederic Grover, asking him to come to Paris to see the SD and try to get his brother released, Yvonne left Paris, heading south on a train to Provence. For the next three weeks she hid out with friends called Garcin in the village of Thorenc, a once-chic health resort in the woods to the north of Grasse.

✠

After his meeting with Yvonne, Robert met Thérèse Lethias, who had come in to Paris to urge him to leave the city as quickly as possible. She then returned to Mery sur Oise in the late afternoon.

Having received instructions from Robert, Fremont drove to the Benoist property that afternoon but saw German vehicles everywhere and decided that it was best not to stop and drove past the entrance and headed back to Paris with the bad news.

Willy Grover spent the afternoon in a cell at the Avenue Foch, waiting to be interrogated. He hoped that the other members of the group would use the time to go to ground and to destroy as much incriminating material as possible. At seven-thirty in the evening the Germans began questioning both Willy and Maurice. Willy was faced with the wily Vogt while Maurice had another SD interrogator called Auguste Scherrer. The two interrogations took place in adjoining rooms but, according to Maurice, each man could hear what the other was saying through the thin partition and told allied investigators that he heard Willy giving the addresses of two people who had links with Chestnut: Georges Laurent and a Monsieur Hulet, who was a director of the Centrale Électrique at St Ouen. Whether Maurice was telling the truth is difficult to know. He also said that Scherrer showed him a dossier, which included a photograph of a special curfew pass which belonged to him and which he had given to France Antelme to be sent to England to be copied. Scherrer said that Maurice had been under surveillance ever since the pass had fallen into German hands at the end of June.

This is unlikely to have been the case because if the Germans had known all about Chestnut they would have made sure that they captured Robert Benoist and Albert Fremont when they swooped on the rest of the circuit. Maurice also reported that Scherrer told him that all the F Section networks from Belgium to the Spanish border had been sold out to the Germans. Scherrer continued to question Maurice until midnight after which time he was sent off to Fresnes. Maurice told Allied investigators that Scherrer told him that he was recommending that Maurice be released.

While Willy and Maurice were being questioned Robert managed to track down Chiquita Vilain to try to find out what had happened at Auffargis. The maid had not been arrested and had returned to Paris with Suzy's jewellery.

That night at 10 o'clock two German cars arrived at Thérèse Lethias's farm with six German police officers. She was arrested and four men took her away, leaving two policemen at the farm. Thérèse's parents were told to stay in their apartment but that did not stop Lethias's maid travelling into Paris to warn Robert of Thérèse's arrest and telling him about the Germans who were waiting for him to appear. Robert reached the conclusion that his position in Paris had become unsafe and it would be wise to find a hiding place and go to ground. He knew Fremont had a small apartment in a quiet street near the Père Lachaise cemetery in the east of Paris and hurried to get there before the curfew.

At the Avenue Foch the Germans were beginning to get rough with Willy Grover. After the discovery of the arms dumps at Auffargis they knew that they had captured another F Section officer, but he was refusing to say anything. The interrogation went on through the night and into the next day, while the searches intensified for Robert Benoist.

At 07.30 on the Wednesday morning the Germans swooped on Georges Laurent's home at the Porte Champerret and took him into custody. An hour later the Germans raided the Fremont family home at Grand Lac in Le Vésinet, in the western suburbs of Paris. They missed Fremont by a matter of minutes, as he had just left to go to his office in Paris. The Germans seemed to be under the impression that Robert would be hiding out there and departed when they found no sign of a visitor, Madame Fremont was told that her phone line would be cut and was warned not to try to contact her husband. They told her that he was wanted for questioning about one of his friends. An hour later the Germans arrested Fremont at his garage on the Boulevard de l'Yser, close to the Porte de Champerret. That same day Monsieur Hulet was taken into custody.

Out at Mery-sur-Oise the Germans returned to Thérèse's house and searched the premises, taking a large sum of money from the safe that she was forced to open. They ignored all her personal papers but took away all the money and jewellery that she had stored there, fearing that the banks could not be trusted. The contents of the safe were worth 12 million Francs (£850,000 at today's prices).

In the course of that Wednesday Robert tried to follow what was going on from his hideout in the eastern suburbs but in order to make phone calls to had to leave the apartment and visit the local post office in the Place Gambetta.

He felt very alone.

CHAPTER ELEVEN

The reports he received were often contradictory and Robert wanted most of all to speak to someone who had been at Auffargis when the Germans raided. On the Wednesday he heard that Suzy Benoist had been released from Fresnes and he immediately rang Maurice's apartment to get more details. Robert noted almost immediately that Suzy was behaving oddly. The Benoist family had never been very keen on Maurice's second wife and had kept their distance and Robert was very suspicious when Suzy immediately suggested that they meet up. It was out of character. He ended the telephone call quickly.

It had been only 48 hours since the arrests and, Robert concluded, it was an odd decision for the Germans to have released someone who obviously knew a lot about what was going on. Later, when explaining his adventures to an SOE debriefing officer in London, Robert said that he felt sure that the SD had decided to use Suzy as the bait to try to trap him. He admitted that he did not know whether she had been a willing participant in the scheme but her insistence on a meeting seemed odd.

The conversation with Suzy had, however, revealed that his parents had not been arrested in the raid, so he immediately telephoned the family house, hoping to speak to his mother or father. One of the servants answered the phone and explained that, in an effort to bring Robert into the open, the Germans had returned to Auffargis the previous day and had arrested George and Jeanne Benoist. They had been taken to Fresnes. They would be held there as hostages for the next two months. The news was upsetting and Robert returned to his hiding place an unhappy man. He found it impossible to stay there doing nothing and felt that he needed more information. Later in the day, perhaps against his better judgement, he went back to the post office in the Place Gambetta and asked the telephone operator to make a second call to Auffargis. On this occasion a German officer in the telephone exchange near Auffargis, who was under orders to listen out for telephone calls to the Benoist residence, instructed the telephone operator to delay the caller for as long as possible while he rang the SD at the Avenue Foch to report an unknown man, calling from the post office in the Place Gambetta. The Germans rightly concluded that this had to be Robert and a car was sent to the Place Gambetta.

During the war the population was used to waiting for telephone calls to be connected by the operators but as the minutes ticked by Robert became increasingly worried. The delay was not normal and, realizing the danger, Robert abandoned the call and quickly left the post office, worried that the German security police would arrive at any minute. He was walking down the street when a man approached him and said "Bonjour, Monsieur Benoist". Robert remembered later that the man had spoken French with a very strong accent and was almost certainly a German. Benoist ignored the remark. To do anything else would have been highly suspicious. The German repeated the greeting and they were by then so close together that Robert could not ignore the remark without arousing suspicion. He decided to play dumb, looked blankly at the German and tried to bluff his way out of the situation, replying that the man must be mistaken because he was not Monsieur Benoist. The German continued to speak and Robert suddenly became aware that two other men were approaching from behind. A car pulled up at the kerb side and Robert was bundled into the back by the three men. He found himself hemmed in on the back seat, with a German on either side of him. He protested his innocence but the Germans simply ignored him. Benoist knew that he would be driven to the Avenue Foch.

The three men in the back of the Hotchkiss were crushed

together uncomfortably and so Robert put his arms on the back of the seats behind the two Germans. He then realised that the rear doors on the Hotchkiss featured leather straps that operated the latches. These straps extended backwards and were secured on the top of the rear seats. This meant that Robert could get hold of the straps behind the backs of the two Germans and if he pulled them hard enough he might be able to open the latch on either side of the car, without alerting either man as to what he was doing. If he could do that when the car was going around a corner he might be able to open the door and at the same time push against one of the Germans with sufficient force to not only get the door open but also to push his captor out.

The Hotchkiss was driving slowly into Paris, passing through the Place de la République and then up the Grands Boulevards. If it followed the logical route it would pass the big department stores behind the Opéra and then continue up the Boulevard Haussmann until it reached the Arc de Triomphe. From there it was just a few hundred metres down the Avenue Foch to the SD headquarters. Robert reckoned that his best chance of escape would be when they reached the Arc de Triomphe but it would be difficult to get away unscathed in such a large open area. If he jumped and ran the Germans would probably be able to shoot him before he could get to cover. Robert began to worry that there would be no other opportunity to make a break before they reached the SD headquarters. Then things took a different turn. At the junction of the rue de Richelieu the German driver turned sharply to the left, aiming to drive south down the rue de Richelieu, perhaps aiming for the Ministry of the Interior, where the Gestapo had offices in the Rue des Saussaies. The passengers in the back lurched to the right and Robert, seizing the opportunity, launched himself into the German on his right hand side. At the same time he heaved on the right-hand door strap and the door flew open. The German was caught completely unawares and Robert heaved him out of the car and into the road and went with him, using the unfortunate man to break his fall when they hit the cobblestones.

In a second Robert was on his feet and running. The German was not. As he ran Robert may have been aware that behind him there was confusion. He may have heard the Hotchkiss skid to a halt but probably he was just ducking in and out between the pedestrians. The other Germans began to climb out of the car and gather around their flattened colleague in the middle of the road. But by the time the three Germans had figured out that Robert was not sprawled on the road, he had vanished, ducking into a small arcade called the Passage des Princes, which cut through from the rue de Richelieu to the Boulevards des Italiens. This meant that Benoist emerged around the corner from where the German car had stopped but in the opposite direction from which he had been running. By walking smartly across the Boulevard des Italiens, surrounded by people and not drawing attention to himself, Robert was able to disappear into one of the side streets that went off to the north. Cutting through to the Boulevard Haussmann, Robert was able to assess the damage to his clothes. They looked a little out of place and he decided that he needed to phone his chauffeur and get some new clothes. Robert could then make his way to the garage where he had hidden his car. His first thought was to try a friend in the neighbourhood but the man was so frightened that Benoist thought it best to move on and made his way to the Avenue Hoche to find his old childhood friend, fellow fighter pilot and former racing colleague Roger Labric, who had an apartment in a building next to the Salle Pleyel concert hall. From there he telephoned L'Antoine.

"This is Robert," he said before L'Antoine could speak. "Meet me at number sixteen Avenue Hoche."

There was a pause.

"You mean at Bugatti's?" L'Antoine asked.

"Yes," Robert replied and rang off, worried that if he stayed on the telephone for too long the call might be traced.

What Robert did not realise was that when L'Antoine answered the phone he was surrounded by four Germans: two in uniform carrying machine guns and two in plain clothes. They had burst into the apartment moments beforehand demanding to know the whereabouts of Robert Benoist. They threatened to take L'Antoine and his wife to prison if they did not cooperate. L'Antoine had no idea what had happened to his boss.

And then the telephone rang.

The two plain-clothed German officers had heard everything and immediately ordered L'Antoine to drive them in Benoist's car to the Avenue Hoche. Madame L'Antoine was taken away by the men in uniform to ensure that the chauffeur did as he was told.

What only L'Antoine knew was that in his rush Benoist had made a mistake when he said that the Bugatti offices were at 16 Avenue Hoche. In fact there was no-one in that building called Bugatti. Ettore Bugatti's apartment and the drawing office were several blocks further up the street. L'Antoine delivered the Germans to number 16 and they went to find out in which apartment Mr Bugatti lived. The reply they received confused them. There was no-one called Bugatti in the building. The Germans were not quite sure what to do but decided that the best course of action would be to wait in the car and watch to see when Benoist emerged from wherever he was hiding.

Up above in the building Robert had no idea what was going on down below. Unable to see the street from Labric's apartment, and keen to avoid standing on the street, Robert decided to telephone the Bugatti office and talk to Ettore Bugatti's personal secretary Georges Clavel - a man who Robert knew could be trusted. He asked Clavel if he could check to see whether Robert's car was waiting outside. Clavel went outside and spotted the car further down the avenue. He saw two men with the chauffeur as he calmly strolled down the avenue and turned into the building in which Robert was hiding. He explained to Robert that there was a trap and advised him to find another way out of the building. Then, quite calmly, Georges Clavel returned to work.

Labric's apartment was on the top floor of the building. From its window it was possible to climb out on to the roof. Labric had rented the apartment because it meant that he could go up there and sunbathe. It was an obvious place to hide and with Labric inside the apartment, Robert would be safe if there was a search. Just as he was preparing to climb out on to the roof, the air raid sirens of Paris began to wail. Everyone in the building headed for the cellars in case the bombers came. Not wanting to be trapped in the cellars, Robert decided that he would go on to the roof and hope that the air raid was a false alarm. To avoid leaving any clues, Labric locked the window behind him and Robert settled down on the roof, watching the sky. He waited until darkness fell and then, having given up hope of getting back into the apartment, he carefully began to pick his way from roof to roof until he was on top of the Salle Pleyel next door. He found a skylight that gave him access to the building and, as quietly as he could, he broke the glass, opened the latch and climbed through into the concert hall. The room he entered was an empty office but was obviously used during the day and so Robert left a short note of apology for having made such a mess and then snuck out into the corridor and began to look for a way down to the ground floor in order to get out of the building. He was nearly at the ground floor when he bumped into a night watchman, who challenged him.

"I'm not a burglar," Robert replied calmly.

"No," the night watchman said. "I don't believe you are. I think you are Monsieur Robert Benoist."

Robert was surprised but the man was French and did not seem to be a threat.

"I am Robert Benoist," he replied.

"Well," laughed the night watchman, "I used to be Guy Bouriat's valet. You look as though you could use a drink."

Robert relaxed and after a couple of drinks asked the night watchman if he could check outside the building to see if there were any Germans around. He returned and reported that the coast was clear and that Robert was safe to leave. It was getting towards midnight by then and Robert knew he had to get off the streets because of the curfew. He had nowhere safe to go. The various family apartments were close at hand but he could not risk going to any of them and he did not have time to get across town to the Place Gambetta. In desperation he remembered a family called Dupuy who lived in the rue des Fermiers, a brisk walk away at the top end of the 17ème arrondissement. He arrived on their doorstep, just before midnight and explained that he had been caught out in the curfew and asked if he might shelter there until the morning. The family, who knew nothing of his activities, agreed to let him stay. Robert slept badly. He did not know Monsieur Dupuy well and decided that he would leave as early as possible, before the rest of the house was awake. He went to a local café for a cup of coffee and then telephoned the nearby Grand Garage de la Place Clichy in the rue Forest, to find out whether the car he had stored with Charles Escoffier had been found by the Germans. He was told that the Germans had taken the car away.

Benoist waited until office hours began and then telephoned the Bugatti showroom on the Avenue Montaigne and spoke to his secretary Stella Tayssedre. She knew from Clavel that Robert was on the run from the Germans and immediately agreed to help. They arranged to meet and she took him to her family's apartment at 67 Boulevard Poniatowski, in the south-eastern suburbs of Paris. She returned to work, promising that she would keep him informed of what was happening. The next day - a Saturday - Benoist decided once again try to make contact with Henri Déricourt and went to their usual rendezvous at the Ping Pong Bar in the rue Brunel, just off the Avenue de la Grand Armée. He told the SOE Air Movement Officer about his adventures and it was agreed that he must get out of France as soon as possible. Déricourt assured Robert that he would find space for him on one of his secret flights to England. Déricourt said that he would telephone Stella Tayssedre at Bugatti when everything was ready, using the password: "Do you have any news from Maurice?"

In the 12 days that followed Stella Tayssedre acted as Robert's eyes and ears. She passed on everything she heard in the Bugatti offices and made contact with several of the survivors of the networks. There could be no clandestine flights until the middle of August because the moon was not right so Robert had to remain in hiding as the frequent pass checks on the streets of Paris meant that it was best to stay off the streets.

✠

Robert Benoist was not Henri Déricourt's first priority because Nick Bodington, the deputy head of the French Section, was still in Paris three weeks after flying in to assess the damage done to the SOE networks following the collapse of Prosper. The Germans knew Bodington was there and the searches had intensified to such an extent that in the end Déricourt had to insist that Bodington leave the city and hide out in the country. It was not until Monday, August 16, that the moon was finally right for operations and Déricourt was able to spirit Bodington away in a Lysander operation near Tours. He then turned his attention to others who were in trouble. In total there were eight F Section agents who urgently needed to escape to England. To transport that many people meant that Lysanders could not be used. However, the Moon Squadrons also had American-built Lockheed Hudson aircraft available. These were much bigger and heavier than the Lysanders and so needed a larger and more solid landing field. Déricourt had discovered a new landing field for the operation, near the village of Soucelles, to the north of Angers. It was a vast flat water meadow without any trees or electricity poles. In the months that followed the Soucelles field was used to such an extent by the secret squadrons that it became known in the area as "The English Airport".

Déricourt made contact with each of his passengers and gave

them all a map reference for the assembly point. They were told to be there at 10pm on the Thursday. For some of his later operations at Soucelles Déricourt organized bicycles from a rendezvous point at the restaurant in the village of Tiercé, close to the station, but for the early operations the passengers had to walk. Things were complicated by the fact that at the very last minute the number of passengers increased to 10 when Francis Basin, from the Urchin network in Provence, escaped from a German prison with the help of his courier Raymonde Menessier and arrived in Paris, begging Déricourt to get them out. Déricourt knew that the Hudson might struggle to take off with 10 passengers but he gave in. It was Basin's only real chance of escape.

Before he departed Benoist wrote letters to several of his family and to his friends, telling them that he had gone away on a journey and that if they needed to contact him they could send letters to a post office box in the town of Toulon, on the Mediterranean coast. Madame L'Antoine, who had by then been released from Fresnes, took the letters to Toulon and from there mailed them back to Paris. Her husband, who had been ordered to keep the Germans informed of Robert's movements, pretended to be helpful and reported that he had heard that Benoist had escaped to the south. Robert hoped that by doing this he would be able to return to Paris later to continue building up a resistance movement with the men who had survived the Chestnut debacle. He knew that the network might have lost its key members but the rank and file were still there and needed a leader and decided that he was going to be that man when things had quietened down.

Robert left the Tayssedre apartment on the Thursday morning and made his way to the Gare d'Austerlitz for the 200-mile journey to Angers. From Angers he took a local train to the village of Briollay where he stopped and enjoyed a pleasant dinner in a local restaurant before beginning the final three mile walk to his rendezvous point. The sun was going down as he walked and when he arrived at the map reference he found that he was not the only person in the field. In fact he noted with some alarm that there appeared to be people everywhere, lurking in the hedgerows, trying to keep out of sight. If the Germans had known about the operation that night they could have captured some of the leading lights of the SOE's sabotage and escape networks.

"As I looked around at our gathering I did not think it was good security to have so many top agents assembled together," remembered Robert Boiteux, one of three members of the Spruce network from the Rhône Valley who were there. "To my amazement, I learned that Déricourt was not due to arrive for another hour."

Also in the field was Vic Gerson, who ran the biggest and most successful of the SOE escape lines in France. There was Basin of Urchin and the sculptor Octave Simon, who had been running the Satirist network, a Prosper sub-network that operated outside Le Mans. In amongst this bunch of cut-throats sat a middle-aged lady with grey hair. Her name was Marie-Thérèse Le Chêne, the oldest woman agent sent into France by F Section.

It was an incongruous group.

Déricourt did not arrive until a quarter past eleven and he brought with him not only his assistant Rémy Clément but also another celebrated agent, Tony Brooks of the Pimento network. Déricourt told the assembled agents to split into three groups and each group was then guided through the darkness to the landing field, a walk of about half an hour. By the time they arrived it was close to midnight. The agents were surprised to find that there were an alarming number of horses and cattle wandering about.

"If the plane hit any of them there would be no journey home for us that night and so we desperately tried to shoo the animals to the edges of the field," remembered Boiteux. "The horses trotted over to the trees, but the cows moved only a few feet and then immediately came back. They would not stay off the landing area. Had we been able to yell at them perhaps they would have gone, but we could not afford the luxury of noise.

"After much goading and persuasion, we managed to move them to the perimeter of the field and then all ears strained to listen for the plane. The minutes ticked by and the stupid cows slowly edged their way back to the landing ground and so the whole business had to be started again."

The process was not helped when a ground mist began to form, reducing visibility to just a few feet. This had an alarming side-effect for Tony Brooks and Rémy Clément, who had been sent to the end of the field to signal to the plane with torches when it arrived overhead. They could not see one another, let alone the main party at the other end of the field and all Brooks remembered was the strange sound of a silent rodeo.

"I could hear considerable movement," recalled Brooks. "It made me think of booted soldiers."

Such was the activity on the ground that for some of the agents the time passed very quickly, while for the others it seemed to drag on for a very long time. As a result there are widely differing accounts of the time at which the Hudson finally arrived above the field at Soucelles – these varied from twenty past midnight to around three o'clock in the morning. Hudson "O for Orange" was piloted that night by 161 Squadron's commanding officer Wing Commander Lewis Hodges, who would go on to become an Air Chief Marshal and later be knighted. He had only one passenger with him. Hodges saw the lights and lined up for an approach but at the last minute mist obscured the lights and the Wing Commander aborted the landing and took the plane around for another circuit above the field. On the ground the burst of noise from the engines of the Hudson had an alarming effect on the cows, which stampeded across the field. At his lonely outpost at the end of the landing strip Brooks was horrified when about 50 of them thundered past him in the mist. The secret agents all knew they had only a few moments to clear the landing strip before the Hudson returned and so they ran desperately around in the mist trying to round up the frightened animals - all without making a sound.

Hodges began another approach and the cows stampeded again. As the Hudson taxied through the mist the crew caught occasional glimpses of agents and cows running in various directions in front of the plane. Fortunately there were no collisions. Hodges decided it was best to stop rather than proceed further and eventually Henri Déricourt appeared out of the mist and, waving a torch, directed Hodges to where the plane needed to be. The door was opened and the arriving agent jumped quickly out. The 10 departing agents climbed aboard, keen to get out of the way of the passing cows. The loading process was delayed when Menessier - who they had already nicknamed "La Tigresse" because of her fiery red hair - had difficulty getting up the ladder of the plane because she was wearing a dress that, although fashionable, was rather too tight around her knees. Brooks, who had by then arrived from the other end of the field, solved the problem in a rather un-gentlemanly fashion by putting his shoulder beneath the lady's posterior and shoving her indelicately into the plane. The manoeuvre was greeted with a chorus of "Bravo!" from inside the fuselage.

Once aboard the agents were instructed to huddle up as close to the cockpit as they possibly could in order to keep the weight forward for the take-off. Déricourt climbed on board, passed through the plane to the cockpit, and indicated to Hodges the direction in which he should take off. Nothing was visible except a wall of ground mist. Déricourt casually mentioned that the Wing Commander should watch out for stray cows and departed with a flourish. The door was closed and Hodges pushed open the throttles. The Hudson edged forward into the mist and everyone on board crossed their fingers and held their breath, hoping that the plane would get a clear run across the field. The passengers of O for Orange had been living under intense pressure for months on end but, as the Hudson lumbered across the landing field that night, everyone was in a state of high tension. It did not last. The cows scattered, terrified from the sound of the engines and the plane lurched off the ground and immediately popped up above the ground mist. They were in the air and a wave of relief and optimism spread through the aeroplane. The agents could begin to relax. There might be German night fighters out there, looking for the Hudson, but it was unlikely that they would be caught on the 200-mile low-level dash through the darkness. Normally a Hudson can cruise at 150mph but O for Orange, with its heavy load, took a little longer than usual that night. Navigator Flight Lieutenant Alan Broadley plotted the course home while the wireless operator Flight Lieutenant "Lofty" Reed went back into the fuselage and handed around cups of tea laced with cognac which he had brought over in a Thermos. Everyone spread out and settled in for the trip home.

"We did not speak much," remembered Boiteux. "We had lived on our nerves for so long that the sudden lifting of tension acted as a gentle anaesthetic and we all fell asleep."

The Hudson crossed the Normandy coast and headed out across the English Channel. The crew was constantly alert, watching out for fighters or ships that might have anti-aircraft guns on board. But all went well and the Hudson crossed the English coastline near Bognor Regis. In the moonlight, Hodges was able to make out the two long camouflaged concrete runways of the Royal Air Force fighter station at Tangmere and, having received clearance from the control tower, brought the Hudson in to land. Although it was still early in the morning when they arrived, the door was opened and they found that Maurice Buckmaster had come down from London to meet the plane. The gesture was greatly appreciated by the sleepy agents who were in very high spirits. They had escaped to England and were amongst friends after months of living with the enemy. They recounted the mad tale of the cows running around in the field and laughed. Buckmaster marvelled at the men and women he had working for him in France.

The party was quickly transferred by car to a small house that was hidden behind tall hedges opposite the gates of the famous fighter station. Tangmere Cottage was where the pilots of the Moon Squadrons lived during the weeks before and after each full moon - the period in which it was considered safe to attempt landings in France. When the party of agents arrived at Tangmere Cottage they discovered that a pair of sergeants from the RAF Regiment had been warned of their arrival and, as the dawn began to break over the English countryside, were in the process of preparing a fine English breakfast of eggs, bacon and tea.

With breakfast out of the way the agents headed back to the cars and headed off to London on the deserted roads, as the rest of England was beginning to wake up.

CHAPTER TWELVE

Heroes do not always get the welcome that they deserve. Benoist and the other newly-arrived F Section escapers from France who were not known to the British authorities were not allowed to go free. They were taken to the Royal Victoria Patriotic School, a vast Gothic building that sits in the middle of Wandsworth Common. It had been built as an orphanage to house the daughters of British officers killed in the Crimean War. It was constructed from yellow brick with grey stone decoration and featured five ornate towers and two internal courtyards. It was not a very welcoming place and to Robert it felt more like a prison.

The school had been requisitioned by the government in 1940 and had served as a clearing house for refugees arriving in Britain from Occupied Europe ever since. The new arrivals were detained until the Security Service (MI5) had assessed whether or not they were a threat to Great Britain. This was a necessary evil. A year earlier a British-trained radio operator called Laroche had been parachuted to France to work with one of Général de Gaulle's information-gathering networks. He had been captured by the Germans and, to save himself, had agreed to work as a double agent. The Germans decided to send him back to Britain where he tried to convince the authorities that he had had a lucky escape. The Security Service quickly picked holes in his story and he was arrested.

Robert had to undergo a series of interviews and his was an interesting case with his exciting tales of close-calls with the Germans. There was never any doubt about his allegiance and he was soon released and whisked away to one of the SOE safe houses in the West

End. There would be debriefing sessions later on but finally Robert was able to relax. He was allowed to walk around in a free country. He had not been in England much since his races at Brooklands in the 1920s and, if the truth be told, Robert was not really interested in staying any longer than was absolutely necessary. He wanted to get back to France to avenge his parents and his friends Willy Grover and Albert Fremont. The very presence of the Nazis in Paris annoyed him and he was very keen to find out what had happened to Chestnut and how the Germans had found their way to the houses at Auffargis.

Over in France, the same questions were being asked by others. At the end of August Madame Fremont heard reports that Maurice Benoist had been released by the Germans and was rather surprised when he did not attempt to make any contact with her. After her husband Albert's arrest at the beginning of August Madame Fremont had heard nothing about his fate. The Germans had returned to her house two days after his arrest, while she was out, and had confiscated her wireless set and left a message saying that she should take some clothes for her husband to 84 Avenue Foch. She had visited the SD headquarters on August 7 only to be told that Albert had already been sent to Fresnes prison in the south of the city.

Fremont would remain in Fresnes for more than four months before being transferred to the transit camp at Royallieu in Compiègne at the end of November. After a brief period there he was deported to the Buchenwald concentration camp in Germany in January 1944. Madame Fremont had hoped that Maurice might have seen her husband in Fresnes but when she heard nothing she asked Commandant Boillot, an Air Force friend of Fremont, who was related to Maurice's first wife Marguerite Dugrosprez, to approach Maurice and ask about what had happened. Boillot reported that Maurice was blaming his arrest on several people, including his own sister-in-law Paule Benoist. He had told Boillot that he believed that France Antelme was a double agent, working for the Germans.

When she heard about Maurice's responses, Madame Fremont

was confused and angry. She requested a meeting with him and a rendezvous was organized at the Brasserie aux Coupoles at the Porte Champerret, not far from Maurice's apartment on the Boulevard Berthier. In the course of that conversation Maurice told Mme Fremont that the Germans were still looking for Yvonne Grover-Williams but that he was not going to tell them where she was.

"There is no danger of that," he said. "I like her too much."

Madame Fremont left the meeting feeling deeply suspicious of Maurice Benoist. After the war Maurice made many accusations about his friends and relatives. He told allied investigators that many of the stories about their treachery had been told to him by a mysterious secret agent who worked under the code name of Andres, who had been in contact with both Robert Benoist and Antelme. These stories, he said, could not be verified because Andres had been killed later in the war but he claimed that a resistant called Guignard, who had been involved in Wilkinson's Privet network in Angers, has been arrested after a meeting with Willy Grover at the Gare St Lazare.

Maurice said that Willy had told Guignard that he was leaving France and introduced him to a man who was supposed to be his successor. This turned out to be Pierre Cartaud, the turncoat Frenchman known to the Gestapo as Peters. Maurice also said that a French report on the Auffargis affair that had been compiled by the local French prefecture had reached the conclusion that the network "had been sold out by a British officer".

Willy did have dealings with someone called Guignard because in a separate interrogation Maurice mentioned that Willy had given 200,000 Francs (£23,000 at today's values) to Guignard and a Madame Bourges of the Angers network to help them fund the operations after Wilkinson was arrested.

The British do not seem to have paid much attention to Maurice's claims and certainly those involved in Chestnut had other ideas about what had happened. Madame Fremont and others were increasingly convinced that it was Maurice and his wife Suzy who had betrayed Chestnut and that by denouncing others Maurice was simply trying to protect himself. Robert's belief that Suzy had been released as part of a pact with the Germans to trap him is supported by the fact that when it became clear that she had failed to ensnare Robert, she was sent back to Fresnes on August 18 and would remain in jail until the start of October.

✠

In England Robert's debriefing took place in the first week of September, a fortnight after his arrival. The interview went well and it was decided that Robert was exactly the kind of man that the SOE needed in France. He would spend a few months being properly trained in Britain, while the manhunt in France died down, and then he would be sent back in to continue the work that Willy Grover had begun. On September 8 Robert began a three-week explosives course at Special Training School 17 at Brickendonbury, under the watchful eye of George Rheam. Buckmaster had decided that Robert's next mission to France would be only a short one with the specific aim being to set up teams of men to attack a number of targets in the Nantes area, primarily the electricity pylons over the Loire at the Île Héron, which carried around 150,000 volts from the south of France up to Brittany. Robert's training in explosives would be specifically designed to teach him to demolish the pylons using the least amount of explosive necessary. One of those on the same course was 24-year-old Denis Johnson, who remembered that Benoist was very different to most of the trainees.

"I remember him as being older," remembered Johnson. "He was quiet, kindly, dark and very evidently a fervent patriot. His one wish was to return to France for another mission."

Johnson, who would end up working with former Chestnut member Richard Heslop in the Jura, said that everyone was aware that Buckmaster had reservations about sending Benoist back to France.

"He was reluctant to see him go, " said Johnson. "He was obviously a marked man."

If Buckmaster had any worries about sending Robert back to France they do not show up in the official records, although the fact that Benoist would be given a false name for his new mission was evidence enough that he could no longer hope to live under his own name. The new name was considered enough to protect the man who in the 1920s and 1930s had captured the imagination of France with his racing victories. No-one seemed to worry that Robert's reputation, his eagle-like features and feisty personality might give him away. He himself was unmoved by the risks he was facing and refused to listen to friends who warned him to be careful. He considered that the Germans were "too stupid" to catch him.

✠

In Paris the German searches for Yvonne Grover-Williams and Noor Inayat Khan continued. Although she had been identified by the Germans, Noor had managed to slip through their fingers and disappeared again. Neither she nor Yvonne could be found. Yvonne was still in the south. In the first week of September Carmèle Laurent, the wife of Georges Laurent (who was still in jail in Paris) made contact with Yvonne and travelled south to meet her. The rendezvous took place in Beaulieu-sur-Mer where Carmèle told Yvonne that Maurice Benoist was protecting her. At the same time he was trying to find Noor Khan. Yvonne was immediately suspicious and told Mme Laurent that she believed Maurice was working for the Germans. Carmèle said nothing, which Yvonne thought was a little strange but it was only later, when she discovered that Carmèle was Maurice's mistress, that she concluded that Maurice has probably sent Carmèle to try to trap her or get information about Noor. In the end Yvonne refused to tell Carmèle how she could contact Noor and made her promise not to tell Maurice where their meeting had taken place.

Carmèle kept her word. Yvonne was by then staying with Sheila Marteau, an old friend from the 1930s, in St Jean Cap Ferrat. Marteau suggested that Yvonne might try to make an unofficial contact with the Gestapo through a friend called Ida Pfansteil, the wife of a Gestapo officer in Paris. Yvonne took the train to Paris on September 12 but did not return to her house for fear of being arrested. She met Noor at the Café Colisée, telling her what had happened and warning her to be very careful. Two days later she met Pfansteil, who suggested that her best course of action would be to present herself for an official interview with the Germans. The following day, while trying to decide what to do, she left Paris and went north to see her parents, as her mother was very ill. She returned to Paris the same day and finally called Maurice. They arranged to meet at the Rue Weber at 10.00 the following morning. Yvonne arrived early and at 09.55 Maurice rang to check she was there. Five minutes later the Germans arrived. Yvonne was arrested and taken around the corner to the Avenue Foch, where she found Maurice waiting for her with the Germans.

"You have nothing to fear," he told her. "Just tell them what you know. Charles talked. Achille talked. Everyone is talking. For Willy's sake you must tell them where they can find Noor."

Yvonne refused to say anything and after Maurice had departed she found herself with the SD officer Karl Langer, the man who had arrested Willy at Auffargis.

"I don't like Monsieur and Madame Maurice Benoist," Langer told her. "A man who sells his own mother and father. He told us everything, even things we did not ask for."

The statement shocked even Yvonne who already had suspicions about Maurice. Langer demanded a statement about Yvonne's activities with Chestnut and her contacts. However, he was not satisfied with the results and that evening ordered that Yvonne be sent to Fresnes where she was put in solitary confinement until the following day when she was moved to a cell with three other women. She explained her predicament and asked the others to spread the word throughout the prison that Maurice Benoist had betrayed her. Thus Suzy Benoist, who was being held elsewhere in Fresnes, heard the rumours about her husband's treachery.

At the end of the month Carmèle Laurent took Mme Fremont to see Maurice. On this occasion he blamed the arrests on Thérèse Lethias's Polish servants and on a French banker called Fernandez, who was an owner of the celebrated Fernandez & Darrin coachwork company. He told Mme Fremont that Willy Grover had betrayed Monsieur Hulet and also claimed that Dowlen was working for the Germans, sending false messages back to England. At the end of the discussions Maurice told Mme Fremont that "the English are not looking after us and there is no reason why we should sacrifice ourselves for them. If we could give them (the Germans) Noor Khan, I am sure that they would free your husband and Laurent."

Mme Fremont was shocked. She departed convinced that Maurice was working for the Germans.

Back in England Robert Benoist was busy demonstrating to the British that he would be a useful man in the battle against the Germans. The explosives course proved that he was a very capable and energetic saboteur, despite the fact that he was 47 years of age.

"He is a very keen, enthusiastic and capable student, who in view of his standing in French industry could become a first class organiser," said his SOE report. "He has a sound knowledge of explosives and should be capable of carrying out attacks on pylons. He requires further training before he will be able to deal with all classes of target".

Having graduated from Brickendonbury Robert was sent on to another SOE training school at STS 42 at Roughwood Park, a large country house near the village of Chalfont St Giles in Buckinghamshire. This establishment provided revision classes for agents who had returned from France and at the same time kept them out of London and out of trouble. Once again Robert did well in all subjects.

"He is an amusing and kindly personality although at times obstinate," said his Roughwood Park report. "The standard he has reached is considered adequate for employment in the field."

As Robert was finishing his training in England, over in France the Germans were beginning to release some of those who had been involved with Chestnut. After the war Maurice Benoist tried to claim that he was responsible for this, having spent weeks in constant negotiation with the SD. Jeanne and Georges Benoist were freed on September 22 and were followed by Suzy Benoist in the first week of October and Yvonne Grover on October 8. Georges Laurent followed on December 13. Maurice also claimed to have been responsible for the release of Henri Guérin, the father of Pierre Guérin of the Réseau Cohors Asturies at Servon and even told post-war Allied investigators that Thérèse Lethias would have been released if her parents had had more confidence in him. To celebrate the release of Suzy, Maurice threw a party and invited Mme Fremont. She wanted to talk to Suzy to find out if she had any news of her husband but Maurice's wife had no time to talk and Mme Fremont once again found herself in the company of Maurice, who complained that Yvonne was not helping the German investigations.

"She knows many things that her husband told her," Maurice told Mme Fremont. "If she wanted to she could speak."

Yvonne had been released the day before the party. Maurice said this had happened after he had given his word to the Germans that he would "keep an eye on her".

"I can get nothing out of her," he told Mme Fremont at the party. "You must come and dine here and try to get her to talk."

Mme Fremont had no intention of doing any such thing. Maurice however continued his attempts to track down Noor Khan, who was by then involved with a different set of people, independent of all the old networks. The Germans were still on her trail. The arrest of Robert Gieules led to the discovery of a telephone number in his address book that led the Germans to find Noor's apartment on the Boulevard Richard Wallace and the name Jeanne-Marie Régnier, under which she was operating. Fortunately Noor had anticipated the danger and had stopped visiting that apartment. London wanted to her to return to Britain and preparations were being made for that to happen while she was staying at an apartment at 98 rue de la Faisanderie, down near the Avenue Henri Martin.

While Maurice continued to try to track down the elusive Noor in Paris, Robert waited to be sent back to France, living in an SOE safe house in Woodborough Road, Putney and while he was there he wrote a last will and testament, leaving everything to his daughter Jacqueline.

On the same day that Yvonne was allowed out of Fresnes, Robert was appointed to an emergency commission as a Second Lieutenant on the General List of the British Army. The appointment and his posting to something called MO1 (SO) was noted in The London Gazette, although this was never published and, thereafter, he appeared as a British officer only on secret War Office lists. On Monday October 11 Benoist went to Orchard Court to begin his briefings for the mission to France. He had impressed the F Section chiefs to such an extent that they had decided that he should take over what was left of the old Chestnut network but this was to be renamed Clergyman and rather than being based in and around Paris would be given the port of Nantes, close to the mouth of the Loire. Away from Paris Robert would be less exposed to arrest. As he could no longer operate under his own name he was given a new cover name: Roger Brémontier. This meant that he had the same initials as before and so could use most of his old personal effects if they were marked "RB".

Robert's code name - the name by which he would be known to the networks - would be Lionel and the detailed instructions called for the Clergyman organization to consist of four different and entirely separate sub-networks: one to act as a reception committee for arms and explosives; one to attack the electricity pylons over the Loire at the Île Héron; a third to prepare for attacks on railway lines in and around Nantes to be carried out on D-Day which would be sufficient to keep the railway lines out of action for at least a week; and the final one to prepare ways of stopping the Germans from demolishing the port of Nantes. This was important because it would mean that Nantes could be used to help supply the Allied Forces after the invasion had taken place. Benoist was specifically warned to avoid what was left of Wilkinson's Privet circuit in Nantes, working on the assumption that after Wilkinson's arrest the network had probably been penetrated by the SD. He was specifically ordered to steer clear of all contact with Wilkinson's wife. London said that it considered her to be talkative and indiscreet. It was agreed that Robert's mission would be limited to just two months in the field and as a result he was not given his own radio operator. All radio communication would be done through an operator called Hercule, whom Robert could contact through an address in Le Mans. Hercule had been ordered to work only for Robert and one other existing contact he had in Tours. The radio operator would be informed of Robert's arrival with one of the personal messages broadcast on the BBC French Service. In an emergency Robert was told to stay in touch with Déricourt to ensure that there were no problems for him to get out of France during the January moon period.

To fund operations Robert would be given half a million Francs (£35,000 at modern prices) which London reckoned would be enough to last him for three or four months. If he needed more he was to send a message to London via Hercule.

As Robert was preparing to go to France, Noor Khan's charmed life in Paris finally ended. The Germans had been very fortunate. A Frenchwoman telephoned the SD offices in the Avenue Foch in mid-October and said that she knew where to find Jeanne-

Marie Régnier. The Germans were delighted. Ernst Vogt was sent to meet the woman in the Trocadéro Garden and it was agreed that in exchange for the promise of a large sum of money the woman would give him the address of Noor's hideout in the rue de la Faisanderie. Vogt insisted that the woman go with him to his offices and later said that he had seen her identity papers, which were in the name of Renée Garry, the sister of Émile Garry of the Cinema network.

On October 13 Peters arrested the Indian princess at the apartment on the rue de la Faisanderie. The Germans also got hold of her codes, her transmitter and the notebook in which she had noted down all her previous messages. They immediately began to use the transmitter to try to convince London that Noor was still operating in Paris.

"Inayat Khan continued to send normal messages which were accepted as being genuine," Buckmaster wrote in a report to Robin Brook in May 1944. "Various trap questions were answered satisfactorily."

London was by this point heavily reliant on Noor's messages because of the number of arrests that had taken place in Paris. There were several other radios in operation but increasingly, thanks to reports from escaping agents, London became aware that some of them must be in German hands. Finally in February 1944, four months after Noor was arrested, it was decided to send Antelme back to France to establish which networks were in operation and which had been compromised. A parachute reception was organized via Noor and he and two other agents were dropped into a German trap.

When he realized what had happened Antelme was furious with London. He was taken off to the Avenue Foch but once he had regained his composure he said nothing, despite all the efforts of the Germans to get information from him. Eventually Antelme was deported to Germany where early in 1945 he was executed at the Gross-Rosen concentration camp in modern day Poland.

Renee Garry was arrested after the war and in January 1950 was tried by the Tribunal Militaire Permanent de Paris at the Caserne de Reuilly. She admitted that she had been having an affair with France Antelme, who had been living at the Garry apartment in Auteuil before Noor arrived. After that she told the court Antelme had shunned her. There is little doubt that during the time that Noor and Antelme were hiding in the apartment in the Place Malesherbes and at Auffargis in July, the two had embarked on a brief but tragic love affair.

Renée Garry denied that she had sold Noor to the Germans. The witnesses for the prosecution were mainly Germans and her lawyers produced a letter from Colonel Maurice Buckmaster, thanking her for her efforts on behalf of the SOE. The judges could not agree on a verdict and voted 5-4 in her favour. She was freed and immediately vanished, without even returning to her apartment, presumably to begin a new life elsewhere.

✠

After the war there were several accusations against Noor. Maurice Benoist claimed that a resistance worker called Andres had been arrested because Noor had told the Germans where to find him. This allegation appears to have been based on the fact that the Germans had a copy of a report, which had been written by Andres, assessing the damage done in Courbevoie and Boulogne by an Allied bombing raid. Andres had given this to Noor.

Later Maurice had been shown the document by the Germans. In fact it seems that Noor had passed it on to Henri Déricourt and he had given it to the Germans, trying to convince them that he was trying to be helpful while at the same time trying to ensure that the SOE agents in his care were left untroubled. It is generally agreed by everyone that Noor would not have betrayed anyone but it is also accepted that she could easily have been duped by the Germans, as happened when she met the two German officers who were impersonating the two missing Canadian agents, and introduced them to other members of the network.

Five days after Noor was arrested Peters called at the apartment on the rue de la Faisanderie and, posing as an Englishman, asked Émile Garry and his wife Marguerite, to hand over some of Noor's personal effects, showing them a letter written by Noor. When they obeyed the request they were both arrested.

Two nights after the Garrys were arrested Pilot Officer Johnny Affleck, a 23-year-old Scottish pilot, flew Robert Benoist back into France aboard Hudson M for Mother. Affleck had done two trips to France that week and two nights previously had flown through a poplar tree as he came in to land at a secret field near Beaune. He was now going into Soucelles for the first time and had been warned by his squadron mates to watch out for passing cows. If Affleck was tense as he came in to land the Hudson, it was nothing compared to the tension that existed between the group that was gathered on the ground to meet the plane. Henri Frager (Paul) of the Donkeyman network from Auxerre was returning to England, planning to report stories he had heard suggesting that Henri Déricourt was working as an undercover agent for the Germans. Frager had arrived at the landing field with one of his assistants Roger Bardet. Déricourt, who had not known that Bardet would be there and considered his appearance to be a serious breach of security, insisted that Bardet go to England with Frager. Bardet refused to go.

M for Mother touched down and quickly Robert came off the plane, handed his suitcases, containing weapons and a radio, to Déricourt. The pair then helped the other SOE agents off the plane. Frager climbed aboard unaided but then there was pandemonium when Déricourt tried to bundle Bardet on board with him. Déricourt's deputy Rémy Clément and the arriving agents stood, open-mouthed, while the two agents struggled. Finally Bardet managed to break loose. A furious Déricourt shut the door of the plane and gave Affleck the signal to go. The Hudson disappeared into the darkness and the noise of the engines faded. The party headed off behind the seething Déricourt although one of the new agents Albert Browne-Bartoli, who was to set up the Ditcher network in Burgundy, decided that it was all too strange for him and slipped away on his own. Benoist had no such fears. He trusted Déricourt completely.

After the war it emerged that Bardet was playing a similar game to Déricourt, having agreed to work for the Germans after being arrested. Bardet's defenders say that he was simply trying to limit the damage done, just as Déricourt claimed he was doing. There were also claims after the war, based on depositions from Henri Lafont, one of the Bony-Lafont Gang, a criminal group that worked with the Germans, that those arriving at Soucelles were followed to Paris and their addresses reported to the SD. This was a relatively imprecise activity as the gang members were not at the landing sites and only picked up the arriving agents at the train stations. Benoist and Déricourt buried some material, including a radio and weapons, at the landing site and then travelled to Paris. There is no evidence that Benoist was followed to his destination, the Tayssedre apartment on the Boulevard Poniatowski. This remained secure.

Once in Paris Benoist began to put his old gang back together. He discovered from Stella Tayssedre that since the collapse of Chestnut in August Marcel L'Antoine, a Bugatti mechanic who had become his chauffeur, had been gardening and doing other odd jobs at the Benoist estates in Auffargis. He called him back to Paris. Robert then asked Stella's husband Robert Tayssedre if he would be willing to take on a more active role in the organization. Tayssedre had been on the run from the Germans after refusing to work in Germany and agreed immediately. Benoist gave him the task of investigating what had happened to Chestnut and to try to identify the traitor. He also sent Tayssedre to the Grand Garage in the Place Clichy to find out whether his old Citroën truck was still there and during the visit Tayssedre discovered from the garage owner Charles Escoffier that a cousin of Madame Escoffier by the name of Pierre Guérin had been arrested in Servon in August, not long after Chestnut had been broken up. It meant nothing to Tayssedre, but when he mentioned it to Benoist, the old racer remembered the visit he, Maurice and Escoffier had made to Servon the previous summer. Escoffier told Tayssedre that the Germans had brought a Frenchman with them when they arrived to arrest the members of the network. Robert wanted to know more and told Tayssedre to visit Servon and find out exactly what had happened. Tayssedre met Pierre Guérin's father Henri and learned that the Germans had arrived in Servon on August 25, in the company of the mysterious Frenchman. Henri reported that the man had walked with a bad limp. Pierre Guérin had been the first to be arrested but Henri had also been questioned and during that interrogation the man with the limp had put his hand on Henri Guérin's shoulder and said: "You can talk. These gentlemen know all about your network. It is in your interest to talk." In the days that followed there were nine arrests in and around Servon.

The news shocked Benoist because he knew that it could mean only one thing: Maurice, his own brother, was the traitor. The only link between Chestnut and the resistance group in Servon had been the visit he and Maurice had made together the previous summer and Henri Guérin's description matched that of Maurice. Robert took the painful decision to avoid all contact with Maurice and instructed Tayessedre to send anonymous letters to all of Maurice's friends, warning them about what had happened. A few weeks later an indignant Maurice told Tayssedre that someone was trying to smear his name. He explained to Tayssedre that he had had the Guérin address in a notebook and concluded that the Germans must have made the connection from that. He insisted that he had not told the SD about the Servon network. After the war Maurice continued to deny that he had anything to do with the arrests at Servon but he was forced to admit to Allied investigators that he had been present at Servon when the arrests were made.

While Robert Tayssedre investigated the fall of Chestnut, his wife Stella was busy trying to find out what had happened to the members of the group. The news was disturbing: Willy Grover and Robert Gieules had already been deported to Germany. Thérèse Lethias was being held in Fresnes but there was no news at all of Albert Fremont. Mme Fremont had refused to give up her search for her husband and to discover how he had been arrested. On November 3 she visited Yvonne Grover at the rue Weber. They discussed Maurice and Yvonne warned her that Robert's brother was capable of anything. Yvonne told Mme Fremont that the previous day she had met Stella Tayssedre and had discovered about the betrayal of the Servon Group.

The next evening Yvonne and Mme Fremont met again at a dinner in Maurice's apartment. It was a tense affair during which the visitors felt that Maurice and Suzy were once again trying to find out as much information as possible about Noor Khan. Yvonne admitted to having met Noor in September but refused to say more. Whether Maurice knew that Noor had been arrested was not clear but as the Germans were keeping her capture secret, in an effort to catch other members of the F Section networks when they tried to make contact with Noor, they may not have bothered to tell him.

CHAPTER THIRTEEN

With the network in Paris reviving, Robert wanted to return to Soucelles to unearth the radio transmitter he had buried close to the landing site. The radio would go to Hercule and there were also some of the handguns for use by Clergyman. Robert concluded that this would have to be a night operation and checked with Henri Déricourt to make sure that he had nothing planned that evening. He then went back to Soucelles, dug up the equipment and took it back to a safe house. His next problem was to find Hercule.

Jean Dubois was as brave and as reckless as Robert. He had been a professional radio operator in France in the 1930s and in the summer of 1942 had been recruited to Raymond Flower's Monkeypuzzle. He had tried to transmit messages to London using the British transmitter that had been sent out from London, but without proper training this proved to be very difficult and so it was decided that the best course of action was for him to go to England and complete a radio training course. While he was away the Germans took his wife and daughter hostage. Dubois was so highly-rated at the SOE training schools when he finished his training that it was decided that when he returned to France he would work not for one network like most of the other SOE operators but for as many as needed him. He would have the right to choose, if only for his own security. It was a very dangerous role but Dubois knew it was necessary. In the months that followed Dubois managed to stay one step ahead of the Germans at a time when the F Section networks were under enormous strain. During that period he transmitted for at least six different networks and sent a remarkable 138 messages.

His secret was that he was always on the move, travelling from safe house to safe house, never staying more than one night in the same location. The Germans could never keep up and did not know where next he would appear.

Before trying to make contact with the elusive Dubois, Benoist decided to first set up a headquarters for the Clergyman network in the Nantes area and set off in his Citroën truck with L'Antoine and Robert Tayssedre to visit the city. Concealed in the truck were the radio transmitter and weapons that Robert had brought with him. They travelled down the RN10 highway but decided as they approached Chartres that they would skirt through the suburbs to avoid any German checkpoints on the main road. As they were doing this, they ran into a German military policeman, who took an interest in the truck and flagged them down. After examining their papers, he decided that they had too many bottles of gas in the back (these were used to power the truck) and, thinking they were working on the black market, ordered them to the German police headquarters at a hotel in the Places des Épars in the centre of the city. The problem was that there were too many of them to travel together in the cab of the Citroën and so Benoist volunteered to move to the back of the truck with the German's bicycle, while L'Antoine and Tayssedre stayed in front with the policeman. Within a few yards Robert had jumped from the truck, taking with him as much of the incriminating evidence as he could gather. He stole the bicycle and cycled the 22 miles from Chartres back to Auffargis, where he hid in the outbuildings on his farm for several days, fearing that it would not be safe to return to Paris.

When the truck arrived at the headquarters of the German military police in Chartres, it was found that Benoist had disappeared. L'Antoine and Tayssedre explained that they did not know him and that they had simply been giving him a lift but the Germans did not believe the story and ordered the pair to unload the truck. They knew that this process would end in their arrest and so they agreed in whispers to make a run for it if an opportunity arose. For a moment the guards were distracted and Tayssedre and L'Antoine made their break, running into the narrow streets of the old town. The Germans chased after them, firing at the fugitives but missing. The two men were separated when Tayssedre slipped and fell, but he managed to get himself into a pharmacy where the owners hid him under the counter of the shop until the immediate danger had passed. Two flower sellers helped L'Antoine to hide. The chauffeur was lucky because he later discovered a bullet hole in his clothing. The Germans could not find either man and were forced to abandon the search and in the days that followed both L'Antoine and Tayssedre made their way back to Paris.

A few days later Robert returned to the Tayssedre apartment and announced that it would be best for him to move elsewhere to reduce the dangers and so he rented a small apartment in a quiet street close to the Val-de-Grâce military hospital in the 5ème arrondissement, in the south of the city. The apartment in the rue Fustel de Coulanges became his safe house in Paris. The arrests in Chartres had been a disaster for the network as all of its equipment had been lost, including a wireless transmitter, crystals and a number of blank German passes. Worse still, Robert had lost a suitcase full of clothing. Hidden in the lining of a suit had been his false documentation in the name of Roger Brémontier. The Germans quickly found it and it was soon in the hands of the SD and Maurice Benoist was called in for an interview at the Avenue Foch, where he was told that his brother was back in France, operating under a new name. Maurice was asked to identify the articles of clothing, which had belonged to Robert.

As he could not operate under the name Brémontier, Robert took on a new identity, choosing the name of Daniel Perdrigé. Perdrigé had been a young Communist mayor in the commune of Montfermeil, one of the "Red Belt" working class suburbs in the east of Paris. Arrested for inciting resistance in April 1941 he was one of the

99 hostages executed by the Germans at the Fort du Mont-Valérien in Suresnes, in December that year, in a reprisal for the killing of a German officer. He was 35 and left two small children.

His sister Charlotte had begun working with Robert as a courier during the Chestnut period and had survived the arrests that summer. Now that Benoist was back, she was ready to continue the work and was operating from an apartment in the Rue Nicolo in the 16ème arrondissement , posing as Robert's sister. She was known in the group by the code name of Sonia.

Robert soon disappeared off to Le Mans to try to make contact with Hercule in order to tell London about the problems in Chartres. His contact was a Monsieur Brault at the Hotel de la Calandre in downtown Le Mans. When he got there, he discovered that Brault had been arrested some time earlier. There was no way that he could make contact with Hercule. Once again Robert was stuck without a radio operator. He would never find Dubois.

Within a fortnight the gallant radio operator was captured after a dramatic gun battle with the Germans in the eastern Paris suburb of Neuilly-Plaisance. Dubois was caught by accident, finding himself in the wrong place at the wrong time. He had been staying in a safe house that belonged to the Inventor network, one of the lesser-known Prosper sub-networks, which was being run by Sidney Jones, an Elizabeth Arden representative in Paris before the war. Jones had recruited Hercule to the Monkeypuzzle network. The Germans knew about Inventor from the start, but it was not until Jones was arrested on November 19 that the address of the safe house was discovered. A number of SD men went immediately to the apartment in Neuilly-Plaisance where Ernst Vogt and Auguste Scherrer, posing as British agents, went into the building. They were introduced to Dubois and explained that Captain Morel from London had told them that he should return to England via Spain. They were obviously not very convincing because Dubois laughed, said that he preferred to travel by air, and then pulled out a revolver and shot both of them, killing

Scherrer outright and injuring Vogt seriously.

Dubois collected all the incriminating papers he could find but, as he was doing this, two more SD officers burst through the front door of the building, having heard the shooting. They gunned down the owner of the house, who had stepped out of his rooms to see what was happening. Dubois caught the two newcomers by surprise as he burst out of his apartment, firing at both men, and reached the top of the staircase before one of the Germans tripped him and sent him tumbling head-first down the stairs. He landed in a heap at the bottom and as he tried to get up, two more Germans came through the front door and shot him. Dubois's gun was empty but he still managed to get out of the house and was 50 yards down the street before he collapsed from loss of blood. He had five different bullet wounds: one in each thigh, one in the stomach, one in the right shoulder and the final one in the neck. He was taken to the Pitié-Salpêtrière hospital, near the Gare d'Austerlitz, which had been taken over by the Germans and had a special guarded section for prisoners.

Robert knew nothing of this. There might have been rumours of a gun battle in the east of the city but the Germans ensured that news was strictly controlled. The newspapers were thin and radio broadcast only what was allowed by the censors.

Deprived of the planned route to communicate to London, Benoist moved on to the fall back plan and went looking for Henri Déricourt at their usual rendezvous at the Ping Pong Bar in the rue Brunel. The barman told him that Déricourt was away in the south and would not be back in Paris before the start of December. Robert had no means of escape and no way of contacting London and so concluded that his best course of action would be to go to Nantes and concentrate on building up the sabotage teams. He would then return to Paris later to meet Déricourt.

Nantes had suffered badly during the latter part of the war, because of its strategic importance, being the first point on the

Loire river where there a bridge. As a result it had become a major railway centre and it was because of this that in September 1943 the Allies carried out two devastating bombing raids within a week of one another on the city. The first destroyed 700 buildings and badly damaged thousands more. Fourteen hundred people were killed. A week later the second raid destroyed another 800 buildings and although casualties were much lower, 200 people were killed. The fires after the second raid burned for three days.

Robert returned to Paris on December 1 and that day met Yvonne Grover-Williams and Mme Fremont at the Brasserie Sherry at the Rond Point des Champs-Élysées. The two women had arranged to have a meeting with Stella Tayssedre and were surprised when Robert appeared in her place. They discussed the collapse of Chestnut and Robert, calling his brother "un salaud" (a swine), explained that it was Maurice who had betrayed the Servon network. Benoist then asked Mme Fremont if she could collect some of his clothing from a cleaner as he had lost most of his clothes in Chartres. As a result they met again the next day.

Déricourt returned from the south later that week and Robert gave him a message to be sent to London. An abbreviated version was broadcast by one of Déricourt's radio operators - the recently-arrived Arthur Watt (Geoffroi) - on December 10. The message was very clear: Robert warned London that his brother was "dangerous".

In mid-December, following the intervention of the Swiss Legation in Paris, the Germans released Georges Laurent, who had been in Fresnes for four months. Mme Fremont learned of his release and immediately telephoned his apartment and requested a meeting. They met at Laurent's office at Pathéphone on the Boulevard des Italiens just before Christmas and he explained that he had shared a cell with Albert Fremont and told Mme Fremont that after his arrest he had been shown a detailed account of the activities of Chestnut, which he was told by the Germans had been supplied by Maurice Benoist.

"Achille (Dowlen) did not say anything," he told Mme Fremont, "Sebastien (Willy Grover) said nothing. Only one person talked. That was Maurice."

Nine months later, after Paris had been liberated, Laurent and his wife paid a visit to Yvonne Grover at the rue Weber. By then Stella Tayssedre was staying with Yvonne and Laurent told the two women of Maurice's involvement in his arrest. He added that Maurice had distributed pictures of Antelme among his friends, telling them that it was the Mauritian who had betrayed Chestnut.

After meeting Déricourt Robert went back to Nantes where he continued his work recruiting and training men for the four Clergyman sub-networks. He completed a reconnaissance of the electricity pylons at the Ile Héron but having no explosives and no means of contacting London there was little that he could do to demolish the vast metal structures. It was during this same period that Robert made contact with a man called Alphonse Partouche, whom Antelme had suggested might be a good recruit for the SOE networks. Partouche was a 38-year-old from Algeria who had been a successful boxer before moving to France. They met in a café and initially Partouche was extremely wary. Gradually Robert won his confidence and soon they were planning to create a new sub-network that would kidnap and assassinate important members of the SD and those who were collaborating with the Germans. The plan was to gather information about the SD and at the same time make the Germans aware that they could not operate with the same freedom as before. Robert and Alphonse wanted the Germans to live in fear and drew up a list of targets which included Karl Boemelberg, the head of the Gestapo in France, who worked from headquarters in 82 Avenue Foch; the SD chief Josef Kieffer, whom Robert knew had led the interrogation of Willy. He lived on the fourth floor at the Avenue Foch, just below where the SOE prisoners were held. The list also included Henri Lafont, a criminal whose gang was working openly for the SS from a house in the rue Lauriston.

Robert and Alphonse rented a villa in the suburbs that they transformed into a prison. When he returned to England Benoist requested further equipment to carry out this work, asking for silenced pistols and Sten guns, incendiaries, grenades and knives. Partouche proved to be a most useful recruit because he was able to obtain information about random German raids that were taking place around Blois and Amboise. The Germans would arrest around 40 people in each raid, hoping that they would sweep up resistance helpers. Most of the people arrested were of no interest to the Germans and were quickly released but there was always the possibility that someone important might fall into the net. Alphonse posed as a collaborator and was able to warn Robert where to expect the next raid. Benoist did his best to ensure that the information was passed on to the local resistance leaders. Throughout this period Robert avoided all contact with his family. He spent some of his time with his mistress Huguette Stocker, who had houses in both St Nazaire and Paris. At Christmas Robert went back to Paris to see the family. He discreetly asked his son-in-law André Garnier if he would be interested in helping out as a wireless operator with the new Clergyman network and Garnier agreed. From then on Garnier and Robert met every week.

On that same trip to Paris Robert again met Déricourt. The SOE's Air Movement Officer had no news for him and so Robert concluded that he should follow the original plan and return to England in January. He asked Déricourt to make the necessary arrangements. On his way back to Nantes, he stopped off at the family estate at Auffargis to see if any of the arms dumps had survived the German raid. There was nothing left. He went on to Angers where, early in January, he met an F Section agent called Philippe Liewer (Clement), who was running the Salesman circuit in Normandy.

Liewer had been a journalist before the war and had then become involved in one of the earliest resistance groups in France but was soon captured by the Vichy police and put in a prison camp at Mauzac in the Dordogne. In October 1941 he and a group of SOE agents talked the French guards into allowing them to escape and they travelled to Lyon where, with the help of Virginia Hall, they were able to escape to England via Spain. Liewer was then recruited by the SOE and after completing his training was sent back to France in March 1943 to run the Salesman network. With the help of Liewer's radio operator Isidore Newman (Athlete) Robert was able to get a message through to London, explaining the problems he had been encountering. London was surprised. They thought that Robert had been arrested and replied to Athlete: "For Lionel. Delighted to hear from you. Come back with Clement."

But the winter weather in the January moon period meant that the Moon Squadrons could not venture to France and it was not until the first week of February that they ventured across the English Channel again. Robert got word of the flight from Déricourt and went to Paris and the day before his departure he telephoned Maurice and arranged a meeting for the day of his departure. Afterwards they went their separate ways, Robert making his way to the Gare Montparnasse and, having made sure he was not being followed, taking a train to Angers. There he met up with Liewer and his assistant Robert Maloubier, who had been wounded while escaping after being arrested by the Germans. The three men made their way to the now-familiar landing ground at Soucelles, where they met Henri Déricourt. There had been no operations in January and Déricourt had 10 passengers that night, including the owner of the restaurant in Tiercé and his wife, who were being flown out of France for their own safety, as their establishment had been used rather too often as a rendezvous point by the F Section agents. That evening Squadron Leader Len Ratcliff was flying Hudson P for Peter, but instead of carrying 10 incoming agents as Déricourt had expected, the Hudson arrived with only one man on board. F Section's Operations Officer Major Gerry Morel had been sent to France to take Déricourt back to London, where F Section wanted to question him about allegations that he was working with the Germans. There had been so many allegations made about Déricourt (notably by Henri Frager) that the F Section chiefs in London felt that they had to act. Morel's orders were to bring back Déricourt, at gunpoint if necessary. The arrival of Morel was intended to surprise Déricourt, allowing the Operations Officer to get him on board the plane without drama. Morel was dressed in an RAF uniform in case the plane was shot down and he was captured. But things went wrong as soon as the door of the Hudson was opened. Morel emerged with a flourish but the backwash of air from the propellers blew his neat RAF cap away into the darkness. Déricourt's assistant Rémy Clément chased after it, aware that if it was not found the landing site could be compromised and could not be used again. As Clément scurried around in the dark looking for the hat, Morel tried to explain over the noise of the engines that Déricourt must board the plane immediately to return to England. Déricourt refused point blank, explaining that he had expected 10 incoming agents and that it would not be fair to leave Clément in a position where he had to disperse the 10 bicycles by himself. If they were left hidden in the bushes above the landing site they could be discovered and that would be the end of "The English Airport".

Morel was not prepared for that argument and in the end agreed on a compromise. Déricourt must be at the same landing field five nights later to be taken to England. The Air Movements Officer gave his word that he would be at the rendezvous and, with all the passengers by now safely on board the plane, the door of the Hudson was closed and Squadron Leader Ratcliff opened up the throttles. The Hudson bounced away across the field, all those on board perplexed by the charade which they had just witnessed.

It was only when Robert was being debriefed in London that it became clear that Déricourt was under suspicion. Robert was shocked and reacted strongly in Déricourt's favour. Henri had done nothing to harm the Chestnut network Robert rejected any suggestion of disloyalty. He had no reason to doubt his friend, a man who had twice helped him to escape from France.

A few days later, as he had promised, Henri Déricourt returned to London to face the F Section investigation. He was confronted with the allegations but simply replied that in order to work effectively for F Section it had been necessary for him to be on good terms with the Germans. He added that he had supplied them with black market oranges. He did not explain all his connections with the Germans but gave a very convincing performance.

✠

In some respects F Section did not want to discover the truth. Déricourt was at that point in the war F Section's star performer and had been recommended for a Distinguished Service Order when he returned from France the first time, which would have been F Section's first such award. The medal was stopped when the investigations began into his conduct.

Déricourt was not in the clear until a secret official enquiry had been held. This took place in the old Northumberland Hotel on Northumberland Avenue. The conclusion reached was that no case could be proved against Déricourt but it was decided that it would be best if he were not to return to France. For a few weeks Déricourt stayed at the Savoy Hotel and dined one evening with Benoist at Madame Prunier's famous fish restaurant in St James Street.

Déricourt and his wife Jeannot, who had accompanied him to England, spent the next few weeks having a rest before Henri found a job with the Free French, flying General Pierre Koenig and his staff around. By September 1944 he had switched to doing reconnaissance work and crashed near Châteauroux, suffering a fracture to his skull, a broken wrist, shoulder and several ribs and a small haemorrhage in one of his lungs. He spent five months in hospital.

An official report into the accident concluded that he had flown into some overhead cables. After the war he went back to professional flying but in April 1946 he was arrested on gold-smuggling charges at London's Croydon Airport while apparently transporting some of Général de Gaulle's wartime gold stocks back to France. He was fined £500 and deported. Someone else paid the fine. Later that year Déricourt was arrested in Paris and charged with having collaborated with the Germans. He spent several months in jail before the trial began in May 1948 at the Tribunal Militaire Permanent de Paris at the Caserne de Reuilly. He was cleared of the charges in no small part due to the intervention in the case of Buckmaster's deputy Nicholas Bodington, who explained that he had known of Déricourt's contacts with the Germans. Déricourt was acquitted although as the years went by more and more evidence emerged suggesting that his links with the Germans had been much stronger than they had appeared at the trial.

The German investigator Ernst Vogt reported that Déricourt was an agent of General Boemelberg of the Gestapo, rather than working directly with the SD, although his contact with the Germans was limited to meetings at an apartment near the Arc de Triomphe where he usually met Joseph Goetz. Neither Vogt nor Goetz had been at the trial but both were quite certain that Déricourt was supplying the SD with documents from the networks. Déricourt also gave details of his operations on the understanding that agents would not be arrested. In this way he was able to protect the majority as the SD did not have the manpower to mount widespread surveillance operations. Déricourt maintained that he had been playing off the Germans and working for the British. The fact that Bodington came to his assistance is perhaps not a surprise as Henri was the only one who could answer the question of whether or not Bodington had knowingly sent Agazarian into a trap at the rue de Rome. The pair was tied together by their past.

After the trial Déricourt returned to flying but was rarely in France. He was employed by various airlines in the 1950s, notably in Indochina and Beirut. In 1957 he hit the headlines once again when he crashed on landing at Orly but he emerged unscathed and returned to

South-East Asia where it appears he was working as a drug-smuggler when he was killed in a plane crash in Laos in November 1962.

Perhaps because of the Déricourt connection or perhaps because of the activities of Maurice, Benoist underwent more than the usual debriefing for an agent returning from France.

"I was favourably impressed by Benoist," wrote one of the SOE debriefing officers, "but in view of the previous escape he made in August 1943 of a rather spectacular nature the following points are worthy of note: He has again made an apparently easy escape from the Germans, this time by jumping off a lorry after his arrest by a Feldgendarme in Chartres. His parents, previously reported shot by the Germans, were actually released. His brother Maurice was released from prison after 12 days and has since been working openly with the Germans."

The SOE report concluded: "it seems strange that Robert, having warned us about his brother and having stated that he was having nothing to do with him, should have gone to see him in Paris before he left for the UK, apparently without any real reason for doing so."

If there were suspicions in London, the fact that Robert had admitted to the meeting with Maurice without any need to do so suggested that this was a personal matter. Perhaps Robert was trying to understand his brother; trying to make sense of the betrayal. If Robert explained his action it was not recorded in official papers, although he did reveal some of the things that Maurice said in the course of the conversation. This led to Robert being asked to attend an interview with MI5, the security service, in Bayswater.

Maurice had talked about a German curfew pass that he had given to France Antelme in June 1943. It had been intended to go to England to be copied but Maurice told Robert that he had seen the very same document at the Avenue Foch when he had been arrested in August. He said that this proved that there was a traitor within F Section in London. When the story was checked it was discovered that

Maurice's original pass had been delivered to London by Déricourt and had not been returned to France. And that meant that Maurice was either lying or had seen a copy of the document at the Avenue Foch.

By 1945 Maurice had changed the story, telling Allied investigators that he had seen a photograph of the pass. By then Déricourt's role as a double agent had come to light and so it was concluded that the Air Movements Officer had allowed the Germans to copy the pass before it was sent to London, another unimportant piece of paper handed over to the Germans by Déricourt as he played his dangerous game with the SD.

Robert also told MI5 that during their meeting Maurice asked Robert if he knew Prosper. Robert, not wanting to give anything away, said he did not. Maurice went on to tell his brother that Prosper was working for the Germans, interpreting all the signals sent to France. In addition, Maurice claimed, Prosper had marked all the British networks on a large map at the Avenue Foch. Robert told MI5 that he had told his brother that such a thing was simply not possible and had then changed the subject. MI5 were curious to ask more questions and asked Robert to return for a second interview on Saturday February 19.

CHAPTER FOURTEEN

For a year and a half Robert had been working secretly in France; he had had several extraordinary escapes, but on the night before his second MI5 interview the Germans nearly got him. After a long period without air raids, London was once again a target, the Luftwaffe had begun a campaign with a 227-bomber raid on the night of January 21 and a similar scale raid the following evening. They returned again on January 29 and raided London five times in the first two weeks of February.

On the night of February 18/19 a force of 200 German bombers dropped 140 tons of bombs on London. The Luftwaffe suffered heavy losses to night fighters and anti-aircraft guns but the damage was extensive. The apartment where Robert was staying was badly damaged but Robert emerged unscathed and the following morning went for a second interview with MI5. Details of that interview were not recorded but afterwards he was promoted to the rank of acting Captain. Obviously MI5 had decided that it had no objection to him returning to France again.

Because of the bombing Benoist ended up staying with Maloubier, which meant that he did not have a very quiet life. The younger SOE agents were drawn to the nightclubs in the West End, despite the bombing raids and, in the company of Maloubier and Liewer, Robert met some of the new generation of agents including the beautiful Violette Szabo, an agent that Liewer had encountered while doing a parachute training course at Ringway. Although Robert would be in London for only 10 days, he also met the Australian Nancy Wake and Harry Peuleve. Security in London at the time was not what once it had been. By early 1944 the London cabbies had started to refer to the Baker Street area as "Spy Headquarters" as the district was filled with people in all manner of different uniforms, speaking all manner of different languages. The cabbies were quick to catch on to what was going on. All along Baker Street and Gloucester Place, which run parallel to one another from Portman Square north to Marylebone Road, the SOE had requisitioned buildings to provide office space and quarters for the large number of personnel. At the centre of the web was 64 Baker Street, which had been the organization's headquarters since 1940. Then there was Norgeby House, at 83 Baker Street and St Michael's House at number 82. Off Baker Street to the west were the apartment buildings Bickenhall Mansions and Montagu Mansions where agents were housed. To the east was Duke Street where Colonel André Dewavrin (Colonel Passy) had set up shop at 10 Duke Street in order for his Bureau Central de Renseignements et d'Action to coordinate the actions of SOE's RF Section, while around the corner was F Section's safe house at Orchard Court.

The neighbourhood was full of spies and saboteurs.

The SOE tried to keep its agents busy when their training was complete but there were times when the weather was bad, the departures had to be delayed and there were agents everywhere.

Colonel Buckmaster was reluctant to let Benoist return to France. The F Section chief was worried about Robert's safety given what had happened during his previous mission. When he expressed these doubts Robert fought back, arguing that there was no reason why he could not return to the Nantes region to carry out the missions for which he had been trained and which he had planned in great detail. Buckmaster had to accept that this was a perfectly valid argument. There was no point in sending over someone else to blow up the electricity pylons over the Loire on the Île Héron, to the east of the city. Robert's people were already in place and he had also put together teams to attack the railways in and around Nantes. It made no sense to send out someone they did not know: mistakes might be made and people lost. It was better to stick with the original plan.

Buckmaster agreed that Robert would return to Nantes. It was logical that he should continue to use the cover name of Daniel Perdrigé, as the Germans had yet to find out about it and his code name was to stay as Lionel, so as not to confuse the networks.

Robert was called back to Orchard Court on February 29. To his original targets was added the task of disrupting the telephone systems in Nantes in the hours after the invasion began. In order to achieve this Robert was instructed to avoid any form of assault on the main telephone exchange in Nantes as it was felt that this would probably result in heavy casualties because the exchange was heavily defended. Instead Robert was given a microfilm, showing maps of the Nantes telephone networks with instructions as to the location of the critical junctions that he and his teams should attack. This would be much more effective in disrupting communications and would take much longer to repair. Robert was given a number of messages to memorize. These would be broadcast on the BBC French Service and would act as signals for him to alert his sabotage groups and go into action. There were two different sets of messages he would hear in the days leading up to the landings. These would warn him that the invasion was imminent. The second messages were the trigger to send the sabotage teams into action.

The attack on the pylons on the Île Héron was not included in the actions for D Day but was to be performed as soon as was possible. Robert was provided with details of a field not far from Nantes that could serve as a landing ground for arms and explosives and was instructed to organise a drop there as soon as he could after his arrival. In order to get as much done in as short a space of time as possible Robert was given another half million francs (around £35,000 at today's values) and told to radio for more money when he knew how much he might need.

F Section insisted, however, that Robert concentrate his

activities in the Nantes region and steer clear of Paris. Once his tasks in Nantes were accomplished he could hand over activities to a deputy in Nantes and move to Paris to continue his other activities there.

To make life easier he would be given his own radio operator, Denise Bloch. Like Robert she was a resistance veteran and knew how to operate underground. Denise was Jewish although this was not immediately evident as she was a striking blonde. When she allowed her carefully bleached hair to grow out she was naturally dark-haired. She was broad shouldered and athletic and had been an early recruit to the resistance movement, coming into contact with F Section through her role as Jean Aron's secretary at the Citroën works at the Quai de Javel in Paris in 1941 before being sent to her home city of Lyon in order to "baby-sit" Brian Stonehouse (Celestin), a British agent who had run into trouble because his French was not good enough for him to survive by himself. He was a member of Henri Sevenet's Detective network. Bloch acted as a courier and looked after Stonehouse for four months before he was arrested by the German radio direction finders. After that she escaped to the south where she rejoined Aron, who was also now working for Sevenet, but after narrowly escaping arrest it was agreed that she should return to Lyon. She travelled with Aron and Sevenet but when they arrived in Lyon Aron was arrested. The Germans had raided his apartment in the city and had found a photograph of him. It was not clear how they discovered that he and Bloch would be travelling up to Lyon but it may have come after a raid on the Bloch family apartment, where they found pictures of Denise and a letter to her mother, explaining that she would soon be back in the city. Sevenet was right behind Aron when he was arrested but managed to walk out of the trap while Bloch was fortunate as she chose a different exit from the station and avoided arrest.

When it became clear what had happened Sevenet and Bloch left Lyon and hid out with a friend in the country. As the Germans had her picture she decided to dye her hair blonde and she then travelled south to the small village of Villefranche-sur-Mer on the

Mediterranean coast, where she hid out between November and January 1943, her only trip being to Nice to visit the hairdresser in order to have her hair dyed again.

Finally Sevenet sent word that he was working in Toulouse and that she should join him there. Hoping to escape into Spain, she headed for Toulouse and was given a guide to take her through the mountains but the snows were too deep and there were too many German patrols, so the attempt was called off and she went back to Toulouse. She began working as a courier for Colonel George Starr (Hilaire) of the Wheelwright network, based in the town of Agen. In April 1943 Wheelwright lost Maurice Pertschuk (Eugene) and his wireless operator Marcus Bloom (Urbain) and Starr decided that Bloch had better leave the region and so sent her across the border into Spain from where she travelled on to London. The journey was remarkably quick and she arrived in Britain just a month after leaving Agen. Bloch was sent off to training school where her reports suggested that she was argumentative. This was because she had more knowledge about life in Occupied France than did her instructors.

When she graduated from the SOE schools F Section found itself in an odd situation. After months when there had been no radio operators available, London suddenly found it had more than were needed. Yvonne Cormeau (Annette) had been parachuted to Starr's Wheelwright organisation and that left Bloch with nowhere to go when she in turn finished her training. She was no longer needed in the south-west of France. Because she was not really known in Paris and Nantes, Buckmaster decided that she should go with Benoist. She would return to France with several sets of false papers: identifying her as Micheline Rabatel, Danielle Williams and a third set in the name of Boitel. She was given the code name Ambroise, although she was also known to other networks as Crinoline or Line.

Benoist and Bloch went back to France on the night of Thursday, March 2. Neither had been trained to parachute and so they travelled in one of the Moon Squadron Lysanders to a reception on the wide-open plains to the south-west of Paris. The closest village was a small farming community called Baudreville. Their pilot that night, Flying Officer Douglas Bell, was new to the Moon Squadrons and had the right to be nervous. On his one previous mission, three weeks earlier, he had watched as a second Lysander on the same mission had crashed and burst into flames as it landed in a field near Vierzon. Bell had had to abort the mission and fly back to England with his passengers still on board.

With Déricourt having been withdrawn from France the mission was organised by the Air Movements Officer of the Secret Intelligence Service (MI6) Pierre Tissier (Pierrot) and it was he was who put Benoist and Bloch on a train at Angerville the following morning. They arrived at the Gare d'Austerlitz in Paris and Robert quickly took Bloch to the apartment in the rue Fustel de Coulanges. A few days later she rented a flat in the rue Raynouard in Passy. This was to be Clergyman's second safe house.

Soon after he returned to France, Robert met a friend called Maurice Henry.

"His face shone as he gave me the information about the material destined for the landings that he had been able to see in England and the training of the men," remembered Henry. "His faith in final victory was unbreakable."

Robert was careful to make sure that his brother Maurice did not know that he was back in Paris but one day, in need of a van, he sent Charlotte Perdrigé (Sonia) to visit Maurice in the Boulevard Berthier, to ask him if he might loan her the Ford truck which he knew that Maurice owned. She carried a letter with her from Robert. It was a dangerous move for Robert but he clearly believed that Maurice would never betray his own brother. Charlotte was given the truck and the Germans did not find out about it. After that Robert stayed away from his brother, although they did speak on the telephone from time to time. Robert and Denise then followed orders and headed off to Nantes in the truck. They would return to Paris on several occasions in the months that followed, Bloch instructing André Garnier in the art of transmitting with a British wireless set and Robert keeping up with his work with Alphonse Partouche. Benoist continued to recruit for the Clergyman network in the Rambouillet area and it was during this period that he decided to approach Jean-Pierre Wimille, the man that Willy Grover had refused to have anything to do with.

☨

Benoist and Wimille had always enjoyed a close relationship, despite the fact that Jean-Pierre was 13 years younger. He had grown up surrounded by motor racing, his father Auguste having been a leading motoring and aviation journalist. Jean-Pierre showed no signs of interest in the sport until after he had completed his military service, during which he served as a chauffeur in the French colonies in North Africa. When he returned to France he started attending races and, so legend has it, soon challenged Benoist and Roger Labric to race their road cars from Maintenon to Rambouillet, a distance of 13 miles. Little is known of this escapade except that Wimille's Sandford cycle car ended up smashing into a tree. The ambitious youngster escaped unhurt and, having been inspired by the encounter, borrowed money to buy himself a private Bugatti Type 37. In September 1930 he headed south for his first race, the Grand Prix de l'ACF at Pau. It was an ambitious start but Wimille did not disgrace himself. The problem was that the rules of Grand Prix racing then changed and what was needed for 1931 was a car capable of lasting for 10 hours of racing.

The Bugatti Showroom in Paris was a meeting place for racing drivers and Wimille was there one day and met Jean Gaupillat, the son of a wealthy ammunition manufacturer, who had started his own precision engineering business in Meudon. Gaupillat was 17 years older than Wimille and too old for a serious racing career, but he enjoyed racing and realised that sharing a car with a young charger like Wimille would bring good results. He was satisfied with that.

The partnership lasted only until the end of July 1931 when the suspension on the car collapsed when Wimille was racing at Dieppe and the Bugatti crashed heavily. Wimille was thrown out, but escaped unharmed. That was the end of his racing season.

In the course of the winter Wimille talked his way into borrowing a Bugatti Type 54 from the Bugatti factory and in March 1932 made an immediate impression by setting the fastest time on the La Turbie hillclimb. He then headed to Africa for the Grand Prix de Tunisie in Carthage but suffered an engine failure although by then Wimille had charmed the wealthy Madame Marguerite Mareuse, one of the first women to race at Le Mans, to loan him her Type 51 in order to take part in the Oran Grand Prix. He won the race and the prize money was such that when he returned to France he was able to acquire an Alfa Romeo 8C-2300 Monza, with which he remained a frontrunner in France for the rest of the year, winning at Nancy. In August he entered the Grand Prix de Comminges on the St Gaudens circuit and was leading the race when he lost control of the car and crashed heavily. He was thrown out of the car and cut his upper lip so badly that he would be scarred for life. It did not bother him because he thought the scar made him look like Humphrey Bogart and thus made him more attractive to women.

Women were an important element in his life.

After the accident Wimille calmed down a little and in the course of the 1933 season, when he teamed up with Raymond Sommer, running a pair of Alfa Romeos, his results began to improve As a result he was chosen by Benoist to drive for the Bugatti factory team in 1934. Wimille's dreams of glory in Grand Prix racing were to be frustrated by the arrival of the Nazi-funded Mercedes-Benz and AutoUnion teams which soon dominated the racing scene. Only Alfa Romeo, which had backing from Benito Mussolini, was in a position to mount an occasional challenge to the Silver Arrows. Bugatti did not have the budget to compete.

Wimille was frustrated, but at the end of 1935 he set off with

Left: When Robert Benoist joined the Special Operations Executive, he became a British officer and was photographed in uniform. He returned to France in the spring of 1944 but was arrested soon after D Day in June 1944. For two months he was held by the Germans in Paris, undergoing interrogation, and then in early August was deported to the Buchenwald concentration camp. On September 10 he met the artist Auguste Favier, who sketched him. The resulting drawing shows the strain that Benoist had been under. He was executed the following day.

244 - The Grand Prix Saboteurs

Top left: Denise Bloch, Robert Benoist's radio operator with the Clergyman SOE network. She was executed by the Germans at the Ravensbrück concentration camp. Top centre: Forrest Yeo-Thomas, the celebrated "White Rabbit", who won a George Cross for his courage and leadership while in captivity. He was with Benoist on the journey to Buchenwald. Top right: The Germans told Robert Benoist that Violette Szabo had betrayed him. Above: The gates of Buchenwald. The windows on the left are the cells in which Benoist spent the last hours of his life. Right: The Leichenkeller under the crematorium at Buchenwald. Prisoners were hanged from the hooks embedded in the walls.

Above: During the war Jean-Pierre Wimille was frustrated at being unable to race and so spent him time planning to build a Wimille road car. When racing restarted he won the Coupe des Prisonniers in August 1945 (below).

Above: The Wimille road car was highly innovative. Jean-Pierre Wimille was the top racer of his era and hoped to translate that success into a commercial enterprise but he was killed in an accident in January 1949 in Buenos Aires (left). His funeral (below) in Paris attracted some famous names, including The Duke and Duchess of Windsor. In the background the great Juan Manuel Fangio prays for Wimille. His wife Christiane (right), known always as "Cric", had fought alongside Jean-Pierre in the resistance. She only narrowly escaped being sent to a concentration camp in Germany in August 1944.

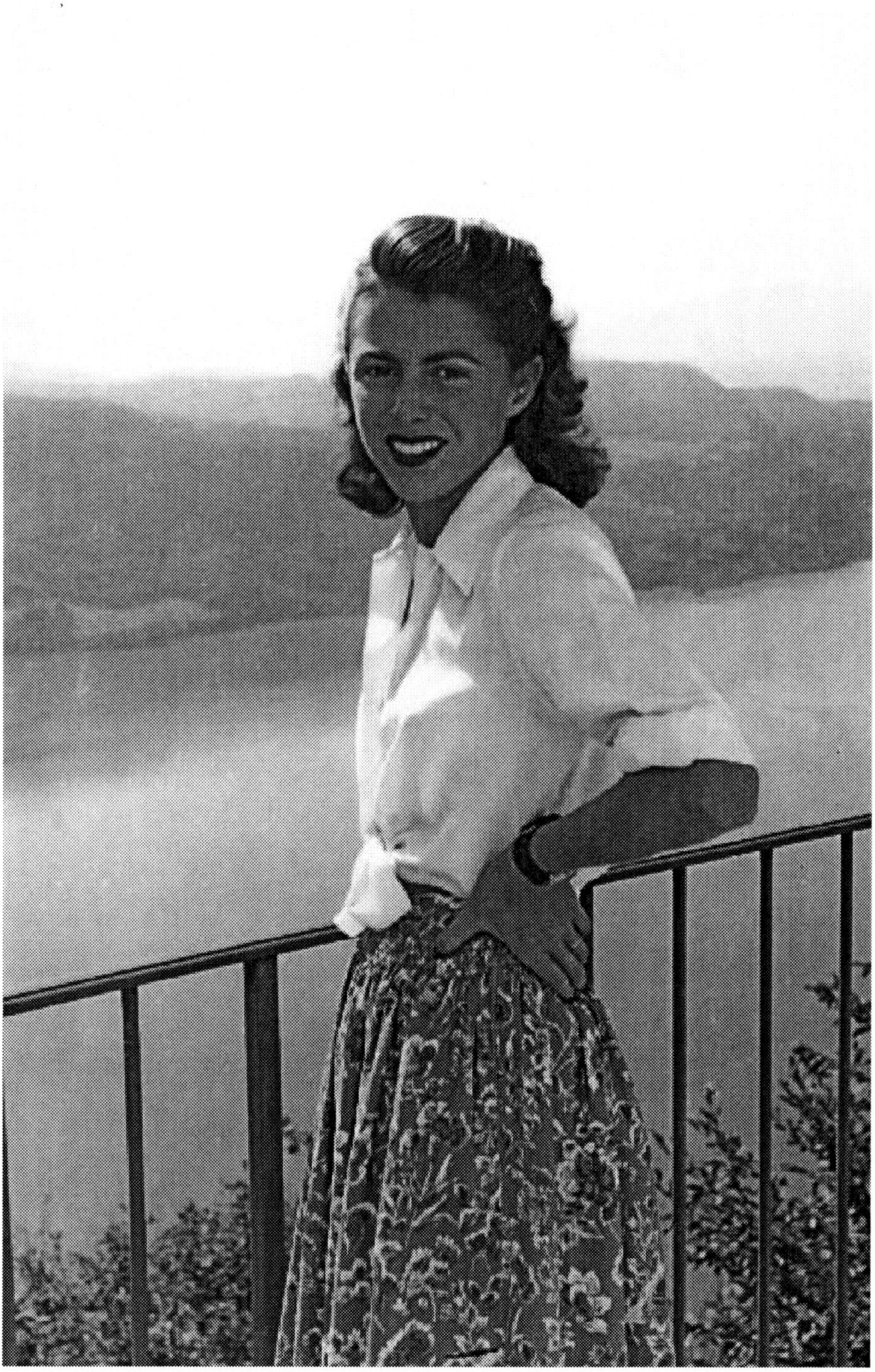

Captains Courageous: Benoist and Williams, together in death on the Brookwood Memorial in Woking, England.

François Sommer, an old friend from national service and brother of Raymond, to fly to South Africa, which in those days was quite an adventure. A Bugatti Type 59 was sent by ship, accompanied by the mechanic Robert Aumaître. The trip provided them with plenty of excitement and after a big storm in East Africa they were actually posted missing for a while. With the plane needing to be repaired Wimille was forced to leave his friends and fly by Imperial Airways from Broken Hill in Northern Rhodesia (now Kabwe, Zambia) to Johannesburg and then take a train to East London, in time to get there for the racing on New Year's Day 1936. He finished second and then flew back to France with Sommer, this time sticking to the coastline and they were back in France by mid-January.

Bugatti had decided to switch its focus to sports car racing, with the aim being to win the Le Mans 24 Hours. Unfortunately the race that year was cancelled because of strikes in France. Desperate for publicity and money to run a racing programme, Robert Benoist sent the team to break long distance records at Montlhéry and in October despatched Wimille to the United States to try to win the Vanderbilt Cup at Roosevelt Raceway on Long Island. The race offered huge prize money and attracted not only Bugatti but also Scuderia Ferrari and private entries from Philippe Étancelin, Raymond Sommer and "Raph", soon to be one of Wimille's closest friends.

Comte George Raphael Béthenod de Montbressieux was a playboy, the son of a wealthy silk manufacturer who had married an Argentine woman. He began racing, sometimes using his mother's maiden name De las Casas and sometimes Raph.

The Vanderbilt Cup took place on a dirt track which was laid out on Roosevelt Field, an aerodrome which had become famous in 1927 when Charles Lindbergh took from there for his solo transatlantic flight aboard the Spirit of St Louis. By the mid-1930s, however, the airfield had been closed and a race track laid out, the design of which would later be copied to create the circuit at Interlagos in Brazil. This featured a series of high-speed curves which were a real challenge on the dirt. Tazio Nuvolari dominated but Wimille came home second and took home a substantial cash prize for Bugatti. This money was sufficient to fund the Le Mans 24 Hours programme in 1937.

Wimille remained as the Bugatti team's lead driver that year and began the programme with a win at Pau in February. This was followed by the 24 Hours, where Wimille, partnered by Benoist, became only the fourth man to win Le Mans at his first attempt. Wimille continued to race that summer but spent much of his time at his family's Villa Tunis in Beaulieu-sur-Mer. That summer Bugatti prepared to race Delahaye to the million franc prize for the French car that could lap Montlhéry fastest by September 1. Jean-Pierre was heading back to Paris from Beaulieu when he was involved in a road accident with a truck and was out of action for some time. Bugatti waited and finally Wimille flew in to try for the money on the last day of the competition, only to be stopped by mechanical trouble.

That winter, while skiing with Raph, he met Christiane de la Fressange, the daughter of the Marquis Paul de la Fressange and Simone Lazard, a member of the renowned Lazard banking family. Cric, as she was known to everyone, was just 17 at the time but would soon become a member of the French national skiing team. Wimille was interested. She was good-looking, wealthy and well-connected and Jean-Pierre, who had political ambitions, recognised the potential of a relationship, particularly as her step-father was Maurice Petsch, a député for the Hautes Alpes departement. He had been Minister of the Colonies in André Tardieu's republican government in 1932.

After the elections of 1936 when the left wing Popular Front swept to power, France's middle class, disenchanted with the general malaise in French politics, looked for a way to avoid a Communist takeover of France. They found Jacques Doriot, who had founded the Parti Populaire Français. A decorated war hero in World War I, Doriot had returned to France from a German prisoner-of-war camp and had risen through the ranks of the French Communist Party. He was elected to the Assemblée Nationale in 1924 and seven years later became the mayor of Saint Denis, a working class suburb to the north of Paris. By then however he had begun to move towards the politics of national socialism, seeing what Mussolini had done in Italy and what Adolf Hitler was doing in Germany. As a result he was expelled from the French Communist Party in 1934. For a time Wimille was a leading PPF supporter and indeed was looking to be a PPF candidate for the elections in 1940, although by then Doriot had begun to style himself on Hitler and had become a strident anti-communist. Wimille and many others turned away.

When war came Doriot's Légion des Voluntaires Français contre le Bolshevisme fought in German uniform against the Russians.

Although he hoped for a political career Wimille continued to race, returning to Grand Prix racing with Bugatti in 1938. By the mid season it was clear that the cars were not competitive and so he did several races for Enzo Ferrari's Alfa Romeo team but in 1939 he agreed to stay with Bugatti and try once again for victory at Le Mans. That was achieved with Pierre Veyron.

By then Europe was descending into war, Wimille's career remained one of frustration. At 31, he knew that his best years as a racing driver would be lost to the war and joined the Armée de l'Air. Being a qualified pilot he soon ended up at the fighter training school at Étampes and after the German invasion he headed south, staying with Marcel Lesurque, an old friend who had won the Monte Carlo Rally in 1939. Demobilisation followed and Wimille found himself at a loose end. It was a good time to decide to settle down and that winter he married Cric in Briançon. As her stepfather was a politician he did not have trouble getting the necessary documentation to cross the Demarcation Line. His best man was Raph, who had by that time become the personal assistant of film star Maurice Chevalier.

Early in 1941 Wimille tried to use his connections in Vichy to organise a trip to the Indianapolis 500 for himself and Raymond Sommer. He applied to Jean Borotra, a famous pre-war tennis star who had become the Minister of Sport in the Vichy government, but received no reply. Frustrated, he spent the summer in Corsica with Louis Chiron and another old racing friend Pierre Leygonie.

Wimille was then asked informally if he would like to join the Vichy government as the director of French automobile racing. The approach was never made official but he told pressmen that if it was he would probably take the job. In 1942 he sold the Villa Tunis to Ettore Bugatti and bought an estate called La Hunière in Sonchamps, a small village to the south of Rambouillet, where he and Cric kept a number of animals to help with the supply of food, which was becoming difficult in Paris. They moved from their apartment on the Avenue de la Grande Armée to a new flat in the rue Murillo, close to Lesurque's garage, where Wimille, Pierre Leygonie and Louis Viel, a former Bugatti engineer, began work on the design of a production car for the post-war era.

✠

After Willy Grover's arrest, Benoist decided that Wimille would be a good recruit for the SOE. Grover, who was well aware of Wimille's politics before the war, refused to have anything to do with him but Benoist was not worried and Wimille joined the Clergyman network and was given the code name of Gilles.

It was during this period that Robert made contact with the Turma-Vengeance resistance movement. This had been formed in July 1943 when the original Action Vengeance network joined forces with another group called Ceux de la Libération to establish Turma-Vengeance, which then became affiliated to the Conseil National de la Résistance.

The first contact was through Paul Beauvallet, a 30-year-old former soldier, who was working as a blacksmith in the village of Granges-le-Roi. This contact led to a meeting with Beauvallet's chief Marcel Bluteau, a garage owner who was chief of the FFI forces in the Dourdan sector, operating under code name Joint, and the man who was in charge of parachute operations.

Curiously, Bluteau told Allied investigators after the war that the first contact between them was made on February 13 1944, although this was impossible because Benoist was in England between February 5 and March 2. Although the Germans often impersonated agents in order to infiltrate resistance networks, in this case it seems that Bluteau simply made a mistake as all the other French records indicate that the first contact came in March. At the first meeting Benoist asked to borrow four machine guns. Bluteau was cautious and asked Benoist to prove that he was a British agent. It was agreed that Robert would arrange for the BBC in London to broadcast the message: "La Fontaine's stories are loved by children". Once this was done, Bluteau and Benoist met a second time and Robert agreed to organise parachute drops for Turma-Vengeance.

Bluteau arranged for Robert to rent the Villa Cécile, a house in the outskirts of Sermaise, just 15 miles to the south-east of Auffargis. Sermaise was a quiet place, nestling in the valley that runs from Dourdan to Arpajon. It was out in the countryside but thanks to a direct railway connection one could be in Paris very quickly. Robert asked Stella and Robert Tayssedre to move to the new house although the radio transmitter in their apartment in Paris remained there.

The link with Turma-Vengeance strengthened quickly with Robert being introduced to Charles Couderc, a 49-year-old legal advisor who was in charge of operations in the region, operating under the code name Commandant Alain. Couderc had been pilot in World War I and so hit it off with Benoist straight away.

Benoist was also put into contact with other senior members of the organisation who asked him whether it would be possible for the Royal Air Force to drop weapons for around 2000 men. Benoist relayed the message to London, and the numbers certainly impressed F Section chiefs.

Robert was put in charge of the arms supply for Turma-

Vengeance and was given the rank of Captain. According to the French records, he appointed Jean-Pierre Wimille as his deputy and had two assistants: Pierre Leygonie and Magahoff Garric. The organisation also listed Stella Tayssedre and Cric Wimille as members of the team, both acting as couriers.

Although Benoist was working closely with the French network, he continued to deal with the F Section activities and at the beginning of April 1944 Philippe Liewer arrived in Paris, bringing the glamorous Violette Szabo with him. When their mission to revive the Salesman network in Normandy ran into difficulties, they went to Robert for help and he arranged for them to spend several days in the apartment in the Rue Fustel de Coulanges.

On April 29 the Turma-Vengeance parachute reception team in Dourdan received the first arms organised by Benoist, with Bluteau and a team of eight locals, including the blacksmith, the plumber and a butcher in action at a landing grand at Granges-le-Roi. Three nights later Benoist and Wimille were present with an even bigger team and a third drop followed on May 5 at Breuillet with almost 20 men collecting the canisters. That haul included 25 machine guns, 15 revolvers, 16 anti-tank weapons, 120 hand grenades, 33 land mines and 45,000 rounds of ammunition, in addition to three radio transmitters and 13 receivers.

With the arms hidden away in various dumps in the valley, Benoist turned his attention to Nantes again and on May 16 he and his sabotage teams blew up the electricity pylons which supplied the city. Electricity supplies were cut and the city's tramway ceased to operate. Nantes was paralysed. It was seven days before the Germans could restore full power and three days after that Benoist and his teams took the power lines down again. Once again the city ground to a halt. Two days later the Allied bombers returned and bombed the railways to the east of the town. Forty-one people were killed. There was another raid two nights later.

Nantes was on its knees.

The Germans were desperately keen to catch the saboteurs and on June 4, during the village fete in Nort, a few miles north of the city, French and German police swept through the merry-makers checking identity papers and arresting a total of 23 men, hoping to stumble upon the saboteurs.

Each evening Robert listened anxiously to the BBC French Service news to see whether or not his D Day messages were broadcast. He continued to try to organize a huge drop of weapons for Turma-Vengeance. The British were working on a plan for a 16-plane parachute drop on June 12, which would include not only weapons for hundreds of men, but also an entire troop of SAS soldiers.

The first hint that the invasion was coming came on Thursday June 1 when the BBC French Service broadcast Robert's two stand-by messages. The word was sent out through the networks that they should be ready to go into action. Robert, L'Antoine and Robert Tayssedre were in Nantes ready to attack the telephone networks while the other Clergyman teams prepared to sabotage the railways, although movement was by then already very restricted because of the aerial bombing and other attacks.

On the evening of Monday June 5 Robert listened as usual to the BBC broadcast from London and heard the messages he had been waiting so long to hear. The invasion was coming. That night Clergyman went into action. The telephone network in Nantes was attacked and the railways sabotaged. All across France partisans working for the British networks felled trees across roads and blew up bridges. The aim was to cause as much disruption to communications and transport as was possible so that the German troops could not move easily around France. That night 950 of the planned 1050 attacks went ahead as arranged and for days afterwards the northern coast of France was isolated from the rest of the country. The Germans tried to restore communication by using despatch riders but the F Section teams had been told to make sure that they ambushed any motorcyclists that they encountered to maintain the upper hand.

Even as the sabotage teams were at work that evening, three Allied divisions of parachute troops were dropping into Normandy, at either end of the planned beachhead. In the east the British 6th Airborne Division landed near Bénouville and seized two vital bridges on the River Orne. At the western end of the beachhead the US 101st and 82nd Airborne Division parachuted from hundreds of Dakota C47s to secure the southern end of the Cotentin Peninsula and by doing so secure the western flank of the attack and cut off the road to Cherbourg. Bad weather meant that the US drop was badly disrupted and units of the 101st and 82nd were scattered. Many dropped into low level land that the Germans had deliberately flooded to secure the area. A lot of the Americans were drowned, dragged beneath the water by the heavy equipment they carried. Another group landed in the village of Ste Mère Eglise and were machined-gunned by the Germans as they were still in the air, the sky having been lit up by a fire in a nearby farmhouse.

Despite heavy losses the two flanks had been secured by the time the first wave of Allied troops hit the beaches as dawn was breaking. On four of the five landing beaches opposition was light but at Omaha Beach the US 1st and 29th Divisions hit trouble when their landing craft became stuck on sand bars before reaching the beach. Hundred of soldiers drowned as they struggled to get to the shore, laden down with heavy equipment and under heavy enemy fire. The defenders at Omaha were not young rookies. They had previously seen action on the Russian Front and they knew how to fight, their heavy and accurate fire, decimating the first wave of Americans. One thousand American soldier were killed, most of them in the first half hour of combat. It took most of the day before the GIs began to win control of "Bloody Omaha".

By the evening of June 6 the Allies had landed around 156,000 troops in Normandy. Hitler's Atlantic Wall had been breached. There were 2,500 Allied dead and another 7,000 wounded or missing. The position was still precarious because the British and American beachheads had not linked up as quickly as expected and the US troops who had been landed on Utah Beach, the western-most of the beaches, were still on their own, although contact had been made with the battered airborne divisions around Ste Mère Eglise. Fighting was still going on at the Omaha beachhead. Supplies and reinforcements were not arriving as quickly as had been planned and, once the initial surprise had been overcome, the Germans were beginning to regroup.

Late in the evening Field Marshal Erwin Rommel, who had been in Germany to celebrate his wife's birthday, arrived back at Army Group B headquarters at La Roche-Guyon, on the Seine, 40 miles to the north-west of Paris, and began to organize the German defence. The Allies had air superiority but the Normandy hedgerows, known as the bocage, favoured the defenders. The patchwork of small fields, divided by thick hedges and sunken roads, made it very difficult for the Allies to move forward. The fighting in the weeks that followed was ferocious as the Germans tried to stop the advance.

✠

German units in central and southern France were ordered north to join the battle but they had to fight their way through constant attacks orchestrated by the SOE and other resistance groups. In Benoist's old stamping ground around Rambouillet there were further attacks by Robert's men and a few days later Denise Bloch was able to radio London with the news that all enemy traffic in the Dourdan-Rambouillet area was at a standstill.

The landings were greeted with jubilation across France. Suddenly everyone wanted to be part of the resistance, or at least wanted to be seen to have been involved.

In most areas there simply were not enough weapons to go around. In some places there was open insurrection but, more often than not, this ended in disaster. The Germans were still very much in control. In Normandy villagers of Graignes joined up with a group of 200 US paratroopers from the US 507th Parachute Infantry Regiment who had landed 20 miles away from their intended target. For a week they held off a Panzer regiment, hoping that the Allied invasion forces would arrive before they were overrun. In the end those who had not been wounded fled into the marshes. Anyone who was left behind was shot when the Germans arrived.

Across France a number of resistance units rose up in open insurrection and paid a heavy price. In the Vercors around 4000 armed men battled the Germans for several weeks before the uprising was crushed with heavy loss of life. In the Dordogne a call to arms and attacks on the Das Reich regiment, en route from Toulouse to Normandy, led to a the destruction of the town of Mouleydier during a battle between the Germans and the resistants. The Frenchmen who were captured after the battle were executed.

Further north frustration caused by the attacks on the Germans led the soldiers of Das Reich to violent retaliation in the town of Oradour-sur-Glane. On the morning of June 10 the Germans arrived in the town, rounded up the population and then put the women and children in the church and split up the men in six different barns. They were then massacred, some being burned alive when the buildings were set on fire. A total of 642 men, women and children were murdered.

Robert and the other members of Clergyman returned to Paris as soon as they could, their next objective being to harass the German forces as much as possible while the battles raged in Normandy. The members of Turma-Vengeance were keen to go into action.

"Paris was full of hope," remembered Stéphane Hessel, an agent working for Général de Gaulle in SOE's RF Section. "There was a feeling of exhilaration. People who had been cautious now had the feeling that the end was coming near. The Germans took advantage of that and there were a lot of arrests in those last weeks."

The war was not over.

CHAPTER FIFTEEN

To those in the Valley of the Chevreuse the fierce battles raging in Normandy seemed a very long way away. Robert and his group had done important work in Nantes but they wanted to fight in the open. Robert, in particular, wanted to take on the Germans head-on. He was lobbying London to parachute weapons for hundreds of men, so that the members of Turma-Vengeance could rise up in open revolt. This was not as outrageous as it sounds as across France Special Air Service (SAS) commando teams, known as Jedburghs, were being parachuted in to organise and support local resistance groups. The June 12 drop designed for Benoist and his two networks was only called off because of bad weather.

While the discussions were going on, Robert had one other thing to worry about. His mother Jeanne had never fully recovered from the four months she had spent in Fresnes prison the previous autumn. She was 68 years old and now very frail. Ten days after the landings in Normandy her condition worsened and she became dangerously ill. It was clear that she needed hospital treatment and, unable to find an ambulance, Maurice Benoist used his connections in the Ministry of Agriculture to get hold of a gas-powered Hotchkiss with all the necessary authorisations. Jeanne Benoist was driven to the Clinique Bizet, a private hospital on the rue Georges Bizet, just off the Avenue d'Iéna in the 16ème arrondissement . Her condition did not improve and it became clear that she was dying. On Sunday June 18 Robert's sister Madeleine Belligand decided that she must tell Robert about his mother's condition. Madeleine knew of Robert's activities in the Resistance and had been involved to the extent that one of the

Clergyman's radio transmitters was hidden in her apartment on the Boulevard Magenta in the centre of Paris. Maurice had no idea of his sister's involvement in resistance work and, although he knew Robert was in France, he did not know how to contact him.

Madeleine was married but was involved in another relationship with a resistance worker called Paul Massonet (Mic). As the Villa Cécile did not have a telephone Madeleine asked Massonet to drive out to Sermaise to see Robert and tell him about the seriousness of the situation and requested that he bring Robert back to the city so that he could see his mother before she died. Madeleine told Massonet that she would make sure that Robert and Maurice did not meet. Massonet set off for Sermaise in a pre-war Simca and arrived at the Villa Cécile as the members of the Clergyman network were sitting down for dinner that evening. There were hurried consultations and Robert announced that he was leaving for Paris immediately. He knew it was a dangerous thing to do but it was his mother and there was nothing he could do about the risk. It was agreed that Charlotte Perdrigé would accompany him and Robert instructed the others that if the two of them had not returned by lunchtime on Monday the gang should abandon the Villa Cécile and go to ground. André Garnier later remembered that they had all thought that Robert was joking. The D Day landings had made victory seem a lot closer and the need for security seemed to be less important than it had been the days before the Allied armies in France gave the nation hope.

After the little Simca had departed Bloch, L'Antoine the chauffeur, Garnier and the Tayssedres settled down to have dinner. It was a quiet summer evening and the war seemed a long way away.

Jeanne Benoist died before Robert reached the Clinique Bizet. Robert, Charlotte and Massonet found Madeleine grieving her mother's death. It is not clear whether Georges Benoist or Maurice were there but that seems unlikely as Maurice later insisted that he did not see Robert at all during his final mission. Robert paid his respects to his mother and then, accompanied by Charlotte, Madeleine and

Massonet, went to his sister's apartment on the Boulevard Magenta. It was already late and none of them was hungry but they ate a sombre dinner with what little food there was available and then Robert announced that he and Charlotte must get on with their work. There would be a funeral but Robert could not risk attending in case the Germans were watching out for him. He and Charlotte took the Métro across town to the safe house in the rue Fustel de Coulanges.

It was too late to go back to Sermaise and they had to move quickly to get to the safe house before the curfew began. The keys to the apartment had always been left with the concierge Pauline Cornet so that if those who used it were arrested there would be nothing in their pockets to give away the safe house. That meant that in order to get into the flat they had to call on the concierge when they arrived. Just before midnight Robert knocked quietly on the door and heard the expected rustling from inside. He was preparing to make his apologies and explain about his mother but when the door swung open, he found himself looking into the barrel of a pistol. Robert and Charlotte were not armed and trying to escape would have been suicide. They were taken at gunpoint by two Frenchmen to the apartment on the fourth floor where they found four SS men waiting for them. It was clear that they had been there for some hours as the apartment had been ransacked. It was later established that the Germans had been in the apartment since eight o'clock in the morning. They had been waiting for Robert.

One of the Germans telephoned the Avenue Foch to say that they had captured Benoist and then, because it was late at night, they waited for instructions. Not long afterwards the telephone rang. It was a pre-arranged call from Paul Massonet, which had been designed to make sure that Robert had not been arrested. It had been agreed in advance by members of the gang that if such a situation occurred they would use a simple code as a warning to the others. If they had fallen into a trap the prisoner would reply with his or her cover name; if everything was well they would use their real name. One of the Germans answered the phone but said nothing. He handed the receiver to Charlotte.

"Ici Sonia," Charlotte said. "Ici Sonia."

Massonet did not appear to have made the connection (or perhaps he did not hear) because Charlotte found that she was talking to Madeleine. She repeated the warning and afterwards was confident that Robert's sister had understood that the group was in danger. She hoped that Madeleine would warn the rest of the group in Sermaise.

Perhaps in her grief or because of the late hour, Madeleine did not realize what Charlotte had been trying to tell her and after a short and meaningless conversation, she hung up and retired to bed.

It had been an awful day but Robert tried to remain positive. There was nothing he could do for his mother and now his priority was to save himself and his group. He knew that if they took him to the Avenue Foch it would be hard to get away and so he decided to act quickly and asked the Germans if he might be allowed to visit the lavatory. Once inside he opened one of the handcuffs and, having managed that, opened a small window that looked out onto the courtyard and tried to climb through, intending to go up to the roof and escape. But the Germans did not give him enough time to get away and he was dragged back through the window. The handcuffs were re-attached and in the early hours of Monday morning Robert and Charlotte were driven across a deserted Paris to the SD offices in the Avenue Foch. They were taken to the fifth floor for questioning.

Karl Wendel, one of the SD officers, told Allied interrogators after the war that Benoist was probably questioned by Karl Langer, the officer who had led the arrests at Auffargis the previous summer. Langer was assisted by two other SD men: Woerle and Wenger. Robert was told that if he gave the Germans the locations of his arms dumps he would be released. Robert, remembering what had happened to the Prosper network, did not believe that the Germans would keep their word. Charlotte refused to say anything.

For a short period the two prisoners were left alone in their separate cells but at four o'clock in the morning the Germans came back and Robert was questioned again. This time he was shown a dossier giving details of some of the activities of the Clergyman network. The Germans told him that he had been betrayed by captured British agents called Charles and Corinne and that it was pointless to say nothing. Charlotte was brought in and questioned in front of Robert, although once again she refused to say anything.

The interrogations continued through Monday while back at the apartment in the rue Fustel de Coulanges, two other members of the gang fell into the same trap as Robert and Charlotte. Roger Soyer, a friend of Denise Bloch from earlier in the war, arrived at the apartment with his courier Marcelle Brion, a close friend of Charlotte, who lived near the Place des Ternes. She had been working with Clergyman for only three months. The pair were held in the apartment for several hours, during which time Soyer was able to whisper instructions to Brion about what she should say when they were questioned. His plan was to make them appear innocent bystanders and he concocted a story that she was visiting the apartment to collect some wool for a sweater she was knitting and that Soyer was her lover and had come along to keep her company. She was to tell the Germans that the affair had only been going for a few weeks after they had met in the Métro and that it was rather embarrassing because she was a married woman and did not want her husband to discover what was going on. This story seemed to have convinced the Germans because the two "lovers" were not held for long.

Benoist had no such escape. The SD officers knew that they had the man they had been chasing for more than a year and they wanted to get as much information from him as possible, using all different kinds of persuasion to break down his defences. The Germans may have threatened and cajoled but there is no evidence to suggest that Robert received the same kind of treatment as Willy Grover or Suttill had suffered a year earlier. Attitudes had changed since then. The Germans knew that they were losing the war and that in all probability it would only be a matter of time before the Allied armies broke out of Normandy and attacked Paris. They did not dare say it, but they knew that it was only a matter of time before they would be going back to their homeland. They were not thinking about victory or defeat, they were simply trying to stay out of trouble. No-one was making long-term plans.

The interrogators asked questions and the prisoners either replied or they did not. Benoist was questioned by a number of different SD officers, including Ernst Vogt. In the course of their conversations the subject of Henri Déricourt came up and Benoist remarked that it was ironic that he had been asked the same questions in England a few weeks earlier. Robert asked Vogt whether Déricourt was really a double agent. Vogt noted down the question but did not give Benoist a straight answer.

In the course of the first day of interrogation, Robert and Charlotte both knew that they must give the rest of the network time to leave the Villa Cécile and go to ground. If the Germans had known about the Clergyman headquarters at Sermaise they would undoubtedly have raided, but for 20 hours after the arrests nothing happened. After Robert and Charlotte had departed with Massonet on the Sunday night the others had dined and gone to bed. The Tayssedres had one of the bedrooms. Denise Bloch had the other. Garnier and L'Antoine slept in the dining room. In the middle of the night Bloch woke Garnier and the two used the radio transmitter to receive a message from London. They slept late on the Monday morning and at around midday Jean-Pierre and Cric Wimille arrived by car and took Bloch away to a nearby farm from where she transmitted a message to London. The three of them then returned to the Villa Cécile and they all had lunch.

No-one thought back to Robert's remark that they should all go to ground if he was not back by midday. It rained heavily that afternoon but towards the evening, when the showers began to clear away, the Wimilles went off in their car to visit the local farmers to see if they could find any eggs. Bloch and Garnier were beginning to worry about Robert and they walked the mile or so down the main road from the villa to the village of Sermaise. They headed for the station, hoping that they would bump into Robert on his way back from Paris. But there was no sign of Robert and the two radio operators eventually turned back and walked back to the villa. They arrived at about eight o'clock and found that the Wimilles had returned and had been successful in their hunt for fresh eggs.

Work began to prepare the dinner. The men went on to a terrace in front of the house to have an aperitif. Garnier, L'Antoine, Robert Tayssedre and Wimille were sitting there at about 8.20pm when they heard a convoy of vehicles approaching along the main road from the direction of St Chéron. Wimille looked up the road, saw that the convoy was headed by a Hotchkiss, a car which was favoured by the SD, and decided instantly that the convoy was probably about to raid the house. He shouted a warning to everyone and even before the first German car turned into the driveway of the Villa Cécile, they were up and running. Wimille, Tayssedre and L'Antoine went down a passage between the house and the garage and from there were able to get out into a small lane, which ran behind the house. Garnier ran into the house to warn the women. The Germans, seeing people running, immediately began shooting, even before the cars had come to a halt. They then charged into the house with guns ready. Garnier had by then jumped out of a window at the back of the house as the Germans began to come through the front door but there was little time left for him to find a hiding place. He ran into the woods and hid in a bush but within a matter of minutes the German soldiers were searching the wood and found him.

When the Germans dragged Garnier back to the villa, he found an SD officer shouting at the women, demanding to know which one of them was Line, one of Bloch's code names. Finally, she stepped forward. Garnier was searched and handcuffed and, as this was happening, he counted no fewer than 11 different cars and estimated that each one must have carried four men. There were Germans everywhere, searching the house, the grounds and the woods. L'Antoine and Robert Tayssedre had both been captured, and Tayssedre had obviously taken a beating from the Germans. Their searches had revealed the radio transmitter and some sub-machine guns that were found hidden inside seat cushions in the garage.

But they could not find Wimille.

He had not gone far but he had found himself a very good hiding place, having run down to the stream in the woods and spotted that there was a gap under the roots of a tree at water level. He had jumped into the water and hid there, with only his face out of the water. From his hiding place he was able to watch the Germans leading Garnier back to the villa. He would remain in the water until night fell by which time the Germans had put the prisoners into separate cars and departed, setting fire to the villa before they left. Wimille emerged from the water and found shelter at a nearby farm, which was run by the Gerber family. When things quietened down in the valley he went back into Paris and moved in with Pierre Leygonie.

After the war some of those arrested at Sermaise blamed Madeleine Belligand and Robert Massonet for not warning them about Robert's arrest but when faced with that accusation Madeleine said that neither she nor Massonet had understood the warning given to them by Charlotte Perdrigé. She also insisted that as soon as she found out about Robert's arrest she had sent a messenger to Sermaise but he arrived too late and found the Villa Cécile burning.

The fact that the raid at Sermaise came around 20 hours after Robert and Charlotte were arrested would seem to suggest that one or the other may have mentioned the hideout, believing that the other members of Clergyman would by then have been warned by Robert's sister Madeleine Belligand after her telephone conversation with Charlotte the previous night. If the Germans had known about the house before that point it would have made sense to raid earlier than they did. The fact is that Robert had warned his colleagues to leave the villa if he had not returned by Monday lunchtime and they did not follow his instructions. If he gave away the address, it was only because he thought his team had gone to ground.

Marcel Bluteau reported that on the evening of the raid at Sermaise he was transferring weapons from the drop at Breuillet, five miles from Sermaise, to a new location in Dourdan. He arrived at Gaston Lamberdiere's garage and found Germans there and so drove on to the Villa Cécile without stopping, intending to warn Benoist about what was happening. When he arrived at Sermaise he found that the villa was in flames.

That night there were other arrests up and down the valley. Bluteau would later investigate the arrests and reported that René Girard (Berthelot Francis) claimed that he had seen a woman answering to Bloch's description showing Germans where transmitters were hidden in the village of Montflix-par-Etrechy. According to the same report, 24-year-old student Gaston Courcimault (Boulon Alphonse) from Guisseray said that he had seen L'Antoine showing the Germans where some of the arms were hidden.

Charles Couderc later wrote in his report that "the chauffeur of Lionel gave away three arms dumps" and added that L'Antoine helped the Germans that day, the next and the day after that.

In the course of Tuesday June 20 there was much activity in the valley and blacksmith Paul Beauvallet (Paul Huon), one of the parachute reception team, was convinced that more German raids were coming and decided to spend that night out in the forest. During the night there was another parachute drop and a gunfight, which Beauvallet heard taking place. In the morning when he returned to his forge he discovered a new F Section agent called Blondet (code name Valérien) waiting for him. Blondet had been briefed for a role as Robert Benoist's assistant and had arrived carrying more than a million Francs (£35,000 at today's prices) for use by Clergyman.

Blondet's reception committee was made up entirely of French turncoats and German soldiers, but the newcomer was fortunate that one of them, mistaking him for a colleague and addressing him in German, alerted him to the trap. Blondet shot the German and, in the confusion that followed, was able to slip away. Bluteau and his team hid Blondet for several days until it was decided that he should be sent out of the region for his own safety. He ended up going south and operating in the Aveyron, around the town of St Afrique.

Blondet left much of the money destined for Clergyman behind with those involved and after the war there was much confusion and controversy over what happened to it. This may have been the root cause of some of the conflicting accusations about what happened to the Clergyman network. Some blamed Benoist but, as Bluteau himself pointed out, although there were a dozen or so arrests, in addition to Benoist's gang, the damage was limited and most of the Turma-Vengeance organisation was left untouched and was able to continue its work against the Germans. Eighty percent of the weapons had been seized and a number of members arrested but many others escaped unharmed. Those arrested included Lucien Courcimault (Boulon Louis) and his son Gaston (Boulon Alphonse). They were followed by Georges Leroux (Boulon Gabin), another member of the parachute reception team, who was shot and seriously wounded while he and his son Lucien (Boulon Gaspar) were being arrested. Pierre Salat (Boulon Jean) was taken into custody two days later. Others arrested were Paul Lespiaux (Anselme Poulain), François Richard, Lucien Clergeon, Émile Daude and François Haugomat.

After the war there was speculation that the arrests could have been caused by two shadowy figures called André Swogel (Petrel) and André Menoud (Fiquet) who were thought to have had some motive to want to see the downfall of the Bluteau network. This pair may be related to a group of "maquisards" who had first appeared in the valley at the start of June. They were from Chelles, on the eastern side of Paris, and were led by a man called "Petrelle". They are reported to have caused considerable trouble, taking arms from resistance groups and murdering various farmers who did not do as they were told.

There were also questions raised about Wimille because of his fortunate escape but again reports were conflicting. In April 1944 Robert told SOE debriefing officers that Wimille was his right hand man. Two months later MI5 advised SOE that there had been claims from France that Wimille was working as a double agent. Maurice Benoist may have been behind some of these stories because Wimille was convinced that Maurice was working for the Germans and was not afraid to say it. On the other hand Wimille's activities in the 1930s had created a certain amount of suspicion. There were, however, no signs that Wimille had anything to do with the Germans, in fact there is plenty of evidence to indicate the opposite. In the weeks that followed the arrests, while his wife was in prison, Wimille busied himself with resistance work with what remained of the networks.

"Wimille tried to renew contacts with England, " Couderc wrote in his report. "But people and radio equipment had been seized and no results were obtained."

In November 1944 after Paris had been liberated Wimille worked closely with the British to try to establish what had happened and went with a British officer to Sermaise to explain the raid on the Villa Cécile and to show how he had been able to get way when all the others present had been caught. The suspicions surrounding Wimille may have been caused in part by what happened to Cric Wimille after her arrest at Sermaise. The cars that took the prisoners back to Paris stopped several times on the way and the first did not get back to the Avenue Foch until about one o'clock in the morning. The Tayssedres, L'Antoine and Garnier were all put in the waiting room on the fifth floor. Before they were interviewed Stella Tayssedre ate a number of documents, including a rental agreement which might otherwise have led the Germans to another hideout in the 16ème arrondissement . Denise Bloch was kept separate from the others, the Germans already knowing that she was a British agent. The odd thing was that Cric was also separated from the main party, taken to the Avenue Foch via her apartment (where she was allowed to pick up some belongings) and then put into a cell with Roger Soyer and Marcelle Brion. She was not there for long and Soyer was convinced that the only reason she had been there was to identify him. This may have been the intention of the Germans but it may have been this that saved Soyer as the SD may have concluded that because Cric did not know either of them, Soyer or Brion were telling the truth about their love affair.

After about half an hour a German officer walked into the waiting room, pointed to Garnier and said: "This is the son-in-law". He also seemed to recognise L'Antoine the chauffeur and growled: "So, you did not get the message the first time around". L'Antoine was searched and papers were found with the name Perdrigé.

"Everyone in this affair is called Perdrigé," the German said.

The SD officers spent the next hour deciding what to do. They wanted first to interrogate the top people in the network, because they were the people who knew most about the activities and could provide more information. They knew that Robert Benoist was the head of the Clergyman network and they knew that Bloch was his principal assistant, although they still did not know her real name. They had identified Charlotte as being an important member of the group because she had been with Benoist at the time of his arrest and her attitude towards them made it clear that she was someone important. They also knew that they might be able to use Cric Wimille to find her husband. The others members of the group were difficult to assess. There was one woman, who had been arrested in the Rue de Mont Louis in the 11ème arrondissement, who had acted as a courier but everyone pretended not to know her and she was soon freed.

In the end the decision was taken to send Robert and Stella Tayssedre, André Garnier, Roger Soyer and Marcelle Brion, in the company of two other prisoners, to the SD's makeshift prison in the Place des États-Unis. This kept them out of the way but cleared out rooms at the Avenue Foch.

Robert, Charlotte, L'Antoine and Bloch were retained in the

cells on the fifth floor at the Avenue Foch. Bloch was of most interest to the Germans because she could send false messages to London. They knew that they had little available time before London would realize what was happening and were keen to have Bloch operate her transmitter. She refused. Josef Goetz and his radio team on the second floor at 84 Avenue Foch began to operate her wireless set instead. Whether or not this contributed to Blondet's misfortune is not certain but it would explain how they knew the location of the parachute drop while the local reception team did not.

For the Germans these were busy times. The number of arrests that were made after D Day increased dramatically and the SD interviewers were overstretched. There were simply too many investigations going on at the same time. It would be four days before the first of the Clergyman group was called back to the Avenue Foch to answer questions. Once they had been questioned they were sent off to Fresnes prison from where, after a few days, Roger Soyer and Marcelle Brion were released. The Germans had fallen for the story about the unfaithful wife and her new boyfriend.

The Germans continued to question Robert Benoist, trying a variety of different approaches to try to get information. On June 24 they called in Maurice Benoist and Robert and Bloch both saw him, in the presence of Obersturmbannführer Josef Kieffer and Josef Placke, one of his more talented investigators. The meeting did not achieve a great deal but it enabled Robert to give his brother a few practical instructions, such as asking him to pay the rent that was due at the apartment in the rue Fustel de Coulanges.

Garnier was questioned on June 26 and on his way to the fifth floor at 84 Avenue Foch, he bumped into Robert on the stairs. On some occasions the Germans made use of such "accidental" encounters to shock or scare agents and it is possible that they wanted Benoist to see that a member of his family was in custody. Garnier was quickly bundled away but Robert insisted that he be allowed to talk to his son-in-law. The Germans must have felt that this would be a good idea and Garnier was eventually taken to Robert's cell. Benoist told him, loudly, that he had nothing to worry about as he had only been at the Villa Cécile to deliver a message and that he would be released. Ernst Vogt then appeared and Robert told Garnier that Vogt would be conducting the interrogation and that the German was very nice.

Vogt's first move was to go through Garnier's address book, asking about all the entries. After that Garnier explained that he knew nothing about Robert's activities except that he had heard about the affair in Auffargis and had only seen Robert when he came to visit his daughter Jacqueline and their new baby - Robert's granddaughter. He then asked Vogt if it would be possible for him to get some new clothes and the German arranged for him to be taken to his apartment, which had been searched by the Germans. The visit gave Garnier the opportunity to talk to the concierge and explain what had happened and he asked her to get in contact with his wife Jacqueline so that she would know where he was. Garnier would remain a prisoner for another two and a half weeks, during which time the Germans seemed to be unable to decided whether or not he was a member of the gang. The fact that he was later released is a clear indication that no-one within the Clergyman group gave anything away about his role as a radio operator.

During the meeting between Benoist and Garnier, Robert told his son-in-law that he had been shown a German dossier that gave the code names of two British agents who had betrayed them: Charles and Corinne.

While waiting in the Place des Etats-Unis Garnier was locked into a room by himself but, hoping to be able to speak to someone else, he tried whispering through the keyhole to the room next door and found out that he was talking to Charlotte.

She too had been shown the dossier implicating Corinne and Charles. And they both knew to whom the Germans were referring.

CHAPTER SIXTEEN

Robert Benoist had been shocked when the Germans showed him the file, which was exactly what the interrogators had intended. He did not know the code names Charles and Corinne, but when he read the dossier he knew exactly to whom the Germans were referring.

The dossier said that Charles and Corinne had been parachuted into France in the Spring of 1944 and, in need of a safe place to stay, had contacted Robert, having known him during his period with the SOE in London. He had let them stay at the apartment in the rue Fustel de Coulanges.

The German report went on to describe Corinne as being a Frenchwoman who had an accent that was "a real menace" because she had not lived in France since she was a child.

The description was that of Violette Szabo.

✠

The suggestion that Violette Szabo betrayed Robert Benoist is one that is bound to cause controversy because since her story first emerged Szabo has always been seen as one of the great legends of World War II. She has been the source of inspiration for the generations that have followed.

She is the perfect heroine, a shining example of courage in the face of adversity. In Britain in the difficult post-war era, Szabo was someone to whom the public could relate, someone who gave them with pride and inspired them to go on battling through the austere times of rationing and rebuilding.

Her story was romantic and compelling: a feisty young shop assistant with film star good looks who transformed herself into a fearsome resistance fighter; parachuted to France and was captured after a gun battle with the Germans. She fought like a tigress, refused to say anything to her captors, despite outrageous torture, and was eventually taken away to Germany and executed.

Szabo was the first British woman ever to be awarded the George Cross, the country's highest award for bravery for a civilian. Instituted in 1940 by King George VI, the medal was designed for people who had performed acts "of the greatest heroism or of the most conspicuous courage in circumstances of extreme danger".

She left a young daughter who after the war went to Buckingham Palace to receive her mother's medal from King George VI.

The problem was that while Szabo used the code name Louise, the name on her false identity papers was Corinne Leroy and the man with whom she parachuted to France in 1944 was Philippe Liewer. He used the code name Clement, but his identity papers were in the name of Charles Beauchamps.

Charles and Corinne.

Implying treachery on the part of a colleague was one of the oldest tricks used in order to undermine the morale of a prisoner during interrogation and Robert Benoist had been taught to expect such things when he was being trained in England. The problem was that the Germans had so much detail that it was hard not to believe them.

✠

Violette Szabo was a remarkable and courageous woman, but there is also no doubt that her story was very different to the one which was first told in the years after the war and which is perpetuated each year by new authors who never look beyond what has been written by others.

The legend of Szabo can be traced back to December 1946 when the citation for her George Cross was first made public. It spoke of her having been "continuously and atrociously tortured" but that "never a word or deed gave away any of her acquaintances or told the enemy anything of value".

In 1956 Violette's story was romanticised in a best-selling book called Carve Her Name With Pride, which was written by the author and film-maker RJ Minney.

Minney had made his name in 1931 with a biography of Clive of India, but he had then moved on to write film scripts in the United States and then became part of the glamour industry, glorifying Hollywood and the film industry in a series of different publications.

When the war came Minney edited a magazine called War Weekly, which was largely government propaganda, before moving on to become one of the key figures at Michael Balcon's Gainsborough Pictures, a film company which was busy making historical dramas which the Ministry of Information wanted to emphasize Britain's history and heritage. The films functioned as both propaganda and escapism, delivering their messages with brilliant subtlety.

Towards the end of the war Minney was the producer of a film called The Wicked Lady, a film which was a huge success in part because it challenged stereotypes and helped change Britain's attitude to women and in part because it featured large amounts of naked cleavage, which at the time was so daring that the prim and proper US censors thought it was too much. The underlying message, delivered amongst the bursting bodices and frills, was that women could be whatever they wanted to be, something which was particularly important given the war work that women were doing.

Carve Her Name With Pride was a follow-up to The Wicked Lady, the major difference being that it was not a fictional historical romance but rather a contemporary story, based on real events. The book was a huge success and two years later it was made into a film, directed by Lewis Gilbert, who had enjoyed considerable success the previous year with Reach for the Sky, the story of the legless fighter pilot Douglas Bader. Gilbert would go on to success with another war film called Sink the Bismarck! (1960) before moving on to make Alfie (1966), a number of James Bond films in the 1970s and the romantic comedies Educating Rita (1983) and Shirley Valentine (1989).

Carve Her Name With Pride starred Virginia McKenna, Paul Scofield, Jack Warner, Billy Whitelaw and even a young Michael Caine. It was a moving tale of the triumph of the human spirit over adversity but, in the same year as the film was enjoying success in British cinemas, Elizabeth Nicholas, one of the early historians of the SOE, published a book called Death be not Proud, the story of some of the women involved in SOE work. She concluded that Szabo's George Cross citation was "in considerable part fictitious".

Eight years later Professor Michael Foot was commissioned by the British Government to write the official history of the SOE in France and after months sifting through the classified documents and writing as much of the story as he was allowed to do, he concluded that "the ghastly story of Violette Szabo's suffering is so far as I can ascertain completely fictitious".

The works by Nicholas and Foot were both based on an academic approach to the subject rather than appealing to the emotions as Minney had done, but the facts were not what people wanted. The British liked having a heroine like Szabo. It was a good story.

It had begun during World War I when Charles Bushell served in France as a driver with the Royal Army Service Corps. He met a Frenchwoman called Reine Leroy and they were married in Abbeville, where the RASC located what was known as the Advanced Horse Transport Depot. When the British troops were sent home at the end of the war Bushell took his young wife with him but after demobilization he found that Britain was not able to live up to Lloyd George's claim that it would be "a land fit for heroes" and he could not find a job. He used his demob money to buy a luxury car and took his wife and new son back to France where he began working as a chauffeur in Paris, as a colleague and rival of Willy Grover.

Violette Bushell was born at the Hertford British Hospital in Levallois in 1921 but she was still only a baby when the family returned to England. There would be a couple of periods when the Bushells went back to France again before they finally settled in the working class London suburb of Brixton in the 1930s. It was there that Violette spent her teenage years, blossoming into an attractive, vivacious and sporting young women, despite the fact that she was only five feet tall. She left school at 14 and for a while worked as an assistant in a hairdressing salon before moving on and getting a job as a shop assistant in the Woolworth's department store in Brixton.

When war broke out Violette was 18. A few months later France was invaded and Britain had its back to the wall. Reine Bushell was aware that thousands of French soldiers had arrived in Britain after the Allied evacuation at Dunkirk and decided that the Bushell family would do something to cheer up one of them on the annual Bastille Day on July 14 1940. She sent her daughter into the West End of London to find a suitable French soldier and Violette came home with 30-year-old Etienne Szabo, a dashing young officer from the French Foreign Legion, who had escaped from France with the remains of the British Expeditionary Force a few weeks earlier. Etienne and Violette hit it off immediately and, after a whirlwind romance, were married on August 21 1940, just five weeks later.

Ten days after the wedding Szabo departed for Dakar with the 13ème Demi-Brigade de Légion Étrangère. Violette joined the Auxiliary Transport Service and after training was posted to Oswestry. The young couple did not see one another again until the autumn of 1941 when they spent a week together in Liverpool, before Etienne was once again sent back to Africa. Violette soon discovered that she was pregnant and in June 1942 gave birth to a baby girl, whom she christened Tania. Four months later Etienne was killed in the fighting for the El Himeimat Ridge during the Battle of El Alamein. He had never seen his daughter.

At 21 Violette was a war widow.

It was not long after Etienne's death that Szabo received a letter from the War Office requesting that she present herself for an interview with a Mr Potter at an address in London. Her name had come up in the searches through the services to find people who spoke foreign languages. When "Mr Potter" made it clear what was wanted, Violette became an enthusiastic recruit to the SOE's French Section. She hated the Germans with a passion.

The SOE liked the look of what they saw, although there were some reservations that she might be a little *too* keen to go into action. Violette was sent off to the SOE training camps. It was while she was doing her parachute training at Ringway that she met Philippe Liewer, a network organizer, recently returned from secret work in France. The two hit it off immediately and when they finished their training it was decided that Szabo would be Liewer's courier for a mission in Normandy in the Spring of 1944.

The code name she was given was Louise and their instructions were to go to Normandy, where Liewer (operating under the code name of Clement) had previously operated. Their mission was to contact the members of the old Salesman network who had not been arrested and see what could be done to revive the old network for immediate action. They did not know it but time was running out as D Day was just a matter of weeks away.

Sending the pair to Normandy was a logical move. Liewer had built the network in the early part of the war and knew all the major players. The only danger was that he might be compromised, having had to get out of Normandy in a hurry after members of the network were arrested and his assistant Bob Maloubier was shot and wounded while escaping from the Germans. He and Szabo had a good rapport and she was a woman who was thirsting to get into action against the Germans.

They were flown by Lysander to a landing site on the plains near Chartres and from there went to Paris and then on to Normandy. Once there they realised that it was far too dangerous a place for Liewer to try to operate. The two retreated to Paris where Liewer was not known, and they made contact with Benoist, hoping that he would be able to give them a place to hide until they could be got back to Britain. It was agreed that rather than give up their mission in Normandy completely, Violette would return on her own and try to find some of Liewer's old contracts, from the details he supplied her. It was a dangerous role but one which she accepted with gusto. They agreed that she would return to Paris before the end of April and meet up with Liewer and that they would then travel back to England together. Liewer lay low in Paris, waiting Violette to return. It seems that during this period he stayed at the apartment in the rue Fustel de Coulanges.

Violette returned after only a fortnight, during which she had had a series of close calls with the Germans. She had discovered that there was nothing much left of the Normandy networks. Back in Paris, popular legend suggests that she stayed in an apartment in St Germain-des-Prés with Liewer's aunt and met Liewer at rendezvous in the Jardin du Luxembourg. However, André Garnier told Allied interviewers in January 1945 that Liewer and Szabo were both staying at the Clergyman safe house in the rue Fustel de Coulanges in the period before they returned to England.

Philippe and Violette departed Paris at the end of April as planned in a double Lysander operation from a small unguarded airfield called Le Fay, close to Issoudun. When they returned to England, they found that Maurice Buckmaster was interested in using them again, but not in the Normandy area where it was deemed to be too dangerous for either to operate. Buckmaster looked elsewhere for jobs that needed to be done. One area where resistance needed to be properly organized was in the Limousin, a quiet rural area in the centre of France, at the centre of which was the city of Limoges. This was strategically important because German troops stationed in the south-west of France would have to pass through the region in order to get to the north when the impending Allied invasion took place. It was clear in the spring of 1944 that an invasion was coming. More and more American troops were arriving in Britain but the date and the location of the invasion remained a mystery.

As it turned out Violette and Philippe did not get back to France until the night of June 7/8 when they parachuted into the Limousin from an American B-24 aircraft belonging to the Special Operations Group of the US Army Air Force. They parachuted with Robert Maloubier and Jean Guiet and landed near the village of Sussac, about 30 miles to the south-east of Limoges. There was much excitement all across France following the D Day landings the previous day in Normandy.

For the first couple of days Liewer assessed the situation and then decided that he would send Violette to meet with Colonel Georges Guigouin, one of the most powerful resistance figures in the Limousin. The plan was for Violette to set off to meet Guigouin in the company of a local resistant called Jacques Dufour (Anastasie). Dufour had a Citroën car and they were travelling in this that morning when, close to the village of Salon-la-Tour, to the south-east of Limoges, they ran into elements of the Deutschland Regiment of the Das Reich division, which was moving north towards Normandy. It was pure bad luck. A passenger they were carrying ran off, but Szabo and Dufour became embroiled in a gun battle with the Germans.

According to Minney's romantic version of the story Violette fought like a tigress but twisted her ankle while trying to escape and, realising that she had no chance, decided to hold off the Germans for as long as possible to allow Dufour to get away. Minney's tale said that a number of Germans were killed and then Violette was taken, kicking and biting, into custody. The citation of her Croix de

Guerre noted that there was a gun battle and that a German corporal was killed but other research has failed to turn up any evidence of the gunfight. What is not disputed is that Violette was taken by the Waffen SS troops and delivered to the SD in Limoges. In some respects she was fortunate because on that same day elements of the Das Reich Division murdered the entire population of nearby Oradour-sur-Glane. It would not have been a surprise if the SS men had simply executed Szabo on the spot.

When she arrived in Limoges Szabo was limping as a result of a sprained ankle and had a minor flesh wound. She remained with the SD in Limoges until the following week when she was escorted to Paris for questioning at the Avenue Foch. Her first interview there began on the morning of Saturday June 17, the day before Robert and Charlotte were arrested in the rue Fustel de Coulanges.

The timing therefore fits in perfectly with the German claim that Corinne betrayed Benoist. There is no doubt that Benoist's description of Corinne from the German dossier fits Szabo almost exactly. There is however one vital element in the story that does not ring true: the Germans told Benoist that Charles and Corinne had both been arrested and had together betrayed Benoist.

Although Benoist did not know it, Liewer had not been arrested and was still operating in the Limoges area. He was not therefore involved in the betrayal of Robert and Charlotte. This information would seem to suggest that the Germans were trying to create a false impression in order to get Robert and Charlotte to divulge information about their activities. However, it is also worth noting that for the news of the treachery to have had any effect on Robert and Charlotte, the Germans must have known that the two prisoners knew Szabo and Liewer. There is nothing to suggest that the SD would have made a connection between the agent captured in Salon-la-Tour in the middle of France and the two who had been arrested in Paris – unless they had been told.

The other details given by Robert were true: Violette was

French, as he had said, but she had not lived in France except for a few years during her childhood; and although she spoke the language fluently she did have a real problem with her accent.

Charlotte Perdrigé and André Garnier discussed the same allegations through the keyhole while they were locked in adjoining rooms in the SD holding prison in the Place des États-Unis. Later when Charlotte was being deported to Germany she told fellow deportees that Philippe Liewer had been responsible for her arrest and she even told them that she had seen him in the corridors at 84 Avenue Foch. This was a curious allegation and suggests that the Germans may have been playing games with her. Liewer was never arrested and was never at the Avenue Foch.

After the war, when confronted with the allegations, Liewer was able to clear his name easily as there were a large number of witnesses who confirmed that he had spent all of his time in the area around Limoges, organizing resistance activities. There was no other evidence to suggest that Liewer was in any way involved in the Clergyman arrests, and no way of knowing why Charlotte Perdrigé thought Liewer had been in Paris. She was never able to explain her claims as she died at the Czarnków concentration camp in Poland at the end of February 1945.

There was, however, other evidence that emerged in the immediate post-war era which linked Szabo to the arrests in the rue Fustel de Coulanges. This included a statement from André Garnier who told Allied investigators that in early July 1944, on the day he was being released by the Germans, he was briefly left alone in a room in the Avenue Foch and was able to read a file which had been left lying on the desk. This was marked "Affaire Normandie" and he saw that all the names of those involved in Clergyman were listed. Garnier said that this had left him puzzled because he knew that Clergyman did not have any operations in the Normandy region. Earlier in the war Chestnut had had a brief link with Normandy, thanks to the activities of Christopher Burney. And Robert Benoist had been in Dieppe soon after the commando raid there, but apart from that there was nothing to suggest that these were facts linked in any way to the demise of Clergyman. The fact that Szabo and Liewer were primarily employed in Normandy on their first mission seems a logical explanation as to why the Germans would have thought that Benoist's network was involved in building up resistance activity in Normandy.

The allegations against Corinne were underlined by another member of the Clergyman network, Denise Bloch's friend Roger Soyer, who told Allied investigators in December 1944 that Corinne had been responsible for the arrests in the rue de Fustel de Coulanges. It is not clear how Soyer knew about this, but it is safe to assume that the Germans presented him with the same dossier that was shown to Benoist, to see if it would have any effect on him.

Soyer's testimony was a lot more precise than the information that had come from Garnier, Robert Benoist and Charlotte Perdrigé and, significantly, it noted that only Corinne had been arrested and that Charles had remained at liberty, something which served to emphasize the identification of Szabo. Soyer's statement was backed up by a report about the arrest of Benoist, prepared by Jean-Pierre Wimille after the events at Sermaise. He noted that when Bloch was deported to Germany from Fresnes prison in August, she went with a group of other SOE agents which included Corinne. There were only three women in the group: Bloch, Szabo and Lilian Rolfe. Rolfe was a British wireless operator who operated for four months with the Historian network in the Loiret region, to the south of Paris and had no known connections with the Clergyman network.

Once again the identification of Szabo as Corinne is clear.

There were many witnesses - and, ironically, Robert Benoist was one of them - to Szabo's bravery during the deportation of the F Section secret agents to Germany. In her defence, it should also be noted that several captured SD officers told SOE investigator Jacques de Guelis after the war that of all the SOE agents that they had interrogated at the Avenue Foch there were two who had stood out as being the least cooperative: Andrée Borrel of the Prosper network and Szabo. One has to be a little bit circumspect about such assertions however as at the time a great deal of trouble was taken to protect the SOE heroines from any form of criticism.

When asked in the 1980s about links between Szabo and Benoist, the Foreign & Commonwealth Office, which then held the relevant documents, replied that there was no connection at all between them. Later when documents were declassified it was clear that André Garnier had told the authorities that Violette knew about the apartment where Robert and Charlotte were arrested and had stayed there in the Spring of 1944.

Further confirmation of this came in 2003 when further documents were declassified including a note which said: "Corinne - Violette, English, interned in Fresnes at the same time as Sonia and Madame Teyssedre, had been sheltered at the rue Fustel de Coulanges for a fortnight".

There is no question that Szabo not only knew Benoist but also knew about the safe house in the rue Fustel de Coulanges. The timing is also correct as Corinne was interviewed for the first time in Paris on the day before Robert was arrested, which would be consistent with the German claims of a betrayal.

What is difficult to accept is that Szabo would have willingly betrayed Robert and Charlotte to the Germans. Those who came into contact with her speak of her anti-German fervour and her unwillingness to help and one is led inexorably to the conclusion that if Violette was the source of the information that led the Germans to stake out the apartment in the rue Fustel de Coulanges, it can only have been as an accident. Perhaps she thought that the address was no longer important; perhaps the address was noted down somewhere.

We will probably never know.

The allegations made against Violette were not the only ones related to the demise of Clergyman. Other people were also accused but there was no evidence to back up any of the claims and as a result no charges were ever brought.

At least some of these claims came from the bad feelings that existed between some of those who were linked to Clergyman and the people involved in the network. Maurice Benoist was named as a potential suspect, probably by Jean-Pierre Wimille, who had heard about Maurice's activities when Chestnut collapsed. These allegations however do not seem to have any foundation. There is no doubt at all that Maurice knew that Robert was back in France in the summer of 1944 but it is also very clear that Robert was very careful to avoid any contact with his brother and made sure that Maurice knew nothing about the apartment in the rue Fustel de Coulanges.

After the war Maurice told Allied investigators that he did not discover about Robert's arrest until Sunday June 24 when Georges Laurent told him that Pierre Tournier, the owner of Le Plantin restaurant on the Avenue de Villiers, had mentioned it to him in conversation. This may seem rather implausible given what was happening with the family that week, but it may be that his sister Madeleine, who knew about the arrest on Monday June 18, decided not to tell Maurice as relationships within the family were already very strained by that point, as a result of the Chestnut arrests.

Maurice told the Allied investigation that he believed that Robert was responsible for his own arrest because of his lack of prudence.

There were also allegations about Wimille, although these seem to have come only from Maurice. These hold little water although Roger Soyer did explain that there were problems within the group, telling Allied investigators that he had the impression that Wimille would do anything for money and that in the final months of Clergyman there was friction between Benoist and Wimille.

Why this was the case is not clear but it is worth noting that there were rumours of disputes over the use of fuel that they had available. According to Soyer, Benoist was annoyed at Jean-Pierre because Wimille was using fuel for private business rather than resistance work. There may have been other more complicated reasons, arising from the fact that relationships within the group were a little complicated. It was an open secret for many years in motor racing circles that Wimille had an illegitimate daughter. What was not obvious was that her mother was Stella Tayssedre, who gave birth to a baby girl in December 1944. This meant that the child was conceived in March that year, which was at about the time that Robert returned from England.

After the war some of those involved raised questions about Cric Wimille's behaviour as a prisoner. Soyer reported that she was put into a cell with him at the Avenue Foch and he believed that she was only there to identify him. After the war there were also questions about how she managed to escape from German custody.

It is certainly an extraordinary story but one that is so strange that it can only be true. Cric was one of 3000 prisoners who were deported in the last convoy to leave from Paris on August 15 (along with Stella Tayssedre and Charlotte Perdrigé). The trains were loaded at Pantin with 110 people in each truck. Hubert de la Fressange, Cric's younger brother and a friend of his called Gérard Bonnet, who was searching for his mother, decided that they would follow the train on bicycles and see if they could do something along the way. They knew that the train could not easily move because of air attacks and concluded that this unlikely plan might work.

It did.

Overnight the train covered just 40 miles before it came to a halt in a tunnel between Luzancy and Nanteuil sur Marne. This had been blocked by an Allied air raid. For several hours the train stayed in the darkness before being reversed out of the tunnel and the prisoners were ordered to walk for several miles, under heavy guard, to the Nanteuil-Saacy station, where another train was waiting for them. Hubert was able to gain access to this station, disguised as a Red Cross official, and by pure chance bumped into Cric, who was fetching water for other prisoners.

Hubert sent Cric back into the train and told her to change her clothes (the prisoners still had luggage) and to dress as much like one of the Red Cross women as possible. While she was doing that, he convinced one of the Red Cross staff to give him a spare armband and Cric was able to slip in amongst the Red Cross party, handing out food to the prisoners until she and her brother were able to get out of the station. She rode back to Paris on the crossbar of her brother's bicycle and went to stay with Pierre Leygonie. Once Cric was safe Hubert headed south from Paris to join up with Free French forces and fought with General Leclerc's Second Armoured Division until he was killed in action six weeks later.

Suspicions about the escape prove only that some of the relationships within the Clergyman network were strained. A post-war investigation of the Wimilles failed to find any evidence of any treachery.

✠

Robert Benoist remained at the Avenue Foch for nearly a month after his arrest, being questioned every day. The Germans wanted to get as much information as possible from him but the cat-and-mouse game does not appear to have yielded any major results, except that either Robert or Charlotte was almost certainly responsible for the raid at Sermaise. It should be remembered, however, that Robert had instructed all of those present to leave the Villa if he and Charlotte did not return by Monday lunchtime.

The instruction had been ignored.

On July 14 the Germans called Maurice Benoist and asked him to bring clothes to the Avenue Foch for Robert. They told him that Robert was being sent to Fresnes. That same day Garnier and Charlotte were taken to the Avenue Foch for their final questioning. André was released but Charlotte was sent back to Fresnes with

Robert. While he was at the SD offices Garnier asked what had happened to his father-in-law and was told by the Germans that Robert "has everything he wants". André then left Paris to find his wife.

Robert remained in Fresnes for only three weeks, but during that period the war entered a dramatic phase. On July 20 Claus Graf von Stauffenberg, a junior staff officer at Hitler's Wolfsschanze (Wolf's Lair) headquarters at Rastenburg in East Prussia, left a briefcase containing a bomb beneath a table during one of Adolf Hitler's briefings. The explosion was planned to coincide with a coup d'état that would end Nazi rule and bring Germany under the control of the military. Hitler emerged from the blast with only minor injuries although for most of the day there was confusion throughout the Third Reich. The German army commander in France General Karl-Heinrich Von Stülpnagel was one of the plotters and that evening army units under his command took over the SS buildings in Paris (including the Avenue Foch) and placed the 1200 Gestapo, SS and SD men in Paris under arrest. It was only when the German navy threatened to intervene with troops that the others were released. In the weeks that followed Hitler wrought his revenge on all those who had been involved in the plot to kill him.

Within a few days of the Bomb Plot, the US 4th Armored Division under General George Patton broke through the German lines at Avranches in Normandy and cut east, behind the Nazi lines, to trap large numbers of German troops. News of the battles in Normandy filtered through to the inmates at Fresnes and word of the Allied break out created optimism. At the same time there were fears that all the prisoners would be executed before the Allied armies reached Paris. Deportation suddenly seemed a much more attractive option. The prisoners could not imagine that it would be any different if they were in prison in Germany.

The world had yet to learn of the horrors of the Nazi concentration camps.

CHAPTER SEVENTEEN

The ground fog on the morning of August 7 was so thick that neither the German attackers nor the US defenders could see more than 100 metres when the battle for the town of Mortain began. Five Panzer divisions moved up through the mists, their plan being to drive through the Allied lines and close the gap at Avranches, cutting off the US troops who were already to the south.

In the early hours of the attack the SS made significant progress, taking Mortain and pushing the US 30th Division back, leaving the 2nd Battalion of the 120th US Infantry Regiment surrounded on Hill 314, to the east of the town.

When the weather cleared later in the morning the RAF Typhoons attacked the German tank formations in such large numbers that there were several mid-air collisions as in the space of a few hours nearly 300 planes engaged the Germans. The armoured columns were decimated and around 150 tanks were destroyed.

In the days that followed Hill 314 held out, despite constant ground attacks and the survivors were able to radio vital information to the US artillery about German troop movements in and around the town. More than 120 guns were then used to make sure that the German advance remained pinned down.

That morning in Paris Robert Benoist was ordered out of his cell in Fresnes and was escorted down to the prison courtyard where he was put into a van and driven across the city to the SD headquarters in the Avenue Foch. The security police wanted to ask him a few more questions about his resistance activities. It was a short interview at the end of which Robert was told by Ernst Vogt that he would be deported to a prison camp in Germany the following day. No sooner had Robert been given the news than his brother Maurice appeared. Maurice had been asked by the Germans to present himself at the SD offices, his instructions being to bring some new clothes for his brother. On this occasion Maurice brought the family maid Chiquita with him. Vogt told him about Robert's deportation order and while Maurice tried to convince the German that his brother should be released, Robert took the opportunity to tell Chiquita that he had been betrayed by an Englishwoman. Robert wanted the truth to be known and was telling everyone he could about what had happened.

The meeting between the two brothers was a short one and then Robert was sent back to Fresnes. There were nearly 3000 prisoners inside the jail by that point, almost half the total numbers of prisoners in the whole Paris area. Fresnes was badly overcrowded and the inmates were on edge. As the Allied armies fought their way slowly out of Normandy the number of executions was increasing: each morning the prisoners waited to see whether it would be their turn to face the firing squad. They found out by listening to the progress of the iron-wheeled carts, which rattled along the open corridors of the prison delivering coffee. If the cart passed by a cell the prisoners inside knew that they were staying. If the cart stopped, the cell door would be opened and the prisoners inside would discover which of them was on the list for execution or deportation.

They did not know which it was going to be.

On the morning of August 8 the trolley stopped outside Robert's cell. He already knew that he was on his way to Germany and so was not unduly worried when his name was called. He bid his cell mates farewell and was escorted to the prison yard where he discovered that he would not to be travelling alone. A very special group of prisoners was being assembled and three prison buses were lined up to carry them. The first two were for male prisoners, most of whom had been SOE agents in France. Robert knew one or two of them. There were quiet exchanges and knowing nods, although because no-one was sure who was operating under which alias it was better to wait for a more discreet moment before greeting an old friend and hearing the latest news. The third coach was for women prisoners and Robert spotted three of them, including his tall blonde courier Denise Bloch. Alongside her was the familiar figure of the petite and beautiful Violette Szabo, the woman whom Benoist believed had betrayed him.

Before they boarded the buses, the male prisoners were handcuffed together in pairs. Then, as each climbed aboard the bus, they were handed a package of provisions, supplied by the International Red Cross. This was a real bonus. The buses departed and were driven quickly through the quiet streets of the city to the Gare de L'Est, where the German forces were in the process of putting together a train to make the run across eastern France to Germany.

By August 1944 such a trip was a very dangerous undertaking. The Allied Air Forces had gained complete control of the skies of France and German trains were an easy target for the American P-47 Thunderbolt fighter-bombers which patrolled the skies looking for anything that was moving. The German troop trains were often painted with Red Cross markings and the American pilots had long ago learned that these could not be trusted and that the Germans were quite capable of shooting them down from a train bearing the Red Cross. At the same time the Germans assumed that the train would be attacked and so included an anti-aircraft wagon.

The train that day consisted of a number of passenger carriages that had been converted to carry the injured from the battles in Normandy back to hospitals in Germany. The prison carriage was coupled to the rear of the train next to the anti-aircraft battery.

The prison wagon was a converted passenger carriage with three separate compartments linked by a corridor and, at one end, a small lavatory cubicle. One compartment was left much as it had been before the war. This housed the guards and the three female prisoners. The other compartments had been completely stripped out so that all that remained were a pair of rough wooden benches on either side, where once there had been seats. The door into each compartment had been replaced with a sliding metal grille, and each of these was secured with a padlock. The windows in the two compartments had been boarded up with thick wooden planks so that very little light got through to the inside of the carriage.

The group of British agents from Fresnes was joined at the station by a second group of special prisoners, who had come from the German holding camp at Royallieu, in Compiègne. Before being loaded into the prison wagon the prisoners were searched, one at a time. One of them, a Belgian called Captain Charles Rechenmann managed to upset the German guards and so was forced to stand naked while his garments were searched.

The senior officer in the group from Royallieu was an RAF Squadron Leader whom the Germans referred to as "Kenneth Dodkin". It was a cover name. In reality Dodkin was Wing Commander Forrest Yeo-Thomas, an agent of Général de Gaulle's RF Section, who operated under the code names of Shelley or The White Rabbit. After his arrest he had masqueraded as a pilot who had been shot down. Despite being seriously beaten by the Germans Yeo-Thomas had maintained his cover story. He was the only man not to be handcuffed to another prisoner, but that situation lasted only until he was searched and a small penknife was found sewn into the lining of his jacket. The result of that discovery was that he was chained to two of the other prisoners.

Nine pairs of male prisoners were put into one compartment and the remaining eight pairs and the trio were locked in the other. Once inside the prison carriage the prisoners were left alone and, as the minutes passed, they began to relax a little and were soon exchanging greetings and stories. Those who were still operating under aliases took the opportunity to warn their colleagues about which names should be used. Benoist was one of the few to be using his own name and word spread quickly in his group that there was a famous racing driver among them. Robert's fame was known to the Germans and official records refer to this group of SOE agents as "The Robert Benoist Group" although not everyone in the group had heard of Robert.

"I did not know the name," remembered Stéphane Hessel, one of Général de Gaulle's secret agents and a friend of Yeo-Thomas. "I was told by some of the group that this was the famous racing driver and that he was there under his own name. Many of us did not know each other at all. Only about half of us were French. The rest were British, American or Belgian.

"None of the 37 of us looked terribly roughed-up or mauled. The positive side was that because of the importance of our jobs we had probably been treated with a greater desire to keep us alive. Benoist did not look roughed up, but neither did I and nor did Yeo-Thomas. When I heard the story of how Yeo-Thomas had been treated by the Germans I was struck by the fact that he looked quite all right. It just shows how quickly one recovers."

Although the men did not necessarily recognise one another, it was a quite remarkable gathering of secret agents and included some of the SD's most important prisoners at the time. In addition to Benoist, Hessel and Yeo-Thomas there was also Major Henri Frager, who had been active since the early days of the Carte network and had gone on to establish F Section's Donkeyman group. There was Squadron Leader Maurice Southgate (Hector of the Stationer network), a legend in the south-west of France. There were survivors from the old Prosper sub-networks, including François Garel, Émile-Henri Garry, Pierre Culioli and the two Canadians Captain John McAlister and Captain Frank Pickersgill. The latter was in bad physical state having been wounded four times while trying to escape from a German prison in Paris. He had attacked one of his guards with a broken bottle and then jumped from a second-floor window before being brought down by a burst of machine-gun fire as he tried to run away. He had lost a lot of weight and lacked strength.

Another member of the group was Harry Peuleve, one of the young SOE agents that Benoist had met through Philippe Liewer in London. He was a friend of Violette Szabo. There were three officers from F Section's Labourer network: Lts Marcel Leccia, Elisee Allard and Pierre Geelen; two from Priest (Lts Ange Defendini and Romeo Sabourin) and Captain Pierre Mulsant and Flying Officer Dennis Barrett (Honoré), two assistant organisers from the Tinker network. In addition there was Captain Gerald Keun, an MI6 officer who had established the Jade Amicol network in Paris.

Benoist was handcuffed to an American agent called George Wilkinson, who had been parachuted into France in May 1944 to set up the Historian network in the weeks before D-Day. He had been arrested in Orleans at the end of June and his wireless operator Lilian Rolfe had been rounded up a month later when the Gestapo raided a house looking for someone else. Rolfe was with Szabo and Bloch in the next door compartment.

Wilkinson showed particular admiration for Robert.

"Benoist was charming," recalled Hessel. "He had great human quality. You can immediately recognise somebody with great valour and he behaved very bravely. Obviously he belonged to the group of people who one would trust."

Hessel also sensed that Benoist was a man whom others would follow.

"Yeo-Thomas had the most natural authority but Benoist gave me the feeling that he was being withdrawn," he said. "He could have been the leader of the group if he had tried."

With the windows of the carriage boarded up, the high August temperatures and the lack of air in the crowded carriage conditions became increasingly unpleasant as the day went on. The guards ignored all requests for water. They occasionally wandered up and down the corridor of the carriage to make sure that the prisoners were not up to any tricks. Otherwise the deportees were left alone. Outside ambulance after ambulance delivered the injured to the train. The Germans were in no hurry to depart and it became clear that they were happy to wait until the evening.

Yeo-Thomas decided that in order to try to keep up morale he would organise the sharing out of the food from the Red Cross parcels that had been given to the prisoners at Fresnes. The men from Royallieu had not been given anything. Some of the Fresnes prisoners refused to share what little they had and this created more than a little bad feeling within the party, although those who were willing to share pooled their resources so that everyone had something to eat in the course of the day. It was agreed that Pickersgill should be given extra rations to help him build up his strength.

When the light was finally beginning to fade, the locomotive was prepared and finally it pulled out of the Gare de L'Est and began to rattle its way out of the city, switching from track to track to avoid damaged lines as it worked its way through the suburbs of Pantin, Noisy, Bondy, Raincy until it reached the River Marne and headed out towards the old battlefields of the Great War. There were constant delays and stoppages. Inside the prison carriage the crush of bodies meant that it was impossible for the men to all sit down at the same time. Yeo-Thomas organised a rota so that the 19 men in his compartment would have a small chance to get some rest. Four men could lie down at the same time and another eight could perch on the benches on either side of the compartment, but the remaining four or five had to remain standing up. Yeo-Thomas worked out that each handcuffed couple could have two hours of sleep on the floor. There were numerous disputes during the night because the painful handcuffs were constantly being pulled as each prisoner moved as he dozed. Yeo-Thomas, Frager and Benoist spent much of the night trying to keep the peace. One of the other prisoners in their compartment, a young man called Yves Loison, worked intently on finding a way to open the handcuffs. The prisoners in the meantime discussed whether or not they should try to make an escape if Loison could figure out a way to release them all.

"A number of us were in favour of trying to get away," Hessel remembered. "Unfortunately the majority did not want to risk it. They were convinced that they were to be put into some jail and would be free when the war was over. Escaping was risky. Had we known what was in store for us I am sure we would have escaped."

Yeo-Thomas was one of the most keen to make an escape but Benoist seemed more resigned although, according to Hessel, he did not express an opinion on the subject, preferring to keep his own counsel.

"I am not sure he would have been pro-escape," Hessel said. "I think he was rather convinced that it would all end pretty soon. Others were more anxious. He may have been anxious within himself but he was not one to show it."

Yeo-Thomas faced open opposition to the idea from several of the men, notably Pickersgill, who would have been too weak to make a run for it.

"Pickersgill was of the leader type," said Hessel, "and there was a little bit of a difference between him and Yeo-Thomas about whether we should escape or not escape. They discussed it, but in a friendly way."

✠

As the dawn broke there were two problems for the prisoners. They were all very thirsty and most of them now needed to use the lavatory. Pickersgill had a particular problem because in the course of the night the tin of treacle he had been given had leaked into his pocket and he was now covered in the sticky liquid. The German guards finally decided to allow the prisoners to go to the lavatory compartment, although this had to be done with the agents remaining handcuffed to one another. The constant delays and stops in the course of the night meant that the train had not even made it as far as the champagne hills of Epernay. Ahead of them lay the wide-open plains and as the heat rose that morning the German guards became increasingly agitated as the train crawled across the exposed countryside towards the town of Châlons-sur-Marne (now Châlons-en-Champagne). The guards were constantly watching out of the windows, looking for Allied warplanes overhead. That day there was considerable aerial activity with the US Eighth Air Force sending B-17 bombers to a variety of targets in France and Germany. One large raid was planned for the Mercedes-Benz engine factory at Sindelfingen, near Stuttgart, but the bomber formations ran into serious weather problems and many turned for home. Their escorts went with them. In addition there were more than 100 P-47s, escorted by P-51 Mustangs carrying out attacks on communications targets across northern France.

In the early afternoon a gaggle of P-47s appeared in the skies above the train and, after swooping down to have a look, they looped around and came in for the attack. There was a loud explosion and the train came to an abrupt halt. The prisoners had little idea of what was going on but gathered from the firing of the anti-aircraft gun on the wagon next to the prison carriage that there were aircraft attacking the train. The guards in the prison carriage panicked and, having locked the prisoners inside, ran away from the train, worried that the flak battery next to the prison coach would be attacked. Inside the carriage some of the prisoners were scared that the coach would be hit by a rocket and they would all be burned alive.

They began to panic.

It was during the attack that Violette Szabo and Denise Bloch, who were chained together by the ankle but otherwise free to move, decided to help the men and crawled backwards and forwards along the corridor, carrying containers of water from the lavatory cubicle to the men in the prison cages. Their coolness and courage under fire provided a great example for the others and helped to restore calm and morale.

The raid did not last long but it was a while before the guards returned to the prison carriage. They were shaken by what had happened. The locomotive had been hit by a powerful rocket and was out of action. Seventeen Germans had been killed at different points along the train and many more had been wounded. The Germans' first priority was to look after their own wounded and it was several hours before the prisoners were finally ordered out of the carriage into the open air. They had been locked in the carriage for 30 hours and the fresh air and sunshine was a much-needed tonic for all of them. The Germans had found and requisitioned two farm trucks from local farmers and the prisoners were immediately ordered to climb aboard to continue their journey to Germany. There was considerable confusion as to what should be done with them and the first stop for the two trucks was the Gestapo office in the centre of Châlons, where the guards went in order to seek orders. Telephone calls were made and a plan devised.

The stop provided the prisoners with the opportunity to wash in the fountain of the courtyard of the building where the Germans had their headquarters. Several of the prisoners scribbled notes to their relatives and these were dropped when the two trucks set off again. Several of the messages were picked up by the local townspeople, who had turned out to watch and some did eventually get through to the families concerned.

The Wehrmacht soldiers escorting them had been ordered to continue on the Route Nationale 3 to Verdun. It was countryside that Robert Benoist would have remembered from his days as a reconnaissance pilot during World War I. Progress was faster but as darkness began to fall the road began to drop downhill into the Meuse valley, towards the city of Verdun. In the late evening the trucks were driven into a barracks in the centre of the city. The prisoners were ordered out of the farm vehicles and directed into a stable block, where they were going to spend the night. There were six to eight prisoners in each box stall and guards were posted at either end of the stable block with orders to shoot anyone who tried to escape.

The prisoners settled into the straw, and grabbed a few hours of much-needed rest. In the morning the handcuffs were removed for a few minutes and the prisoners were allowed to wash in the horse troughs. Each was given a cup of hot bitter "coffee", a brew made from roasted acorns. Then the manacles were re-attached and they were once again ordered to climb aboard the farm trucks, which headed out of the barracks and on towards the German border.

It was a bright and beautiful summer day and, as they passed through the villages between Verdun and Metz, the local people came out of their houses and cheered the prisoners, showing some small defiance to the occupying forces. Everyone knew that the war was coming to an end and that soon the Allied troops would overrun the Germans in the west and head eastwards across France to the border. The war would soon be over. The trucks rumbled on across the old Franco-Prussian War battlefields of Mars-la-Tour and Gravelotte and then the road began to drop downhill once again into the valley of the Moselle river and the great fortress of Metz but the old farm trucks did not stop in the walled city but rather passed through the Porte des Allemands (The German Gate) and continued on towards the border. Gradually the names of the villages began to sound less French and became more German. At Bambesch the little convoy passed through the fortifications of the Maginot Line and at Forbach crossed the border itself. Immediately after the border crossing the trucks turned off the main highway and drove a short distance to the gates of a prison camp.

They had arrived at KZ Neue Bremm, an SS-run transit camp, located in the outskirts of the German city of Saarbrücken. It was a sinister place, surrounded by high barbed-wire-topped fences and watchtowers. At the entrance of the camp the three women were ordered out of the trucks. Neue Bremm had a separate camp for women prisoners. It was the last time the men would see the three women agents. They would go from Neue Bremm to the women's' concentration camp at Ravensbrück, in the forests to the north of Berlin.

The farm trucks then drove into the camp and the men were ordered to climb down. They were immediately beaten and kicked by the SS guards, a great shock to all of them.

"It was the first time we saw how a concentration camp worked," remembered Stéphane Hessel. "We had never seen such things before. We didn't know about Auschwitz then. There were people in a little central square who were being made to put their hands behind their necks and jump around. This seemed terribly barbaric treatment to be given by German officers. We were very British. We knew that the Jews were treated very badly and perhaps killed, but we thought everyone else would be treated like slave labourers. We did not expect this kind of brutality."

The names of the prisoners was noted in the camp register then the handcuffs were removed and the prisoners were chained together by the ankle, in groups of five or six. They had to shuffle across the camp to the latrines. If they stumbled they were attacked by the SS guards. The whole process was humiliating and designed to break the spirit of even the toughest prisoners. The treatment of prisoners at Neue Bremm was particularly vicious, even in comparison to the other infamous concentration camps, and after the war a total of 37 of the guards at the camp were tried and executed for their brutality.

The special prisoners were eventually chained in pairs once again and were then crammed into a small hut behind the camp kitchen. This measured only nine feet by eight. There were narrow benches running along each wall and an oil drum was placed near the door, to act as a latrine. With only a small window in the hut the heat and the smell was overpowering.

"It was Hell," Yeo-Thomas wrote later.

Once again Yeo-Thomas took control and organized a rota so that all of the prisoners would be able to get some rest. Twenty-three of them could sit down at the same time and eight more could lie full-length on the floor. The remaining five had to lean against the wall by the oil drum. The positions were rotated during the night but if someone needed to use the oil drum the whole arrangement was disturbed. There was to be further mistreatment in the morning when they were ordered out of the foul-smelling hut and made to watch as the SS guards played games with other camp inmates, ordering them out of their huts and then beating them when the emerged. This process was repeated several times to show the newcomers that they had no hope.

It was part of a deliberate process of dehumanisation to which the prisoners were subjected. After this pathetic display the prisoners were allowed to wash in a tank full of filthy water in the centre of the square. They were then given a small amount of black bread and a thin soup in which floated pieces of mangel-wurzel.

The prisoners could not believe what they were seeing and demanded to see the camp commandant, insisting that they had certain rights under the Geneva Convention. The commandment told them that at Neue Bremm they had no rights. They were completely at the mercy of the SS guards. Of the various different accounts of the stay at Neue Bremm there are different memories about how long the group of prisoners stayed there. Hessel remembered just one night in the hut but Yeo-Thomas wrote that it was three nights. We will probably never know the real answer. Eventually, however, they were put back into prison vans and handed over to the Wehrmacht military police. The vans were driven into the bomb-damaged city to the Saarbrücken railway station where the prisoners were ordered into two cattle trucks that were coupled to the back of a troop train, carrying soldiers home from France. The atmosphere amongst the Germans was cheerful and the mood rubbed off on the prisoners. The cattle trucks might not have had any comforts but there was plenty of space and the regular army men were less barbaric than the SS men at Neue Bremm. They agreed to leave the doors of the cattle truck slightly open to allow fresh air to circulate. The guards were confident that none of the prisoners would dare to jump from the train if they were handcuffed to one another. The danger of injury was too great. But inside one of the trucks Loison was still trying to open the handcuffs. He did not want to remain a prisoner. It was not long afterwards that the youngster finally worked it out and soon several sets had been opened. The breakthrough offered great hope for those who wanted to make a break for it but it was not long before a dispute broke out. Some of the prisoners wanted to open the doors and simply jump from the train. Others did not want to take any more risks and wanted to avoid stirring up trouble. They were afraid that if some of the prisoners made an escape those who were captured or remained behind would be shot. The experience at Neue Bremm had worried everyone. The debate became increasingly heated and when the anti-escapers threatened to inform the Germans guards that an escape was being planned both Yeo-Thomas and Benoist had to be restrained from attacking those who were against the escape. After the period at Neue Bremm, Benoist had joined the ranks of those who wanted to escape. He was willing to take whatever risks were necessary to escape and find a way of getting back to France.

Discipline needed to be maintained and, in the end, the would-be escapers reluctantly accepted that they could not simply abandon those who were still handcuffed. The decision not to make an escape attempt left bad feelings within the group.

That evening, at a station somewhere in Germany, the prisoners were ordered out of the cattle trucks and transferred to a normal railway carriage, in which they could stretch out on proper seats. Hessel, who spoke fluent German, talked to the officer in charge of the military escort and discovered that their destination was a camp called KZ Buchenwald.

No-one had ever heard of it.

"He painted a glowing picture of the place," remembered Harry Peuleve, "with a fine library with books in all languages, concerts, a cinema, a theatre, a brothel and a hospital."

As this information spread amongst the prisoners the mood

improved a little and they relaxed and some even slept as the train made its way across Germany. The prisoners did not know where they were being taken but after their experiences in Neue Bremm they felt that nothing could be worse than the vicious treatment they has received in the transit camp.

The journey lasted for the rest of the day and it was close to midnight before the train pulled into Hauptbahnhof in the city of Weimar. The carriage in which they had been travelling was uncoupled from the train and was then shunted back up a spur line which led up through the woods to the north of the city to a special enclosure, surrounded on all sides by tall fences, topped with barbed wire.

The regular Wehrmacht guards who had accompanied the group from Neue Bremm handed over the prisoners to the SS. The Robert Benoist group formed up and marched through the night along a road called the Carachoweg towards the gates of KZ Buchenwald.

CHAPTER EIGHTEEN

Buchenwald was once a beautiful place. In his old age the German poet Johann Wolfgang von Goethe would often walk up from the city of Weimar to the hill at Ettersburg and sit beneath the old oak tree on the northern side of the woods, which rise 750ft above the surrounding countryside.

For him it was a magical place. The name "Buchenwald" means "forest of beech trees" but in 1937 the Nazi government selected the hill as the place to establish what it called a Konzentrationslager, to house the opponents of Adolf Hitler's ideas and minorities considered undesirable by the Nazis. It was not the first of the concentration camps but Sachsenhausen in the north and Dachau in the south had both grown to such an extent that they needed to build Buchenwald to ease the pressure.

When the war came, the prisoners in the camps were used as slave labour, working 12 hours a day in the Deutsche Ausrüstungswerke (DAW) factory. Buchenwald was not a death camp like Auschwitz or Treblinka, but discipline was extreme and the inmates were required to work for their food. Buchenwald's notoriety has much to do with its infamous Block 50, the Waffen SS's Typhus and Virus Research Division, where SS doctors carried out medical experiments on live human beings.

Between 1937 and 1945 around 239,000 prisoners passed through Buchenwald. The official records say that 33,462 died there. That may be a terrible toll but it is nothing compared to the death camps which were built later to exterminate people with industrial efficiency. Most of the deaths at Buchenwald occurred in the later years when the camp, which had been designed to hold 10,000 prisoners, housed 82,000 inmates. By August 1944 around 300 people were dying each day.

According to surviving records the 37 secret agents belonging to the "Robert Benoist group" arrived at Buchenwald on August 27 1944. They were handcuffed and dressed in civilian clothing. As it was late at night they were taken straight to the disinfection building where they were locked in a room until morning, sleeping as best they could on the tiled floor. When daylight came the Germans returned and ordered the prisoners to strip. Their heads and entire bodies were shaved and they were then submerged in a large tub of disinfectant to kill lice and bacteria, the Germans being particularly worried about the spread of typhus. The prisoners then had to go to the showers. After weeks of living in filthy prisons and on the road the hot water went a long way to reviving their spirits. They were once again sprayed with a stinging disinfectant and were then sent on through a tunnel to the storehouse, where each prisoner was given one of the blue and white striped uniforms of the concentration camp prisoners. Each prisoner had a red triangle sewn onto his jackets. They laughed at one another's appearance before other inmates warned them that Buchenwald was no place for laughter.

The red triangle indicated that they were political prisoners and they were then marched off to Block 17, an isolation unit that housed around 400 people. Word quickly spread through the camp that a group of captured parachutists had arrived and there was much interest amongst the other Block 17 inmates. For some of the prisoners it was an opportunity to see old friends from the Resistance who had arrived at the camp before them.

From their new home the SOE agents could see little of the main camp. There were a series of long wooden huts, each of them about 50 metres long. Inside each "block" there were three-tier bunk beds crammed in so that the building could house up to 250 prisoners. The huts were ranged on the northern slope of the hillside and were all overlooked by the main camp building, which featured a gatehouse and a wing on either side. On top of the gatehouse was a watchtower from which guards could see the entire camp. In front of the gatehouse was a parade ground where there were roll calls each morning and each evening. Looking up from the camp there was the camp jail, known as the Zellenbau, on the right side of the gatehouse, while on the left side were the camp administration offices. To the right of the parade ground was a canteen where the prisoners were fed and on the left, up near the perimeter fence was the crematorium, which was surrounded by a wall which hid what was going on inside. The new prisoners were told that this was where executions took place. It was a reminder that at Buchenwald life was cheap. The entire camp was ringed by 22 watchtowers, each manned by three sentries. The fencing was electrified and there were guards patrolling in the woods outside the wire.

Block 17 came under the control of a block leader, a German communist prisoner, who explained to the new prisoners how the camp worked. During the first day they watched through the wires that separated them from the rest of the camp and saw a number of prisoners who were just wandering around in a listless way.

"These people were called 'the muslims'," remembered Stéphane Hessel. "They had given up all hope and wandered around the camp very sadly and apathetically. They did not live long. Others, like the resistance workers - managed to keep up their hopes."

That first evening the agents watched the slave labourers return and witnessed the nightly roll call and the brutality to which the prisoners were subjected by the SS guards. As special prisoners they did not have to work but this meant that they had a problem finding things to do to keep themselves busy.

"The block leader wanted us to do exercise in the morning," remembered Hessel. "We spent most of the rest of the time just waiting. Waiting for nothing. We did not know what was going to happen to us."

Yeo-Thomas decided that in order to keep up morale the group should adopt a strict regime and it was decided that they would wash every morning from head to foot and would shave with a razor which Benoist had somehow managed to keep hold of despite all the searches. Whenever they were required to march anywhere Yeo-Thomas ordered that they would do so in columns and they would sing as they marched to keep up their spirits and create the right impression for the other prisoners.

To help pass the time Yeo-Thomas organised a chess competition with a chess set which Desmond Hubble, one of the agents, had managed to hold on to throughout his adventures, while Frank Pickersgill made some playing cards and a bridge competition was soon organized. Hessel decided that he would do his bit for morale by using the playing cards to read fortunes.

"Strangely enough, the card that means 'in a little while' came out for many of them," he remembered. "I told them that in three weeks they would be free."

After a few days some of the agents were given permission to go into the main camp and Yeo-Thomas, Southgate, Frager and Benoist began to study the layout to see if there was any way that an escape could be organised. On one of his trips into the main camp Robert met Professor Alfred Balachowsky, who had been a Prosper agent but was now working with the typhus programme in the notorious Block 50, where the Germans conducted medical experiments.

Balachowsky invited a handful of the agents to dinner – and even managed to acquire a rabbit for them to eat. The artist Auguste Favier was there and drew portraits of several of the SOE prisoners, including Benoist. They learned that a few days before their arrival the US Air Force had bombed the Buchenwald factory, killing 384 prisoners and wounding another 600. During the raid the inmates had cheered the bomber but later, when the death toll became known there seemed little consolation in the fact that 80 SS men had also been killed. The raid was a blow to the German morale, however, particularly as the old oak tree in the middle of the camp - named Goethe's Oak – had been so badly damaged by an incendiary bomb which had drifted into the camp that it had to be cut down.

"The news of the bombing gave us some hope," Hessel remembered, "many people had been killed but we said: 'Ah, now the Allies are coming'."

But the Allied troops would not get there soon enough for many of the inmates. On Saturday September 9, a fortnight after the arrival of the Benoist group, the Reichssicherheitshauptamt (RHSA) in Berlin sent camp commandant SS Oberführer Hermann Pister, an SS man who had been in charge of Buchenwald since December 1941, a list of 16 of the prisoners who should be given "sonderbehandlung" (special treatment). He knew it was an execution order.

Buchenwald did not have gas chambers and while some of those killed at the camp were shot, there was a far more barbaric method used for those who were given 'special treatment'. In the basement of the crematorium was an execution chamber, known as the Leichenkeller (literally the "corpse cellar") where prisoners were choked to death by slow strangulation, their bodies dangling from a series of meat hooks that were mounted on the walls about eight feet above the floor. It is reckoned that by the end of the war as many as 1100 people had been killed in this barbaric way.

After the July Bomb Plot against him Hitler had ordered that some of those involved be killed in this way and the executions were even filmed and watched by the Führer and his staff.

On the Sunday afternoon the Buchenwald loudspeakers announced that "the following Block 17 prisoners should report to the Zellenbau: Allard, Benoist, Defendini, Garel, Garry, Geelen...". There were 16 names. Thinking it was an identity check, the men fell in four by four and marched off with Frank Pickersgill leading the singing as they went. They did not return that evening and the Block Leader told Yeo-Thomas quietly that they would probably never be seen again.

The following morning - Monday, September 11 - Polish orderlies from the main camp reported that the 16 were still alive but had been beaten up and locked in the cells in the Zellenbau. This building had two rows of cells facing one another with a central corridor between them. On the north side the windows looked out over the rest of the camp, on the south side the cells had only air holes. Later on the Monday there were further reports that the 16 had been seen again but on Tuesday morning came news which shook the remaining prisoners. The orderlies reported that at 5.30pm on the Monday the 16 men had been taken to the Leichenkeller and had been killed by slow strangulation. The bodies were then cut down and a hand-operated elevator transported them upstairs to the ovens where they were cremated. No trace of the prisoners remained.

The surviving 21 agents were horrified.

"It was a severe blow to all of us," remembered Hessel.

From then on they lived in fear that the loudspeakers would call their names, but it would be another three weeks before Pister received his next special treatment order from the RHSA. Another 11 prisoners were ordered to report to the Zellenbau. Only 10 of the 11 marched away that day - October 4. The eleventh name on the list was Harry Peuleve and he failed to appear. The Germans were told that he had contracted typhoid and was dying in Block 46, where those infected in the Block 50 experiments were housed. It was in fact a ruse, a desperate plan devised by Viennese lawyer Eugen Krogon and Professor Balachowsky after the first 16 executions to try to save at least some of the SOE men. In the end it saved only three: Peuleve, Yeo-Thomas and Hessel. Each was injected with a mild dose of typhus to give them symptoms of the disease, but not enough to kill them. As soon as another typhoid victim in Block 46 died the agent would switch identities with the dead man. The authorities would be informed that the secret agent had died and the survivor would be returned to a different part of the camp under a new identity.

There was no saving the 10 men who marched away on October

4. They knew they were going to be executed but they intended to die with honour. The senior officer of the group Paul Frager demanded that as officers they had the right to die in front of a firing squad, rather than the barbaric slow strangulation. It was contrary to his orders but Pister agreed and the 10 men were marched to the SS rifle range where they were executed by firing squad.

With 26 of the original party dead and three typhoid 'victims' there were only eight of the Benoist Group now left. Three more were called to their executions in the days that followed but for reasons which have never been clear five were overlooked. One can only presume that they were forgotten amid the bureaucratic chaos into which the Third Reich was sinking by the late autumn of 1944.

The perpetrators of the murders at Buchenwald did not go unpunished. When the camp was liberated the SS guards ran away but some of the prisoners hunted them down and captured around 80 of them. Most were killed. Pister was captured by the Allies and put on trial. He claimed that he had not ordered or condoned any mistreatment, torture or killing but his defence soon broke down. He was convicted and sentenced to be hanged but he died in prison before the sentence could be carried out.

The murders at Buchenwald were not the only ones that autumn and were mirrored by similar - but less barbaric - killings in camps across Germany and Poland.

At KZ Sachsenshausen, to the north of Berlin, there were only two F Section prisoners: Francis Suttill and Willy Grover, the two 1943 network organizers from Paris. Both prisoners were obviously considered to be important. Willy's interrogations at the Avenue Foch had lasted for about a month after his arrest at the start of August 1943. He had stubbornly refused to give anything of any value away - despite very rough treatment.

In September his wife Yvonne had been arrested in Paris and the Germans had tried to use her to make Willy talk. He refused. With each passing day the value of the knowledge he was protecting faded and the Germans eventually seemed to give up. Yvonne was released on October 8 and at some point in the weeks after that Willy was deported to Germany. There are no records of the journey although Robert Benoist radioed London with the news of Willy's deportation in January 1944.

Suttill is known to have arrived at Sachsenhausen in September 1943 but Willy Grover spent some time in the cells at the RHSA building in Berlin. This was the Reich Security Office, the umbrella organization of the SD, the Gestapo and a number of other police divisions. It was located at 8 Prinz Albrechtstrasse, in a vast and ornate building which had once been Germany's School of Industrial Arts and Crafts. When the Nazi Party took power in 1933 it was taken over and the classrooms and studios became the offices of the Nazi police machine. In the basement there were 39 cells where prisoners of particular interest were kept.

The interrogation techniques at Prinz Albrechtstrasse were notoriously unpleasant with vicious beatings and primitive tortures such as thumb screws and racks and more advanced ways of inflicting pain using electricity in order to force information from the prisoners. Some prisoners died under torture, others killed themselves to avoid giving away secrets. Many talked, beaten into submission by the brutal SS. It is not known what, if anything, the Germans got - or tried to get - from Grover.

By that stage of the war the torture was only part of the psychological battering that prisoners in Berlin had to endure. The German capital was a city under siege from the air.

The Royal Air Force heavy bombers had begun pounding the German capital in August 1943 with three huge raids in the space of only 10 days. These attacks provided an important publicity coup for the British and at the same time were a significant blow to the German morale, although the cost of the raids was appalling, with Bomber Command suffering an 8% casualty rate on each raid, its heaviest losses of the war up to that point. The casualties were such that after the three raids the RAF had to turn its attention to less difficult targets in order to win time to replace the air crew and aircraft that had been lost.

Bomber Command went back to Berlin in November 1943, dropping 8,500 tons of bombs in a week of raids on consecutive nights. The bombers returned in December and again in January dropping, another 15,000 tons of bombs in nine different raids during the period. Throughout the bombing the RHSA building emerged unscathed.

Early in March Grover was ordered out of his cells at the Prinz Albrechtstrasse and taken by prison van through the city, across the River Spree, and northward to the town of Oranienburg. Just outside the town was the KZ Sachsenhausen.

This had been established in 1936 but like Buchenwald was seriously overcrowded by the start of 1945. It was operated on the same system as Buchenwald with the prisoners working in the local factories to earn their food. There were no gas chambers but starvation, disease and executions resulted in the deaths of around 100,000 people at Sachsenhausen in the course of its existence.

Grover remained a special prisoner and was locked into the Zellenbau, which was slightly different to the prison at Buchenwald. At Sachsenhausen the Zellenbau was a self-contained compound within the main camp. It was completely surrounded by a nine foot high wall, topped with electrified wire. The building was a T-shaped construction with the three corridors meeting in the middle by the main entrance door. In this central area was an interrogation room, a room for the warders, a room for orderlies, a cell where the barber worked, a boiler room, a lavatory and a store.

Around the building was a garden, although by March 1944 part of this had been dug up to create an air raid shelter, following the heavy RAF night raids. Being 17 miles from the city centre, Sachsenhausen avoided most of the bombs aimed at Berlin but during the last big RAF raid - shortly after Grover arrived - high winds caused the attacking streams of RAF bombers to be spread out much more than usual. When German night-fighter aircraft attacked the bombers were further split up and in the course of the night Bomber Command suffered its heaviest losses of the war. Planes jettisoned their bombs wherever they could and headed for home. A string of seven phosphorus bombs fell on the Zellenbau, one landing on either side of the block. Fortunately they were not close enough to set fire to the building. The raid gave some of the inmates the chance to meet other prisoners in the bomb shelter, although Grover arrived too late to make any lengthy contact with the other British prisoners. The best known of these was Captain Sigismund Payne-Best, a pre-war British secret agent who had been snatched by the German intelligence service in a cross-border raid at Venlo in Holland in November 1939. He had been in the Zellenbau for five years.

Another prisoner was the famous Royal Air Force escaper Wing Commander Harry "Wings" Day. He too had been a prisoner since 1939 and had led the famous Great Escape from Stalag Luft III at Sagan. He had been fortunate to escape execution as had three other survivors of The Great Escape: Flight Lieutenants Sydney Dowse and "Jimmy" James and Major Johnny Dodge, a man who was always known as "The Dodger". Despite their escaping skills none of them could find a way out of the Zellenbau.

There was also a Lieutenant-Colonel Jack Churchill. He was no relation to the British Prime Minister Winston Churchill but the Germans were somehow convinced that there was a connection and were holding him as a possible hostage. It was a similar story for another of the Zellenbau prisoners: Russian Lieutenant Wassilli Kokorin Molotowsk, a nephew of Soviet Foreign Affairs Minister Vyacheslav Mikhaylovich Molotov. There were members of several deposed royal families from Eastern Europe and a number of important German dissidents, some of whom had been in the Zellenbau since before the war broke out.

And there was Suttill but even inside the compound the

security was extraordinarily strict. The names of the prisoners were never used, the inmates being referred to only by the number of the cell in which they lived. They were not allowed to talk.

They were forgotten men.

Despite this, Payne-Best's many years in the camp had enabled him to build up good relationships with some of the guards (although to avoid this happening they were regularly changed) and he was able to use them to arrange for some of his English books to be given to other British prisoners.

In the summer of 1944 news of the Allied invasion did leak into the Zellenbau and there was some optimism for the future. But then came the July Bomb Plot against Adolf Hitler and the cells in the Zellenbau became a stopping-off point for a string of high-ranking German officers on their way to execution. Later, more British servicemen arrived in the Zellenbau, saboteurs who had been caught operating behind enemy lines. There was Lieutenant-Commander Claude Cumberlege of the Royal Navy and three non-commissioned officers: Sergeant Thomas Handley (Royal Signals), Company Sergeant-Major James Steele (Black Watch) and Corporal Jan Kotbra (who was imprisoned under the alias of Sergeant Davies) of the Czech Field Forces.

The six saboteurs were treated badly by the German guards and Paul Schröter, a prisoner who was employed as an orderly inside the Zellenbau reported that Willy Grover in particular was picked out for rough treatment.

"He received the most brutal treatment of the six men," Schröter told Allied investigators after the war. Schröter reported that the adjutant of the camp Heinrich Wessel often visited the Zellenbau, even at night, and beat and kicked the prisoners. Wessel was eventually tried for war crimes. He was sentenced to seven and a half years in prison.

"Their health can well be imagined on a diet of wurzels cooked in water," reported Schröter. "They never received any Red

Cross parcels. Some officer prisoners of war helped them with Red Cross things. There was Captain Best and some of the greatest of the British escapers and a number of others including American and Danish officers in transit - all of whom received a better diet. They helped as much as they could by passing food to the six. We orderlies, too, when it was possible, gave them extra 'swill' if there was any left over, which we smuggled into them at night. Despite this the six were very emaciated. They never required the attendance of the medical officer though they suffered from skin complaints and teeth ailments."

The six were held in cells which were seven feet by five feet in size. They contained a bed, a small table, a cupboard, a stool and a bucket to act as a latrine. The windows in each cell were made from frosted glass and were covered outside with a fine wire mesh. Every morning prisoners were each allowed only 15 minutes of exercise out of doors but they were never allowed out at the same time.

In this dismal place Grover and Suttill lived out the final months of the war, hoping that liberation would finally come and that they would be able to return home. At least a dozen prisoners gave up hope and tried to commit suicide by cutting their wrists or hanging themselves. Winter came and as the German armies retreated in the east and the west. Conditions in Germany became worse and worse and the camp began to suffer desperate food shortages.

Thirty miles to the north of Sachsenhausen, in the Ravensbrück concentration camp Violette Szabo, Denise Bloch and Lilian Rolfe, the three SOE girls who had travelled to Germany with Robert Benoist, were still alive. They had survived the work camps of Torgau and Königsberg, helping to build airfields, but then in February 1945 they were suddenly summoned back to Ravensbrück and put into the high security Zellenbau cells there. On February 5 the three were led from their prison to the wall of the cemetery, next to the crematorium. Camp Commandant Fritz Suhren read out an order for their execution. The camp's deputy commandant Johann

Schwarzhuber reported that the three were brave until the end.

"I was deeply moved," Schwarzhuber told SOE investigators after the war. "Suhren was also impressed by the bearing of these women. He was annoyed that the Gestapo did not themselves carry out these shootings."

The executions were carried out by a corporal, who fired a small-calibre revolver into the back of the neck of each girl. The corpses were taken to the crematorium and immediately burnt.

They had ceased to exist.

That same day the Yalta Conference opened in the Crimea, with the Allied leaders planning for the new post-war world.

By the end of February 1945, when the wind blew from the East, the prisoners in the Zellenbau at Sachsenhausen could hear the gunfire from the Oder Front, as the Red Army battled on towards Berlin. Inside their high-security prison the inmates began to worry about liberation. There were fears that if the prisoners in the main camp were released they would seek retribution. There were a few SS prisoners in the cells in the Zellenbau and the Allied captives were worried that they might be killed in error.

On March 7 the 27th Armoured Infantry Battalion of the US Ninth Armoured Division reached the Rhine at the town of Remagen and discovered that one of the bridges over the Rhine was still standing. Hitler had ordered all bridges to be blown up but the Ludendorff Bridge at Remagen had not been destroyed. It was a railway bridge but the Germans had covered the rails with wooden planks to allow normal vehicles to get across. General William Hodge realised the significance of the bridge and ordered his troops to cross the river immediately before the bridge was demolished. As the first American units approached the bridge there was a huge explosion but the bridge remained intact. Within a few hours a bridgehead over the Rhine had been established. Hitler was furious that his orders had been disobeyed and four German officers were executed in the days that followed. The damage was done. The Americans were across the

Rhine. The German High Command knew that there was now no hope. Hitler refused to countenance the idea of a surrender.

A week after the Remagen disaster Hitler made his last journey out from the bunker beneath the Reich Chancellery in Berlin, visiting the Oder Front, where the German forces were desperately fighting to hold back the mighty Red Army. As the inevitability of defeat began to sink in, the Nazi bureaucracy embarked on the appalling policy of murdering its important prisoners. The RHSA in Berlin sent out a list of political prisoners who should be given 'special treatment'. That list included the names Suttill and Grover.

"I saw them for the last time round about March 15-18," Schröter told SOE investigator Vera Atkins. "They were transported by ambulance car to the Industriehof, where they were most certainly executed by either hanging, shooting or lethal chamber. I was not an eyewitness of the execution but we knew only too well from the usual procedure that they were done to death. After the execution I assisted Petzke, the Head Camp Orderly, in packing their effects, and taking them to the Kommandatur, from where it was said they were despatched to the Gestapo HQ at Columbia Haus in Berlin."

Schröter collected up the papers belonging to the prisoners and with the help of the boiler room attendant burned them all.

"Their prison garb was handed back to us by mistake," remembered Schröter. "We sent it to the quartermaster stores, where it ought to have gone in the first place."

The other four saboteurs disappeared in similar fashion three weeks later. For many years no-one knew for certain how Willy Grover and Suttill died. After the war many of the SS who had been at Sachsenhausen disappeared without trace. The Russians spared no-one wearing the hated SS uniform. If SS men were captured they were immediately shot. Some fought to the death in the ruins of Berlin, some slipped away, disguised as regular soldiers or civilians.

SOE investigators were never able to find any trace of the two men but they knew that the Industriehof was where Sachsenhausen prisoners were executed. The SS jokingly nicknamed it "Station Z" because prisoners arrived at Sachsenhausen by way of Building A and exited at Station Z. The British concluded that they died on March 18 1945, the last date on which they were seen alive.

In 2006 documents finally emerged from the old KGB archives in Moscow relating to the trial of an SS Sergeant called Kurt Eccarius, the man who had been in charge of the Zellenbau. These revealed that in December 1946 Eccarius told Russian investigators that at "the end of February 1945" he took Grover, Suttill an Italian officer called Bacigalupi and a Norwegian Peer Nilsen to the crematorium.

"All these people were shot," he said.

The dates do not tally but it was clear evidence of what had happened. Another statement from the trial, however, caused a certain amount of confusion as it quoted a Soviet officer called Nowikow reporting the existence of a book which listed all the inmates who had passed through the Zellenbau and what had happened to them. This book mentioned that Suttill was "released to the crematorium" on March 23 1945, on the orders of Horst Kopkow's IV-A2 department of the RHSA.

The suggestion that he had been released led to some curious suggestions that Will Grover had ended up working for MI6 before returning to France and living under an assumed name with Yvonne.

It was a romantic idea but the reality was sadder. "Released to the crematorium" meant execution.

On the evening of March 23 - the same day - Allied armies under General Bernard Montgomery launched an all-out attack across the Rhine river, into the German heartland. A 30-mile stretch on the eastern bank of the Rhine, around the town of Wesel, was subjected to a massive bombardment by allied artillery and bomber aircraft. After two hours of pounding by guns and bombs, the German defenders had to face a brigade of British commandos, crossing the river and attacking what was left of the old medieval town. To the north of the town units of the British Second Army went across the river while in the south there was a similar movement by elements of the US Ninth Army. At dawn two parachute divisions - the British Sixth Airborne and the American 17th dropped at the German rear. The carefully orchestrated attack met strong resistance but after a period of heavy fighting the Germans began to fall back and the Allied advance into Germany began on a broad front, the British armies moving quickly across the ground in the north and the Americans flat-out in the south. There was little resistance.

By April 11 the armies had reached the River Elbe, which was only 60 miles to the west of the German capital Berlin. But there, the advance halted as had been agreed by Winston Churchill, Joseph Stalin and Franklin D Roosevelt.

Five days later the Russian armies under Marshal Grigory Zhukov burst out of the bridgeheads on the German side of the River Oder, while the armies under Marshal Ivan Koniev crossed the Neisse River to the south of Berlin and attacked towards the city. By April 25 the two armies had encircled the German capital and on the same day American and Russian troops met amid much rejoicing at the town of Torgau. That evening the Italian dictator Benito Mussolini tried to flee Italy but was intercepted by Communist partisans. The following morning he was taken out and shot.

The Russian armies drove on into Berlin. KZ Sachsenhausen was liberated but by then the whole of Nazi Germany was disintegrating. As the Russians tightened their grip on Berlin, Hitler stayed in his bunker under the Chancellery on the Wilhelmstrasse. On the night of April 30, the situation having become hopeless, Hitler committed suicide. The Third Reich, which he had boasted would last for a thousand years, survived him by only eight days.

The German surrender on May 8 was greeted with widespread rejoicing around the world. The war was still being fought in the Pacific but in Europe attention turned to rebuilding a continent that had been destroyed by six years of war and the deaths of tens of millions of people. As the full horror of Nazi Germany was revealed, thousands were left asking what had happened to missing relatives. Organizations such as the International Red Cross tried to track down some of the missing but with many of the German records from the camps having been destroyed as the Nazis tried to hide what they had been doing and other information having ended up in the hands of the Russians there was no easy way to establish facts.

There have been many estimates of the number of Frenchmen and women who were deported to Germany but the accepted figure now appears to have been something in the region of 140,000. Seventy-five thousand of these were Jews. Only 2,200 of the 75,000 came back from the death camps in the East - a survival rate of only one and a half percent. The other 65,000 French deportees were either political prisoners or resistance fighters and about 26,000 of them - 40% - returned from the camps in Germany and Poland. Many were in very poor health but they had survived.

The intense secrecy surrounding the activities (and indeed the existence) of F Section made things more difficult for the relatives of the missing secret agents and things were not helped by the fact that the organization was very quickly disbanded. The task of tracking down the missing SOE agents was doubly difficult as the Nazi administration had gone to considerable lengths to leave no trace at all of the saboteurs.

In London the staff at F Section headquarters knew the numbers. They had sent a total of 393 agents into France, although a large percentage of these had been "Jedburgh" commando units, which had been dropped into France in the period leading up to and immediately after the D Day landings. As news filtered back to London from Germany a depressing picture began to emerge. F Section established that 119 of its agents had been either captured or killed in France. Of those who had been taken prisoner only 17 returned from Germany.

The remaining 100 were left unaccounted for.

CHAPTER NINETEEN

The bells of the church of St Pierre in Neuilly-sur-Seine were tolling on the morning of May 29 1945. A memorial service had been organized in memory of Robert Benoist and many of his friends from the automobile world were there to remember the sacrifice he had made for his country. There were many wreathes, including a discreet one from the British Embassy, and a small party from the British Consulate was present at the service. Captain FW Hazeldene reported later that the presence at the ceremony of Maurice Benoist was for many "an unpleasant surprise". At the time there were only rumours about Maurice and he defended himself robustly against any claim that he had worked with the Germans.

Robert's many admirers from the racing world decided that they wanted to create an event in his honour and as soon as the war in Europe was over the Association Générale Automobile des Coureurs Indépendants, under its president Maurice Mestivier, began planning for a race meeting. The war in the Pacific was still grinding on but in Europe peace had returned and Europe was beginning the process of rebuilding. Mestivier and his colleagues agreed that a major racing event would be good for morale, particularly if the race could be held in the Paris area, at a venue where thousands of people could attend the race.

Mestivier, a racer himself, had worked his way up through the ranks, starting out as a mechanic at Amilcar in 1921. Four years later his brother Marius was killed when he had a brake failure early in the Le Mans 24 Hours. Maurice would eventually become the chief development engineer at Amilcar, working closely with André Morel.

When the company closed its competition department he continued to work there, selling road cars. In this role he found himself in competition with Benoist at Bugatti, although the Amilcars were rather less luxurious (and a great deal cheaper) than Bugattis. Mestivier became the president of the AGACI in 1937 and was not a man to back down in the face of a challenge. Running a motor race in the months after the war was not an easy thing to achieve, despite the fact that the event had the backing of one of the largest resistance associations - the Groupement National des Réfractaires et Maquisards (GNRM). It was agreed that any profit made would go to a fund, which had been set up by the GNRM for former prisoners and war victims.

The major problems were not to do with the authorities but rather of a more practical nature. There were, for example, no new racing cars; many of the pre-war machines had been hidden away during the fighting, but these were all at least six years old and a lot were in a very poor state of repair. Racing tyres were almost impossible to find in any large quantity. The easiest task was to find a venue and the club quickly came up with a road circuit to be laid out in the Bois de Boulogne, a vast public park in the west of Paris. The circuit was to be 1.72 miles in length and would be within easy reach of the Paris Métro station at the Porte Dauphine. This meant that tens of thousands of Parisians could attend the event using public transport.

The start-finish line was located close to the Carrefour du Bout-des-Lacs, a crossroads located at the end of one of the man-made boating ponds in the middle of the park. The pits were on the Route de Suresnes, running from the crossroads down to the Porte Dauphine, one of the gates of the old city, although the fortifications were now overgrown and falling down. This was just a couple of hundred metres from the old SD headquarters on the Avenue Foch. At the Porte Dauphine there was a hairpin where the road curled to the right went back into the park, running down a section of road known as the Allée des Fortifications, until it reached the Avenue de Saint Cloud and curled around to the right before arriving at a second hairpin at the junction of the Avenue de Saint Cloud and the Chemin de Ceinture du Lac Inférieur. From there it headed back towards the pits on to a very challenging section of track, about 600m in length with the cars going through two consecutive sets of esses, with the boating lake on the left, until they arrived back at the Carrefour du Bout-des-Lacs, which had become a high-speed right hand corner.

Preparations for the race went on throughout the summer of 1945 as Europeans watched the fighting in the Pacific gradually moving towards to its inevitable conclusion. And then came a shock. President Harry S Truman, who had taken over when Franklin D Roosevelt died in April, decided that in order to speed up the end of the war and save American lives, he would use a terrifying new secret weapon called an atomic bomb to convince the Japanese that it was impossible to win the war.

On the morning of August 6, a Boeing B-29 bomber called the Enola Gay, piloted by Colonel Paul Tibbets dropped the first atomic bomb, nicknamed "Little Boy" on the city of Hiroshima. The temperature of the air at the moment of detonation was calculated to have been more than one million degrees C, with a fireball 280m in diameter. The shock wave created by the explosion was such that thousands of people were picked up by the 1000mph wind and hurled through the air or crushed in their collapsing houses. Every wooden building within two kilometres was destroyed. More than 100,000 people died and more would die in the months and years that followed as the deadly radiation added to the death toll.

The power of the new weapon shocked the world. The Japanese government reeled but tried desperately to fight on and so on the morning on August 9 a second B-29 nicknamed Bockscar set off to bomb Kokura in the south-west of the country. Bad weather forced the pilot to switch to his secondary target, the city of Nagasaki, where a bigger bomb called "Fat Man" was dropped, killing another 150,000

Japanese. The attacks were a devastating blow to the country and on August 14, the Emperor Hirohito accepted the American terms of surrender and ordered the Japanese forces to lay down their weapons. It took two weeks for the official surrender to be organized but on Sunday September 2 the official surrender documents were signed aboard the battleship USS Missouri in Tokyo Bay.

The world was at peace again.

Seven days later, somewhere between 90,000 and 200,000 Parisians, depending on which account one believes, turned up in the Bois de Boulogne to watch the first post-war motor race - and to celebrate the fact that they were at liberty again.

The first event that day, the first motor racing competition of the new era, was called the Coupe Robert Benoist. A 36-lap race for a field of small capacity cars with engines between 750cc and 1.5-litres. There were 17 cars entered for the race, including three prepared by engine wizard Amedée Gordini for himself, Jean Brault and Robert Cayeux; there were two old Salmsons for AGACI vice-president Just-Émile Vernet and Robert-Aimé Bouchard; there were a pair of Rileys for the engineer Pierre Ferryand and Georges Brunot. There was a DB, designed and driven by engineer Charles Deutsch and a Singer entered by Jacques Savoye who had a showroom in the nearby Rue Brunel. Victor Polledry drove an Aston Martin and the rest of the field was made up of an Adler, an Amilcar, a Fiat and even a small Bugatti.

Before the race began Ettore Bugatti, Le Patron himself arrived in his magnificent personal Bugatti Royale. The crowd was barely contained by the Paris police, who were helped out by the US Military Police.

At the start of the race Gordini took the lead and he went on to lead the entire 62-mile event, coming home ahead of his team mates Brault and Cayeux but the result was not important. The noise and the speed of the cars had thrilled the crowd and then they pulled off the track one by one and fell silent. A lone bugler sounded the Last

Post and the crowd rose and for a minute stayed silent in memory of Benoist, a man who had done so much for French motor racing. A bouquet of flowers was presented to Jacqueline Garnier, Robert's daughter.

The tribute was finished and the sadness passed as the engines began to fire up for the second race of the day, which was called the Coupe de la Liberation. This was for cars with engines between 1.5 and three-litres and attracted a good field of 15 cars including six Amilcars, one of them driven by Mestivier; René Bonnet, the co-founder of DB was in one of his own cars, while Auguste Veuillet, a motorcycle racer who went on to become Porsche's importer in France, was in an MG Magnette. Polledry reappeared in an Alfa Romeo 1750 but the race was won with ease by Henri Louveau in a Maserati 6CM, the only driver in the field to have a three-litre machine at his disposal.

The main event was open to cars with engines of more than 3-litre capacity and the winner would receive the Coupe des Prisonniers. There were 16 entries, seven of them being pre-war Delahaye 135Ss, with the drivers including 38-year-old Eugene Chaboud, the winner of the 1938 Le Mans 24 Hours. The machinery was all rather outdated but almost all of the big name drivers from the 1930s were present, a little older and in some cases a little greyer. At 49 Philippe Étancelin was a little past his prime but he was driving an Alfa Romeo 8C with his usual gusto. Louis Gerard (46) was at the wheel of a Maserati 8CM, a car which had been racing 10 years earlier, while Raymond Sommer (39) was at the wheel of an old Talbot Lago T26. Pierre Levegh drove a second Talbot, a 150C.

There were five Bugattis, including a Type 55 which was being driven by Paul Friderich, the son of Ernest Friderich, the Bugatti dealer from Nice and Maurice Trintignant, who at 28 was hoping to make a name for himself in the sport, having lost some of his best years because of the war. He was at the wheel of a Bugatti Type 35/51, which he called "Grandma" and dated back to the early 1930s when it had originally been owned and raced by Maurice's brother Louis

Trintignant. It had been at the wheel of that very car that Louis had been killed while practising for the 1933 Grand Prix de Picardie. Maurice had been 16 at the time and the mourning family had sold the car but five years later Maurice bought it back and began racing in the months before the war broke out. In fact he did so well that he quickly became something of a protégé of Jean-Pierre Wimille, the big Bugatti star of the day. During the occupation of France the old Bugatti had been hidden under a haystack in a barn in the Vaucluse region but when the war ended Trintignant took "Grandma" out from under the haystack and went to work to restore the car.

René Dreyfus was missing. He had been in the United States when France was invaded in the summer of 1940 and had taken the decision to stay in America and had opened a restaurant in order to make a living. It did very well but when the United States entered the war after the Japanese attack on Pearl Harbor in December 1941 Dreyfus joined the US Army and later served as a GI in the European theatre before returning to his new home where he would soon open his first restaurant in New York City, to be called Le Gourmet. Dreyfus would live in the US for the rest of his life.

Another man who was missing was Louis Chiron, who had spent the war living quietly in Switzerland and would return to racing later although he was by then well past his best. He would win French Grands Prix in 1947 and 1949 and would take part in the official FIA Formula 1 World Championship when it began in 1950 although by then he was in his fifties. Chiron would retire in 1955 but remained around the racing scene, acting as Clerk of the Course for the Monaco Grand Prix until the end of the 1960s.

The biggest star present for the Coupe des Prisonniers was Wimille himself. After his escape from the Germans during the raid on the Clergyman headquarters at Sermaise, Wimille had fought alongside the surviving members of the Turma-Vengeance movement in the Dourdan area. As soon as Paris was liberated in August 1944 he began working as a liaison officer between the Allied forces and the resistance and then, when some sense of order had begun to return to France, he enlisted in the Forces Aériennes Françaises Libres and after completing his training became a member of the Groupe de Reconnaissance III/33 which was based in Cognac, flying Bell P-63s in missions against the German pocket around Royan.

The group was then sent to Germany in the final months of the war. Lieutenant Wimille was still in the Armée de L'Air but thanks to the intervention of his old friend Captain François Sommer (brother of Raymond), he was able to fly back from Germany for the race. Sommer had been an early resistant with Ceux de la Libération and had then escaped to Britain at the start of 1943 and had joined the Free French Air Force. By the end of 1944 he had become chief staff officer of General Martial Valin, the commander-in-chief of the Armée de l'Air.

The whole process was completed at the last minute and Wimille arrived in Paris too late to be able to take part in the practice and qualifying. He would have to start from the back of the grid while Sommer was at the front in his factory Talbot. The Bugatti 59/50B was a factory car which had been raced in 1939 but had been hidden away by Robert Benoist during the war before the Germans could steal it. It had an eight cylinder engine producing 450bhp and was much more powerful than all the other cars, Sommer's Talbot boasting only 250bhp.

The state of preparation of many of the other cars was just as suspect and the race for the Coupe des Prisonniers had a very high attrition rate, with nine of the 16 cars retiring before they got to the finish. Wimille's progress from the back of the grid had the crowd on its feet. He was ninth by the time he reached the first corner and fourth by the end of the first lap. It was not long before he was up to second place and after a brief fight for the lead Wimille went ahead and pulled away.

"The car was extraordinary," Wimille told reporters after the race. "With this car I think I could win other races."

On the podium Wimille received the Coupe des Prisonniers and then a frail man with a shaven head stepped forward and handed him a second trophy. Albert Fremont had survived Buchenwald and was there to present the winner of the Coupe des Prisonniers with a special silver trophy called the Coupe Williams. This had been donated by Jean Boudon, an old friend of Willy and Yvonne Grover, who was running a restaurant in the rue Rennequin.

After the presentations Wimille returned to the paddock where he found the young Trintignant mulling over "Grandma", the old car having broken down during the race. Trintignant had tried to find the problem and discovered that the fuel filter was full of rat droppings, a family of rats having apparently made their home in the Bugatti fuel tank, during the time when "Grandma" was buried in the haystack. Wimille asked Trintignant what the problem had been and the miserable youngster replied "petoule" (rat shit), a remark that so amused Wimille that he immediately started calling Trintignant by the name of "Le Petoulet". This sobriquet stayed with Trintignant for the rest of his long racing career and when in 1960 he finally hung up his helmet he went back to running the family vineyard and renamed his wine "Le Petoulet".

The event had been a huge success and raised a large sum of money for the families of missing members of the resistance. It was left to the racing press to put it into the right perspective.

"Each spectator understood that the moral winner of the day," wrote Charles Faroux, the leading racing writer of the era, "was the country itself."

The race in the Bois de Boulogne was of great symbolic importance but also established France as the leading racing nation in the immediate post-war era and there was a strong field when the new season kicked off in Nice in April 1946, including not only the best French entries but also three Maseratis from the reformed Italian Scuderia Milan. There was an unpleasant interlude involving Robert Mazaud, a talented pre-war driver who had set the fastest lap at Le Mans in 1939 in a Delahaye. Mazaud was accused of making money from the German occupation forces and the drivers refused to compete with him. The problem was sorted out when it was revealed that Mazaud had also been involved with helping Benoist, supplying him with trucks for his resistance work.

There were races in Marseille and Forez and then in May the racers were back in the Bois de Boulogne, although on a different circuit to the previous autumn. Wimille had by then been demobilised from the Armée de l'Air and returned home to Paris where he quickly talked his way into a drive with Denise Depois's Écurie Naphta Course, alongside his old friend Raph. Depois was a wealthy woman but her husband had been jailed for collaborating a little too closely with the Germans, providing them with furniture for their barracks – a very lucrative business. As Depois was also a shareholder in the Naphta oil company, it was logical for the team to use that name for the team. The opposition came from Sommer's Maserati, which had been the most competitive car in the earlier races. The event also marked the return to the international scene of pre-war star Tazio Nuvolari but the Italian dropped out early with mechanical trouble and Sommer spun and so Wimille was able to win again.

Nine days later Wimille was back in an Alfa Romeo factory car, having been asked by Alfa Romeo's Competition Manager Giovanbattista Guidotti to drive for the Italian company alongside the pre-war ace Dr Nino Farina in the races on the streets of St Cloud, the event having been organized to celebrate the opening of France's first stretch of motorway which stretched from St Cloud out to Orgeval. The mayor of St Cloud had served with Wimille in the Armée de l'Air and paid some of the costs involved. The event was called the Grand Prix de l'Autoroute de l'Ouest and while Wimille failed to finish the race, it was nonetheless an important event for him as it marked the unveiling of the prototype Wimille road car, which he had spent the war working towards, having been frustrated that his racing career was interrupted.

Wimille had dreamed of a revolutionary sports car and at the end of 1943 he recruited two of Bugatti's designers Louis Viel and Pierre Leygonie and put them to work, designing the Wimille road car. Leygonie had been a friend of Benoist and had been a member of Turma-Vengeance with him and Wimille, while running a garage on the rue Murillo in Paris. Wimille was keen to have an aerodynamic car and engaged the carriage-builder Henri Chapron to create the bodywork. The resulting car was a dramatic prototype that drew considerable attention. Unusually, it had three seats side by side. The centrally-mounted engine was inside a tubular chassis and the gearbox was electrically-operated and fitted to the front of the engine. The plan was for the car to have a 1500cc V6 engine capable of producing 70 horsepower, but this was not ready for the launch and so the prototype had a Citroën engine. Initial tests gave the car a top speed of 75mph although when the V6 engine did appear that improved to 95mph. Wimille was rather disappointed with the testing and decided quite quickly that he would build a second car.

In the meantime "Cric" was pregnant and that year produced a boy who was named François.

Jean-Pierre continued racing that summer with wins for Écurie Naphta Course at Perpignan and Dijon, brushing off suggestions that he had somehow been involved in betraying Robert Benoist, despite accusations from Maurice Benoist. Wimille had always blamed Maurice for the arrests in 1943, while Maurice fired back with allegations that Wimille had had connections with the Vichy police chief René Bousquet which had enabled him to travel, using diplomatic papers, to Spain and Tangiers. Bousquet, so Maurice said, had also arranged special papers for Madame Wimille – who came from a Jewish family - so that she could avoid deportation. While it is clear that in the late 1930s and during the early part of the war that Wimille had some sympathy with Jacques Doriot's politics and seems to have used his connections in high places to his own advantage, there is no doubt that later in the war he did become involved with active resistance work and the conclusion is that the accusations made by Maurice were in response to his assertions that Maurice was himself a collaborator.

The question marks over Wimille faded and his racing career flourished. In mid-July he rejoined the Alfa Romeo factory team for the Grand Prix des Nations in Geneva, the first international race after the war. This time he was alongside the entire team of pre-war aces: Farina, Achille Varzi and Carlo Trossi, although he and Trossi used the year-old Alfa Romeo 158s which were fitted with a single compressor compared to the twin compressors in the cars of Varzi and Farina. Wimille won the first heat and in the final was able to stay with Farina without too much difficulty although in the end he was knocked off the road while lapping Tazio Nuvolari and ended up a lap behind. A week later he went back to Écurie Naphta Course for a race in Nantes but the chassis broke and he had to retire. Alas, the race was marked by the death in an accident of Robert Mazaud, In September he joined the Alfa Romeo factory team in Turin, the first Grand Prix to be held in Italy since the war. This took place in the Valentino Park alongside the River Po, around the Castello del Valentino, and Wimille proved to be the dominant force, although he obeyed team orders at the end of the race to allow Varzi win. He had shown, once again, that he was more than a match for the old Alfa Romeo aces.

By this point Wimille had taken on an executive role at the Champion Garage in the east of Paris, which was at the time the biggest garage in the world. It was importing Austin Morris cars from England. This gave him an income while his engineers worked on the Wimille prototype, which in October that year, was displayed at the Paris Salon de l'Automobile in the Grand Palais. By then he was already looking ahead to the design of a second prototype. In the racing world he was a man in demand. Amédée Gordini offered to let him race the brand new Simca-Gordini 15 in French national events while Alfa Romeo wanted him for its factory team in international races. In the end Wimille agreed to drive for both teams but it was to be a season of mixed fortunes. There were a number of wins for Gordini but the new car was not reliable and he retired on several occasions. On June 1, however, on a road circuit near Nîmes, Jean-Pierre won the Coupe Robert Benoist, beating his ever-present rival Raymond Sommer, despite a failing engine in the final part of the 80-mile race. It was a victory that meant a great deal to Wimille. A week later he was back with Alfa Romeo factory team for the Swiss GP at the Bremgarten circuit in Berne, which he won and there would be another victory in the European GP at Spa at the end of the month. Alfa Romeo, wanting an Italian driver to win a few races, then made the controversial decision and dropped Wimille for the Italian GP which allowed Trossi was able to take the victory, while Wimille had to be content winning national races in France.

That summer Ettore Bugatti died of a stroke at his post-war home in the rue Boissière in Paris's 16ème arrondissement . He had spent the last years of life fighting officialdom, hoping to become a naturalised French citizen and to recover his old factory at Molsheim, which had been seized by the French authorities after the war because the post-war government felt that the deal Bugatti had struck with the Germans smacked of collaboration. Le Patron protested his innocence and fought the decision in the courts and, just days before his death, the confiscation of the factory was overturned. By then the damage had been done. Without someone to lead it, the Bugatti company was fading away.

Wimille continued to race for both Alfa Romeo and Simca-Gordini in 1948 and began his season in South America where in January 1948 he took on the local drivers with a Naphta Course Alfa Romeo 8C. In the Gran Premio del General Juan Peron in mid-January he retired with gearbox trouble. A week later he raced in Mar del Plata and was third but for the Grand Prix of Rosario he switched to the Gordini team and found himself with a new team mate called Juan-Manuel Fangio. The local hero, who had made his name in the road races of Argentina, was a serious competitor and the two men battled hard in the race. Wimille took an early lead but then Fangio managed to outfox him and get ahead. Wimille fought back and moved ahead again and then ensured that Fangio was never given another chance to pass him. Towards the end of the race Fangio retired with an engine failure but although great he went on to become the Formula 1 World Champion five times in the 1950s he never forgot the battle with Wimille, one of the few drivers ever to beat the great Argentine.

Jean-Pierre went back to Europe to sign a deal with Maurice Dollfus, the president of Ford France, to use Ford V8 engines in his new road car. He had recruited a new designer in Philippe Charbonneaux, a man who would go on to become a famed automobile designer with Renault in the 1960s and 1970s. The new car was progressing well and Wimille went back to racing with the start of the international season being at the beginning of July with the European Grand Prix at Bremgarten, in Bern, Switzerland. The track was wet in qualifying but the sun had come out and the road was drying. Achille Varzi, a man who had never had a really serious accident, lost control of his car at just over 100mph and the Alfa Romeo 158 spun several times and then hit a barrier and flipped over. Varzi was crushed beneath the vehicle. The Alfa Romeo team took the tough decision to press on with the event. There was further tragedy at the start of the race when Christian Kautz, a Swiss who had made his name in the 1930s as a Mercedes-Benz and later an Auto Union driver, was killed in a multiple collision. Wimille led the race but the pit stops put Trossi in the lead and, knowing that the Italian aristocrat was dying of a brain tumour, he allowed Trossi to win. It was a last generous gesture. Wimille was the undisputed team leader of the Alfa Romeo factory team and after years of letting others win, he began to show his true class, taking all the wins for himself. He dominated the French, Italian, Monza and Turin Grands Prix. If there had been a World Championship – as there would be two years later – Wimille would have won it.

At the end of that year Wimille's second prototype road car appeared at the Salon de Paris. It was a more elegant car than the original and powered by a Ford V8 engine. It looked very promising and plans were made for it to go into production.

In January 1949 Wimille set off again for South America for the annual Temporada series in Argentina. The first race was the Gran Premio del General Juan Peron y de la Ciudad de Buenos Aires, which was to be held on the roads in and around Palermo Park in Buenos Aires. The park is often likened to the Bois de Boulogne in Paris and features a wide range of facilities, including five lakes, sports fields, a golf course, botanical gardens, a zoo, a horse racing track and polo grounds. The Équipe Simca-Gordini had a pair of 1.4-litre cars for Wimille and Amédée Gordini and they were competitive.

On Friday January 28 the drivers got up early for the third practice session, the organizers wanting to get the qualifying done before it became too hot. The sun had only just risen when the cars went out at six thirty and soon Wimille was out on the circuit, lapping quickly. The times were promising and the Gordini team waited each lap to see what its star driver could do. Then Wimille failed to come through. Other drivers came into the pits and reported that the little car had gone off in the fast corner by the Municipal Golf Club and had hit a small tree. The damage did not look to be too bad.

But at the scene of the crash it was clear that Wimille was badly hurt. The Gordini had gone off the track and hit one of the straw bales that had been placed beside the circuit to act as a safety barrier. In fact it had acted as a launch pad and the car had flown through the air, turning slightly as it did and hit the tree. It was not a big tree and the only obvious damage to the car was a dent in the side of the cockpit. Wimille however had taken the full impact with his head and chest and was unconscious and the Argentines rushed him to the nearby Hospital Juan A Fernandez. On the way to the hospital Wimille regained consciousness and asked what had happened before falling back into unconsciousness. When the ambulance arrived at the hospital the doctors found that he had died, the victim of a fractured skull and a crushed chest. A distraught Cric was looked after by Prince Bira and his wife Ceril, who were joined by Alberto Ascari and Gigi Villoresi. There was nothing they could do but mourn.

The death of the top racing driver is always a tremendous shock because the best men seem somehow indestructible. Often there is no clear idea of why an accident occurred and no-one has ever been able to establish with any certainty what happened. There were stories that Wimille had swerved to avoid hitting spectators who had crept forward onto the track to watch him; others said that the car suffered an axle failure as it skidded sideways; there were even suggestions that he might have lost control after being blinded by sunlight as he came around a corner, with the early morning sun low in the sky.

Wimille was interred in one of the many small chapels in La Recoleta cemetery in Buenos Aires, his coffin carried by his old teammate Giuseppe Farina (who would become the first World Champion in 1950), Luigi Villoresi, Oscar Galvez and others from the racing community. Later the body was sent home to France, where President Vincent Auriol announced that Wimille had been posthumously awarded the Ordre de la Nation. His funeral took place at the church of St Philippe du Roule in Paris and was attended by the Duke and Duchess of Windsor, Fangio and many others. One person who was not invited was Wimille's mistress, the young and beautiful Juliette Greco, who at 22 was already a movie star. She snuck into the back of the church with the help of a young journalist called Jabby Crombac. Wimille was buried in the Cimitière de Passy, close to the Place du Trocadéro.

The AGACI would later erect a monument to him at the Porte Dauphine, close to where the first hairpin had been on the Bois de Boulogne circuit. Behind the monument is a sports ground, named after Jean-Pierre Wimille. It runs up the side of the Bois de Boulogne, towards Willy Grover's old house on the rue Weber.

CHAPTER TWENTY

While Jean-Pierre Wimille was carving out a place for himself in the pantheon of great racing stars, Squadron Leader Vera Atkins of the SOE's French Section embarked on a sad but necessary mission to discover the fate of the 100 missing F Section agents. Atkins had no illusions about what she would discover but wanted to know the details so that the families of those who had been executed would know the fate of their loved ones. Atkins travelled around Europe, piecing together the stories, interviewing former inmates from the concentration camps and Germans who were now prisoners.

She soon discovered that the missing agents had all been designated "Nacht und Nebel" prisoners. The words mean "night and fog" and the expression came from a secret directive issued by Hitler in December 1941, known as the Nacht und Nebel Erlass. This decreed that anyone who endangered German security would be executed immediately or would be imprisoned and vanish without a trace. The order added that if "foreign authorities inquire about such prisoners, they are to be told that they were arrested, but that the proceedings do not allow any further information".

In documents the letters SB were put on the records of most of the executed men and women. This was short for "Sonder behandlung", meaning "special treatment". The camp authorities understood very well what that meant.

There were around 7,000 prisoners designated as Nacht und Nebel inmates, most were from the French Resistance and all were deliberately murdered on the orders of the RHSA in Berlin. Atkins discovered that there had been two distinct waves of executions, the first being in the late summer of 1944; the second in the spring of 1945, by which time it was clear that Germany had lost the war.

The first killing of F Section agents took place in July 1944 at the Natzweiler-Struthof concentration camp, in the hills of the Vosges, not far from Strasbourg. After the war there was much confusion as to which women agents had been killed but it eventually emerged that the four were Prosper's brave and resourceful assistant Andrée Borrel and another Prosper courier Sonia Olschanesky, Vera Leigh of Inventor and Diana Rowden of Acrobat. Atkins was fortunate that Natzweiler-Struthof was an all-male camp as the arrival of the four women made a big impression and they were seen by several prisoners, including Albert Guérisse, the famous Pat O'Leary of the Pat escape line, and by SOE agent Brian Stonehouse. The four women were injected with phenol, a poison that attacks the central nervous system and causes respiratory failure. Their bodies were immediately cremated so that no trace remained.

Such small execution parties proved to be the most difficult for Atkins to uncover and there was often confusion as to which agents had been involved. For a long time it was thought that Noor Inayat Khan was one of the victims at Natzweiler, but it later emerged that she was one of the four women executed at Dachau in September 1944. Atkins's investigations into the murders at Natzweiler led to the arrest of the officers responsible and to a trial in Wuppertal in May 1946. The names of the agents were suppressed to avoid relatives being upset by the gruesome details – Borrel, the court was told, woke up after the supposedly lethal injection and scratched the face of her executioner, Peter Straub, as he was pushing her into the ovens.

The identity of the dead girls would not be made public until 1948 when a memorial for the members of First Aid Nursing Yeomanry was unveiled at St Paul's Church, Knightsbridge in London.

Atkins discovered that it was in September 1944 that most of the killing took place, beginning at the Mauthausen camp, near Linz in Austria, where a group including Prosper's assistant Gilbert

Norman, Ely Wilkinson and Sidney Jones were murdered. Within a few days another 10 F Section agents were executed at Gross Rosen, near Striegan (now Strzegom) in Poland. Among that group were France Antelme and Jean Dubois. The biggest of the F Section executions, however, remained the Benoist Group at Buchenwald.

Atkins discovered that a second wave of killing on the orders of the RHSA began in March 1945 when Jack Agazarian and 12 other F Section officers, including Chestnut's Roland Dowlen, were hanged at Flossenbürg, a camp close to the Czech border. In the same period the four SOE women in Ravensbrück were also executed.

There were cases where F Section agents died alone of starvation and disease and these left almost no trace.

Many of the local recruits to the SOE networks also died in the camps in Germany and little trace left of them. Benoist's childhood friend Thérèse Lethias died at Ravensbrück on August 6 1944, one of 50,000 women who perished in the camp. When the war ended the village of Auffargis erected a memorial to her on a house in the village square and at Mery sur Oise, her adopted home, a street was named in her honour. Charlotte Perdrigé, Robert's courier, was also a victim of the camps, dying at the age of 34 in a work camp at Czarnków in Poland at the end of February 1945.

Robert Tayssedre failed to return from the camps but his wife Stella was more fortunate. When she was arrested in June 1944 she was heavily pregnant. After two months in Fresnes prison she was taken to the Gare de l'Est during the mass deportation from Paris on August 15, when around 3000 prisoners were sent to Germany. In the course of this she fainted and so was separated from the main group. The carriage in which she was put did not depart with the others and she ended up back in Fresnes prison. She was freed when a Belgian consular official visited the prison looking for his countrymen. Stella was a Belgian and spoke Flemish and this convinced the Germans to let her go. She was taken in by Yvonne Grover-Williams and lived in the house on the rue Weber. At the end of the year she gave birth to a daughter whom she named Annie. Stella Tayssedre lived for another 57 years, dying in Paris in April 2001.

Robert Benoist's chauffeur Marcel L'Antoine survived the camps and returned to live quietly in Paris until his death in 1968.

Of the Servon Group only three of the nine arrested by the Germans survived the war. Pierre Guérin died in the Dora-Mittelbau camp in the course of February 1944.

There was little official recognition from the British Government for the exploits of F Section officers and their networks. The post-war Victory Parade took place through the streets of London on Saturday, June 8 1946, and it included a small contingent of Special Forces personnel. The SOE was allotted four Jeeps, each containing four agents, one of which was a woman. The sight of women with parachute wings on their uniforms impressed everyone and the crowds gave them a rousing welcome. It was an emotional experience for all concerned. As the little convoy passed the royal box, which had been set up outside Marlborough House on The Mall, they were saluted by King George VI. There was then a spectacular fly past by the Royal Air Force and that night the River Thames in Westminster was lit up by a huge firework and searchlight display.

It was not until 1948 that the King held a number of discreet investitures in Paris for SOE agents who had been decorated for their wartime activities. After one of these events, Maurice Southgate - one of the survivors of the Benoist Group in Buchenwald - held a very special dinner party. Throughout his captivity Southgate had dreamed and planned the entire meal in every detail. It was intended to be the dinner party to end all dinner parties and those who attended remember it as having been exactly that. Everything was perfect.

Maurice Buckmaster was showered with honours after the war, being appointed an Officer of the Order of the British Empire (OBE), a Chevalier de la Légion d'honneur and being appointed to America's Legion of Merit. He had never been a professional soldier and after he was demobilised in 1946 he returned to work with the

Ford Motor Company. He became head of its European department until 1950 and then spent 10 years in charge of the company's public relations activities in Europe.

It was not long before accounts of the adventures of F Section agents began to be published in Britain. A film called Now it can be Told revealed some of the first details of SOE activity and gradually the organisation became more widely known. Maurice Buckmaster's Specially Employed and They Fought Alone were published in the 1950s and related stories he remembered from his days in Baker Street. They were not always accurate and all the characters had pseudonyms. Buckmaster retired in the late 1960s and stayed out of the spotlight until his death in 1990, at the age of 89.

The British Government decorated a lot of the F Section agent and it was the women agents who were the best rewarded. Forrest Yeo-Thomas (The White Rabbit) of RF Section was awarded a George Cross for his work with SOE and the bravery and leadership he showed after his capture. The citation for his award gives a clear understanding of the suffering he had undergone.

"He underwent four days continuous interrogation, interspersed with beatings and torture, including immersions, head downwards, in ice-cold water, with legs and arms chained," it read. "Owing to his wrist being cut by chains, he contracted blood-poisoning and nearly lost his left arm. He made two daring but unsuccessful attempts to escape. He was then confined in solitude in Fresnes prison for four months, including three weeks in a darkened cell with very little food. Throughout these months of almost continuous torture, he steadfastly refused to disclose any information."

Yeo-Thomas was one of the three members of the Robert Benoist Group to avoid execution by switching identities with dead French prisoners. His George Cross citation records "his determined opposition to the enemy, his strenuous efforts to maintain the morale of his fellow-prisoners and his brilliant escape activities" that demonstrated "the most amazing fortitude and devotion to duty".

The French Section of the SOE received three George Crosses, but all of them went to the women agents: Noor Inayat Khan was singled out for refusing to abandon "what had become the principal and most dangerous post in France, although given the opportunity to return to England." The citation noted that she had been arrested with all her codes and messages but when asked to cooperate with the Germans she refused.

Violette Szabo's citation was inaccurate and spoke of her being "surrounded by the Gestapo in a house in the south west of France. Resistance appeared hopeless but Madame Szabo, seizing a Sten gun and as much ammunition as she could carry, barricaded herself in part of the house and, exchanging shot for shot with the enemy, killed or wounded several of them. By constant movement, she avoided being cornered and fought until she dropped exhausted. She was arrested and had to undergo solitary confinement. She was then continuously and atrociously tortured but never by word or deed gave away any of her acquaintances or told the enemy anything of any value".

The third award went to Odette Hallowes, who had the good grace to always maintain that her award was not to be seen as having been to her but was recognition for those known or unknown who had served the cause of liberation in France.

Several other F Section women agents were recommended for the George Cross but their awards were turned down. There were few other options for the women and a number of them received what were known as "civil MBEs", which meant that the agents became Members of the Order of the British Empire (Civilian Branch). One such award went to the American Virginia Hall, a reward that in no way reflected her importance to F Section, nor her skill and bravery in the early part of the war. Pearl Witherington, another F Section agent, was recommended for the Military Cross but as women were not eligible for that award she was given a civil MBE.

She returned the medal with a note saying that she did not deserve the award as she had done nothing civil.

Decorations do not always go to those who deserve them most. It is a fact of war that if there is no-one to recommend an award, it cannot easily be made and bureaucratic logic deemed that one could not be a member of the Order of the British Empire if one was dead and so awards could not be made posthumously. This meant that those who were recommended for an MBE but died before the award was made ended up with no recognition at all. One such victim of this injustice was Prosper's steadfast assistant Andrée Borrel, the least rewarding SOE prisoner to have spent time with the SD in the Avenue Foch, who died clawing at the eyes of her executioner.

The F Section men collected a total of 32 Military Crosses, which included awards for many of the network organisers including Tony Brooks, Ben Cowburn, George Starr, George Millar, Roger Landes and Robert Boiteux. There was a Military Cross for Philippe Liewer, another for Christopher Burney and even one for Denis Rake, who returned to France on two occasions after his accident-prone first mission and became an experienced and successful organiser.

There were 27 awards of the Distinguished Service Order, including one for Richard Heslop, who ended the war as a Lieutenant Colonel and a legend in the Haute Savoie where he operated under the code name of Xavier on his second mission to France. Suttill was awarded a DSO before his arrest and so the award was upheld, even though he never received the medal in person. For those who died in Germany there was little or no recognition: Gustave Bieler and Michael Trotobas were two highly-effective F Section organisers who went undecorated. Trotobas was gunned down by the SS in November 1943 having been betrayed by one of his assistants, while Bieler was captured in December 1943 and impressed the Germans to such an extent that he limped to his death by firing squad at Flossenbürg with an SS Guard of Honour.

Jean Dubois, the fiery radio operator who tried to shoot his way out of a German trap, was recommended for an MBE but received nothing when news got back from Poland that he had been executed. Jack Agazarian, who was sent into a German trap by his senior officer Nicholas Bodington but stubbornly refused to talk after his capture, was treated terribly by the Germans, who knew that he had an enormous amount of important knowledge about the Paris networks. He received no recognition at all.

France Antelme also underwent terrible beatings after his capture, the Germans at the Avenue Foch knowing full well that the Mauritian knew details of all the major British resistance groups in northern France. He had been appointed an Officer of the Order of the British Empire before his death but received nothing for his stubborn refusal to talk to the Germans.

Robert Benoist was posthumously mentioned in despatches in November 1945, although this recognition, along with many similar awards, was suppressed and not made public. Roland Dowlen received a similar posthumous mention in despatches.

For Willy Grover there was a recommendation for an MBE in September 1945, written by Major General Colin Gubbins, the head of SOE. This document was in part inaccurate, stating that Grover-Williams had landed by sea, but it concluded that "this gallant officer performed outstanding work over a long period in organising clandestine resistance". When it emerged that Grover had died, the award was not made.

The dead secret agents were also not remembered on any single memorial until the unveiling of an F Section monument at Valencay in the Sologne in the 1990s. Until then the agents with no known graves were commemorated on memorials across Europe, depending on the circumstances. The Canadians and a number of others were added to a memorial in the Canadian Cemetery at Groesbeek near Nijmegen in Holland. Others were listed on the Royal Air Force memorial to the missing airmen at Runnymede or on a memorial for the missing army officers in Brookwood Cemetery, near Woking, Surrey.

The one exception was Dubois. He was the only British-trained member of SOE who was not commissioned as an officer, apparently due to a bureaucratic oversight.

There is no memorial to him.

The French motor racing fraternity erected a number of monuments to Benoist and "Williams". Streets and grandstands were named after them and there is a memorial on the approach road to the old Montlhéry racing circuit to the south of Paris. The Robert Benoist Cup and the Williams Cup both faded away in the post-war years but today the Bugatti Owner's Club in England holds a race each year for the trophy which "W Williams" won at Monaco in 1929.

But while the two men slipped quietly out of the limelight after the war, the loss remained vivid for those who were left behind. Yvonne Grover-Williams was heartbroken when her beloved "Willy" did not return from Germany.

"I have seen her lie on the ground and beat her head on the gravel, weeping for him," said a friend Gladys Garcin. "She never believed he was dead."

But there was no doubt. After the war Yvonne obtained a British Army widow's pension and went on living at the house in the rue Weber until plans were announced for a high-rise block to be built next door. She sold the house and moved to the Villa Ramby in Beaulieu, which she had retained as a summer home. Eventually she settled in the village of Amfreville-la-Campagne, near Elbeuf in Normandy, where she ran a kennel breeding terriers, just as she had in the old days at La Baule. Yvonne died in Évreux on December 17 1973, not long after her 77th birthday.

Robert Benoist's wife Paule was sorting out Robert's estate after the war and discovered that he had an old Bugatti stored in the Garage Banville. She decided that the car should be put up for sale, but this was challenged by Huguette Stocker, Robert's mistress, who insisted that before his arrest he had given her the car. The matter went to court with the judge finally deciding that the best course of action was to sell the car and split the proceeds between the two claimants. Madame Benoist died in May 1988 and is buried in the family grave at Auffargis, which is also a memorial for Robert.

For those who had lost relatives during the war there was little hope that justice would ever be done. Heinrich Himmler, the head of the SS, and the man who carried out Hitler's Nacht und Nebel order to execute all saboteurs, tried to escape when the Allied armies crushed Germany. For two weeks after the surrender nothing was heard of him but then, on May 21, he was captured at a British army checkpoint in Bremervörde, near Hamburg. He was disguised but his false identity papers attracted suspicion and he was arrested. Finally he admitted his identity. When the authorities ordered him to undergo a medical inspection Himmler was forced to decide his own fate. He had a phial of cyanide hidden in his mouth. Rather than face trial and execution, he chose the poison.

The trial of the other surviving Nazi leaders began in October 1945 in Berlin but was then transferred to Nuremburg, where the courts listened to the sorry tales of Nazi excesses. One key witness to the crimes and medical experiments at Buchenwald was Dr Alfred Balachowsky, who had been one of Prosper's men.

In October 1946 ten of the Nazi leaders were sentenced to hang among them Ernst Kaltenbrunner, the Austrian who had taken over the RHSA following the assassination in Prague of the hated Reinhard Heydrich by agents of the SOE's Czech Section.

Kaltenbrunner went to the gallows on October 16.

Horst Kopkow, the RHSA officer who sent out the "Sonder behandlung" execution orders for most of the SOE agents, was facing a war crimes trial when he was spirited away by MI6 to its Combined Services Detailed Interrogation Centre (CSDIC) at Bad Nenndorf, near Hanover. There, he convinced the Secret Intelligence Service that he would be a valuable asset in the new fight against Soviet Russia. Later, when pressure increased for him to be released for trial, the SIS announced that he had died. The truth was that he returned to his family in 1950 and lived under the assumed name of Peter Cordes, working for the British. He died in 1996.

Another who escaped punishment was Karl Boemelburg, the man who had been in charge of the Gestapo in Paris. He left the French capital in September 1944 with instructions to escort the Vichy France head of state Marshal Pétain to Sigmaringen in southern Germany. He managed to get Pétain into Switzerland and then disappeared without trace. It is believed that Boemelburg assumed the identity of a dead non-commissioned officer and slipped through the Allied net at the end of the war, settling in a small village near Munich. He died, still living under an assumed name, in 1947.

Of the SS men who had been in Paris, the most senior was Dr Helmut Knochen, who was the man in charge of all RHSA activity in France. He was caught by the British after the war and was sentenced to hang but was then handed over to the French to face other charges. In the end he was sentenced to death by them as well but that ruling was later commuted to life imprisonment and eventually Knochen was pardoned by French President Charles de Gaulle.

They did not all get away as lightly. SS Sturmbahnführer Josef Kieffer, Boemelberg's deputy and the man who had led the SD in Paris, was captured by the French and imprisoned in Strasbourg. He was later transferred to a British-run prison in Gaggenau in Germany where he was hanged in March 1947.

The main Nuremburg Trial for the Nazi leadership was followed by 12 other processes involving members of the Nazi administration, the eighth of these trials was for members of the RHSA.

The eight trials resulted in around 5,000 convictions and there would be another 5,000 convictions in the German courts in the years after that. Well into the 1950s concentration camp guards were still being arrested and tried, although a large number of the soldiers involved were never brought to justice.

Almost all of the concentration camp commandants were caught or killed when Germany collapsed. In the course of 1947 Forrest Yeo-Thomas was called to give evidence for the prosecution in the US Military Tribunal which had been established to try the Buchenwald commandant Hermann Pister and 30 members of his staff. Twenty-two of them were sentenced to death, although ultimately only 12 were executed. Pister himself died in prison.

Fritz Suhren, the commandant at Ravensbrück, managed to escape from custody after the war and lived under a false name until he was recaptured in 1949. He was executed by a French firing squad in June 1950.

Franz Ziereis, the Mauthausen commandant, fled with his family before the camp was liberated in May 1945. Around 30 of the SS guards who were left behind were lynched by the prisoners. A fortnight later Zereis was found in a hunting lodge in the mountains to the south of Linz. He tried to escape, was shot, and died the following day at a US hospital in the old Gusen camp. Zereis's corpse was hanged on the camp fence by former prisoners. Sixty-one Mauthausen officials were later tried and 58 were executed.

Anton Kaindl, the Sachsenhausen commandant, and 15 of his men were tried by the Russians in October 1947. They were sentenced to life imprisonment as, at the time, Russia had eliminated the death penalty. They were sent to a work in coal mines on the Polar Sea. Kaindl was dead within a few months.

Kurt Eccarius, the man who had run the Zellenbau at Sachsenhausen, survived the Russian coal mines and was released after an amnesty in 1955. The West German government, however, then arrested him and in 1962 he was found guilty of shooting six prisoners during the evacuation of Sachsenhausen in April 1945. He was sentenced to four years in prison. When he was released, the Germans arrested him again, this time for his involvement in the murders of other Sachsenhausen prisoners. He was convicted and in December 1969 was sentenced to another eight and a half years in prison.

In post-war France accounts were settled in different ways. The French nation had been torn apart under the German occupation and in the immediate post-war period many collaborators were not given the luxury of a trial. In the violent days after the liberation of Paris in August 1944 gangs took swift revenge on the most conspicuous traitors. This was followed by hundreds of thousands of investigations into claims of collaboration. In many cases the allegations were met with counter-claims, while in other cases the accused adopted the defence that they had been working for the resistance but had no-one to vouch for them, as their superior officers had all been killed. It was virtually impossible to disprove this argument and even men who had been photographed in SS uniform and had German military papers were able to avoid being held accountable for their actions.

There were so many claims made about the F Section networks related to Robert Benoist that in the spring of 1945 the French authorities launched an investigation. The result was a 26-page report which would remain classified until the spring of 2003. This condemned Maurice Benoist, revealing how early in the war he had supplied his friend Marcel Peyrouton, the Interior Minister of the Vichy government, with lists of Jews and other undesirables.

It went on to reveal that through his friend Achille Boitel Maurice had met Boemelberg as early as 1941 and it concluded that Maurice had been the cause of the arrests of the Servon Group and of Yvonne Grover-Williams. The report also noted that on several occasions he had tried to get information in order to have Noor Inayat Khan arrested. It concluded by calling for the arrest of Maurice and Suzy Benoist.

But Maurice and Suzy were not arrested. After the war there was no communication between Maurice and Robert's family. It is believed that Maurice died in the mid 1950s. The question of why he was never punished remains unanswered. Clearly he was well-connected and was thus able to avoid prosecution.

The only hint we have was amongst the other British documents that remained classified until 2003. These included two important notes. The first was a memo from February 1945 that noted that "an enemy source now in this country, whose information is considered to be reliable" had made a statement that "a certain Benoit (sic) formerly of 47 Avenue Brocard, Paris, worked for the Germans and denounced to them the well-known racing driver Grover Williams who was paracuted into France in 1942". At this point in the memo a comma was left out and so it read "and was working under Gestapo control in may 1943" which seemed to suggest that Willy was a double agent. It seems, however, that it was nothing more than a punctuation error.

The second memo was from a March 1945 interrogation of a German secret agent codenamed Marcus that had been carried out by a Captain Kressman (This may be the same source as above). Marcus was asked about German agents in France and said that he had been present at a meeting between Walter Schellenberg, the head of SS foreign intelligence, and Helmut Knochen in Berlin in September 1944, during which Knochen had reported that he had left his best agent behind in Paris.

"This was Maurice Benoist (known as Beliot) who lived in the Boulevard Berthier, Paris," the report said. "It was through him that Dr Knochen contacted Fernand de Brinon, Pierre Laval and other Vichy circles. Benoist had also enjoyed a good liaison with circles close to de Gaulle. He wanted to remain behind as he felt confident that he was unsuspected. He had given information to Knochen which led to a large number of British parachutists being captured including a certain racing motorist Grover Williams, who had driven for Bugatti pre-war."

In the same interview Marcus said: "Benoist was certainly an important agent for Knochen. He worked under the name Beliot and probably made large sums of money from the Gestapo."

Marcus added that Benoist "has excellent relations with all of Général de Gaulle's entourage, which means that he can extricate himself from all difficulties, thanks to his very powerful protection."

It is only in recent years that such treachery has started to come to light in France, but there are still many secrets about the days under the Occupation which the establishment in France do not want revealed. In 1993 René Bousquet, the head of the Vichy police and a friend of Maurice Benoist, was put on trial for crimes against humanity. On the eve of his trial the 84-year-old was shot dead by a man who later told police that all he wanted was to be remembered for doing something.

The assassin was sentenced to 10 years in prison.

There were in total around 158,000 court cases in France relating to the Occupation years but these resulted in only 3,750 executions. By 1950 France had turned its back on the war and was trying to forget. The number of former collaborators in prison dropped to only 5,000.

Heroism and treachery will ultimately come to the surface and if there was little recognition for the dead SOE agents, their memory lived on with the friends they had made during the war. But there was also bitterness at the way that the world changed and how some of the Nazis were allowed to escape unpunished. The war had been over for less than a month when Britain went to the polls on July 5 for its first general election since 1935. The result was a shock as the Conservative Party, led by national hero Winston Churchill, was defeated by Clement Attlee's Labour Party.

Churchill turned down all honours and took his place as the leader of the opposition and began to warn the country about the dangers of Communism. The socialists promised full employment, a National Health Service and a welfare state.

It was a brave new world.

In the 1950s Forrest Yeo-Thomas found himself beginning to doubt the reasons for which he had fought and which had caused him and others so much suffering and, although he was a much-respected and decorated war hero, he found that he had begun to envy those who had died.

"They gave their lives willingly, gladly, and they died happy, for they died with an ideal, with the feeling that they had sacrificed everything for something good, something enduring," he wrote.

"They did not live to see the sham that it all was, to see the wasting of all their efforts, the shameless scramble for personal satisfactions."

Many of those who fought in the war felt the same way as the world changed in the 1950s and 1960s.

But they did not forget the sacrifices made.

One of the seventeen F Section agents who survived the concentration camps in Germany was Bob Sheppard, the youngster who had been through the SOE training schools with Willy Grover. He had been parachuted into Burgundy in the same week as Grover and Burney dropped near Le Mans but had had the great misfortune to land on the roof of a French police station. He was arrested before his feet ever touched French soil. Later he escaped from captivity and made his way south towards the Spanish border, hoping to cross the frontier by the same route he had used in 1940 when escaping from France after the German invasion. Within a few miles of the frontier Sheppard was recaptured and sent to Germany. He survived the concentration camps of Buchenwald and Dora-Mittelbau and was eventually liberated by the advancing Allied armies.

Sheppard did not forget the arrangement he had made with his friend Vladimir when they had lunched at the Café Royal just before their missions began. When he got back to England he asked Vera Atkins what had happened to his old friend Vladimir and was told that it did not seem that he had survived the war.

Twenty years later Sheppard found himself in London one day on a business trip and he had lunch by himself at the Café Royal.

"There was a table full of German businessmen nearby," he remembered. "They were joking and drinking happily, and for some reason I was reminded of my last lunch with my friend Vladimir.

"I asked the waiter if I could have the table that we had sat at for that last lunch before going to France and, with an empty seat facing me, I drank a toast to my old friend Vladimir - who never came back."

A NOTE ABOUT SOURCES

Uncovering the story of Willy Grover, Robert Benoist and Jean-Pierre Wimille involved a huge amount of research and thousands of documents. These are to be found in a variety of different places, notably The Public Record Office in Kew, England. This now houses the records of the Special Operations Executive Advisor at the Foreign & Commonwealth Office. There are also important records in the National Archives of Canada and in France at the Bibliothèque de Documentation Internationale Contemporaine (BDIC) in Nanterre. Other documents were found at the Archives départementales des Yvelines in Montigny-le-Bretonneux.

There were very few private documents made available.

BIBLIOGRAPHY

AMOUROUX Henri, Les Francais sous l'Occupation, Fayard 1964
ARNOLD Bruce, Orpen, Mirror of an Age, Jonathan Cape 1981
AUBERT Philippe, Les Bugattis, Editions Jean-Claude Lattes 1981
BLEICHER Hugo, Colonel Henri's Story, Kimber 1954
BOWER Tom, Klaus Barbie Butcher of Lyons, Michael Joseph 1984
BOWMAN Martin & BOITEN Theo, Raiders of the Reich, Airlife 1996
BRADDON Russell, Nancy Wake, Frederick Muller 1956
BRADLEY WF, Bugatti, Motor Racing Publications 1948
BRYANT Arthur, The Turn of the Tide 1939-1943, Collins 1957
BUCKMASTER Maurice, Specially Employed, Batchworth Press 1952
BUCKMASTER Maurice, They Fought Alone, Norton 1958
BURNEY Christopher, Solitary Confinement, Clerke & Cockeran 1952
BURNEY Christopher, The Dungeon Democracy, Heinemann 1945
BUTLER Josephine, Churchill's Secret Agent, Blaketon-Hall 1983
CARPENTER Humphrey, Geniuses Together, Unwin 1987
CAVE BROWN Anthony, Bodyguard of Lies, WH Allen 1976
CONWAY Hugh, Grand Prix Bugatti, GT Foulis & Co 1968
COOKRIDGE EH, They Came from the Sky, Heinemann 1965
COX Geoffrey, Countdown to War, William Kimber 1988
CUNNINGHAM Cyril, Beaulieu, the finishing school for secret agents, Leo Cooper 1998
DELARUE Jacques, Histoire de la Gestapo, Fayard 1962
DE HOYOS Ladislas, Klaus Barbie - the untold story, WH Allen 1985
DE VOMÉCOURT Philippe, Who lived to see the day, Hutchison 1961
DREYFUS Rene & KIMES Beverly Rae, My Two Lives, Aztex 1983
DUBREUIL Jean Pierre, Des Bolides en Or, Lieu Commun 1984
FOOT M R D, SOE - An outline history, BBC 1984
FOOT M R D, SOE in France, HMSO 1966
FORD George, The Pickersgill letters, McClelland and Stewart 1948
GUILLAUME Paul, La Sologne au temps de l'heroisme et de la trahison, Imprimerie Nouvelle 1950

HAMILTON Alexander, Wings of Night, William Kimber 1977
HARMAN Nicholas, Dunkirk - the necessary myth, Coronet 1990
HASTINGS Max, Das Reich, Michael Joseph 1981
HESLOP Richard, Xavier, Rupert Hart-Davis 1970
HIGHAM Peter, International Motor Racing, Guinness Publishing 1995
HINCHLIFFE Peter, The Other Battle, Airlife 1996
HMSO, British Intelligence in the Second World War, 1984
HOWARTH Patrick, Undercover, Routledge & Kegan Paul 1980
JONES Liane, A Quiet Courage, Corgi Books 1990
KING Stella, Jacqueline, Arms and Armour Press 1989
KNIGHT Frida, The French Resistance, Lawrence and Wishart 1975
KNOWLSON, James, Damned to Fame, The Life of Samuel Beckett, Bloomsbury 1996
LABAN Brian, Winners, Orbis 1981
LABRIC Roger, Robert Benoist - Champion du Monde, Edicta 1945
LE CHENE Evelyn, Watch for me by moonlight, Eyre Methuen 1973
LITTLEWOOD Joan, Milady Vine, Jonathan Cape 1984
LORAIN Pierre, Armement Clandestin France, L'Emancipatrice 1972
LOUCHE Maurice, Un Siecle de Grands Pilotes Francais, Editions Louche 1995
MARSHALL Bruce, The White Rabbit, Evans Brothers 1952
MARSHALL Robert, All the King's Men, Collins 1988
MATHIESON T A S O, Grand Prix Racing 1906-1914, Mathieson 1965
McCALL Gibb, Flights most secret, Kimber 1981
MERRICK K.A, Flights of the Forgotten, Arms & Armour 1989
MICHEL HenriI, Paris Allemand, Ets Albin Michel 1981
MICHEL, Henri, Paris Resistant, Ets Albin Michel 1982
MINNEY RJ, Carve Her Name with Pride, Newnes 1956
MONKHOUSE George & KING-FARLOW Roland, Grand Prix Racing Facts & Figures, Foulis 1964
NICHOLAS Elizabeth, Death be Not Proud, Cresset Press 1958
NOGUERES Henri, Histoire de la Resistance, Robert Laffont 1967-1976
OVERTON-FULLER Jean, Dericourt, The Chequered Spy, Russell 1989
OVERTON-FULLER Jean, Madeleine, Gollancz, 1952

OVERTON-FULLER Jean, The German Penetration of SOE, William Kimber 1975
PAKENHAM Simona, Pigtails and Pernod, Macmillan 1962
PAYNE-BEST Sigizmund, The Venlo Incident, William Brendon 1950
RAFAELLI Antoine, Archives d'une Passion, Maeght Editeur 1997
RAKE Denis, Rake's Progress, Frewin 1968
RUBY Marcel, F Section SOE, Leo Cooper 1988
SEAMAN Mark, Bravest of the Brave, Michael O'Mara 1997
SHELDON Paul, A Record of Grand Prix and Voiturette Racing, St Leonards Press, 1990
SHEPPARD Robert, Missions Secrètes et Deportations, Editions Heimdal 1998
STAFFORD David, Britain and European Resistance 1940-45, University of Toronto Press 1980
ST GEORGE SAUNDERS, Hilary, The Red Beret, Michael Joesph 1950
SWEET-ESCOTT Bickham, Baker Street Irregular, Methuen 1965
TARRANT V E, The Red Orchestra, Arms & Armour 1995
TICKELL Jerrard, Moon Squadron, Allan Wingate 1956
TICKELL Jerrard, Odette, Chapman & Hall 1949
TOMMASI Tommaso, Dizionario dei Piloti, Mondadori 1977
VERITY Hugh, We landed by Moonlight, Ian Allen Ltd 1978
WAKE Nancy, The White Mouse, Macmillan 1985
WEST Nigel, Secret War, Hodder & Stoughton 1992
WIGHTON Charles, Pin-Stripe Saboteur, Oldhams 1959
YOUNG Gordon, The Cat with Two faces, White Lion 1957

INDEX

Abbaye des Vaux de Cernay 46, 47, 170
Abbeville 73
abrasive grease 106
Abwehr (German military intelligence) 113, 150, 151, 156
Acrobat (SOE network) 337
Action Vengeance network 118, 131, 185, 252
Affleck, Pilot Officer Johnny 217
Africa 89, 277
Afrika Korps 131, 139
Agazarian, Francine (Marguerite) 156
Agazarian, Jacques (Marcel) 136, 138, 142, 152, 156, 162, 177-179, 232, 338, 343
Agen 27, 141, 239
AIACR, automobile federation 54, 62
Aigrain, Germaine 173, 174
Air Ministry 12, 74, 104, 111
Aisne, River 74
Aisner, Juliette 145
Ajustron, André 184
Ajustron, Marie 184, 187
Ajustron, Paule (see Benoist, Paule)
Ajustron, Paulette 184
Ajustron, Robert 184
Aldeamuro, Spain 54
Alfa Romeo 39-40, 53-56, 60, 65, 66, 67, 242, 248, 251, 325, 329, 331, 332, 333
Alfie, movie 276
Algeria 33, 115, 139, 227
Allard, Elisee 294, 308
Alsace 69
Amboise, France 228
America 90
Amersham 25
Amfreville-la-Campagne 345
Amies, Hardy 99
Amiens 47, 52,
Amilcar 321
Amps, Jean 134, 136
Anchor and Wheatsheaf pub 111
Andres 207, 216
Angers, France 91, 124, 126, 141, 152, 153, 177, 198, 199, 207, 228, 229, 245
Angerville, France 240
Angoulême, France 75
Antelme, France (Antoine, Rattier) 137, 138, 144, 153, 154, 157, 173, 175, 176, 189, 206, 207, 215, 216, 227, 231, 233, 338, 343
Antibes 119, 122
Anton (German agent) 156
Antoinette aviation company 52
Arc de Triomphe, Paris 78, 156, 193, 232
Archer, Fred 26
Argenteuil hillclimb 52

Arisaig 92, 99
arms drops 142, 143, 149, 253, 254, 255, 259
arms dumps 187, 228, 262, 267
Arnaud (German agent) 156
Aron, Jean, 136, 238
Arpajon, France 253
Ascari, Alberto 335
Ascari, Antonio 53, 54, 55
Assemblee Nationale, Paris 243, 251
Association Générale Automobile des Coureurs Indépendants (AGACI) 321-322, 324, 335
Atkins, Squadron Leader Vera 161, 317, 336, 337, 338, 351
Atlantic Wall 103, 256
Attlee, Clement 350
Auchinlake, General Claude 131, 132
Auffargis, France 46, 50, 74, 128, 129, 142, 144, 150, 175, 176, 183-189, 191, 192, 206, 207, 210, 216, 218, 222, 228, 247, 253, 262, 338
Aumaître, Robert 71, 249
Auriol, Vincent 335
Auschwitz, camp 300
Austin-Morris 331
Austria 154
Auteuil 148, 156, 216
Autogiro (SOE Network) 20, 121-122, 125, 134, 136
Automobile Club de France 37-38
AutoUnion 68, 242, 333
Auvety, Suzanne (see Benoist, Suzy)
Auxerre, France 217
Auxiliary Transport Service (ATS) 277
Avenue Foch, Paris 22, 146, 154, 159, 160, 178, 182-184, 187-189, 192, 193, 206, 210, 214, 215, 223, 227, 233, 234, 247, 261, 262, 269-271, 281-283, 286-287, 310, 322, 343
Avenue de la Grande Armée, Paris 197, 252
Avenue Henri Martin, Paris 213
Avenue Hoche, Paris 78, 79, 194, 195
Avenue Iena, Paris 184
Avenue Montaigne, Paris 44, 45, 70, 76, 79, 110, 246
Avenue de Suffren, Paris 49
Avenue de Villiers, Paris 285
Aveyron, France 268
Avranches, France 288, 289
Avus, Germany 68
Aylesbury 97
B-17 297
B-24 Liberator 132, 280
B-29 323
Bablot, Paul 33
Bad Nenndorf, Germany 346
Bader, Douglas 276
Baille, Gaëtan 64, 67

Baker Street, London 19, 236, 340
Balachowsky, Professor Alfred 137, 173, 174, 307, 309, 346
Balachowsky, Madame 158, 164
Balcon, Michael 275
Ballot automobiles 33
Baltimore 110
Bambesch, France 299
Banville Garage, Paris 62-67, 155, 170, 345
Bar de la Faubourg St Honoré, 124
Baracca, Francesco 65
Barbès Métro Station 18
Barbie, Klaus 160
Bardet, Roger 217, 218
Barlier, Maurice 18
Barnard College 120
Barrett, Flying Officer Dennis (Honoré) 294
Barrett, Thomas 54
Basin, Francis 199, 200
Bastille Day 176, 277
Battle of Britain 77
Battle of Midway 131
Baudreville, France 240
Bay of Bengal 163
Bayswater 233
Beach, Sylvia 30
Beaugency, France 157
Beaulieu Abbey 98-102, 109, 119
Beaulieu-sur-Mer, France 43, 209, 250, 345
Beaune, France 217
Beauvallet, Paul (Paul Huon) 252, 267
Beckett, Samuel 30
Bégué, Georges 20, 127
Beirut 232
Belgian Grand Prix 54, 166
Belgium 65, 70, 71, 72, 73, 95, 189
Bell P-63 aircraft 327
Bell, Flying Officer Douglas 240
Belligand, Madeleine (see Benoist, Madeleine)
Ben Nevis 92
Bend Or, race horse 26
Benes, Edvard 11
Benoist, Gaston (Georges, Pape) 46, 184, 185, 212, 260-261
Benoist, Jacqueline 50, 129, 213, 272, 325
Benoist, Jeanne 184, 185, 191, 212, 259
Benoist, Madeleine 259, 260, 261, 262, 266, 285
Benoist, Marguerite 206
Benoist, Maurice (Beliot) 46, 47, 129-130, 146, 149, 150, 155, 175, 182, 183, 185-189, 191, 197, 206-212, 216, 219, 220, 223, 226-229, 233, 234, 240, 259, 260, 269, 271, 285, 287, 290, 321, 330, 331, 348, 349
Benoist, Paule (Paulette) 50, 129, 184, 206, 345

Benoist, Robert (Lionel, Roger Brémontier, Daniel Perdrigé) throughout
Benoist, Suzy 130, 175, 182, 183, 184, 186, 187, 189, 191, 207, 208, 210-212, 220, 349
Benouville, France 256
Bentley car company 64, 65
Berlin, Germany 23, 68, 162, 311, 312, 313, 316, 317, 319, 338, 348
Berne, Switzerland 332, 333
Bertarione, Vincent 53
Bertoni, Flaminio 136
Béthenod de Montbressieux, Comte George (Raph, De Las Casas) 69, 249, 250, 251, 329
Bickenhall Mansions, 236
Bieler, Gustave 343
Billotte, General Gaston 73
Bira, Prince 335
Birkigt, Marc 31
Birmingham 25
Blitzkrieg 73
Bloch, Denise (Ambroise, Line, Crinoline, Micheline Rabatel, Danielle Williams, Mlle Boitel) 238-241, 246, 257, 260, 264-265, 267, 269-271, 283, 291, 294, 297, 315-316
Blois, France 74, 75, 123, 228
Blondet (Valerien) 267-268, 271
Bloom, Marcus (Urbain) 239
Bluteau, Marcel 253, 254, 267, 268
BMW 69
Bockscar 323
Bodington, Nick 121, 127, 177, 178, 198, 232, 343
Boemelberg, General Karl 178, 181, 227, 232, 346, 348
Boer War 17
Bogart, Humphrey 242
Bognor Regis 203
Boillot, André 41
Boillot, Commandant 206
Boillot, Georges 47, 52, 55
Bois de Boulogne, 176, 247, 322, 324-328, 329, 335
Bois-Colombes, France 76, 142
Boitel, Achille 186, 348
Boiteux, Robert 200, 203, 342
Bol d'Or race 51
Bonnet, Gerard 286
Bonnet, Rene 325
Bonnie Prince Charlie 92
Bony-Lafont Gang 218
Bordeaux, France 19, 72, 75, 78, 185
Bordino, Pietro 53, 60
Borrel, Andrée (Denise Urbain) 134, 135, 140, 156, 158, 159, 160, 244, 284, 307, 346
Borotra, Jean 252
Borzacchini, Baconin 38
Botulism 23
Bouchard, Robert-Aime 324
Boudon, Jean

Boulevard Berthier, Paris 175, 183, 207, 240, 349
Boulevard des Capucines, Paris 30
Boulevard Gouvion St Cyr, Paris 130
Boulevard Haussmann, Paris 193, 194
Boulevard des Italiens, Paris 150, 194, 226
Boulevard Magenta, Paris 260, 261
Boulevard Poniatowski, Paris 197, 218
Boulevard Richard Wallace, Neuilly 176, 213
Boulevard St Germain, Paris 158
Boulevard Suchet, Paris 148, 155
Boulevard Victor, Paris 74
Boulevard l'Yser, Paris 190
Boulogne, France 31, 108, 146, 216
Bourges, France 48, 52
Bourges, Madame 207
Bouriano, Georges 41
Bouriat, Guy 66, 67, 196
Bourlier, Edmond 33, 57, 58, 60
Bournemouth 100
Bousquet, Rene 186, 330, 349
Brasserie aux Coupoles, Paris 187, 207
Brasserie Sherry, Paris 226
Brault, Jean 324
Brault, Monsieur 224
Bremgarten 332-333
Brescia, Italy 65
Brest, France 75
Breuillet, France 254, 267
Briançon, France 251
Brickendon Bury 105, 106, 136, 208, 211
Brie-Comte-Robert, 155
Brille-Peri, Gastone 54, 55, 56
Briollay, France 199
Brion, Marcelle 263, 270, 271
British Chemical and Biological Warfare Research Centre (Porton Down) 23
British Army 73, 91
- 1st Parachute Brigade 108
- 4 Commando 108
- 6th Airborne Division 256, 318
- 8th Army 131, 132
- 12 Commando 110
- Advanced Horse Transport Depot 276
- Black Watch 314
- Central Purchasing Board 73
- Coldstream Guards 89
- Commandos 108
- First Armoured Division 73
- High Command 77
- Home Forces 77
- Military Police 89
- Parachute Regiment 95
- Parachute Training School 95
- Royal Army Service Corps

(RASC) 73, 78, 95, 147, 276
- Royal Signals 314
- Special Air Service (SAS) 255, 259
British Broadcasting Corporation (BBC) 87, 90, 115, 142, 143, 214, 237, 253, 255
British Expeditionary Force (BEF) 19-20, 72, 73, 159, 277
- 50th Division 19
Brittany 42, 86, 104, 108, 121, 208
Brixton, 277
Broadley, Flight-Lieutenant Alan 203
Brockenhurst 98
Broken Hill, 249
Brook, Robin 164, 215
Brooklands 36, 51, 55, 57, 60, 206
Brooks, Tony 200, 201, 202, 342
Browne-Bartoli, Albert 217
Bruneval Raid 108
Brunot, Georges 324
Buchenwald camp 206, 246, 302-308, 310, 312, 328, 338, 340, 347, 351
Buckmaster, Maurice 19, 21, 103, 110, 122, 127, 136, 138, 154, 164, 177-179, 203, 208-209, 215, 216, 232, 236, 237, 239, 243, 279, 340
Buckingham Palace 274
Buckinghamshire 12, 211
Buenos Aires 248, 334
Bugatti 15, 31, 34, 35, 37-42, 45, 53-58, 60, 62, 65-71, 74, 76, 79, 110, 121, 124, 129, 142, 164, 172, 194, 195, 197, 198, 241, 242, 246, 249, 250, 251, 321, 324, 325, 327, 349
Bugatti, Ettore 32, 35-38, 41-42, 45, 58, 62, 65, 67, 69, 70, 71, 78, 118, 119, 165, 195, 252, 324, 332
Bugatti Grand Prix 65
Bugatti, Jean 67, 68, 71, 72, 172
Bugatti, Roland 71
Bulovka Hospital, Prague 11
Bureau, Jacques 152
Bureau Central de Renseignements et d'Action (BCRA) 236
Burgundy 217, 350
Burney, Christopher (Charles) 13-17, 111, 112, 125, 210, 342, 350
Bushell, Charles 29
Bushell, Violette (see Szabo, Violette)
Café Colisée, Paris 179, 210
Café de la Paix, Paris 30
Café Royal, London 109, 351
Caine, Michael 276
Cairo 132
Campari, Giuseppe 53, 54, 55, 60
Campbell, Malcolm 36, 55, 60
Camusdarach 94
Cannes, France 122, 127
Cap Gris Nez, France 107
Caracciola, Rudi 40, 166
Cartaud, Pierre (Peters, Capri,

Von Kapri) 185, 207, 215, 216
Carte network 139, 150, 293
Carthage 32
Carve Her Name with Pride 275
Caucasus 131
Cauvin, Fernand 155
Cayeux, Robert 324
Central Electricity Board 106
Centrale Electrique 188
Central Intelligence Agency (CIA) 140, 244
Ceux de la Liberation 252, 327
Chalfont St Giles 25, 211
Châlons-sur-Marne 297, 298
Champion Garage, Paris 331
Champs-Élysées 21, 29, 137, 173, 179, 226
Channel Islands 108
Chapron, Henri 330
Charbonneaux, Philippe 333
Charing Cross 80
Charron car company 52
Chartres, France 74, 222, 223, 226, 233, 279
Château de Forcilles 155
Château de Lesigny 155
Château de Nanteuil 123
Châteaubriant, France 90
Châteauroux, France 127, 231
Châtellerault, France 75
Châtillon-sur-Cher, France 157
Cherbourg, France 75, 256
Chery-Lury, France 126
Chesham, Bucks 25,
Chestnut (SOE Network) 20, 113, 121, 124/129, 131, 133-6, 138, 142, 144, 146, 147, 149, 150, 152, 155, 157, 162, 164, 176, 179, 180, 183, 186, 188, 189, 199, 206, 207, 208, 210, 212, 213, 218, 219, 224, 226-8, 230, 244, 245, 283, 285
Chevalier, Maurice 251
Chevreuse Valley 37, 46, 47, 259
Chez Tutulle 156, 182
Chiron, Louis 33, 37, 38, 39, 42, 60, 65, 252, 326
Chrysler car company 64, 65
Church of Cyril and Methodius, Prague 23
Churchill, Lt-Col, Jack 313
Churchill, Winston 16-17, 21, 77, 119, 132, 133, 134, 151, 243, 313, 319, 350
Cimitiere de Passy, 335
Cinema (SOE network) 215
Circuit de la Garoupe 37
Circuit de Picardie 47
Citroën 136, 150, 238, 244, 246, 280, 330
Chabaud, Eugene 325
Clamart, France 145
Clark, Captain Nobby 100
Clavel, Georges 195, 197
Clech, Marcel 121-123, 126-127
Clément, Rémy (Marc) 145, 146, 157, 158, 200, 201, 217, 230
Clément-Rochelle car company

145
Clergeon, Lucien 268
Clergyman (SOE network) 213, 221, 222, 228, 241, 246, 252, 255, 258, 260, 263, 264-268, 270-272, 279, 282-285, 287, 326
Clermont-Ferrand, France 126
Clinique Bizet, Paris 259
Clive of India 275
Cliveden House 26
Coatalen, Louis 33-34, 35
Cognac, France 327
Cole, Harold 184
Cologne, Germany 12-13,
Colonel Remy 185
Combined Services Detailed Interrogation Centre (CSDIC) 345
Commandant Alain, (see Couderc, Alain)
Commando raids (Cross-Channel) 107, 109
Comminges, France 37, 242
Communist Resistance 90, 116, 135, 140, 223
Compiègne, France 76, 206, 292
Conelli, Count Caberto 37, 41, 43, 60
Conseil National de la Résistance 252
Conservative Party 350
Costantini, Meo 57, 65, 66, 68
Coppa Florio 65
Cormeau, Yvonne (Annette) 239
Cornet, Pauline 261
Corre car company 79
Corsica 252
Côte d'Azur 119
Cotentin Peninsular, France 256
Couderc, Charles (Commandant Alain) 253, 267, 269
Coulommiers-Voisin 155
Coupe de la Liberation 324
Coupe des Prisonniers 325, 326, 327
Coupe Robert Benoist 247, 324, 332, 344
Coupe Williams 328, 344
Courbaize, Louis 63
Courbevoie, France 48, 79, 146, 216
Courcimault, Gaston (Boulon Alphonse) 267
Courcimault, Lucien (Boulon Louis) 268
Cowburn, Ben 342
Crombac, Jabby 335
Crosmières, France 15
Croydon airport 231
Culioli, Pierre 123, 134, 157, 158, 159, 293
Culloden Moor 92
Cumberlege, Lieutenant-Commander C M 314
Curie, Marie and Pierre 46
Czarnków, camp 282, 338
Czech Field Forces 314

Czechoslovakia 11, 17
D Day 133, 176, 178, 214, 237, 245, 255, 256, 260, 271, 278, 280, 294, 320
Dachau camp 304, 337
Dagan, Hermance (see Grover, Hermance)
Dakar, 277
Daladier, Édouard 90
Dansey, Claude 19
Darlan, Admiral Jean-François 139
Darling, Captain George 159, 162, 179
Daude, Émile 268
Dauvergne, Christian 40, 62, 63, 64
Davis, Sammy 60
Day, Wing Commander Harry "Wings" 313
Daytona Beach, Florida 36
DB, car company 324, 325
De Bernard de la Fosse, Countess Anne-Marie 123, 125
De Bernard de la Fosse, Count Pierre 123
De Brinon, Fernand 349
De Courcelles, Gerard 35
D'Estienne d'Orves, Honoré 18
De Gaulle, General Charles 18, 75, 97, 179, 205, 231, 258, 293, 347, 349
De Guelis, Jacques 283
De La Fressange, Christiane (see Wimille, Christiane) 250
De La Fressange, Hubert 286-287
De La Fressange, Marquis Paul 250
De La Fressange, Simone 250
De Marmier, Lionel 50
De Rothschild, Baroness Charlotte 46
De Rothschild, Baron Henri 46, 47
De Rothschild, Baron James 46, 47
De Rothschild, Baron Nathaniel 46
De Rothschild, Baron Philippe 40-41, 46, 68
De Sinety, André 46
De Sterlich, Diego 40
De Vere, Cyril 65
De Voméclourt, Pierre 20, 136
De Wesselow, Major Roger 89, 90
Death be not Proud 276
Defendini, Ange 294, 308
Dehn, Paul 99
Delahaye car company 69, 250, 325, 328
Delage 31, 35, 40, 47, 48, 52-59, 62, 67, 170
Delage, Louis 51-52, 54, 57, 58, 62
Demarcation Line 104, 119-121, 123, 126, 127, 139

Depois, Denise 329
Derby 101
Derby horse race 26
Déricourt, Henri (Gilbert) 134, 144, 146, 156, 157, 158, 161, 176-179, 197-200, 202, 214, 216-218, 221, 225-234, 245, 264
Déricourt, Jeannot 231
Detective (SOE network) 238
Deutsch, Charles 324
Deutsche Ausruestungswerke (DAW) 304
Deuxieme Bureau 18
Dewavrin, Colonel André (Colonel Passy) 236
Dewoitine aircraft company 49
Dhuizon, France 157
Diaghilev, Serge 45
Dieppe, France 30, 128, 242, 283
Dijon, France 124, 130, 330
Distinguished Service Cross 140
Distinguished Service Order (DSO) 145, 231, 343,
Ditcher (SOE network) 217
Divo, Alberto 35-6, 41, 53-60, 68
Dix-Sept Tournants hillclimb 37
Dodge, Major Johnny 313
Dollfuss, Maurice 333
Domino, Georges 48, 71
Don, river 131
Doncaster, race horse 26
Donkeyman (SOE network) 217, 293
Donovan, Bill 140
Doornik, Yan 18
Doret, Marcel 49
Doriot, Jacques 250, 251, 330
Dorset 107
Douglas Dakota C47 256
Doullens, France 73
Doumergue, Gaston 55, 170
Dourdan, France 253, 254, 257, 267, 326
Dowlen, Roland (Achille, François Perrier) 144, 146, 149, 155, 181-184, 186, 210, 211, 226, 245, 328, 343
Dowse, Flight Lieutenant Sidney 313
Dreyfus, Rene 24, 43, 66, 326
Dublin 30
Dubois, Jean (Hercule) 214, 221, 222, 224, 338, 343, 344
Dubonnet André 31, 58
Duesenberg car company 51, 56
Dufour, Jacques (Anastasie) 280
Dugrosprez, Marguerite (see Benoist, Marguerite)
Duke Street, London 236
Duke and Duchess of Windsor 248, 335
Dumbarton 92
Dunham Massey Hall 94-95
Dunkirk 74-75, 277
Dunlop 43

Dupuy Family 197
East Africa 249
East India Company 163
East London, South Africa 249
Eastern Front 131, 151
Eaton, Cheshire 26
Eccarius, Kurt 318
École Militaire, Paris 49
École Nationale d'Agriculture 137, 164, 173, 174
École Normale de Musique 163
Ecurie Naphta Course 329, 330, 331, 332
Educating Rita, movie 276
Egypt 78, 131, 132
EHP car company 130
Eiffel, Gustave 43
Eiffel Tower, 244
El-Alamein 139, 278
El Himeimat Ridge, 278
Elbe river 319
Elizabeth Arden 224
"The English Airport", landing ground 198, 230, 245
English Channel 203, 229
Enola Gay 323
Epernay, France 296
Escoffier, Charles 155, 197, 218, 219
Esterel hillclimb 32
Etampes, France 251
Etancelin, Philippe 40, 249, 325
Eton College 19
Ettersburg, Germany 304
European Grand Prix 38, 59, 332
Euston Station 92
Evans, Major General Roger 73
Evreux, France 183
Execution of SOE agents 178
Eysserman, François 33
Eyston, George 35-36, 60
Fairfield, Pat 69
Falmouth, England 75
Fangio, Juan-Manuel 248, 332-333
Farina, Giuseppe 329, 331, 335
Farman, Maurice 48
Faroux, Charles 328
Farrier (SOE network) 145
Favier, Auguste 307
Feluccas 104, 122
Ferrari, car company 249
Ferrari, Enzo 53, 65, 66, 67, 251
Ferme de la Haute Borne, 129
Fernandez 211
Fernandez & Darrin 211
Ferryand, Pierre 324
Fiat car company 51, 53, 60
Fildes, Paul 23
Filipowski, Ferdi 177
First Aid Nursing Yeomanry 111, 338
Fitzgerald, F Scott 30
Flossenbürg camp 338
Flower, Raymond (Gaspard) 123, 221
Foch, Marshal Ferdinand 72
Foot, Professor Michael 276

Forbach, France 299
Ford Motor Co. 19, 243, 333, 340
Foreign & Commonwealth Office 284
Foresti, Giulio 38, 53
Forez, France 329
F1 World Championship 326
Formula Libre 35, 58
Fort William 92
Frager, Major Henri (Paul) 217, 229, 293, 295, 307, 310
Franco, General Francisco 103
Frazer-Nash car company 69
Free French Forces 231, 327
Fremont, Albert 116-117, 118, 119, 128, 136, 142, 143, 146, 153, 157, 188, 189, 190, 206, 220, 226, 328
Fremont, Madame 129, 190, 206, 207, 211, 212, 220, 226
French Army
- 1st Aviation Group 130
- 131e Regiment Infanterie 48
- Armée de l'Air 48, 63, 70, 75, 118, 251, 327, 329
- Cadre Noir Cavalry School 75
- Chasseurs d'Afriques 130
- École de Perfectionnement 70
- First Army Group 73
- Foreign Legion 277
French Grand Prix (See GP de l'ACF)
Fresnes, prison 184, 191, 199, 206, 208, 210, 211, 213, 220, 259, 271, 283, 284, 287, 288, 289, 292, 295, 339, 340
Friderich, Ernest 37, 41, 44, 65, 67, 325
Friderich, Paul 325
Gabčík, Josef 10-11, 17
Gaggenau, Germany 347
Gainsborough Pictures 275
Galvez, Oscar 35
Gamelin, General Maurice-Gustave 72
Garcin, Gladys 188, 345
Gare d'Austerlitz, Paris 126, 158, 160, 199, 225, 240
Gare de l'Est 291, 295, 338
Gare Montparnasse, Paris 16, 158, 229
Gare du Nord 159
Gare St Lazare 177, 207
Garel, François 293, 308
Garnier, André 129, 228, 241, 260, 264-267, 269-272, 279, 282, 284, 287-288
Garnier, Jacqueline (see Benoist, Jacqueline)
Garramor, Scotland 93
Garric, Magahoff 254
Garry, Émile-Henri (Cinema) 157, 164, 173, 215, 217, 293, 308
Garry, Marguerite 217
Garry, Renée 164, 214, 215, 216

Gatacre, Vladimir (See Grover, William)
Gaupillat, Jean 241
Gaynor-Beard, William 123
Gebhardt, SS-Brigadeführer Prof Dr Karl 22
Geelen, SOE agent 294, 308
Geneva, Switzerland 331
Geneva Convention 109, 301
George, Lloyd 276
George VI 274, 275, 339
George Cross 245, 246, 274, 275, 276, 340-342
George Washington University 120
Georges, Pierre (Colonel Fabien) 18
Gerard, Louis 325
Gerber Family 266
German Army
- 6th Army 131
- Army Group B 257
- Das Reich Division 258, 281
- Deutschland Regiment 280
Gerson, Vic 200
Gestapo (Geheime Staatspolizei) 125, 178, 187, 193, 207, 210, 227, 232, 288, 294, 311, 316, 317, 341, 346, 349
Ghica, Prince Jorgu 60
Gibraltar 91, 103, 119, 132
Gielgud, John 81
Gielgud, Lewis 80, 87, 88, 90
Gielgud, Val 80
Giers, River 53
Gieules, Robert 174, 176, 179, 180, 213, 219
Gilbert, Lewis 276
Gilles (see Wimille, Jean-Pierre)
Girard, Rene (Berthelot Francis) 267
Gisors, France 159
Givors, France 53
Glasgow, Scotland 92
Gloucester Place, London 236
Gnome & Rhône 52
Goering, Hermann 186
Goethe's Oak 308
Goetz, Dr Joseph 180, 183, 232, 271
Gordon, Frederick 80
Gordon Bennett, James 43
Gordini 248, 332
Gordini, Amédée 324, 331
Gott, Lt-Gen. William 132
Gouju, Marcel 183
Goux, Jules 47, 53, 57
GN car company 50
Graignes, France 258
Grampian mountains 92
Gran Premio del General Juan Peron, 332, 334
Grand Garage de la Place Clichy 197, 218
GP de l'ACF 15, 35, 41, 47, 51, 52, 53, 54, 56, 58, 165, 170, 241, 320
GP d'Antibes 37

GP de l'Autoroute de l'Ouest 329
GP des Nations 331
GP de l'Ouverture 34, 58
GP de Picardie 67, 326
GP de Provence 32-33, 84
GP of Rosario 332
GP de Tunisie 242
Grands Boulevards, Paris 193
Grands Fonds, France 27, 82
Granges-le-Roi, France 252, 254
Grasse, France 188
Gravelotte, France 299
Great Escape 313
Great Missenden, 25
Great North Road 111
Greco, Juliette 335
Gregoire, Jean-Albert 48
Grenoble, France 54
Grignon, France 137, 158, 164, 173, 174
Grimaldi Family, Monaco 44
Groesbeek Cemetery, Holland 344
Gross Rosen camp 215, 338
Grosvenor, Hugh Lupus (See Westminster, Duke of)
Groupement National des Refractaires et Maquisards (GNRM) 322
Grover, Elizabeth 27, 82, 97
Grover, Alice 27, 82, 83
Grover, Frederic 27, 29, 31, 34, 38, 43, 74, 77, 96, 107, 108, 141, 142, 155, 156, 183, 188
Grover, Frederick 25, 27, 82
Grover, Hermance 27, 82
Grover, Willy (William Grover-Williams, "W Williams", Vladimir Gatacre, Sebastien, Charles Lelong) - throughout
Grover, Yvonne ("Didi", Yvonne Aupicq) throughout
Guadalcanal 131
Gubbins, Major-General Colin 120, 150, 344
Guderian, General Heinz 73
Guidizzolo, Giovanbattista 329
Guiet, Jean 280
Guigouin, Georges 280
Guepin, Renée 159
Guérin, Henri 155, 212, 219
Guérin, Pierre 155, 212, 218, 219, 339
Guérisse, Albert (Pat) 337
Guerne, Armel 137
Guignard 207
Guildford, England 88, 92
Guinness, Kenelm Lee 53-55
Guisseray, France 267
Guy (SOE trainee) 92, 97
Guynemer, Georges 63
Guyot, Albert 47
Guyot Special automobile 35
Halder, Max 125
Halford automobile 35
Hall, Virginia (Marie Monin)

120-123, 125-127, 140, 228, 244, 342
Hallowes, Odette 342
Hamilton, Raymond (see Heslop, Richard)
Handley, Sergeant TF 314
Handley-Page Halifax bomber 12-14, 112
Hardelot, France 108
Harding, Thomas 25
Harmsworth Family 128
Harriman, Averill 132, 133
Harris, Air Chief Marshal Arthur "Bomber" 12,
Harvard University 23
Haugomat, François 268
Haussman, Baron Georges-Eugene 20
Haute Alpes departement, France 250
Haute Savoie departement, France 343
Hazeldene, Captain FW 321
Hazells Hall 111
Heinrich, Jean 50
Hemingway, Ernest 30
Henry, Maurice 240
Hercule (see Dubois, Jean)
Hertford British Hospital, Paris 277
Hertfordshire 105, 111
Heslop, Richard (Raymond Hamilton, Rene Garrat, Xavier) 89, 94, 98, 99, 119, 124, 127, 128, 141, 152, 153, 157, 158, 208, 343
Hessel, Stéphane 285, 293, 294, 296, 300, 301, 302, 306, 308, 309
Heydrich, Lina 22
Heydrich, Reinhard 9-11, 17, 22-23, 346
High Wycombe 12
Hill 314, 289
Himmler, Heinrich 22-23, 162, 345
Hirohito, Emperor 324
Hiroshima 323
Hispano Suiza 24, 31-32, 72, 83
Historian (SOE network) 294
Hitler, Adolf 9, 22-23, 67, 72, 73, 103, 109, 131, 139, 243, 251, 256, 288, 304, 308, 314, 316, 319, 336, 345
Hodge, General William 316
Hodges, Air Chief Marshal Sir Lewis 201, 202
Hofer, Walter 186
Hog's Back 89
Holdorf, Karl 162, 179
Holes'ovickách Highway 10
Holland 73, 95
Hollywood 75
Holz, Lt-Col Karl 18
Honel, J 50
Hospital Juan A Fernandez, Buenos Aires 334
Hot Club, Montmartre 137
Hotchkiss car company 192, 193,

194, 259, 265
Hotel Astoria, Paris 29
Hotel de la Calandre, Le Mans 224
Hotel Daunou, Paris 85
Hotel Magrazan, Paris 158, 160
Hotel Majestic, Paris 29-30
Hotel Northumberland, London 231
Hotel Plaza Athenée, Paris 45
Hotel Savoy, London 231
Hotel Splendide, Bordeaux 75
Hotel Victoria, London 79, 80
Hradčany Castle, Prague 9-11
Hubble, Desmond 307
Hulet, Monsieur 188, 190, 211
Huntziger, General Charles 76
Île Héron, France 208, 214, 227, 236, 237, 254
Imar, Inspector 153
Imperial Airways 249
Indian Motorcycle Company 29, 31, 83
Indianapolis 500 33, 52, 58, 252
Indochina 232
industrial sabotage techniques 106
Inter Services Research Bureau See SOE
Interlagos, Brazil 250
International Red Cross 80, 118, 286-287, 291, 295, 315, 319
interrogation techniques 161, 263, 274, 281, 311
Invasion of France 72, 73, 91
Invasion of Vichy Zone 139
Inventor (SOE network) 224, 337
Isle of Skye 92, 93
Italian Air Force
- La Squadriglia degli Assi 65
Italian Grand Prix 54, 55, 58
Issoudun, France 279
Istres, France 32, 70
Itala car company 63, 64
Jade Amicol network 92
James, Flight Lieutenant "Jimmy" 313
James Bond films 100, 276
Jano, Vittorio 53, 65
Japanese Navy 131
Jardin du Luxembourg, Paris 279
Jedburgh teams (SAS) 259, 320
Johannesburg, South Africa 249
Johnson, Denis 208-209
Jones, Sidney 224, 338
Joyce, James 30
Junior Car Club 51
Jura 208
Juvisy, France 126
Kaindl, Anton 347
Kaltenbrunner, Erst, 346
Karlsruhe, Germany 154
Kautz, Christian 333
Keller, Mme 124, 141, 152, 154, 214
Kent 77
Keun, Captain Gerald 294

Khan, Hyder Ali 163
Khan, Princess Noor Inayat (Madeleine, Jeanne-Marie Regnier) 157, 158, 162-164, 173, 174, 175, 176, 179, 180, 182, 209-217, 220, 245, 337, 341, 348
Khan, Tippu 163
Kieffer, Obersturmbannführer Josef 154, 160, 161, 162, 227, 271, 347
Kiev, Russia 27
Kinross, Scotland 78
Kippeurt, Rene 69
Klein, Johannes 9-11
Knocken, Helmut 346, 349
Koenig, General Pierre 231
Kokura 323
Kommandobefehl order 109
Koniev, Marshal Ivan 319
Konigsberg, Germany 315
Kopkow, Horst (later Peter Cordes) 346
Kotrba, Corporal J (Sergeant Davies) 314
Kressman, Captain 348
Krogon, Eugen 309
Kubiš, Jan 10-11, 17, 23
L'Antoine, Madame 195, 199
L'Antoine, Marcel 129, 194, 195, 218, 222, 223, 244, 255, 260, 264-267, 269, 270, 271, 339
La Baule, France 42-43, 67, 71, 86, 168
Labour Party 350
Labourer (SOE network) 294
Labric, Roger 69, 194, 195, 196, 241
La Flèche, France 15, 153
Lafont, Henri 218, 227
Laffrey hillclimb 54
La Hunière 252
La Licorne car company 79
La Turbie hillclimb 32, 58, 242
Lamberdiere, Gaston 267
Lancashire 94
Land Speed Record 36
Landes, Roger 342
Langer, Karl 184, 185, 187, 210, 262
Laos 232
La RÉcoleta cemetery, Buenos Aires 335
La Roche Guyon, France 257
Laroche 205
Laurent, Carmèle 209-210, 211, 227
Laurent, Georges 150, 188, 190, 211, 212, 226, 227, 285
Laval, Pierre 18, 349
Lazard Family 250
Lazard, Simone (see De La Fressange, Simone)
Le Bourget 71, 72, 74
Le Camp hillclimb 32, 52
Le Canadel, France 28
Leccia, Marcel 294
Le Chene, Marie-Thérèse 200

Le Fay, airfield 279
Légion d'honneur 61, 170, 340
Legion des Voluntaires Francais contre le Bolshevisme, 251
Legion of Merit, 340
Le Gourmet, New York 326
Les Halles, Paris 62
Lehoux, Marcel 33, 40
Leichenkeller (The Corpse Cellar) 246, 308
Leigh, Vera 337
Lelong, Charles (See Grover, William)
Le Mans, France 13-16, 41, 51, 65, 130, 157, 164, 172, 174, 200, 214, 224, 350
Le Mans 24 Hours 43, 64, 65, 68, 69-70, 249, 250, 251, 321, 325, 328
Leopold, King of Belgium 71
Le Perray en Yvelines, France 182
Le Plantin restaurant, Paris 285
Le Plessis-Belleville, France 49
Le Puy-en-Velay, France 141
Les Quatre Vents 15
Leroux, Georges (Boulon Gabin) 268
Leroux, Lucien (Boulon Gaspar) 268
Leroy, Reine 276
Les Sept Chemins 53
Lespiaux, Paul (Anselme Poulain) 268
Lesurque, Marcel 251, 252
Lethias, Ernest 129
Lethias, Thérèse 129, 146, 181, 182, 188, 189, 190, 211, 212, 220, 338
Letourey, Robert 51
Le Trou dans le Mur bar 30
Le Vésinet, France 146, 153, 157, 190
Levallois, France 277
Levegh, Pierre 325
Lewis machine-gun 48
Leygonie, Pierre 252, 253, 266, 287, 330
Lidice, Poland 23
Liewer, Philippe (Clement, Charles Beauchamps) 228, 229, 235, 254, 263, 272, 273, 278-283, 294
Lille, France 30
Limoges, France 126-127, 153, 279-282
Limonest hillclimb 52
Limousin 124, 279, 280
Lindberg, Charles 249
Lionel (see Benoist, Robert)
Liverpool 277
Loch Lomond 92
Loch Long 92
Lockheed Hudson aeroplane 198, 199, 201, 202, 203, 217, 229, 230, 245
Lohse, Bruno 186
Loire, river 75, 91, 134, 208, 213,
214, 225, 236
Loison, Yves 295, 302
Lombard, André 50
London throughout
London Gazette 213
London Midland and Scottish Railway 92
Long Island 249
Lory, Albert 52
Louveau, Henri 325
Lovat, Major The Lord 108
Low, Nigel 136-137
Ludendorff Bridge, Remagen 316
Luftwaffe 72, 74, 77, 235
Lurcy-Lévis, France 46
Luzancy, France 286
Lycée Janson de Sailly 28, 41
Lycée Michelet 63
Lyon, France 52, 55, 120-122, 125-128, 136, 141, 228, 238, 244
Lysander (see Westland)
Madagascar 138
Madame Pruniers, London 231
Madras, India 163
Madrid, Spain 17
Maggi, Count Aymo 60
Maginot Line 72, 299
Maid Honour Force 107, 108
Maintenon, France 241
Maison Blanche 69
Maloubier, Robert 229, 235, 278, 280
Mall, London 339
Manchester 95
Manoir Ramby 42-43, 166, 168
Marcay car company 49
Marce, France 152
Marcus, German agent 348
Mareuse, Marguerite 242
Marlborough House, London 339
Marne, river 295
Marquis of Salisbury 43
Mars la Tour, France 299
Marsac, André 139, 150
Marseille 133, 134, 221, 224
Marteau, Sheila 210
Marylebone Road 236
Maserati 39-40, 67, 325
Maserati, Ernesto 38
Masetti, Count Giulio 56
Masson, Captain Robert 118
Massonet, Paul (Mic) 260, 261, 262, 264, 266
Materassi, Emilio 36-38, 59, 60
Matford car company 19
Mathis car company 19
Mauritius 138
Mauthausen camp 338, 347
Mauzac, France 127, 228
Mazaud, Robert 328-329, 331
McAlister, John (Valentin) 157, 158, 159, 162, 179, 293
McKenna, Virginia 276
Medal of Honor 140

Melun-Villaroche 155
Menessier, Raymond 199, 202
Menoud, André (Fiquet) 268
Mercedes-Benz car company 9-10, 40, 52, 68, 166, 242, 297, 333
Merlimont, France 107
Mers-el-Kebir 115
Mery-sur-Oise, France 129, 152, 181, 182, 188, 190, 338
Mestivier, Marius 321
Mestivier, Maurice 321, 322, 325
Métro, Paris 188, 261, 263, 322
Metropolitan Railway 25
Metz, France 299
Metz, Joseph 71
Meudon, France 241
Meuse, river 298
MG Magnette 325
Michelin 43
Mi-Corniche hillclimb 32, 58
Middlesex Hospital, London 23
Milan, Italy 52, 59, 65
Milan Grand Prix 60
Military Cross 342,
Military Operations 1 (Special Projects) See SOE
Millar, George 342
Miller, Major (SOE) 93
Ministry of Economic Warfare 19
Ministry of Information 275
Ministry of Works 79
Minney RJ 275, 280
Minoia, Ferdinando 57
Miramas circuit 32-33, 56, 70
Miranda de Ebro 103
Misbourne, River 25
Molotov, Vyacheslav Mikhaylovich 313
Molotowsk, Lieutenant Wassili Kokorin 313
Molsheim, France 37, 69, 70, 71, 72, 332
Monaco 44
Monaco Grand Prix 39, 166, 326
Mongin, Marcel 65
Monkeypuzzle (SOE network) 123, 124, 134, 221, 224
Monsieur Jean 184, 185
Mont Agel hillclimb 32, 52, 56
Montagu Family 98
Montagu Mansions, London 236
Montaigu hillclimb 52
Mont des Mules hillclimb 32
Mont-Valérien 18
Montceau-les-Mines, France 123-124
Monte Carlo 28, 33, 40, 169
Monte Carlo Rally 31-32, 37, 83, 251
Montfaucon d'Argonne, France 48
Montfermeil, France 223
Montflix-par-Etrechy, France 267
Montgomery, Lt-General Bernard 132, 139, 318

Montlhéry 34-36, 51, 54, 55, 58, 68, 69, 84, 249, 250, 344
Montreal, Canada 132
Montrouge, France 27
Mont-Valérien, France 223
Monza, Italy 38, 58, 59, 60
Morane-Parasol aircraft 48
Morel, André 35, 57, 58, 321
Morel, Major Gerry 224, 229, 230
Morel, Raymond 155
Moreuil, France 47
Moriceau, Jules 33, 35, 57
Morocco 130, 139
Morse Code 90, 92, 180
Mortain, France 289
Moscow, Russia 28, 131, 163
Moselle, river 299
Moulin, Jean 160
Mountbatten, Lord Louis 108
Mountford, Ely (see Wilkinson, Ernest)
Moyenne Corniche hillclimb 58
Mulsant, Captain Pierre 294
Munich, Germany 346
Munich Crisis 70
Murphy, Jimmy 51
Mussolini, Benito 242, 251, 319
Mysore, India 163
Nacht und Nebel prisoners 317, 336
Nagasaki, Japan 323
Nancy, France 242
Nantes, France 15,18, 90, 152, 208, 213, 214, 222, 225, 227-228, 236-240, 254, 255, 259, 331
Nanteuil-sur-Marne, France 286
National Health Service 350
Napoleon Bonaparte 148
Narvik, Norway 111
Natzweiler-Struthof camp 337
Nazi Party 22, 311
Nazzaro, Felice 51
Neisse river 319
Neuilly-Plaisance, France 224
Neuilly-sur-Seine, France 176, 321
Nevers, France 140
Neu-Bremm, camp 299-303
New Forest 98
New York Herald newspaper 43
New York Post 121
New York Stock Exchange 66
Newman, Isidore (Athlete) 229
Newmarket 104
Nicholas II, Tsar of Russia 27
Nicholas, Elizabeth 276
Nice, France 37, 44, 67, 239, 325, 328
Nijinsky, Vaslav 45
Nimes, France 332
Noisy, France 295
Noregby House, London 236
Norman, Gilbert (Archambaud) 135, 136, 151, 156, 158-164, 177-178, 180, 183, 338
Normandy 77, 104, 125, 203, 228,
254, 256-259, 264, 278-80, 282-3, 288, 290, 337
Normandy Dock, St Nazaire 108
Nort, France 255
North Africa 18, 131, 139
Northumberland Avenue, London 79, 80, 231
Now it can be Told 340
Nuremburg Trials 346
Nuvolari, Tazio 38, 55, 66, 67, 250, 331
Occupied Zone (France) 104, 124
Oder Front 316, 319
Office of Strategic Services (OSS) 140, 244
Oise, river 147
Old Gibraltar Farm 112
Olschanesky, Sonia 337
Omaha Beach 256, 257
Onival, France 107
Opera, Paris 193
Operation Millenium (See Thousand Bomber Raid)
Operation Blue (German) 131
Operation Torch (US) 139
Orabona (SOE agent) see Guy Oradour-sur-Glane, France 258, 281
Oran Grand Prix 242
Orchard Court 87, 98, 109, 110, 213, 236, 237
Order of the British Empire
- Member 342
- Officer 343, 340
Oranienburg, Germany 312
Orleans, France 126, 294
Orly, France 232
Ormonde, race horse 45
Orne, river 256
Orpen, Sir William 29, 31, 39, 83, 85
Oswestry, England 277
P-47 Thunderbolt 291 297
P-51 Mustang 297
Packenham, Simona 30
Palermo Park, Buenos Aires 334
Panhard car company 52
Pantin, France 286, 295
Pappenheimer, Alvin 23
Paris, throughout
Paris-Nice Trial 49
Paris Peace Conference 72
Paris Salon 50
Parry-Thomas, John 36
Parti Populaire Francais (PPF) 250, 251
Partouche, Alphonse 227, 228, 241
Passage des Princes, Paris 194
Passy, France 112, 240
Pat escape line 337
Pate, Henry 51
Pathephone 150, 226
Patton, General George 288
Pau, France 31, 42, 49, 241, 250
Payne-Best, Captain Sigismund 313, 314, 315
Pearl Harbour 94, 326
Peilfunkdienst 148, 181
Père Lachaise, Paris 189
Petit, Émile 50, 130
Perdrigé, Charlotte (Sonia) 224, 240, 260, 261, 262, 264, 266, 270, 271, 272, 281, 282, 283, 284, 286-288, 338
Perdrigé, Daniel (Communist mayor) 223
Perdrigé, Daniel (pseudonym for Robert Benoist) 223, 237
Péronne circuit 67
Perpignan, France 330
Perrier water company 128
Perrot, Albert 50
Pertschuk, Maurice (Eugene) 239
Pétain, Marechal Henri 75, 121, 346
Petsch, Maurice 250
Peters (see Cartaud, Pierre)
Petrelle, maquisard 268
Petzke 317
Peugeot car company 47, 52
Peuleve, Harry 235, 294, 302, 309
Peyrouton, Marcel 186, 348
Pfansteil, Ida 210
Pharamon restaurant, Paris 62
Physician (SOE network) see Prosper
Pickersgill, Frank (Bertrand) 157, 158, 159, 162, 179, 293, 295, 296, 307, 309
Pimento (SOE network) 200
Ping-Pong Bar, Paris 197, 225
Pister, SS Oberführer Hermann 308, 309, 310, 347
Pitié-Salpêtrière hospital, Paris 225
Place de Clichy, Paris 218
Place des Epars, Chartres 222
Place des Etats-Unis, Paris 184, 270, 272, 282
Place de l'Etoile, Paris 188
Place Gambetta, Paris 190, 192, 197
Place Malesherbes, Paris 163, 173, 174, 175, 216
Place de l'Opera, Paris 24, 30
Place de la République, Paris 193
Place de Ternes, Paris 263
Place du Trocadéro, Paris 112
Placke, Josef 162, 179, 271
Planchon, Charles 52
Poissy, France 48
Poitiers, France 75
Poland 72, 215, 282
Polar Sea 347
Polledry, Victor 324, 325
Pont Long, France 49
Pont de Sevres, Paris 74
Popular Front 250
Porsche 325
Porte de Champerret, Paris 129,
187, 190, 207
Porte Dauphine, Paris 248, 322, 335
Porte Maillot, Paris 20, 29, 70
Porte de Ternes, Paris 64
Porte St Denis, Paris 158
Portman Square, London 87, 236
Porton Down (See British Chemical and Biological Warfare Research Centre)
Portugal 121
Pound, Ezra 30
Pourville, France 30
Prague, Czechoslovakia 22-23
Priest (SOE network) 294
Prinz Albrechtstrasse, Berlin 311, 312
Privet (SOE network) 141, 147, 207, 214
Prohibition 29
Prosper (SOE network) 133, 134, 136, 139, 140, 150, 151, 152, 156-162, 173, 175-179, 181, 198, 200, 224, 234, 244, 245, 262, 307, 337
Prosper (see Suttill, Francis)
Provence 121-122, 188, 199
Purdy, Harold 36
Puteaux, France 48
Putney 213
Pym Family 111
Pyrénées, France 38, 49, 75
Quai de Javel, Paris 238, 244
Qualliot, Monsieur 146
RAC Grand Prix 36, 57, 60
Radcliffe College 120
Radio France 155
Radio game 173, 180, 215
Raincy, France 295
Rake, Denis (Dieudonne) 122-127, 141, 153, 342
Rambouillet, France 47, 142, 241, 252, 257
Raph (see Béthenod de Montbressieux, Comte George)
Rastenburg, East Prussia 288
Ratcliff, Squadron Leader Len 229, 230
Ravensbrück camp 246, 299, 315, 338
Reach for the Sky 276
Rechenmann, Charles 292
Red Army 316-317
Red Orchestra network 140, 180
Reed, Fl.Lt Lofty 203
Regent Street, London 109
Reich Chancellery, Berlin 23, 317, 319
Reichssicherheitshauptamt (RHSA) 22, 308, 309, 311, 312, 317, 336, 338, 346, 347
Remagen, Germany 316-317
Renault, car company 333
Réseau Adolphe 134, 135, 157
Réseau Cohors Asturies 155, 212
Resslova Street, Prague 23
Resta, Dario 53, 55
Rethondes, France 76

Reuilly, France 215, 232
Reuters 121, 177
Reynaud, Paul 75
Rheam, George 106, 208
Rhine, river 316-318
Rhône, river 32, 200
Richard, François 268
Riley, car company 324
Ringway aerodrome 95, 96, 235, 278
Risacher, Louis 62, 63, 64
Rites of Spring 45
Roanne, France 54
Rolfe, Lilian 283, 294, 315-316
Rolls Royce 28-31, 39, 101
Romain-Pilain car company 53
Rome, Italy 42
Rommel, Erwin 131, 257
Ronin, Colonel George 118
Roosevelt, Franklin D 132, 319, 323
Roosevelt Raceway 249
Rost, Maurice 43
Roth, Fritz 69
Rouen, France 37
Roughwood Park 211, 212
Rousset, Marcel, 184
Rowden, Diana 337
Royal Air Force (RAF) 77, 78, 91, 101, 104, 108, 114, 132, 253, 311, 313, 339
- 138 Squadron 12-13, 104, 112
- 161 Squadron 105, 201
- 419 Flight 104
- 1419 Flight 104
- Bomber Command 12, 112, 312, 313
- Ferry Command 132
- Fighter Command 77
- RAF Abingdon 164
- RAF Tangmere 203
- RAF Regiment 204
- Special Duties Squadrons (Moon Squadrons) 104, 105, 198, 203, 240, 245
Royal Bank of Canada 147
Royal Navy 103, 104, 115
Royal Tunbridge Wells 77
Royal Victoria Patriotic School 205
Royallieu, France 206, 292, 295
Royan, France 327
Royce, Sir Henry 28
Ruby engine company 145
Rudellat, Yvonne (Jacqueline Gautier) 134, 157, 158, 159
Rue Berlioz, Paris 42
Rue Boissiere, Paris 332
Rue Brunel, Paris 197, 225, 324
Rue de Courcelles, Paris 197
Rue Dardanelles, Paris 64
Rue du Débarcadère, Paris 70, 78, 79
Rue Erlanger, Paris 156, 174
Rue de la Faisanderie, Paris 213, 215, 216
Rue des Fermiers, Paris 197

Rue Forest, Paris 197
Rue Fustel de Coulanges, Paris 223, 240, 246, 254, 261, 263, 271, 273, 279, 281, 282, 283, 284, 285
Rue Georges Bizet, Paris 259
Rue Hautefeuille, Paris 158
Rue Lauriston, Paris 227
Rue de Mont Louis, Paris 270
Rue Murillo, Paris 252, 330
Rue Niccolo, Paris 224
Rue Ordener, Paris 50, 64
Rue de la Pompe, Paris 28
Rue Pergolèse, Paris 22, 145, 155
Rues des Petits Ecuries, Paris 156
Rue Pierre Demours, Paris 63
Rue Raynouard, Paris 240
Rue de Rennequin, Paris 328
Rue de Richelieu, Paris 193, 194
Rue de Rome, Paris 177, 178, 232
Rue de Saussaies, Paris 125, 193
Rue St Didier, Paris 70
Rue Troyon, Paris 156, 182
Rue Vineuse, Paris 112, 116, 142
Rue Weber, Paris 20-22, 29, 39, 86, 112, 141, 145, 153, 155, 165, 210, 220, 227, 335, 338, 345
Runnymede, 344
Russia 18, 131, 347
Russian Front 256
Rymills, PO Frank 12-15, 112
Saarbrücken, Germany 299, 301
Sablé-sur-Sarthe, France 15
Sabourin, Romeo 294
Sachsenhausen camp 244, 304, 310, 312, 315-319, 347
St Afrique, France 268
St Alban les Eaux hillclimb 54
St Avold airfield 48
St Cheron, France 265
St Cloud, France 163, 329
St Cyr, France 74
St Denis, Paris 251
St Gaudens, France 37, 165, 242
St Germain des Pres, France 279
St Germain-en-Laye, France 51
St Jean Cap Ferrat, France 210
St Leger horse race 26
St Leger-en-Yvelines, France 50
St Malo, France 75
St Michael's House, London 236
St Nazaire, France 75, 108, 228
St Ouen, France 188
St Paul's, Knightsbridge 338
St Petersburg, Russia 26
St Philippe du Roule, Paris 335
Ste Devote corner, Monaco 40
Ste Mère Eglise, France 256, 257
Salat, Pierre (Boulon Jean) 268
Salesman (SOE network) 228, 229, 254
Salle Pleyel concert hall 194, 196
Salmson car company 50-52, 130, 324
Salmson, Émile 50
Salmson, Georges 50
Salon de l'Automobile 331, 334
Salon-La-Tour, France 280, 281

San Sebastian, Spain 34, 38, 54, 56, 57, 65
Sandford cycle car 241
Sandri, Guglielmo 40
Sandringham Estate 100
Sark 109
Sarthe, river 13, 164
Satirist (SOE network) 137, 200
Sauerbruch, Prof Ferdinand 22
Saumur, France 75
Savoye, Jacques 324
Schellenberg, Walter 348
Scherrer, Auguste 188, 189, 224
Schmid car company 53
Schneider car company 52
Schröter, Paul 314-315, 317
Schutzstaffel (SS) 22, 23, 99, 162, 184, 227, 261, 281, 288, 289, 300, 301, 303, 306, 310, 317, 319, 343, 345, 346,
Schwarzhuber, Johann 316
Scofield, Paul 276
Scotland 78, 79, 87, 119
Scotland Yard 80, 98, 109
Scott, William 36
Scuderia Milan 328
Sebastien (see Grover, William)
Second Front 133
Secret Intelligence Service (MI6) 19, 121, 145, 178, 240, 294, 318, 346
Security Service (MI5) 87, 205, 233, 234, 235, 269
Sedan, France 73
Seine, river 257
Sénéchal, Robert 57, 58
Seringapatam, India 163
Sermaise, France 253, 260, 261, 262, 264-267, 269, 283, 287, 326
Servon, France 155, 212, 218, 219, 220, 226, 348
Sevenet, Henri 238, 239
Shakespeare & Co, Paris 30
Shelsley Walsh, England 71
Sheppard, Robert (Roland) 91, 93, 94, 96, 97, 98, 99, 101, 109, 110, 350-351
Shirley Valentine, movie 276
Sicherheitsdienst (SD) throughout
Sicily 42, 56, 147
Sigmaringen, Germany 346
Sigrand, Gaston 62, 63
Silver Arrows 249
Simca car company 260
Simca-Gordini 331, 334
Simon, André 88, 90, 91, 92, 96
Simon, Octave 137, 200
Sindelfingen, Germany 297
Singer, car company 324
Sink the Bismarck, movie 276
Small Scale Raiding Force 108
SOE in France, book 276
Sologne region 134, 157, 344
Sommer, François 249, 325, 327

Sommer, Raymond 68, 242, 249, 252, 327, 329, 332
Sonderbehandlung (special treatment) 308, 309, 317, 336, 346
Sonchamps, France 252
Sorbonne 163
Soucelles, France 198, 199, 201, 217, 218, 221, 229, 245,
Sound of Sleat, Scotland 92
South Africa 249
Southgate, Squadron Leader Maurice (Hector) 293, 307, 340
Southampton, England 98
Souville, France 49
Soviet Russia 116, 346
Soyer, Roger 263, 270, 271, 283, 285, 286
Spad aircraft 65
Spa 24 Hours 65
Spa-Francorchamps 43, 54, 332
Spain 54, 91, 97, 103, 121, 148, 189, 224, 229, 239
Spanish Civil War 17
Spanish Grand Prix 34, 57, 65
Special Operations Executive (SOE) throughout
- Czech Section 346
- French Section throughout
- République Francaise Section (RF) 97, 179, 236, 258, 292, 320, 340
Special Training Schools 17, 19, 24, 89, 93, 94, 97, 98, 105, 117, 133, 136, 138, 157, 164, 208, 211, 221, 239, 350
Specially Employed 340
Spirit of St Louis 249
Spooner, Colonel Frank 164
Spree, river 317
Springfield, Massachusetts 29
Spruce (SOE network) 200
Square Clignancourt 156, 158
Stade J-P Wimille, Paris 248
Stalag Luft III 313
Stalin, Joseph 132, 133, 134, 319
Stalingrad 131
Starr, Col. George (Hilaire) 239, 342
Stationer (SOE circuit) 293
Steele, CSM J C 314
Stein, Gertrude 30
Stocker, Huguette 228, 345
Stoffel, Henri 65
Stonehouse, Brian (Celestin) 238, 337
Strasbourg, France 347
Straub, Peter 337
Stravinsky, Igor 45
Stucchi & Prinetti car company 65
Stumpfegger, Dr Ludwig 22
Stuttgart, Germany 297
Stutz car company 64
Suchet, Marechal Louis-Gabriel 148
Suez Canal 131

Suhren, Fritz 316, 347
Sukulov, Victor (Anatoli Gurewitsch and Kent) 140
Sunbeam car company 52-56
Sunbeam Talbot Darracq (STD) 33-36, 57, 58
Suresnes, France 18, 163, 164, 223
Sussac, France 280
Suttill, Francis (Prosper, François Despree) 133-138, 140, 150, 151, 152, 156, 157, 158, 160, 162, 234, 242, 244, 263, 310-313, 315, 317-318, 342
Swiss Grand Prix 332, 333
Swiss Legation, Paris 226
Switzerland 72, 103, 326, 333, 346
Swogel, André (Petrel) 268
Szabo, Etienne 277
Szabo, Tania 277
Szabo, Violette (Louise, Corinne Leroy) 235, 246, 254, 263, 272-284, 290, 291, 294, 297, 315-316, 341
Talbot 33, 35, 38, 57, 58, 59, 84, 327
Talbot-Lago 325
Tambour, Madeleine 134, 135, 140, 150, 151
Tambour, Germaine 134, 140, 150, 151
Tangmere, England 203, 204
Taplow, England 26
Tarana 104
Tarbes, France 75
Tardieu, André 250
Targa Florio 42, 56, 65
Tarragona, Spain 51
Taylor, Philip 158
Tayssedre, Robert 218, 219, 222, 223, 246, 253, 255, 260, 264-267, 269, 270, 338
Tayssedre, Stella 129, 197, 198, 199, 218, 220, 226, 244, 253, 254, 260, 264-267, 269, 270, 284, 286, 338-339
Teager, Jessie 42, 44, 73, 97, 98, 107, 108
Teheran 132
Tempsford aerodrome 111, 112
Terrisse, Henri 63
Thames, River 25-26, 339
The Wicked Lady, movie 275
Theatre des Champs-Élysées, Paris 45
Thevenon, Daniel 109
They Fought Alone 340
Thomas, Rene 52-54, 56
Thomas Specials 36
Thorenc, France 188
Thorgau, Germany 315
Thousand Bomber Raid 12
Tibbets, Colonel Paul 323
Tiercé, France 199
Tinker (SOE network) 294
Tirpitz battleship 108
Tissier, Pierre (Pierrot) 240
Toile d'avion clothing store 173

Tokyo Bay 324
Tolstoy, Leo 43
Tony-Robert, Suzanne 155
Torchy, Paul 54, 56
Toulon, France 28, 70, 199
Toulouse, France 50, 126, 239
Touring Club de France 131, 186
Tournier, Pierre 285
Tours, France 52, 75, 123, 176, 198
Trafalgar Square, London 80
Tre Fontane circuit 42
Treblinka camp 304
Trepper, Leopold
Treaty of Versailles 72
Tremoulet, Jean 69
Tribunal Militaire Permanent de Paris 215, 232
Triechâteau, France 159, 162
Trintignant, Louis 325
Trintignant, Maurice 325, 326, 328
Tripoli 139
Trocadéro Garden, Paris 214, 335
Trossi, Count Carlo 331, 332, 333
Trotobas, Michael 343
Trubetskoy, Prince Ivan Yurievich 26-28
Truman, Harry S 323
Turin, Italy 331
Turkey 120
Turma-Vengeance network 252, 253, 254, 255, 258, 259, 268, 326, 330
Two Thousand Guineas horse race 26
U-Boat Headquarters 155
Unic 48
United States Army
- 1st Division 256
- 4th Armoured Division 288
- 8th Air Force 297
- 9th Armoured Division 316
- 9th Army 318
- 17th Airborne 318
- 27th Armoured Infantry Battalion 316
- 29th Division 256
- 30th Division 289
- 82nd Airborne Division 256
- 101st Airborne Division 256
- 120th Infantry Regiment 288
- 507th Parachute Regiment 258
- Military Police 324
- US Army Air Force 280, 307
US Military Tribunal 347
University Hospital, Prague 22
Unterturckheim, Germany 9
uprisings 257-258
Urchin (SOE network) 122, 199
USS Missouri 324
Utah Beach 257
Val de Grace hospital, Paris 223
Valencay, France 344
Valentino Park 331
Valin, General Martial 327
Van Lith, Beatrice 272
Vanderbilt Cup 249

Vanderkloot, William 132
Vanderwynckt, Professor Maurice 137, 173, 174
Vanves, France 63
Varzi, Achille 43, 66, 67, 331, 333
Vaubecourt, France 48
Vaucluse, France 326
Vaux, France 146, 147, 181
Venlo, Holland 313
Vercors, France 258
Verdun, France 48-49, 298, 299
Vernet, Just-Émile 324
Vernon hillclimb 37
Versailles, France 18, 47, 74, 130, 137
Versailles Cycling Club 47
Veuillet, Auguste 325
Veyron, Pierre 68, 70, 172, 251
Vichy 77, 90, 104, 118, 120-124, 127, 138-141, 186, 228, 251, 252, 330, 346, 348, 349
Vic-Dupont, Dr Nicolas 118
Vidal, General Emilio Mola 17
Viel, Louis 252, 330
Vienna, Austria 120
Vierzon, France 126, 240
Vilain, Chiquita 184, 186, 189, 290
Villa Cécile 253, 260, 264-267, 269, 272
Villa Mimosa 28
Villa Ramby 43
Villa Tunis 250, 252
Villecresne, France 155
Villefranche-sur-Mer, France 239
Villoresi, Gigi 335
Vineyards (SOE house) 99
Vionnet, Madeleine 45
Virolle, Georges 62
Vogt, Ernst 154, 183, 185, 187, 188, 214, 215, 224, 232, 264, 272, 289, 290
Volkswagen 67
Von Goethe, Johann Wolfgang 304
Von Stauffenberg, Claus Graf von 288
Von Stülpnagel, General Karl-Heinrich 288
Vosges 337
Wagner, Louis 35, 53, 57, 58
Wake, Nancy 235
Wall Street Crash 41
Wanborough Manor (STS 5) 89-93, 99, 119, 122
Wandsworth Common 205
War Office 19, 80, 88, 91, 164, 213, 278
War Weekly magazine 275
Warner, Jack 276
Warsaw, Poland 120
Warrington 94, 97
Waterloo Station 88, 98
Watt, Arthur (Geoffroi) 226
Weimar, Germany 303, 304
Wellington bomber 95
Wendel, Karl 262

Wenger, SD officer 262
Wessel, Heinrich 314
Western Desert 78
Westland Lysander 105, 144, 156, 176, 198, 240, 245, 279
Westminster, London 339
Westminster, Duke of 26
Weybridge 36
Wheelwright (SOE network) 239
Whitelaw, Billy 276
Whitley bomber 12
Whitworth, Richard Wright 28, 74
Whitworth, Elizabeth (see Elizabeth Grover)
Wilkinson, Ernest (Ely Mountford, Alexandre) 90, 97, 98, 99, 105, 124-128, 141, 147, 152-154, 155, 157, 207, 214, 338
Wilkinson, George 294
Williams, Danielle (see Bloch, Denise)
Wimille automobile 247, 252, 329-331, 334
Wimille, Auguste 241
Wimille, Christiane (Cric) 250, 251, 254, 264-265, 269, 270, 286-287, 330, 335
Wimille, François 330
Wimille, Jean-Pierre (Gilles) 67, 69-71, 129, 172, 241, 242, 247-253, 254, 264-265, 269, 270, 283, 285, 286-287, 326, 328-335, 336
Witherington, Pearl 342
Woerle, SD officer 262
Wolfsschanze (Wolf's Lair) 288
Women's Auxiliary Air Force (WAAF) 163
Woolworth's 277
Worms, Jean 151
Wright Brothers 52
W Williams (see Grover, William)
Wuppertal 337
Wurzburg radar system 108
Xavier (see Heslop, Richard)
Yalta Conference 316
Yeo-Thomas, Wing Commander Forrest (Kenneth Dodkin, Shelley, The White Rabbit) 292-296, 300, 301, 302, 307, 309, 340, 347, 350
Zenith Carburetors 70
Zenklova Street, Prague 10
Zhukov, Marshal Grigory 319
Zirn, Ernst 40